THE CHALLENGE OF RELIGION

Edited by
Frederick Ferré,
Joseph J. Kockelmans,
John E. Smith

THE CHALLENGE OF RELIGION
Contemporary Readings in Philosophy of Religion

THE SEABURY PRESS • NEW YORK

1982
The Seabury Press
815 Second Avenue
New York, N.Y. 10017

Printed in the United States of America.
Design by Nancy Dale Muldoon

Library of Congress Cataloging in Publication Data
Main entry under title:

The Challenge of religion.

"Bibliography by George L. Kline": p. 354
Includes index.
1. Religion—Philosophy—Addresses, essays, lectures.   2. Philosophy and reli-
gion—Addresses, essays, lectures.   I. Ferré, Frederick.   II. Kockelmans, Joseph
J., 1923-   III.   Smith, John Edwin.
BL51.C478   200'.1   81-16609
ISBN 0-8164-2368-7 hbd   AACR2
     0-8164-0520-4 pbk

In memory of Dr. Gerhard Brand

CONTENTS

vii

PART THREE

RELIGIOUS EXPERIENCE AND RELIGIOUS EXPRESSION
Introduction by John E. Smith 161

PART FOUR

RELIGION AND THE HUMAN PREDICAMENT
Introduction by Joseph J. Kockelmans 265

PREFACE

To use a book like this, either for the professor who may have adopted it for a course or for the person who may simply be reading it out of interest, is to call for creative imagination. There are many different ways in which these readings might be approached. Our own editorial discussions about groupings and orderings were themselves quite lively.

Many readers may decide to take the course of least resistance and read right on through, from beginning to end, after the manner of our final editorial consensus. The book makes sense that way: it begins by attempting to get hold of the religious phenomenon itself; then it tries to explore the possibilities and limitations of religious reasoning; then it proceeds to dig into the nature of meaning and its expressions in religious language or other forms of symbolism; finally, it concludes with a section on "applied" topics that look to our current situation and on into the future.

We are pleased with this ordering, which is eminently sensible and capable of providing the backbone for a stimulating course of study with a beginning, a development, and an end. But we hope that some of our readers will avail themselves of the greater variety of approaches that our book makes possible. Considering only the four major sections, sixteen different logical possibilities of arrangement exist. Many of them—perhaps all of them—make good pedagogical sense. To take a few examples, it might be stimulating to move directly from Part One, in which the religious phenomenon in general is explored, to Part Four, in which the phenomenon is seen variously in connection with aspects of contemporary culture. Then, with keener realization of the relevance of the more abstract issues, the nature of religious expression and experience in Part Three might be examined, concluding in Part Two with a look at the cognitive questions and the old arguments in a new context.

Other users of this book might wish to dive immediately into Part Four, where the juicy issues of contemporary relevance are uppermost, and next to drop back to Part Two, where the question is seriously addressed why one might be expected to believe (or disbelieve) any of this. The issues of religious reasoning lead naturally on to the questions dealt with in Part Three about the nature and limitations of religious expression, and these topics might well precede a final look at Part One in order to ponder what this strange phenomenon called *religion* might be, and to rethink the way it relates to philosophy.

Still other feasible approaches might be considered. Many people, for example, might feel drawn first to examine the question of how much we might reasonably claim to know about fundamental religious claims, such as the existence of God, and thus open first to Part Two. Such concerns would logically lead on to the issues of meaning explored in Part Three, but those issues, relating as they do to fundamental religious experience, must draw the reader back to the nature of the religious phenomenon, which is discussed in Part One, and finally to the way in which this phenomenon is related to contemporary concerns, presented in Part Four.

It would be tedious to spell out all the logical possibilities. Our hope is merely that our readers feel free, as they approach the pages to come, to follow their own interests and to be their own editors. But in illustrating these possibilities we are also seeking to show something significant about philosophy itself. In philosophy, everything is really related to everything else. It is a comprehensive way of thinking. It is impossible, except provisionally and for practical purposes, to isolate important philosophical questions from one another. All the significant topics in philosophy both lead to and spring from one another. This crucial fact about philosophy, that every question presupposes all the other questions, is sometimes a hindrance to early students in our field. Often they feel frustrated and hardly know where or how to begin. The upshot of our approach is that it hardly matters where one begins, since everyone who takes up a philosophic question *has already begun* at some level of sophistication or unsophistication, however little examined or made explicit, and therefore the process of philosophical growth is more helical than linear: one continues to cycle around the same basic axis of questions, but finds greater depths (or heights) each time around. This is well illustrated in Plato's *Dialogues*, where every participant already has some beliefs before he begins, and where solutions are always provisional and open to further discussion another day.

Invoking the model of a Platonic dialogue, moreover, reminds us of another significant truth about philosophy: it is not only *comprehensive* and without any neutral starting points, it is also highly *critical*. Not only is everything linked to everything else, but those linkages need to be logical, explicit, and warranted. Philosophy, including the philosophy of religion, cannot give up on the careful use of discourse, therefore, and the attempt to bring thought from inchoate to increasingly explicit forms. This is not only true of contemporary analytical philosophy, though analytical philosophy puts a great deal of emphasis on the quest for critical explicitness, but is essential to the philosophical enterprise, whatever its chosen modality.

By contrast, as will be seen from the pages that follow, this essential trait of philosophy illustrates something no less significant about religion, our subject matter. Whatever religion is, we agree that it is not primarily to be found at the level of critical discourse on which philosophy plants its flag. However it may be further specified and described, the living heart of religion is somewhere "behind" or "below" or "transcendent to" the domain of theory. It is something about which we may (and as philosophers we must) theorize, but it is much more than theory. This poses one of the first problems of philosophy of religion: how can something so different from theory be adequately approached by—much less expressed through—theory? That question is wrestled with below, but it should be noted that the general issue is not unique to philosophy of religion, since most of the objects of theorizing, like the solar system or our own digestion, are distinct from theory too. The question for philosophy of religion then becomes why one might hold that there is something about the nature of religion that makes it even harder to handle explicitly through critical discourse than other subject matters.

We may leave the fuller treatment of this question for the essays below, but it should be noted that this is one of the primary themes of our book. And in this connection we may also note one more significant fact about religion: namely, no matter how far from theory it may be, it seems to have an irresistible power to draw theorizers to speak about it. Religion is the sort of thing that attracts, repels, lures, seduces, terrifies, comforts, converts, and confirms. We may not always know what to say about it, but as thinking human beings we are driven to speech in story and song as well as in theory and myth. As philosophers of religion, the authors of these readings do not all take up the same attitudes towards our subject matter; for all of us, however, it is a vital source of fascination.

These observations lead to one final, general reflection: on the differences of style and content among our contributors. We are a diverse group, despite our common commitments to philosophy as a comprehensive and critical way of thinking and to the importance of religion as a valuationally vibrant subject matter demanding our best efforts of thought. We were brought together, in fact, more for our diversities than for our commonalities.

To characterize these diversities, we must describe the history of our book. It is the product of an unusual process, beginning with a form of foreign aid that most of us on this side of the Atlantic find aid "in reverse": *from* a West German foundation *to* scholars in the United States and Canada. The Fritz Thyssen Stiftung, which had previously taken an interest in philosophers of religion in

Europe, turned its generous attention to their counterparts in North America in 1976, when the contributors to this volume were first invited to meet on a regular semi-annual basis for the purpose of free and frank discussion.

The group of eight were deliberately selected to cover a wide range of viewpoints. It was with astonishment and delight, therefore, that we found from our first meeting, held at the Barclay Hotel in Philadelphia, we were able to cut across the barriers of different philosophical traditions and religious (Catholic and Protestant) backgrounds. We did not fall into immediate agreement—that was hardly expected—but we discovered that we could communicate and, what is more, that we wanted to nurture and deepen the discoveries that this communication made possible.

We abhor labels, like "analyst," or "existentialist," or the like, and will not perpetuate their misleading and divisive use by characterizing our diversity in their terms. In the light, however, of our earlier remarks about the nature of philosophy and the character of religion, we might invite the reader to consider our diversity on two separate continua, both vital to our enterprise. The first continuum has to do with the degree of philosophical *comprehensiveness* that we attempt in our work. It can be taken for granted that all of us, as philosophers, are employing the most *critical* methods we know in the handling of issues that admit no neat boundaries, but some of us are intellectually drawn toward dealing with more particular problems of conceptual explication and others toward issues with inclusive scope. This style, or temper of thinking, will make itself evident as the reader moves from essay to essay in the pages that follow. In our lively discussions over the years, these differences of temper have made for fascinating reflections on the many complementary ways to approach a single problem in philosophy of religion. Despite our years of communication, these differences of style and approach have not been eroded away, but we have found it mind-expanding to learn to see our subjects from a variety of points on the philosophical continuum, and that is what our readers, also, will come to enjoy.

The other major continuum on which we find ourselves significantly separated has to do with the extent to which the religious phenomenon itself is actually or potentially intelligible. All of us realize that religion is not merely a matter of theory, but on the spectrum beginning, on the one hand, with complete intelligibility according to ordinary logical standards, and shading off, on the other hand, into total mystery and ineffability, we found ourselves standing—and still stand—in different places. Again, we suggest that the discerning reader might try to locate the various authors from one end of this continuum to the other.

Are the two continua logically related? Can one show a regular correlation between preference for the more particular *versus* the more global philosophical approach, for example, and a position nearer one end or the other of the spectrum dealing with ordinary intelligibility *versus* the ineffability of religion? Judging from the essays to follow, there appears to be no such easy correlation. Should one have been expected? Why or why not?

Such questions are the stuff of still another way of reading this book: looking at the stance of the various authors on different topics to identify the way in which different styles of thought may handle similar issues. If there are surprises—if, for example, the same author should adopt different philosophical styles to approach different issues—what does this say about the nature of philosophical method? Is method, in any case, independent of content? How is communication across methodological style and religious commitment possible? All these are matters that we hope will continue to enliven the thinking of our readers: to stimulate them as we have been stimulated and to help their horizons grow as ours have grown.

For the support which led to the initial meeting of our authors and which nurtured the convivial confrontation of these issues, we reiterate our thanks to the trustees of the Thyssen Stiftung, adding special gratitude to the late Professor Dr. Gerd Brand, Director, who made it all possible.

Frederick Ferré
Joseph J. Kockelmans
John E. Smith

PART ONE

The Religious Dimension: God and the Sacred

INTRODUCTION BY JOHN E. SMITH

THIS section deals with three fundamental topics: first, the interplay between philosophy and religion and the need for the former to do justice to the religious dimension; second, the delineation of what religion is and means; and, third, the nature of God and of transcendence.

In the opening essay, "Philosophy of Religion and the Redefinition of Philosophy," Kenneth Schmitz considers how religion can become a valid subject matter for philosophical reflection, and shows that religion can be treated philosophically only if there is a broadening of the conception of philosophy itself. A theory of meaning is called for, capable of accommodating all the modes of meaning, symbolic no less than strictly conceptual, so that room is made for those forms of expression

1

which embody the presence of their referent and are thus *transformative,* as distinct from representations which are *informative* in a theoretical way. Religion thus appears as a challenge and a goad to philosophy; the encounter between the two cannot leave philosophy unchanged.

The succeeding two essays are devoted to the task of determining the nature of religion and of delineating its distinctive features. In "The Structure of Religion," John E. Smith, approaches the problem posed for a philosophy of religion by the existence of a plurality of religious traditions by attempting to disengage a common pattern or structure manifest in these traditions. The pattern proposed is threefold, embracing a vision of the divine and of man's ideal fulfillment, a diagnosis of the flaw in actual man which separates him from this fulfillment, and a means of deliverance whereby this flaw is overcome and it becomes possible for man to reach his ideal destiny.

In "The Transcendent and the Sacred," Louis Dupré maintains that the object of religious worship has traditionally been identified as the *sacred,* and that its opposition to the profane has made it a simple, unambiguous mode of referring to the transcendent. Yet archaic societies, he insists, know no such rigid dichotomy between a sacred and a profane sphere of life. Moreover, the direct experience of the transcendent implied by the term sacred is no longer universally available to religious men and women of our secular age. He concludes, therefore, that the *sacred,* though useful in the interpetation of traditional forms of religion, is not an essential category of transcendence.

The final two essays in this section deal with the concept of God. In "The Person God Is," Peter Bertocci characterizes God as the reality who answers questions of ultimate importance to the believer. He approaches the difficult problem of expressing the divine nature through the concept of the Person, which is, for him, the most adequate model in our experience. As the Ground of the unity and uniformity of nature, God is envisaged as Cosmic Knower, Loving Agent, Cosmic Creator, and the Creator of Cocreators or human persons. Stress falls on the importance of individuality, both Divine and human, as opposed to any form of Monism wherein individual persons are absorbed.

Kenneth Schmitz, in "The Element of Mystery in the Conception of God," compares Hegel's view of God as a Trinity with that proposed by the Greek church Fathers. The author attempts to reconstruct the sense of religious mystery in Hegel's approach as something quite distinct from the claim that God is unknowable. The most significant difference between Hegel and the ancient thinkers is that he describes the Trinity as a movement from the Father to the Holy Spirit that allows for the role of the negative as well as for a rational process of development and fulfillment. The Greek Fathers, on the other hand, stress the position of the Father, his ontological superabundance, to which the other Persons are the response. The author insists that Hegel did not rationalize and secularize the Trinitarian model, as has been claimed, but rather that he catches the somber shadows of religion and, above all, its relentless energy.

Chapter 1

PHILOSOPHY OF RELIGION AND THE REDEFINITION OF PHILOSOPHY

Kenneth L. Schmitz

PRESENT philosophical fashion uses big words to talk about little ones. It is proper, therefore, to ask about the meaning of *of* in the phrase "the philosophy of religion." The word is English but the genitive function is built into such venerable names as "ontology," "epistemology," and "psychology." Does the tiny genitive preposition bear the same meaning in each of its uses? For example, does it have the same meaning in "the philosophy of religion" as in "the philosophy of knowledge"? Most philosophical curricula indicate that the philosophy of knowledge is adjudged more essential and more appropriate to philosophy than the philosophy of religion. The phrase "the philosophy of knowledge" seems normal, proper, and reassuring, because the relation of philosophy to knowledge seems obvious and secure. Many of us may not think that knowing is fully transparent to a philosophical inquiry; but what does seem certain is that we know that we know, and that we know when we know, and that we know what criteria and conditions must be satisfied if we are to know. Because many of us hold this we see the appropriateness of a philosophical examination of what it is to know or claim to know. By heritage we are better Cartesians that we may care to admit.

We meet the genitive again in the phrase "the philosphy of man." Here the subject of inquiry is a being rather than a process, activity or state. What is the relation of philosophical scrutiny to such a subject? Few of us think that man is a subject of exhaustive clarity, for self-understanding is a hard-won achievement. But here too we may be Cartesians in good standing. Whatever difficulties lie along the path, and however puzzling we are to ourselves, still the inquiry

From: *Man and World*, 3(1970): 54–82. A paper read to the Graduate Seminar on the Philosophy of Religion at the School of Philosophy, The Catholic University of America, Fall, 1969.

is launched and carried out by the very subject who is called into question. It has been noticed that this causes a problem of method. For we can rightly ask: How can objectivity be achieved when the investigator is also the judge, and when the one under investigation is the inquirer himself? Of course, if philosophy is a court trial, the situation is impossibly absurd. But there are methodological advantages too. It is a satisfying circle, this questioning of man by man, and it may be rendered innocent because we can't possibly get ourselves out of it. We may not be the unshakable foundation which Descartes took us to be (*subjectum fundamentum inconcussum*), but we can surely serve as a foundation for our inquiry into ourselves.

The usage finds still another variant in "the philosophy of law." Here, of course, the inquiry is made into a practical domain. The law is engaged in the contentious matters of human life, tracing a balance between contested claims and contriving a reasonable reparation of wrongs done and claims entered. And yet there is an appropriate proportion between philosophy and the law. Reason in its practical judgmental form is already operative in the law, being ordered to urgent imperatives. Legal reason, then, anticipates the reflective reason of philosophical inquiry. There is a continuity between the rationality of the law and a philosophical reflection upon its foundations.

The phrase "the philosophy of art," however, poses a different problem, for art is dominated by a factor that is not easily amenable to rational discourse and evaluation. A reflective inquiry into law may lead eventually to very general moral and social principles in harmony with the theoretical and practical ideals of reason. But art introduces the nonrational principle of sensibility, a principle which remains insubordinate to the demands of reason. The law institutionalizes the guiding role of reason in practical affairs, but there is no such need or possibility in many forms of art. Is a syllogism ever likely to change the taste of an artist, critic or art-loving public regarding the value of a piece of art? If it were alleged from general principles, for example, that Schubert's Trout Quintet has a ridiculous gap between a rumbling bass viol and the nearest treble instrument three and one half octaves higher, that the distance is therefore too remote for harmony and the tones too disparate—the reply would come quickly. "Listen! It is an artistic victory!"

Further difficulties arise with such phrases as "the philosophy of God," or "the philosophy of religion." The former suggests an unbridgeable chasm between the inquirer and the inquired about; and the latter threatens to introduce factors that are either beneath rational consideration or beyond it. These illustrations are enough to suggest that it is easier to say "the philosophy of . . ." than to understand what is meant by it. Indeed, what is this *philosophy* which recurs in all these phrases? Is not its very unity and identity problematic? Is there a unitary mode of reflection which engages its matters in diverse ways? Or is *philosophy* simply a word standing for the ultimate but disparate acts of reflection prompted from within the various regions of human interest? Does *philosophy* stand for a single enterprise or at least a family of them with common parentage? Or is it simply a collection? But if philosophical inquiry is unified, in what sense is it so? Is philosophy a hard, sure core of distinctive rational principles which is loaned out for various matters? And has it a right to the consideration of everything? From the point of view of philosophy, art may seem to be a sublogical dramatization of meaning; but from within, art may feel itself gripped by an inner and meaningful necessity which makes philosophical reflection upon art seem trivial and alien. Or again, from the point of view of philosophy, religion may be held to be incomprehensible and dubious in its truth claims; but from within religion, philosophy may seem doubtful and its rights to criticism questionable. What is the ground for the resolution or balance of these tensions between philosophy and its neighbors? And within philosophy itself, is the philosophy of religion philosophy in the same full sense as the philosophy of knowledge?

A BRIEF CONSIDERATION OF RELIGION

There are many different philosophies of religion, and their differences stem both from differing conceptions of philosophy and of religion. A philosopher of religion, therefore, must make explicit his own understanding of what religion is, rather than abandon his readers to infer what that understanding might be. The present abbreviated consideration of religion is offered in order to suggest those features of religion which are important for the reflection that follows.

The possibility of more adequate definitions of religion is only a recent one, and was prepared for by several important developments. As long as the Christian religion was effectively dominant in the minds of all but the Jewish people in our culture, the variety of ways in which religion has in fact manifested itself was obscured. Moreover, the materials for the study of religion were presented often in a controversial context and spirit either within Christianity or against non-Christians. Individual data were often misreported and the overall presentation was highly selective. Fortunately, the establishment of the intellectual discipline of the history of religions over the past hundred years has given a methodical and objective focus to the study. In addition, the remarkable advances in archaeology, linguistics, anthropology, sociology, and psychology have contributed to the scholarly understanding of religion. Only within the background of this rich variety of data and approaches can a discriminating search for pervasive and resilient features be carried out. More recently, the phenomenology of religion in its prephilosophical phase has been of great help in framing descriptive definitions of religion.

A review of the history of religions will disqualify several notions that were sometimes thought to be essential to the nature of religion. First, as exhibited in its history, religion does not consist principally of private thoughts and spiritual feelings in the "inner" man. Second, it cannot be equated unqualifiedly either with the irrational and emotive or with the rational and conceptual, for it includes something of both.

Third, the history of religions will not permit an identification of religion with morality. It follows, therefore, that the religious man is not unqualifiedly the morally good man. Religion has shown itself to be a great power in human affairs, but the sacred contains the demonic as well as the blessed. Moreover, the distinction between morality and religion, so easily obscured in Judaism, Christianity, and Islam, has received confirmation in more recent times from the struggle of freethinkers and atheists against the institution of religion. Internecine "religious" wars, the preservation of social privilege in the name of religion, abuses of religious power, and sometimes an open hatred of religion, have led some men to shape for themselves a morality that does not owe its force or legitimacy to religious grounds. Although the alliance between religion and morality is still operative for many people and is an essential ingredient in the religious spirit of the major religions today, the two have been separable in fact at least since the Enlightenment.

Fourth, the history of religions also warns us against insisting that belief in God or gods is an essential element of every form of religion. All religions confess an extraordinary power to which man is called upon to respond, but it is not always understood to be personal. The removal of this familiar focus renders a descriptive definition of religion more difficult. We might be tempted to fall back upon a description of the subjective disposition of the believers, and to say, for example, that religion is "an institutionalized way of valuing most comprehensively and intensively."[1] On these grounds, however, a good university, art gallery, or library might qualify as religious. Moreover, it would be arrogant in the face of the stern disclaimer made by secular and atheist humanists to insist that they "really" are religious, especially when what they value most intensively may include getting rid of the mantrap they take religion to be. Any definition of religion, then, must be broad enough to permit the various forms shown in the history of religions, and yet distinctive enough to permit a clear meaning for the irreligious, nonreligious, and antireligious.

On the positive side, three sources seem especially helpful: sociology, anthropology, and phenomenology.[2] From a sociological viewpoint,[3] religion fans out into three dimensions: a) There is a community or fellowship, the collectivity within which and through which most religious life is carried out. b) There are rites through which devotees participate in the good that religion offers and through which they avert the evil it threatens. c) There is a system of symbols which embody and express the teachings of the religion and any truth claims it makes. In short, community, rite, and symbol form the institution of religion.

An anthropological viewpoint[4] highlights the functional role of religion. It is experienced as a dimension of reality answering to men's needs. It is a bonding power which enables a group to meet situations of crisis. The rites of passage of traditional religions enable a believer to accept the difficult transition from one state of being to another. These rites are numerous and varied, but they arise in the typical moments of death and birth, puberty, marriage, and ascension to high office; they assist in the hopes for food, safety, and victory, and in the commemoration of important events and theophanies in the memory of the people. The emphasis on the functional role of religion for society has the advantage of showing that religion has not been concerned only with another world or afterlife. If religion is taken up with the dead, its warrant for dealing with them comes from its effectiveness in dealing with the crisis that death brings into the midst of life. In sum, religion provides a group with a consecrated bond which helps to secure basic needs and to preserve both individual personalities and group identity from disintegration in the face of recurrent crises. Through myth men come to know how they stand with regard to the profound forces of life; through a system of values they are given norms with which to measure actions in relation to the basic needs of the group and its members; through rite they know how they might come into touch with ultimate reality and receive help or protection from its power.

The third major source for an understanding of religion is the prephilosophical phase of the phenomenology of religion. To catch something of the distinctiveness of the ultimate reality with which religion is concerned, Rudolf Otto[5] has coined the now famous term *numinous,* from a word which means "nod, command, power, deity." It stands for a vague Something, a "highly exceptional and extremely impressive 'Other,' " the *holy.* It is encountered as a commanding presence, pressing itself paradoxically as an absolute reality, and yet always in a historically determinate form, manifesting itself in particular times and places, through definite theophanies, rituals, symbols, and myths, things, persons, and communities. Such a demand is experienced as having extraordinary power, value, and meaning. Each believer does not himself have to undergo such an intense experience, but the particular religion will be grounded and renewed in original and ritual encounters with the sacred.

Joining these sources together with a comprehensive study of the history of religions, Mircea Eliade[6] has called religion a practical ontology which traffics in the holy and in the passage of man from profane to sacred time and place. It is able to touch everything in human life, and calls upon the human personality at all levels. It is not simply an appeal to the theoretical intelligence of man. In its roots, religion is not a matter of propositions but of deeds, not of truth claims but of imitable actions. In a preliterate society, men dance out their encounter with the sacred.[7] Rite is the existential expression proper to religion, and myth in its full embodiment is more a sacrament which transforms men and events than a story which merely recounts them. *The proper (though not exclusive) vehicle of meaning for religion is the symbol and not the concept, precisely because the symbol does not only signify the thing intended but also embodies its presence and calls upon the hearer to enter the world which the symbol reveals.* The point is a controverted but important one: Participation is the intention of the symbol. The parables of Jesus are not stories but invitations to go and do likewise. Indeed, the religious symbol transcends the distinction between theory and practice, and proclaims a dimension of reality which is at once a demand for action and a revelation of meaning. The symbol calls for a response from man's intelligence, sensibility, emotions, and choice.

The history of religions, then, assisted by sociology, anthropology, and phenomenology, can offer a reasonably adequate account of what religion has been for man from earliest to recent times. It is rooted in the group; it has a theoretical dimension which provides its adherents with a way of apprehending reality; and it is a practical affair which guides and transforms their lives in the precarious ecology between human and divine powers.

It would be unfortunate for a philosopher of religion today to proceed without some such understanding of religion, just as it would be unwise for him to philosophize without a sound knowledge of the history of philosophy. The parallel continues. Just as the history of philosophy cannot define for us today what philosophy must be and do, so too, the history of religions cannot define for us today what religion is or is to become. However, we learn one more lesson from the history of religions. It is that religion itself is not a fixed and unchanging essence, and that it has changed in important ways. During the millenium before our present era a number of religions assimilated the moral imperative to themselves. Also, in Hinduism and Buddhism, and in medieval Islam, Judaism, and Christianity, religion showed a dexterous ability to absorb the views of ancient science into their fabric. Religion has proven both conservative and flexible in the past; and, confounding as it is to both its friends and critics, its future lies open but not visible to us. For example, if ancient puberty rites have almost disappeared as religious rites in industrial societies, and if marriage becomes wholly secularized, we cannot be certain that religion itself will disappear, say in the forms of sacrament and prayer. Nevertheless, what is sure is that the spread of urban, technological society has issued a prolonged and fast-moving challenge: Is religion an essential perspective in human life and part of the fabric of reality? The challenge has many salients, but two of them are especially important for a philosopher of religion. They are religious pluralism and the process of secularization. It is not easy to say in what each consists. The terms point to and mask such vital phenomena that they are in continual but various use.

Religious pluralism is not simply the actual existence of a multiplicity of religions, for that is age-old. Nor is it the awareness of such a multiplicity for that knowledge has been with us a long time. Educated Christians in the Middle Ages, for example, in some fashion knew of Judaism and Islam as well as of the remnant pagan folk religion. Religious pluralism as a contemporary phenomenon consists rather in *the compelling recognition that several different religions have proven their adequacy by organizing fundamental values through different systems of rites and symbols.* This may not mean that every religion has done it equally well, but it does mean that no one of them can so preempt the religious essence that it is in exclusive possession of religious values and meanings. Their diversity also means that religious teachings and imagery are not best understood in a strictly factual, literal, and commonsense way. It is clear that such a challenge forces the philosopher of religion to think through what the character of truth or meaning might be in religious terms.

The related challenge of secularization is not to be confused, of course, with secularism. Secularism is a philosophy which thinks that religion has already failed the challenge, and if it ever has played a role in human affairs, it is incapable of playing a constructive one now. It declares the bankruptcy of religion. On the other hand, secularization or secularity is not a philosophy but an actual contemporary process. It is the emergence of man and his world into a new realization of their intrinsic importance. More and more spheres of life—politics, social welfare, business, art, medicine and education—have come to be valued without direct reference to religious claims. The world has come to be validated in its own terms and not primarily as an instrument for the divine purpose or in terms of enclosure within a sacral order.[8] The process of secularization and the values of secularity have advanced the autonomy of man and his world. Some students of religion see this as a threat to the continued existence and role of religion and its values, while others hail it as a vindication of those religious values which are most important. Still others think that secularism and not religion will be vindicated. What is sure is that the challenge has made problematic the transcendent dimension to which religion has characteristically pointed.

In summary, then, the double challenge is one which has reverberations for a theory of being and a theory of meaning. Secularization poses the problem of reality (transcendence), and religious pluralism poses the problem of truth (diversity of meanings).

CONCEPTUAL RATIONALITY

Before formulating a philosophy of religion a philosopher must become conscious, not only of the character and development of religion, but also of the considerations which have shaped his own philosophy. How does the history of philosophy teach us to view philosophy itself? In the host of different and sometimes conflicting philosophies the unity and consistency of philosophical inquiry seem to waver. Yet, if we do not become too particular we can say some things generally true of most philosophical inquiry. It is a form of *rationality*, but not the only form. There is also common sense, science, morality, law, and technology. Philosophy is *reflective* rationality, and so it deals with more primary forms of experience. For the problematic of this essay, the most important feature of philosophical rationality is its *conceptual* character. The history of philosophy exhibits many theories of conceptuality and even philosophers who deny that there are concepts. The use of the term *conceptual* in this essay, however, is not meant to adopt any one of these theories, for example, Aristotle's universals, scholastic abstractions, Husserl's *eidoi* or Wittgenstein's family resemblances. Nor is it necessary here to enter into whether the character of conceptuality arises out of the nature of things or is a function of linguistic structure. Only a very general, though arguable, point is assumed: *Not all meaning is conceptual, but the form in which philosophy has tolerated meaning has been thoroughly conceptual.* It is assumed in this essay that meaning presents itself to us in many guises, so that we can say that a painting or poem has meaning for us, and that an encounter, action or gesture is meaningful. Most of us, however, would not insist that the meaning of these things is equivalent to a set of concepts carefully contrived to describe them. A conceptual description is a form of meaning in which clarity is sought for the sake of thorough penetration, in which precision is sought for the sake of determinate definition, and in which meaning at a distance from the unreflecting complexities of life is demanded for the sake of an objective understanding. Common sense, poetry, theater, and other modes of expressive life employ concepts for the sake of communication; but, unlike philosophy, the context of these life forms is not itself rigorously conceptual. Concepts are embedded in a conversation, poem, or play, but the mode of meaning is not itself wholly given over to a self-conscious and resolute conceptualization. Philosophy, then, is not unique in using concepts, but (along with science) it also defines and systematically integrates its descriptions and interpretations in a mode and context that is methodically conceptual. It is incurably argumentative and must proceed consequentially by giving reasons, and so it is *methodical* and *logical* rationality. It must test those reasons, and so it is *critical* rationality, raising questions within a framework that appears to itself as autonomous and final. It is answerable only to itself, though it is responsible to the truth. Finally, it is ambitious rationality, seeking to be *radical, comprehensive,* and *fundamental.* It asks the last questions or the first. Of course, it is not easy to say just what the appropriate questions are, and it is even more difficult to decide whose reflections are most radical. But he is a philosopher who furthers the investigation of the general and fundamental principles of meaning, value and reality by raising the most sweeping and profound questions and by opening up new apprehensions of these questions and their responses.

This fundamental, self-prescribing, reflective, conceptual rationality has a history, and if the philosopher is to become conscious of his own philosophical inquiry, he is obliged to pay a good deal of attention to the general considerations which have gone into shaping that expectancy for meaning and demand for conceptuality that characterizes philosophical rationality. One of these considerations is the origin of philosophy among the Greeks. These origins have persisted in their influence in a remarkably decisive way. The conception of rationality which was hammered out by the early philosophers bears the marks of its association with religion. Then, and ever since, the relations between philosophical reflection and religious faith have shown a variety of ways in which the two coexist. Of one thing we are certain: Philosophical reason took its origin within a context shaped importantly by the poetic religion of Greece. We can speak less surely of the exact relation between the incipient philosophical rationality and the popular religion. The Pythagorean brotherhood gives evidence of reflective rationality in the service of religious values. But Xenophanes' strictures and the Athenians' threat against Anaxagoras indicate that the new rationality could be or seem severely critical of the popular religion. Abstractly, we can picture two extremes. At the one pole, philosophical reflection would have placed itself so much in the service of religion that it would have lost its autonomy and its powers of criticism—the power to frame its own questions, establish its own criteria, and seek out its own methods. At the other pole, philosophy would have assumed such an imperial stand towards religion that it would have recognized only its own rights, and would have sought to transform, erase, or ignore religion. In the first stance we would look towards the withering away of philosophy and in the second to the disappearance of religion. Yet most philosophies actually find themselves at some point between the two extremes. The tension between philosophical reflection and religious faith which characterizes the beginnings of philosophy has continued to manifest itself in a variety of ways. Each way is a somewhat different rational expectancy.

The tension between the critical and conceptual standards of philosophy and the intuitive and revelatory claims of religion has been partly constitutive of philosophical rationality. For the tension *between* philosophy and religion finds a reflected tension *within* philosophical rationality itself. For simplicity's sake we might trace two very general expectancies. The one would look for rational satisfaction in terms of a strict, formal, and even narrow criterion. The other would look for rational satisfaction in terms of a broader, more flexible, material standard. To describe these expectancies fairly we must use pejorative and laudatory terms for each, for there seem to be no neutral ones. Thus, if we seem to speak pejoratively of a certain strict narrowness over against a generous breadth, we must compensate by adding that the strict caution is also a firm demand that meaning be adequately tested. On the other hand, if we seem to speak pejoratively of a certain flexible breadth over against a hardheaded firmness, we must in balance add that flexibility may allow reason to adapt itself to different sorts of evidence. The strict formal expectancy calls for an emphasis upon argument, method, and precision; in a word, upon *logos* or *ratio*, upon the discursive and systematic facet of reason. The flexible rationality is more sensitive to extraphilosophical claims (some will say more credulous), and it places greater emphasis on an open, discriminating dependence upon the evidence; in a word, upon *nous* or *intellectus*, upon the intuitive and apperceptive. Of course, it is too simple to speak of these as absolute expectancies, and each philosophy is a compounding of them in varying degrees. The tension between these aspects of human rationality, between the logical and poetic, between arguing and seeing, is constitutive of philosophical reflection. This inner philosophical tension is made even more crucial because of the emphasis given to the intuitive by the popular religion out of which and over against which the new mode of reflection strove to identify itself.

The more immediate background of our present conception of rationality takes shape in the emergence of scientific rationality in the sixteenth and seventeenth centuries. In the flood of scientific demands for precision and method, the rational came to be equated with the logically conceptual, backed up usually by the empirically verifiable. Within this strict view of reason, much that had hitherto been considered rational came to be rejected as nonrational, noncognitive, or emotive. The great seventeenth-century philosophers gave expression to an expectancy for meaning which leaned to the stricter and more formal conception of rationality. Shored up by brilliant successes in empiriomathematical science, which was pursuing its own form of strict rationality, an understanding of philosophical rationality emerged which confirmed the more formal traditions in past philosophy. Under the influence of this expectation modern philosophy, as we have seen, has generally forged a distinction among themes of philosophical investigation. There is a core of investigations which are held to be indispensable to philosophy. These are the major disciplines: epistemology and methodology, ontology and metaphysics, ethics and politics. These core disciplines are generally held to be the bread and butter of the philosophical meal. It is thought (by the most tolerant) that to them can be added some lesser nonparadigmatic disciplines, such as philosophical inquiries into art, history, and religion.

The point of reciting this familiar history is to notice that the disposition of what is core and what is peripheral in philosophy is itself a function of a definite (and historically developed) conception of rationality. Such a distribution of disciplines within philosophy is based upon a conception of meaning that restricts meaning in its philosophical form to abstract concepts, verified by a definite interpretation of evidence, and related by a systematic logical interconnection that also reflects this stricter conception of rationality. There is, undoubtedly, a salutary caution in this wary understanding of the philosophical circle. Certainly the demand that any purported evidence make its way by meeting rational standards and that it be consistently integrated with other philosophical results is a demand that is indispensable for philosophy. If it gives up this demand, it forsakes its traditional role of passing upon its own truth claims, and threatens to become an exercise in interpretation or even in opinion.

At the same time, however, the history of philosophy has examples of philosophers who accepted that demand but pressed it with a minimal or flexible emphasis in order to accommodate the different kinds of evidence they sought to understand. From its beginnings there have been philosophies moved by the more ample and generous conception of rationality *(nous, intellectus)*. Indeed, the natural-law tradition affords examples, in which rationality is equivalent to reasonableness in the face of difficult and recalcitrant data. Perhaps Aristotle's remark that we ought not to demand more certainty of any study than its subject matter can reasonably be thought to provide is a classical statement of the broader and more flexible conception. What is reasonable becomes very nearly a prudential judgment. Presumably, however, the limits of this wider rationality are reached when a philosophy can no longer give reasons consistent with its own integrity and its own rational expectations. And yet despite Aristotle's broad conception of rationality and his omnicurious interest in all fields of investigation, he studied these from a definite conceptual point of view. This has been the history of philosophical reflection in both its strict and its flexible practice. In a word, philosophy has been fiercely or mildly abstract and conceptual until some very recent and problematic exceptions.

CONCEPTUAL RATIONALITY AND ANALOGY

The conceptual rationality characteristic of philosophy has not been stretched more vigorously at any time in its history than in the high Middle Ages. In the thirteenth century a sophisticated philosophical reflection was brought to bear upon new questions proposed by religion: questions about creation, the end of human life, and the existence and nature of an infinite God. It is well noticed that these questions caused a crisis in the religious circles of Christendom, but it is less remarked that they also posed a crisis for philosophical rationality. Under the pressure of the religiously inspired questions, a philosophical theology developed which distinguished between the ordinary and extraordinary use of terms. True to the dominant philosophical conception of rationality, the main discussion moved within a theoretical perspective that identified meaning with conceptuality. Even so symbolic a thinker as Saint Bonaventura used the common language of Aristotelian science. Nevertheless, this conceptual perspective was strained to its limits (some will say, beyond) in its efforts to cope with the new problems of predication about God.

Saint Thomas's doctrine of analogy was perhaps the most thoroughgoing conceptual attempt made at the time. It was a device for coping with the extraordinary language of God talk. Indeed, analogy can still serve today as a way of cutting between any precipitate demand for either/or. It is not uncommon today to suppose that the choice is either confident speech about God or silence. The doctrine of analogy, on the other hand, suggests that it may be too easy to assume that a term, such as *wise*, said of God, either has a merely human meaning or none at all. To assume a simple dichotomy between finite and infinite, man and God, may be a subtle extension of the verifiability principle, with all that that assumes. A doctrine of analogy, then, may still be able to marshal the hesitations of human speech before God. For the classical medieval theologians, there was need to speak of and to God, for an underlying religious sensibility moved beneath all their rationality. So much so, that their philosophy was properly a religious use of philosophy, buoyed up by a religious life. For Saint Thomas, an extraordinary rationality was operative from the beginning of his reflection; and so all his data, questions, and principles were already open to a transcendent dimension of reality and were not caught within an immanent human order. His religious apperception showed him a kind of rationality that only the perspective of faith could then offer him; and the doctrine of analogy was shaped as a device for accommodating talk about and to God. It was an instrument of a religious philosophy; and yet it was a philosophical answer to needs which came from a life in which religious speech was already an actuality.

The point most germane to the present consideration, however is not the religious origin and service of the doctrine of analogy but its conceptuality. Analogy is a move to salvage God talk within a mode of rationality that is radically conceptual. It is a way in which religious language is salvaged within a theory that identifies meaning with abstract concepts and their employment in judgments.

By introducing negativity into the analogous term, Saint Thomas was able to break the literal continuity of meaning between the same term said of creatures and of God. He did this in two ways. First, he accepted and developed the dialectic of *viae, affirmativa* ("God is good"), *negativa* ("God is not good in the sense in which creatures are good") and *eminentior* ("God is subsistent Goodness"). The latter was not a simple return to affirmation but an accentuation of the negative as well as the affirmative. Second, he distinguished between the thing signified *(res significata)* and the manner in which it is signified *(modus significandi)*.[9] In ordinary language the referent and the predication are tailored for one another. In the extraordinary language of speech about or to God, they are not. Whereas the speech intends the thing signified (God), the manner of signification (the language) is wholly inadequate to represent the referent. Analogous speech incorporates the tension between manner and intention, and is the bold attempt to cope with an infinite distance in meaning and reality by a shattered but not wholly obliterated conceptual scheme. Analogous God talk, then, is a way of trying to handle an incomprehensible distance and nonidentity by conceptual means within a conceptual mode of rationality, that is, within an expectancy for philosophical meaning that is satisfied by concepts and their employment in judgments.

RELIGION AND SYMBOLIC MEANING

Most students of religion agree that religious language is not simply literal, and various ways have been taken to mark this nonliterality. The Bible itself uses language in several different ways, and the Christian Fathers began a long discussion of the several senses of sacred scripture. Others speak of the "more-than-human" meaning of religious language and of the element of mystery in religious speech. Religious language has been called extraordinary and heteronomous. And we have just considered analogy as a way of handling the distinction between ordinary and religious language. In more recent times, however, the long association of philosophy and religion has assumed a new form different from the traditional rational theology or philosophy of God. This modern way of handling the problem of nonliterality is to distinguish between conceptual and symbolic orders of meaning, and to consider one kind of symbol a proper religious mode of meaning.[10] The distinction within the whole field of meaning between concept and symbol represents an advance for the philosophical study of religion. The history of religions confirms the distinction and offers a foundation for the contemporary philosophy of religion.

The history of religions suggests that religious symbols are one of the early apprehensions of man. The term is used variously today and its use in this essay needs to be made more precise. A symbol is not a signal, such as a traffic light; nor is it a physical sign, such as smoke; nor is it a mental sign, such as a concept. A concept may be understood as a sign which is abstract and indicative of its referent. A conceptual theory of judgment, then, would explain how the concept comes to be related to the concrete. A theory of symbolic judgment, however, would not understand such a judgment to simply intend, refer, or relate the mind to the object. A symbolic expression is, rather, a reference beyond itself which also paradoxically embodies its referent. It is not simply significative, for it "delivers" its referent in a more than conceptual way, and through it the referent is purportedly in some sense actually present. Yet it is in another sense less than conceptual, because the referent escapes the limitation brought about in the process of symbolization. The paradox consists in the inability to separate the symbol from something which would supposedly lie "behind" it. If we can do that, we do not have a symbol, but an allegory which is subject to conceptual translation. It is important to insist that the present attempt is to describe the religious symbol as fully operative within a religious context, and primarily within religious rite. The religious symbol relapses into a dead form when it is disengaged from that context. The ancient myths, to us, can be taken simply as stories, unless we deliberately recreate the religious context in which they were more sacrament than story. Only through such a reconstruction can the symbol of a dead religion be understood as once having had a religious force. The symbols of a living religion—the wine and bread consecrated, the holy waters of the Ganges, the sacred words of Passover—these are held to have not only an indicative and significative presence but the presence of power. The symbol invites the religious initiate to encounter in and through it the embodied presence of that to which it refers. The holy places, the sacred object, the mountain, the burning bush, the rock, the host—all reveal and mask a holy presence and power. To Saint Bonaventura, for example, the natural world itself was a sacrament of the Holy Trinity and revealed itself as such to an eye cleansed by faith.

The doctrine of analogy is a bold attempt to conceptualize the symbolic dimension of meaning, and it may come as close as such an effort can. But an analogous concept differs from a symbol in several ways. First, it is highly reflective, whereas the traditional symbol can strike home at a primordial level of meaning and experience. Second, analogy ends by distinguishing the thing signified from the predication which signifies it, whereas the symbol unites them. Zwingli is said to have drawn a conceptual distinction between the order of signs in the institution of the Eucharist and the result in reality, saying that the words, "This is my body," are predicative signs which only signify by way of commemoration the distant scene in the upper room where Christ broke bread with his disciples. Luther is said to have replied: "I have not come here to discuss whether *is* means is." For him, the words of consecration were the very symbols which referred beyond themselves and yet could embody the very presence of the divine, subject to the conditions for receiving the sacrament. Both concept and symbol have negativity in them. The general concept leaves out much of what is designated by it: Socrates is much more than a man or white or Greek. But it leaves out complexity for the sake of determinate formal precision. The symbol, on the other hand, hides more than it reveals, and yet evokes what is hidden. For that reason the symbol does more than unite the predication and the referent; it calls for the participation of the believer, because only in that way can he experience its saving power.

Religious symbols undergo a history, and their character and function can be changed. There are five relevant features under which symbols function today as vehicles of religious meaning. First, the traditional symbols come to the more educated in our society as "broken " symbols. They cannot be accepted without challenge. Moreover, they are not continuous with a conceptually intelligible line of meaning, as they were for medieval theologians. Second, they are therefore grasped and used in a reflective manner. They have entered the domain of reflection in a fully explicit way. Third, they are not the extension of analogous concepts into the context of religious faith, but rather rise from a reflective grasp of the totality, of the whole context of religious faith. Thus, they are grasped as another "language," or another "modality" of experience, or another "dimension" of meaning. Fourth, they do not function like a concept *manqué,* which lacks a proportion between referent and predication, but rather in their own right as a way of apprehending and expressing a transconceptual reality and meaning.[11] Fifth, they embody conative, emotive, and life-oriented power as well as intellectual meaning. They fulfill themselves when they inspire a response in conduct as well as a recognition in thought. This response is often engendered as a shared experience and activity. The religious symbol suggests a dimension of meaning that cannot be fully articulated in concepts, and evokes an order that claims more meaning and power than concepts can express or empirical facts verify.

PHILOSOPHICAL RESPONSIBILITY: THE TENSION BETWEEN AUTONOMY AND OPENNESS

It may be easy enough for a religion to endorse the claim that religious symbolism discloses a dimension of meaning inaccessible to conceptual theories of meaning, including empirical ones. But such a claim is not easily reckoned with from the point of view of philosophical rationality which has been conceptual in theory and practice. If a philosophy were to adjust its basic conceptions because of pressure from religious symbolism, would it not betray its own rational standards and expectations? Can a philosophy incorporate a symbolic dimension of meaning *into its own mode of reflective rationality* without so transforming its rationality as to be philosophy no longer? The question brings us to Heidegger's meditation by another route. We can even understand why he hesitated to use the word *philosophy.* Attempting to retrieve a certain poetic kind of meaning at the very origins of philosophy, he turned to the poet Hölderlin—and to the gods.

Nevertheless, philosophy cannot easily abandon its allegiance to conceptuality, for it cannot deny its historical career as a critical, fundamental, conceptual, reflective rationality. Even if it could forget its history, it cannot ignore its ambition to be a comprehensive yet self-consistent rational account of nonreligious as well as religious matters. Out of a responsibility inherent in philosophy itself, therefore, a philosophy of religion should be integrated with the general principles of meaning, value, and reality that are operative in the philosophy as a whole.[12] An alleged philosophy of religion which was so adapted to the mode of meaning offered by religion that it couldn't handle nonreligious problems would be a flawed philosophy, a reflective *deus ex machina.* As well as its need for internal coherence, a responsible philosophy also demands an autonomous exercise of reflective rationality, even in the face of the powerful symbolism of religion. It must never surrender its own rational expectation. But how is it to relate to religion, and even to other domains, such as art, history, and science?

Its past, as well as its need for a comprehensive self-coherence, and its autonomous integrity put philosophy in tension with other domains of human life, especially with that of religion.

It is not uncommon to assume that philosophy is a sort of gatekeeper to all rational discourse. On that assumption, two extreme positions may be taken regarding religion. (1) It may be considered a matter of indifference to philosophy. (1a) Thus, philosophy can withdraw itself from all but the duty of being keeper of the merely formal rules of discourse. This is tantamount, however, to denying the more ambitious understanding philosophers have usually had of their task, and so it claims too little for philosophy. (1b) Another way of being indifferent is to permit religion to pass over into a cloud of unknowing outside the realm of significant and controllable discourse, but this claims too little for religion. After all, even to those who do not accept its truth claims at face value religious speech is not gibberish. (2) The other extreme position holds that philosophy has governance over religious discourse. Some philosophers write as though religious language will be legitimated or condemned only after and because of their reflections. Or more modestly, they think that philosophy has the task of determining in what sense religious language can or cannot be meaningful. This view that philosophy exercises a kind of hegemony over religious expression or, more precisely, over the rational values in religion finds no sure parallel in science, history, or poetry. A philosophy of science certainly does not legitimate scientific discourse; a philosophy of history does not confirm the validity of historical writing; and a philosophy of poetry does not vindicate poetic language. Of course, if history were merely the art of the particular, and poetry merely decorative imagery, there would be no rational values peculiar to history and poetry. On that view, then, philosophy might be understood as the keeper of the general principles and basic notions of all rational discourse. To this general rational core the empirical particulars of history and the imagery of poetry would presumably be added, but not as *rational* values. To this view poets and historians might rightly protest that their discourses do have rational values which can be achieved *only* through history and poetry. Many philosophers are ready to acknowledge this claim to other unique forms of rationality, and to admit the distinctiveness of the ''language of poetry,'' the ''realm of historical discourse,'' or the ''world of science.'' It may, therefore, be unwise to expect a philosophy of religion to legitimate or illegitimate religious language.

Philosophical attempts to proscribe the rationality of religion can take several forms. (2a) Obvious attempts to subordinate religious discourse to a priori criteria include appeals to the verifiability principle. (2b) Still other attempts are frankly reductive. Hume did useful philosophical work when he restricted his account of religion to the origins of religious belief in the human emotions; and Kant reinforced a genuine alliance between religion and morality. Both of these analyses are indispensable elements in the formulation of an adequate philosophy of religion; but it remains true that the first reduced religious discourse to its noncognitive functions, and the second to its moral or regulatory role. (2c) Classification can be a more subtle form of hegemony, in which the philosophy of religion is placed alongside other "philosophies of . . . ," and is *expected to conform to a context of discourse which takes its possibilities exclusively from nonreligious speech.* If religious speech is excluded from the nonphilosophical discourses (such as science, morality, and common sense) in response to which philosophical discourse is shaped, then it is bound to sound alien in the courts of philosophy.

Between the extremes of indifference and subordination there lies the possibility of a negotiated settlement between philosophy and religion, a settlement which respects the autonomy of philosophical reflection and the integrity of religious symbolism. If analogy is a medieval example of an attempted settlement, Hegel's concrete universal is a more recent attempt. He transformed religion into its speculative philosophical account, but not without altering the very conception of rationality. Still, his treatment of the symbol emphasizes its theoretical, allegorical, and representative features, and betrays a framework that is basically conceptual. More recent studies in the nature of religious symbolism may invite philosophy to consider the relationship anew.

In any rapprochement, of course, it must be clearly understood that the basis of the relationship cannot include any compromise of philosophical autonomy, such as a readiness to accept the truth of a particular religious symbol, or even the vague sentiment that religion in its general claims to the transcendent is a true representation of reality. Philosophy simply hasn't the resources with which to cope with the negative transcendence and nonliterality of the religious symbol. Religious faith is needed if one is to affirm a reality in and beyond the symbol; and the philosopher must not base his consideration on an act of religious belief or disbelief. The curiously contingent yet absolute claims made in the name of a religion lie outside the scope of any position that can be established by philosophical rationality. Philosophy must leave in an indeterminate state the relation which religious symbols claim to have to transcendent reality. On the other hand, religion must not be expected to compromise its own integrity; for example, by reshaping itself into the merely noncognitive or moral. Religious discourse expresses an aspect of human experience that has its own meaning, features, and laws. Such an integrity and autonomy is also found in other realms of discourse, to be sure, such as art, science, history, and law. What differentiates these from religious discourse, and makes religion a special challenge to philosophy, is the negativity and claim to transcendence inherent in religious symbolism.

The philosopher, of course, has the right and duty to ask why the religious symbol ought to be taken into serious consideration in his reflection. What in its claim to meaning promises that a consideration of it will be philosophically significant? Religious faith claims to be a distinctive mode of apprehending reality, an openness to a dimension which has extraordinary power and a meaningful though mysterious presence. On the other hand, the extravagances and dangers of religion are notorious. It is, for that reason, much easier to admit that a chemist should be the judge of what is good chemistry, or a lawyer good law, than to leave it to the religious man to say what is good religion. Yet, even if the philosopher respects the integrity of the religious man as much as that of the chemist or lawyer, there remains a properly philosophical question: What is the enterprise of chemistry, law, or religion within the whole order of human knowledge, values, and activities? Such a fundamental probing arises out of a framework of questioning that is the traditional fabric of philosophical reflection. The autonomous character of philosophy is grounded in the transcendental questions it asks and the answers it accepts. In the pursuit of a radical, comprehensive, and integral questioning which is sensitive to the evidence, however, it may be necessary to go beyond previous understandings of conceptual rationality itself in order to accommodate a newly recognized demand for meaning.

In asking about its relation to religious language, philosophy must ask about the very structure of meaning and language itself. It is helpful in the present reflection to see language in three of its constitutive elements: the subjective intent of the speaker, the objective intentionality of what is meant, and the modality in which the meant is expressed. The modality of the meaning determines the possibilities and the limitations of saying what is meant, but the full structure of the language is constituted through the interplay of the three factors. These three factors are not extrinsically interrelated. The subjective intent arises out of the larger context of a life oriented towards linguistic expression. So, too, the modality and intentionality are open to one another and impose their demands upon each other and upon the speaker. In religious language the reality is transcendent and yet all-encompassing, and the modality is the symbolism which both points beyond itself and yet also embodies the reality as a presence and power. In philosophical language, the modality has been deliberately conceptual. Nevertheless, the character of the modality and its ultimate intent may come to be qualified by its attention to other modes of meaning.

PHILOSOPHICAL RATIONALITY AND TRANSCONCEPTUAL MEANING

Religious symbols may be translated into concepts, but in their fullness they contain nonconceptual elements, including reference to what is conceptually inaccessible. In this sense, then, they are extra- or transconceptual. On the one hand, religious symbolism claims to be constitutive of meaning and reality; words of consecration or blessing allegedly create a presence and power. On the other hand, abstract conceptuality does not claim to be constitutive but only representative or significative. Religious symbolism shows us a kind of meaning which purportedly unites theory and practice, knowledge and power. It is evident, even to a nonbeliever, that religion does in some fashion move men with its symbols, and is sometimes capable of transforming them. If we were to ask for a religious account of that transformation, we would be told that the symbol is a sacrament which carries with it the power of the holy. Without accepting or rejecting that religious interpretation, philosophy can recognize that a certain form of originative meaning is capable of "invading" a human psyche, meeting a response and bringing about a transformation. Furthermore, philosophical reflection can recognize that such a transformation is not accounted for by a theory of meaning which sees meaning as the result of applying or referring concepts to reality. Neither application nor reference is the source of the power. Rather, the believer is encaptured, even overwhelmed, by the symbolism which works through his response to transform him. It gathers intellectuality, sensibility, affectivity, and conation together into a single concrete meaning. It throws the believer out into a purported reality which lies inexpressibly beyond his capacities. Concrete presence and mysterious negation are constituent elements of religious symbolic meaning. This projection into reality is not simply the reference of abstracted meanings in judgments, but is the throwing forward of the whole many-levelled personality into a commitment which may bring comfort or high risk. The power is not experienced as coming from within man, but is a response evoked in man by the symbol, so that man is moved by the presence of the meant in the symbol. Such meanings operative in man evoke a vision of ultimate values and urge him to act upon them, although not in the same way that moral ideals do. A discussion of the different sorts of performative utterances would help to develop this difference, but that is beyond the present essay.[13]

What can the philosophical significance of such purported meanings be? The answer hinges upon the character of philosophical reflection. If such reflection finds adequate expression in abstract, general, ordinary conceptual language, then religious symbolism will acquire philosophical significance only by being translated into such language. It will, therefore, be translated into regulatory moral categories (as in Kant), or into analogous ontological categories (as in Thomas Aquinas), or into some similar conceptual scheme. *There are reasons for supposing, however, that the philosophical enterprise itself is not adequately expressed by ordinary conceptual language.* Its form of reflection has usually been held to be unique in its drive for completeness, depth, and ultimacy. Obscured in medieval times by religion and in modern times by science, philosophy still has ambitions that are not fully satisfied within conceptual theories of meaning. While Socrates sought to bring moral values to conceptual clarity, nevertheless he took up the life of philosophical reflection as a way which in its totality was intended to transform the seeker. Self-understanding intended self-transformation. Now, whereas conceptual theories grasp meaning as a constituted result, Socrates' own understanding of the examined life was an apprehension of meaning as constitutive, that is, as capable of transforming human life. It is this transformative seed in the philosophical enterprise which provides philosophy with its own grounds for openly recognizing transformative power in other domains. The comprehensive, radical, and sapiential ambitions of philosophical reflection lead it beyond a conceptual theory of constituted meaning; so that, without accepting or rejecting any truth claims on behalf of a religion or of religion in general, philosophy can still recognize a dimension of meaning which contains a transforming power that comes from the interplay of the ordinary perception of reality (the profane) and the extraordinary apperception of a reality purportedly apprehended in faith (the sacred). In this way, religious symbolism can play a role in calling upon philosophy to recognize philosophical grounds for adjusting its theory of meaning. The adjustment would accommodate the symbolic form as an openness to rootage beyond conceptual meaning. With this adjustment, a more than merely negative sense of mystery becomes ingredient in philosophical reflection.

At the same time, however, such a philosophy would be "empirical" in the fullest sense, unable to disengage its fundamental meanings from its matrix in experience and unwilling to formulate them into abstract, definite, and closed concepts devoid of the larger transconceptual context. The tension is here at its height, for philosophy must balance the claims of rational precision with the claims of sensitivity to all modes of experience.

Such a transcendental "empiricism" demands not only a new theory of meaning but also a new way of distributing meaning. Among a number of phenomenologists the *eidos* is understood in a way not incompatible with such an "empiricism." Heidegger's *existentialia* are by no means essences or properties in the classical sense. Moreoever, *Dasein* is neither universal humanity nor a particular man. Such a theory of meaning does not distribute meaning into the Aristotelian universal and particular, nor into class and member, nor into law and instance. It transcends these distinctions. A symbolic theory of meaning must account for the concretion of the universal and the singular in the unity of the symbol. It may be a helpful analogy to consider one's experience of a great work of art. Here universality means the recovery of the one in the many. The art work brings many elements into a unity, and is available to many participants in its excellence. The same is true of religious symbolism. It unifies its theophanies and recovers the disintegration or falling away of its believers.

Such a theory of meaning will also express itself in a new mode of procedure in philosophy. Philosophy is discursive and will always appear as a *way*. It has usually appeared as a rational way, moving from a beginning (evidence or first principles) to a conclusion (the effect or cause, ground or consequent, the explanation). But in order to carry on its reflection in the light and power of a theory open to the symbolic dimension of meaning, philosophy will have sometimes to proceed in ways different from that of logical conceptual analysis and argument. We already have some suggestions of such a procedure in the reflections of Marcel, Heidegger, Sartre, and Nietzsche. Even though only one of these is known as a religious believer, all of them strove to incorporate into their reflection something of the symbolic dimension of meaning revealed by religion.

THE PHILOSOPHY OF RELIGION AND A THEORY OF MEANING

Some readers may concede that some mode of meaning exists as has here been described; and some of these may even concede that philosophy ought to be cognizant of religious symbol as an extrinsic limit to its own conceptual analysis, just as art, science, and common sense also impose extrinsic limits upon philosophical reflection. But it may still be asked, why should a philosophy rework its own view of the foundations of meaning in order to incorporate a symbolic transconceptual mode of meaning? As has been suggested in the previous section, the imperative lies in its own understanding of itself as manifested in much of its history. Philosophy has traditionally claimed to be the guardian of the intelligibility of discourse in its more general and necessary conditions, conditions without which discourse itself would lack a rational basis. And yet an observer cannot but feel a more restrictive distinctness in the way in which philosophy has carried out its mandate. Poetic discourse, for example, continues even in the face of violations of consistency rules which philosophy cannot tolerate in its own procedure. And yet poetry violates these in the need to find a richer meaning. In a word, philosophy proves to be somewhat curious. It claims to be the guardian of the conditions which make any and all discourse possible, and yet it practices a kind of discourse which is more restrictive than the field of all possible meaningful discourse. In overcoming all points of view, it finds itself to be a point of view of a paradoxical sort. Neither the more formal nor the more flexible traditional conception of rationality is adequate to cope with the kinds of discourse that include the symbolic as well as the conceptual.

It is here that the philosophy of religion may provide the key and instrumentality for transforming the understanding of rationality operative until recent times in philosophy. What, then, is the challenge which a philosophy of religion poses for philosophy in general? It can be the instrument for asking what would philosophy have to be in order to acknowledge such a mode of meaning, value, and power as religious symbolism manifests? And it must answer that question without determining the validity of the truth claims of particular religions or religion in general, just as it must be open to the modality of meaning in science and in art without deciding upon *their* truth claims.

This is the inherent condition of philosophical reflection. A philosophical rationality carries about with it the prephilosophical districts from which it has come and the extraphilosophical districts which lie adjacent to its interest. But, more than that, a philosophy is changed by the regions it invades in its philosophical exercise. It is not changed merely in its externals, like a chameleon which takes on different colors easily as it moves into new surroundings. Rather, an alert philosophical reflection is altered in its structural principles, its aspirations, motivations, and criteria, and even in the way in which it seizes and understands itself. Reflection is transformed by what it feeds on. If it feeds on itself it will become sterile, like those grammatical logicians whom logic had detained, as John of Salisbury said of his former friends in twelfth-century Paris. And if it feeds only on its past history, it will also become frigid and will not conceive. If, on the other hand, it feeds upon some other mode of experience, such as science, certain emphases are bound to show, certain conceptions of rationality will gain a hearing, certain matters of importance to science will perhaps have a privileged hearing, and may even become overdeveloped while others remain underdeveloped, ignored, or even denied. The same might be said of a philosophy nurtured primarily upon art or politics—or religion. A philosophy is a human undertaking, and its own ambition condemns it to be malformed, bearing a suspicious resemblance to the special interests, to the intellectual gene pool, of the philosopher whose parent it is. There is no cure for this imbalance, only a cautious and limited palliative.

Nevertheless, in the face of its constitutional affliction, a sense of philosophical responsibility can drive the more conscientious philosopher to attempt to reserve room *in principle at least* for dimensions of meaning and reality that are not in the foreground of his interests. Bound to fail, he mitigates his failure as best he can. Perhaps the history of philosophy can even provide a rough rule of thumb. The formation of a theory of meaning and reality will reflect the pre-, extra- and properly philosophical interests and evidence of a philosopher, but he will be needlessly unreflective and uncritical if he refuses to face up to several typical accomplishments of man. Philosophy has known these long before Kant and Hegel, who called them the works of the spirit: science, history, art, politics (and with it ethics), and philosophy itself. But they also included religion. The rule of thumb, then, is this: A contemporary philosopher ought not to develop his basic conceptions of knowledge and reality without at least seriously listening to these voices. He does so at his peril. He may, of course, in the end judge himself impelled to exclude one or more of these voices on grounds of his theory of evidence or of rationality. What, it can surely be asked, has Jerusalem to do with Athens? What has a paintbrush to do with critical rationality? What have the marketplace and the hustings to do with a theory of knowledge? And does philosophy really need to contemplate itself in its history before redefining itself? There are conflicting answers to these questions, but it is perilous to frame one's philosophy without putting them.

A philosophy which takes seriously the symbolic dimension of meaning exhibited in religion is called upon to rethink the long history in which the meaning appropriate to philosophical rationality has been identified with conceptuality. It will have to enlarge its theory of meaning and its expectation of truth so as to build into philosophical rationality a transconceptual dimension of meaning. This is the challenge which a serious philosophy must meet in its philosophy of religion. If it meets that challenge and rejects religious symbolism, and perhaps the whole order of symbolic meaning, as irrelevant to redefining philosophical rationality, it will at least be the better for having rethought its theory of meaning. If, on the other hand, a philosophy opens itself out towards the symbolic so as to incorporate it into its own conception of philosophical rationality, it will be called upon to overhaul its theory of meaning, value, and reality, to rework its conception of truth, freedom, transcendence, and all of its central conceptions. In the end it will have transformed its expectancy for meaning.

To sum up:

1) The tension between philosophy and religion reveals a difference between two modes of meaning. Conceptual theories have played and must continue to play an important role in philosophy; they present meaning as a result, that is, as constituted, significative, and even representative. A theory of meaning open to religious symbolism, however, must recognize and accommodate three features: a) meaning that is transconceptual because the referent purports to be not completely conceptually inaccessible; b) meaning that purports to incarnate the presence of the referent while it masks its presence; and c) meaning that has transformative power.

2) There are grounds in philosophy itself for recognizing constitutive as well as constituted meaning: for this is the attempt at self-understanding.

3) Moreover, philosophy must formulate its theories of meaning so as to accommodate all modes of meaning; this is the demand for completeness or comprehensiveness.

4) In religion, then, philosophy finds a challenge as well as a risk, and yet also an opportunity to reformulate its theories of meaning so as to make room for the symbolic modality of meaning exhibited in religion; and yet to do this without granting or denying religious truth claims.

The philosopher who ventures into the philosophy of religion may think that he is going to add a new application to his basic principles; but if he takes seriously the modality of experience and behavior exhibited by the religious man—then he may find that he will have to retrace his steps and recast his entire philosophy.

NOTES

1. This is mentioned as only one element in an extensive discussion about the definition of religion by Frederick Ferré, *Basic Modern Philosophy of Religion* (New York: Scribners, 1967), p. 73.

2. The contributions of psychology to an understanding of religious belief come into play in a perspective somewhat different from the present consideration.

3. As in Joachim Wach, *The Comparative Study of Religions* (New York: Columbia University Press, 1958), chaps. 3–5.

4. As in E. O. James, *Comparative Religion* (New York: Barnes & Noble, 1961).

5. *Das Heilige,* translated as *The Idea of the Holy,* trans. John W. Harvey, 2d ed. (New York: Oxford University Press, 1958).

6. *The Sacred and Profane* (New York: Harper & Row, 1959), p. 95.

7. G. Van Der Leeuw, *Phenomenologie der Religion,* translated as *Religion in Essence and Manifestation,* 2 vols. (New York: Harper & Row, 1963), 2: 374ff.

8. James Collins, *The Emergence of Philosophy of Religion* (New Haven: Yale University Press, 1967), p. 434. This excellent book is a study of the classical founders of the philosophy of religion: Hume, Kant, and Hegel. The last two chapters are filled with penetrating and sagacious observations of the problems and issues in this field.

9. See the valuable discussion in G. Smith, *Natural Theology* (New York: Macmillan, 1951).

10. See, however, J. Heywood Thomas, "Religious Language as Symbolism," *Religious Studies* 1(1965–66) : 89–93, for a wise reminder that symbolism is not the only kind of language which religion uses. On the other hand, I do not find telling his objections to the view of the symbol put forth below.

11. The descriptive term *transconceptual* will be clarified later in this essay.

12. Collins, *Emergence of Philosophy,* p. 435ff.

13. Antonio S. Cua, "Morality and the Paradigmatic Individuals,"*American Philosophical Quarterly* 6(1969), : 324–29.

Chapter 2

THE STRUCTURE OF RELIGION
John E. Smith

THE popular belief that religion is the same everywhere or that all religions are "at bottom" identical in essentials is a widespread falsehood that is saved from being completely worthless by the fact that religion does exhibit a universal or common *structure* wherever it appears. This structure is intimately related to the structure of human life in the world. The enduring pattern that enables us to understand religions widely separated in both time and space depends largely on the fact that man and the process of human life in the world have their own structures which remain, despite the undeniable variety introduced by vast differences of culture, ethnic features, geographical location, climate, etc. Structure means pattern or form; it is reality significantly organized. It can be grasped as that which endures above and beyond changing historical details. Because human life has a structure, we are able to understand the wrath of Achilles or sympathize with the love of Abelard for Héloïse although we are separated from both by centuries of time.

It should not be necessary to point out that neither the structure of religion nor of human life exists apart from historical embodiment, but it is important to avoid the supposition that the structure of religion itself represents a universal or "natural" religion freed from detail that is parochial or merely historical. The structure in question has a genuine persistence in all instances of concrete religion, and the chief value of seeking to discover it resides in the assistance it provides in understanding religion as a pervasive factor in human life. The philosophy of religion in any case is not directed towards the creation of a "rational" or "philosophical" religion by abstracting the generic structure of historic faith and endowing it with separate existence. The task of the philosophy of religion is

From: *Religious Studies* 1(1965–66) : 63–73.

to understand, to interpret, and to criticize religion, not to create it—something that is, at any rate, an impossibility.

Returning to the concept of structure itself, we may say that it is best understood in correlation with function. Structure means contemporaneous pattern or related elements, and function means a temporal development or process in which each structured element plays a particular role. To perform functions, an element must be structured, and a structured element can participate in a process only by performing some function. The two features are correlative and neither can be reduced to the other. A world of pure functioning is impossible since function itself requires structure, and a world of pure structure is likewise impossible since every element of a structure has a purpose or is "for" something. The pervasive fact of change does require, however, that the dynamic side of things, the side of function, be regarded as a primary datum; it is through the study of actual functioning that all knowledge of structure is attained. This fact is of special importance for the philosophy of religion, since religion appears as embodied in the most complex set of functions that exists—individual and corporate human life. The only manner in which the structure of religion can be grasped is through its historical manifestation in the lives of individuals and in the religious community or church.

Religion, wherever we find it, manifests a threefold structure than can be set forth in generic terms.[1] These terms can be further specified for interpreting a given religious tradition and can be used as a powerful tool in the task of understanding the plurality of world religions and of introducing order into what might otherwise appear to be but a chaos of historical information. Religion demands *first* an Ideal or religious object that is at once the ground and goal of all existence. As ground this object is the source of all that is and constitutes the reason why there is anything at all; as goal this object defines the ultimate destiny of all that is, especially the ideal being of man and what he may become. *Secondly,* religion lives in the conviction that natural existence or life as we find it is separated from that Ideal or religious object by some flaw or defect. Contrary to popular belief, religion does not thrive on an undiluted idealism or optimism; high and profound religion reveals a vivid sense of the distorted or broken character of existence and of some deep need on the part of man not only for the form of life manifested in the Ideal or religious object but for the removal of the flaw that infects his being and separates him from what he essentially is or was meant to be. Finally, there is a *third* element that takes the form of the deliverer or power that overcomes the need or flaw in existence and is able to establish the Ideal on the far side, so to speak, of broken or distorted existence. The three elements, then, that go to make up the structure of religion are the Ideal or religious object, the defect in existence or the Need, and the saving power or the Deliverer. Prior to the interpretation of these elements in terms appropriate for a particular religious tradition, they remain general and open to some variety of content. We must resist the temptation to supply this content from the Judeo-Christian tradition at the outset, lest we diminish the interpretative power of the structural scheme.

Every historical religion and a considerable number of substitutes that have functioned as religions can be shown to exhibit the structure just indicated. A clear description of this structure depends on the clarity with which the three basic concepts can be set forth and related to actual religion. Prior to this analysis it is necessary to understand the internal connections between the three elements and to see that these connections enter essentially into their meaning. The nature of the Ideal serves to interpret the task of the Deliverer by making clear what form of existence the deliverer must establish. The nature of the Need clarifies both the Ideal and the task of the Deliverer by contrast. The flaw that separates us from the Ideal makes us more vividly aware of the life abundant that we do not yet possess and shows us clearly what it is that the Deliverer has to overcome. Finally, the Deliverer shows forth the Ideal as that which is genuinely real despite the existence of the flaw that separates man from it.

The relations between the structural elements are not only logical in character but ontological and temporal as well. Ideally, the religious life should include the temporal or historical character of actual existence. We should begin with a vision of the Ideal, from which should follow the sense of being finite and unclean in comparison with the Ideal, leading on in turn to the quest for the Deliverer. In view of the variety in human individuality, the ideal logical pattern will not be repeated exactly in every case; the important point, however, is not mere conformity to a pattern but rather the acknowledgement of the historical nature of life. It is extremely doubtful whether a religious tradition can contain the truth about human life in its day-to-day movement unless it acknowledges the reality of time and relates the progress of human life to the cosmic process of redemption. For those religious traditions in which the dynamic character of concrete life is lost, redemption becomes a timeless affair that seems without relevance to ordinary life and experience. When the redemptive process is thought to take place entirely apart from historical life with all of its tragedy and distortion—as indeed it does for some forms of Hinduism and Buddhism and for Christianity when it stresses only *Heilsgeschichte*—actual life is abandoned or becomes no more than an incident in a myth of cosmic proportions. This undesirable consequence is avoided if we view the structure of religion not as a timeless pattern but as marking out a progression of the religious life, a movement, that is, from a vision of the Ideal to the awareness of the Need that separates us from it and on to the quest for the Deliverer.

In order to employ the three structural concepts to describe the universal structure of religion, it becomes necessary to set them forth in abstraction from what is distinctive of any singular religion. We must not conclude, however, that emphasis on the universal structure necessitates the loss of what is distinctive and thus essential in the singular religious traditions. On the contrary, the opposition often envisaged between the universal and the singular is a false opposition, for it is only through the use of universal conceptions making possible significant critical comparisons between singulars of the same kind that we are able to discover and express clearly what is distinctive of the singular phenomenon.[2] We may begin, for example, with the concept of Deliverer as universal and then select from each religious tradition the element or feature in it that functions as Deliverer, compare the several cases, and finally arrive at an understanding of the utter distinctness of each singular religion in the respect chosen for comparison. Such comparison by means of a structural concept, far from obscuring what is distinctive in the singular, enables us instead to grasp it more clearly just because we now know it through explicit contrast with other examples of the same kind.

THE STRUCTURAL CONCEPTS—IDEAL, NEED, DELIVERER

Ideal. The Ideal is the central element in all religion since it comprehends within its meaning the meaning of the Religious Object itself. As a consequence, the Ideal takes on a twofold meaning corresponding to the two aspects of the Religious Object—ground or standard guiding and judging life on the one hand, and goal or fulfillment of life on the other. In relation to the Religious Object, ultimate concern as experienced by the individual takes on a double meaning. There is a concern by the self for knowledge of its present status, the ground upon which it lives, and there is a concern directed away from the present self and towards a perfection of life which everyone but the most complacent person knows that he does not possess. A present imperfection can, however, be apprehended only through a *contrast effect* in which the actual situation is compared with the Ideal. In the legend of Job, for example, we can readily see the function of such contrast. The traditional conception of God called for prosperous life for the righteous and punishment for the wicked; Job's condition as both a model of the righteous man and yet one who suffers and does not prosper stands in sharp contrast with the Ideal as then conceived. The same point can be seen in Augustine's claim in *De Beata Vita* that the self cannot know its present condition without a standard of perfection by which to judge. By consulting the Ideal, the person gains knowledge both of his present state and of what he is meant to become.

Every religion contains more or less clear teaching concerning the Ideal or Religious Object in the dual sense of standard or truth about human life in the world and of goal expressing the ultimate purpose of life. It is characteristic of most religion that it is realistic because it views human life as standing under the judgment of a truth in contrast with which all other forms of life are regarded as defective and as carrying within themselves the seeds of destruction. This truth about life is revealed in the nature of the Ideal and is regarded as a present perfection not entirely dependent upon a process of realization in the future. As standard and truth about life within the world, the Ideal provides the guiding principle of morality. Understood as already embodying the final form of life, the Ideal exemplifies the properly religious meaning of life since it takes us beyond what we are *to do* and makes plain what we are *to be*.

From an ontological and theological point of view, the Ideal appears both as the Religious Object or God and as that life in God most completely in accord with the divine nature. From a psychological and historical point of view—considering the matter as it appears to the individual believer concerned for the pattern of his life—the Ideal is the object striven for and the life abundant defined by the divine nature.

Christianity has a clear view of the Ideal in the sense in which it is here understood. The New Testament reaffirms the one God of earlier biblical religion, with the radical added belief that the final nature of God is found in the figure of Jesus as Christ. In Christ the concept of God as loving kindness and as merciful, so much emphasized by the Old Testament prophets and vividly expressed in the later chapters of the Book of Isaiah, is brought to completion in the form of sacrificial love. The justice of the divine nature is also preserved in the New Testament picture of God, for the coming of the final manifestation of God is itself regarded as a form of judgment. Justice, however, is seen as comprehended within the divine love since the element of vengeance is eliminated and replaced by the idea of the divine persuasion aiming at preserving the life rather than bringing about the death of the sinner.

From the Christian perspective, the Ideal appears as a center of understanding that transcends the world while also dwelling within it. The divine nature is seen as providing the clue to the truth about human life in the world, including the standard that should determine the relations between man and man. The writer of the First Epistle of John expresses the point in a forceful way—"If a man say, I love God, and hate his brother, he is a liar."[3] For Christianity, what we have here been calling the Ideal incorporates still more. It presents not only the divine nature and the law of life in the world, but it includes a doctrine of the ultimate purpose of life and a vision of the perfect life. In Christianity, the doctrine of the Kingdom of God and of the life that is described as eternal, represent that part of the ideal from which we discover the true end of man. Much of the direct teaching of Jesus concerns the Kingdom, the quality of life it demands, its nature, it relation to the world of time and history and its final consummation in God. The Kingdom is described as a community of persons whose relations with each other are governed by the principle of the divine *agape*. This community of selves constitutes the ideal of man's life and the quality of life envisaged is the "eternal life" of Christian belief.[4] The so-called farewell prayer of Jesus as recorded in John contains the classical description of eternal life: "And this is the life eternal, that they should know thee the only true God . . ." (Jn. 17:3). The knowledge of God, that is, with all the implications of loving and willing that the term connotes, defines eternal life, the perfection of human existence.

Central as the Ideal is for every religion, it does not exhaust religion. For, though the Ideal be the final reality, religion is incurably realistic in the sense that it points us to a deep awareness that, as we presently are and stand, we are separated from the Ideal. Each religious tradition has its own diagnosis of what was earlier called the Need, the obstacle, flaw, deficiency that must be overcome if the Ideal is to be established in its fullness. A poet has written, "Between the promise and the fulfillment falls the shadow"; this shadow finds its place in the structure of religion as the concept of the Need.

Need. In view of the fact that religion is so frequently associated with hope and triumph it may seem strange to assert that the concept of the Need—the dark side of religious insight—is, in many respects, the most important of the three concepts. Despite the seeming incongruity, its importance remains. Between the Ideal as it stands before man in the form of a goal that has, in fact, not yet been realized, and its final realization, stands the Need as a stubborn and intractable obstacle. The religious perspective, that is, cannot be summed up in the complacent claim that all is well with the world, that the Ideal is real regardless of the tragic distortion of human life. On the contrary, all religions of scope and depth are filled with a clear sense of the negative judgment on existence. Life as it exists—the life of the "natural" man—is distorted; it is not as it ought to be because it harbors within itself some flaw or deep Need that has to be met with and overcome before we can speak confidently of the reality of the Ideal. Far from being the complacent celebration of a transcendent goodness existing above and beyond historical life, the religious perspective forces us to acknowledge the reality of evil and of some deep-seated obstacle that stands between us as we naturally exist and the attainment of the Ideal. As will become clear, the concept of the Need provides us with a powerful tool for the comparative interpretation of the world religions. When we can specify exactly where a given religion finds the Need and what nature it assigns to the flaw in existence, we have a clue not only to its diagnosis of the human predicament, but also to its understanding of the task set for the Deliverer or the power that is to effect the resolution.

Although attention has already been called to the temporal aspect of the structure of religion and its reflection of the movement of human life, it is not literally the case that the awareness of the Need falls neatly between the awareness of the Ideal and the quest for the Deliverer in the case of every individual person. A general description cannot hope to express adequately the variety to be found in individual experience. It is clear, nevertheless, that the awareness of the Need depends upon confrontation by the Ideal, and a serious acknowledgment of the reality of the Need is required if we are to have the quest for the Deliverer. In this sense the Need does fall between the other two elements in the structure.

To the extent to which the self knows the imperfect character of its present life, it can be said that the self begins to be aware of the Need. The person, that is, becomes aware, perhaps vaguely and dimly at first, of an incongruity, an incompleteness, and a lack of satisfaction within himself. The first sense of the Need corresponds to the common experience of *feeling that* a situation is unsatisfactory without having at the same time any clear understanding of exactly *what* is the cause of the deficiency. The first sense of the Need is negative; it appears largely as the lack or absence of something, like the experience of a void unaccompanied by a clear grasp of what would fill it or overcome the emptiness.

When the Ideal becomes more explicit to a person—usually in a vivid way through example, as in the model set by the Buddha or the pattern of love exemplified in Christ—the contrast between the norm and present life begins to define itself more clearly. As the awareness of the gulf between the actual and the Ideal becomes more insistent, the sense of Need becomes more and more acute and, as a result, it assumes a different form. The Need now presents itself as a positive obstacle; it appears no longer as a "privation" or deficiency. The Need now takes on an active and powerful existence the overcoming of which becomes a matter of serious concern.

When the Need is finally grasped as a positive power separating the person from the Ideal, a new distinction becomes appropriate. It is the distinction between the Need as an obstacle which can, in principle, be overcome or removed by man himself as he now exists in the world, and Need as something that cannot, in its own nature, be overcome by the being who has the Need. The internal connection between the three structural concepts becomes especially clear at this point. The nature and office of the Deliverer depends to a very large extent on the sense in which the Need is understood. For it is the task of the Deliverer—whatever precise form it may take—to overcome the Need and establish the Ideal. It is, therefore, crucial whether the one who has the Need is able to function as his own deliverer or whether the Deliverer must be another existing above and beyond man and capable of performing what man in his natural existence is unable to accomplish. Several possibilities present themselves. At one extreme is the humanistic view according to which the being in need still retains sufficient resources within himself to overcome the Need through some form of discipline and effort. At the other extreme is the view of radical discontinuity according to which the being in need is so radically separated from the Ideal that no basis whatever exists within the nature of the being in need from which the process of recovery or redemption is possible. Between these extremes, that of total continuity and total discontinuity between man and the Ideal, other views are possible that would seek to do justice to both elements while accepting neither extreme position as the final truth.

The differing interpretations are of central importance not only for the theory of man, but in relation to the concept of the Deliverer. The office of the Deliverer must be understood in relation to the being who is to be delivered, and to what it is that he is to be delivered from. Where man is seen as, in principle, capable of redeeming himself, i.e., where the Need is regarded as something that is pliable or respondent to human effort, the Deliverer inevitably becomes no more than an *example* of what man would have to be and to do in order to achieve his own salvation. On the other hand, if the Need is understood as involving a recalcitrant factor, something that resists human ingenuity and power, the Deliverer has a far different office. In this latter case, the Deliverer is no longer merely an exemplar, but must become a source of power available to the being in need, a source of power that man is unable wholly from his own resources to provide for himself.

These differences in understanding concern the precise nature and office of the Deliverer; they do not alter the fact that the Deliverer remains a necessary element in the structure of religion generally. For, as was previously pointed out, religion always contains within its interpretations and items of belief a diagnosis of man and the world aimed at revealing the flaw in existence separating us from the Ideal. The grand strategy of the enduring world religions has been to diagnose that flaw and then to point to some form of Deliverer able to overcome it. The decisive fact is that the major religions have not agreed in their diagnosis and consequently differ in their view of what sort of Deliverer is required for making up the deficiency. After brief comment on the concept of the Deliverer, I shall propose a threefold comparison illustrating these differences and at the same time showing how the theory of a general structure of religion provides us with a powerful conceptual tool for finding patterns of intelligibility among the world religions and of making critical comparisons. For if it could be shown that human life itself has a universal structure relatively independent of ethnic and cultural conditions, it might then be possible to discuss the question as to which of the major religions possesses the most faithful and relevant account of the human predicament and of its resolution.

Deliverer. Much has already been said to indicate the meaning of this concept. The Deliverer has two aspects, a function or office to be performed and filled and a specific nature that makes this operation possible. The task of the Deliverer is, as we have said, to overcome the Need and establish the Ideal on the far side, so to speak, of distorted existence. Whether the Deliverer need be identical with Ideal, as in the case of Christianity, or an instrument through which the redeeming process is accomplished, will depend on several factors. It is well, however, to notice that the Deliverer need not be a person. Unfortunately, the term itself connotes a person, and perhaps another term should be found that does not have this restriction attached to it. For in actual fact, the Deliverer has assumed a variety of forms; in some religions it is knowledge that delivers, or a law or a sacred discipline. And in the case of some of the secular substitutes for religion the Deliverer has been a political system or even the course of history itself. But if what we have called the structure of religion is to be adequate for the interpretation of religion wherever it appears, variety must be allowed for in the structural concepts themselves. Christianity views the Deliverer as assuming the form of a person, whereas other religions do not, although there will always be a counterpart for the Deliverer in every tradition. It is interesting to note, moreover, that the classical Christian theologians were not insensitive to the problem of the exact form the Deliverer must assume, which is precisely why Anselm's well-known question *Cur Deus Homo?* has continued to be of theological interest.

The explanatory value of the structure of religion can best be seen, not from further general analysis, but from actual comparison. Let us consider, in brief compass for present purposes, the conception of the Need and the Deliverer to be found in three traditions—the Vedanta form of Hinduism, Buddhism in its nontheistic form, and Christianity. A comparison involving so much in a short space need not be superficial in view of the fact that we need attend only to certain precisely selected features.

The Vedanta says that what separates man from the realization of the true self, that is, the Need, is a misapprehension of the true nature of things. The Need is located in a failure to understand reality as it really is. The true self (Atman) is that underlying unity most closely approximated in human experience by the dreamless sleeper who is effectively beyond the distractions caused by the separateness of things and by finite individuality. There is a tendency in this position to regard the fact of individuality itself as the obstacle standing between the self and its realization of the truth. What needs to be overcome is this mistaken view of things as finite, individual, separate, and sundered from each other. What is demanded as the Deliverer is knowledge, a form of insight which, once attained, teaches the believer that individuality is not the final truth and that the true self cannot be found among the items of the plurality. If the Need appears as the defect, including partiality of insight, inherent in finite individuality itself, the Deliverer must assume the form that overcomes the partial insight and the limitations of individual existence. The Deliverer is itself knowledge and insight, the insight that individuality is not an ultimate form of existence.

In Buddhism as it can be derived from the ancient legends that were passed on concerning the original experience of the Buddha and his illumination, we find a different diagnosis of man's plight and a different interpretation of the Need. Once again the quest is for the true self and the proper path towards self-realization. The Need, however, appears not as a form of ignorance or misunderstanding but rather as the boundlessness of desire. In some of the early tales, the Buddha specifically refuses to answer questions about the state of Nirvana, but insists instead that his task is to disclose the cause of suffering and to show that it consists in the ever-recurring cycle of desire, limited satisfaction, renewed desire, and so on without end. The Need is, therefore, for a way of overcoming the formlessness of desire and of subjecting it to discipline. The function of the Buddha as Deliverer is to offer the illumination he has gained, an illumination that teaches, theoretically, about desire as the cause of suffering and, practically, about the noble eightfold path that leads to life. Alfred North Whitehead, in his most instructive comparison between Buddhism and Christianity, claims that whereas in Christianity Christ gives his life in performing his role, the Buddha gives only a doctrine. This claim is only partially true. The Buddha does not give himself in the fashion Christians understand the life of Christ to be given, but we must not overestimate the contrast. The Buddha gives a doctrine, to be sure, but we must not neglect the sense in which Buddhists take inspiration from the actual attainment of the Buddha, the fact of his illumination, and of his example for others.

It is of the greatest moment that the Buddhist conception of the Need is not entirely an affair of knowledge. Desire, that is to say, cannot be overcome in its destructive effects through the attainment of an insight alone. Since the defect is located more nearly in the will and in human striving, a contemplative insight will not suffice to dispel the Need. Insight and understanding are there, but something more is required, something closer to moral wisdom, and the power to desire and to act in accordance with the noble virtues. The Buddha functions as Deliverer both through the moral insight he attains and through the fact of his actual achievement, showing that it is possible for man to reach the good life.

If the Vedanta finds the Need in the partiality and imperfection of individuality and Buddhism in the destructive force of desire that is without form, the Judeo-Christian tradition finds it more deeply rooted in the freedom of man. The Need does not in a literal sense belong to the necessary structure of natural existence, but rather to the capacity of a free being to make himself his own end and thus deny the sovereignty of the true God. Here the Need resides neither in the structure of being individual or separate, nor in desire as a part of natural being, but in the capacity of a free being to deny God and the divine law. The Need is internal to the individual, but it does not at all consist in the fact that he is individual.

The task of the Deliverer is to provide a norm for man's freedom and a source of power to perform without at the same time denying that freedom by reducing man to the status of an object or thing. The Deliverer is to save man from the self-destructive consequences of his own misuse of freedom and make possible a measure of the eternal quality of life envisaged in the Ideal.

It is not difficult to see from this brief comparison that the traditions in question exhibit a common structure, directing their attention to an Ideal, diagnosing a Need or flaw, and proposing a resolution in the form of a Deliverer. It is equally clear that the three do not understand the three elements in the same way; each has its own understanding of the tragic flaw and of the resolution that enables us to overcome it. But, viewed from the standpoint of a common structure, the differing traditions do not seem so strange. Not that we shall pass lightly over differences in the interests of merely diplomatic agreements; on the contrary, the differences stand out vividly by comparison, but these differences now appear within the framework of a common endeavor. We are better able to consider the relative merits of the different diagnoses offered and the possibility of overcoming the Needs defined by the Deliverers that appear. We come ultimately to a clearer understanding of where we all stand.

NOTES

1. William James, in *The Varieties of Religious Experience* (New York: Collier, 1969), suggested the idea of such a structure, and the concept was further developed by J. Royce, *The Sources of Religious Insight* (New York: Scribner, 1963); neither, however, went on to employ the concept of a general structure of religion as it is employed in this paper.

2. This point is well made by E. Cassirer, *Substance and Function* (New York: Dover, 1953).

3. 1 Jn. 4:20; the great commandment of Mat. 22:37ff., Lk. 10:27ff. is, of course, presupposed.

4. Some New Testament scholars such as Amos Wilder and Paul Schubert incline towards the view that the Kingdom idea is not a basic one for Christian belief derived from the New Testament sources. On the other hand, in addition to the many passages in the synoptic Gospels, especially the so-called parables of the Kingdom, there are many references to the Kingdom of God, e.g., Rom. 14:17; 1 Cor. 4:20, 6:9–10; Col. 4:11; 2 Th. 1:5.

Chapter 3

THE TRANSCENDENT AND THE SACRED
Louis Dupré

SINCE the beginning of this century man's relation to the transcendent has been formulated mainly in terms of an opposition between the sacred and the profane. Introductory college courses in religious science are often restricted to an exploration of this dialectic. Though much in our past justifies referring to the object of the religious attitude as sacred, the equation cannot be assumed to be universal. Not only does it fail to account for the primitive mentality, but, of more immediate concern, it appears less and less appropriate to describe modern man's awareness of transcendence. Yet contrary to a common opinion today, it is not the *objective* nature of the sacred that makes it unfit to symbolize an experience which the modern mind tends to regard as purely interior. Even in it most intimate self-possession the embodied mind requires objective symbols.

THE SACRED AS PARTICULAR CATEGORY OF TRANSCENDENCE

But the sacred is *one* symbolic complex in which man expresses his encounter with transcendence; it is not the only one. It no more covers the entire range of religious experience than the beautiful exhausts the realm of aesthetics. Indeed, some religious cultures seem to do very well without it. Remarkably enough, the category of the sacred appears to be most questionable in the one instance to which it has been most confidently applied,

From: Louis Dupré, *Transcendent Selfhood: The Loss and Rediscovery of the Inner Life* (New York: Seabury, 1976), pp. 18–30.

that of the primitive society. Advocates of the opposition sacred/profane as a universal priniciple belong to a variety of schools. Initiated by Robertson Smith,[1] it soon spread to French ethnologists, first Durkheim then Hubert and Mauss, and finally became the central principle of interpretation with the phenomenologists Otto, Van der Leeuw, Eliade. It may appear foolhardy to challenge a position established with such imposing credentials. Yet I remain unconvinced that the category of the sacred plays a crucial role in the primitive or in the contemporary mentality. To be sure, primitives, as all people, regard certain areas of experience as more important than others. It is not unwarranted to attribute a religious significance to a distinction which may in some instances lead to the one between the sacred and the profane. But the two do not coincide, for the original distinctions take place within one diffusely "sacred" sphere. I see little use for a category that covers all aspects of primitive society and for which its members possess neither name nor concept. To say this is not to make the absurd claim that nothing is sacred to the savage, but, on the contrary, to assert that, in varying degrees, all of life is, and, consequently, that nothing is entirely profane.

An attentive reader will discover traces of this position in the selfsame authors who popularized the distinction. Thus, Durkheim, for whom the separation of the sacred and the profane constitutes the very essence of religion, nevertheless assigns to the taboos which are supposed to enact it not only the function of separating the sacred from the nonsacred but also that of introducing structure and hierarchy within the sacred realm. "All these interdictions have one common characteristic; they come not from the fact that some things are sacred while others are not, but from the fact that there are inequalities and incompatibilities between sacred things."[2] Recent studies confirm this intrasacral function of taboos.[3] Yet Durkheim never drew the conclusion from this fact. He continued to regard those taboos which distinguish the sacred from the nonsacred as "the religious interdicts par excellence" and devoted his attention exclusively to them. It is the very point on which later students of primitive religion have most challenged his theory.

E. Evans-Pritchard denies the existence of any rigid dichotomy in the primitive mind. "Surely what he (Durkheim) calls "sacred" and "profane" are on the same level of experience, and, far from being cut off from one another, they are so closely intermingled as to be inseparable. They cannot, therefore, either for the individual or for social activities, be put in closed departments which negate each other, one of which is left on entering the other."[4]

Claude Lévi-Strauss, himself schooled in Durkheim's thought, all but eliminated the distinction as an illegitimate transposition of contemporary categories to the primitive mentality. Besides, it is hard to conceive what the notion of the sacred could contribute to an understanding of archaic myths such as the ones analyzed in his trilogy on structuralist interpretation. The significance of this critique for our subject is that the very theories from which the universality of the sacred/profane distinction was derived are being questioned today.

Yet the distinction has received its strongest support from the phenomenological school and, so one might argue, their descriptions stand, regardless of the historical origin of the descriptive concepts. Since the remainder of this chapter consists precisely in an attempt to prove that a description of the religious attitude in our time by means of the concept of the sacred is no longer adequate, I need not go into the matter at this point. I would nevertheless mention that those phenomenological descriptions which favor the primary importance of the sacred are based upon a *particular stage* of religion. Mircea Eliade, whose penetrating insights and seductive style have done so much to secure the sacred a primary place in the study of religion, supports its crucial significance by arguments that are convincing only when they are drawn from advanced religions.[5] Even among them I doubt whether we can justifiably attribute a *universal* significance to it. At least I have been unable to detect much "sacredness" in the original forms of Buddhism. One may read one's way through the canonical writings of the ancient Buddhists without ever encountering the term or needing the concept.

Of course, such difficulties may be circumvented by enlarging the meaning of the concept "sacred." A sacred that is no more than a common nomer for the object of all possible experiences of transcendence remains immune to attacks. But such a general definition fails to convey the specification required by the concept of "experience." The term *sacred* as most students of comparative religion use it, refers to a *direct, immediate experience,* characterized by some degree of passivity. Such a passive immediacy is not what determines the use of sacred in the biblical and Christian literature. Here the sacred is the main attribute of God, revealed by God as such. It is not, or not primarily, an object of direct experience. Holiness expresses what God is in himself. He may bestow this quality upon persons, places, or objects. But they do not possess it in their own right.[6] Repeatedly we read in the Bible that God is the source of all holiness: "It is I Yahweh who sanctify you."[7] Even where Israel is requested "to sanctify" God, the source of all holiness is God himself. "But I will hallow Israel so that they will sanctify me. For this reason does it say: And ye shall be holy unto me, for I the Lord am holy who made you holy."[8] The sacred, then, appears to be the quality of transcendence *par excellence* which more than any other distinguishes the divine as such.

Even attempts to retain the sacred as a universal and central religious category by sacrificing its ultimacy prove inadequate when we come to the Old Testament. Paul Mus was probably the first to feel the need for an ulterior category. In a remarkable essay on the Brahman sacrifice he posited the divine as such a category which founds the sacred and enables it to be mediated with the profane.[9]

Henri Bouillard developed his conclusion into the general principle: as the emphasis on transcendence increases, the divine becomes more and more separate from the sacred. In some forms of mysticism one may eclipse the other altogether.[10] Yet this principle (which I believe to be valid in other instances) cannot be applied to the Bible, which both strongly emphasizes divine transcendence *and attributes the sacred to God himself.* In the Old Testament the sacred fulfills a unique function which is by no means typical for all religion. For it is *neither beyond* God as a more primitive form of being in which both God and some creatures partake, *nor below* God as an intramundane category that is totally surpassed by divine transcendence. Rather it is the main attribute of the divine itself, which belongs by nature exclusively to God.

I can think of no other reason why Western students of religion have generalized this category, except that it played such a central part in their own religious tradition. There lies a particular irony, then, in the fact that this concept, as it was eventually developed, least applies to the biblical faith from which it was drawn. Nonetheless, the dialectical opposition within which they conceived the relation between the sacred and the nonsacred still reflects the infinite distance between the Holy One and the mere creature. Only in a biblical perspective could the sacred be regarded as *the wholly other*. Yet opposition is definitely not the primary characteristic of the sacred in most religious cultures. The sacred is rather that which encompasses all human experiences and gives them their ultimate integration. One may well wonder whether a category that is defined primarily by *opposition* to the nonsacred adequately accounts for this function. "The sacred is not in the first place a separate, reified reality, nor is it *in itself* as the profane is, but it is an *objective relation, present to and coextensive with all being, all reality*."[11] All this raises some serious questions about the universal applicability of the concept. Does the concept after all the shifts of meaning still remain sufficiently coherent and specific to function as a primary religious category? I doubt it.

THE DECLINE OF THE SACRED

My doubts increase when I consider the religious condition of our own age. To what extent is the contemporary awareness of transcendence a ''sacred'' experience? Of course, if one defines as sacred any experience which relates man to the transcendent, there is no problem. But the preceding analysis showed that such an equation must remain unsupported. Two factors, one doctrinal and one general-cultural, are essential for understanding the modern situation: an unprecedented emphasis on the transcendence of God and an equally unprecedented secularization of the world. Whether they are causally connected or not, the two have certainly converged in drastically decreasing the very possibility of a worldly experience of transcendence. Hence a decline of the sacred and of its primary effect: the integration of life. As man discovers the control over his universe to reside within himself, the need to relate each aspect of existence to a transcendent principle ceases to be felt urgently. Yet to relate them is a primary effect of those religious phenomena to which we refer as sacred. In the Judeo-Christian tradition the relation may well constitute the entire experience, since the sacred here is not perceived as a self-enclosed phenomenon but one that refers itself, and through itself all worldly reality, to God.

To be sure, any society as it grows more complex will eventually experience difficulty in integrating the various aspects of life. If I am not mistaken it is precisely out of this complexification that the need arises for a differentiation between the so-called sacred and profane areas of existence. Yet nowhere before have the latter ever grown *entirely independent* of the former. In our own secular age art, science, philosophy, and morality have virtually lost all need for religious support in their development. Nor do most educated men still relate them to a transcendent source.

But as the need for a transcendent integration disappears, the perception of the sacred becomes increasingly weaker. Today most of our Western contemporaries are totally unacquainted with the religious awe and irresistible attraction which are supposed to have manifested the sacred presence in the past. For people living in this technological age, nature no longer holds the sacred meaning which their ancestors detected in its works. Modern men frequently can claim no direct experience of the sacred at all, either in the world or in themselves. I saw this interpretation confirmed in a poll of my students in a course on the philosophy of religion, a group that, by selecting this subject, had already expressed serious interest in the topic. Asked what the sacred meant to him or her, one respondent stated forcefully but not atypically: "Nowhere in my world and at no time in my experience is there anything that I can point to as a manifestation of the sacred. I'm not even sure that the notion of the sacred can be meaningful to modern man. I doubt, at any rate, that I have a conception of it."

Equally revealing is the fact that those who claim to experience certain aspects of life as sacred are unable to share this experience with their contemporaries. On a discussion devoted to this topic, in which I participated some months ago, no agreement of any kind could be attained about what specifically would be sacred. A prominent Catholic writer remarked that the Supreme Court decision to legalize abortion had suddenly brought home to him that human life at least was sacred, particularly that of a helpless fetus. A Protestant professor equally opposed to abortion responded that he did not in the least experience life as sacred, but that he had made up his mind on this issue on the basis of a rational reflection about the dignity of man. His statement eloquently expresses the autonomy of the moral sphere even in the mind of the modern believer. Yet more immediately, it illustrates the totally private character of the sacred when it is still experienced today. Those who hold a particular value or reality sacred are reluctant to defend it on that basis, knowing full well how little understanding their argument is likely to encounter.

Now, increasing numbers of our contemporaries have grown disenchanted with the secularist fragmentation of modern life. They are searching for a new synthesis and nostalgically recall how a sense of the sacred provided their ancestors with what their existence so sadly misses. Not surprisingly, interest increases as experience declines. Quite a few theologians, anxious to assist man in his present predicament, proclaim that he has found already what he was looking for, and dignify with a halo of sacredness any state of mind that lifts a person beyond the unquestioning acceptance of existence. Today that is principally a feeling of dissatisfaction. As man becomes aware of the limitations of our society's commitment to the technical and the pragmatic, he is now told that his dissatisfaction itself constitutes a rediscovery of the sacred, since it questions the satisfactoriness of a purely immanent world view. According to the teachings of Augustine, Luther, and Kierkegaard, is the feeling of being estranged in this world not in itself religious?[12]

Unfortunately, matters are considerably more complex. For even if we grant that modern man's spiritual need forcefully reopens the question of transcendence, it does not follow that the question itself places life in a transcendent perspective and, even less, that it constitutes a return of the sacred. The religious mind lives indeed in a constant awareness of its own insufficiency. But does that entitle every alienated consciousness to the attribute "religious"? The question of man's homelessness has received multiple answers, most of them excluding the very possibility of an absolutely transcendent principle. But even to invoke such a principle by no means restores the direct, intramundane experience of transcendence to which alone the term *sacred* applies.

However, do we not positively witness a return of the sacred in the current interest in symbolism, mythology, and heterogeneous spiritual phenomena ranging from black magic to yoga exercises? Undeniably, something new is afoot and much of it seems to consist in a quest for the kind of integration which sacred signs provide. The sharing of common symbols and ritual gestures in small groups all suggest an attempt to recapture the ancient wholeness of life. But do those phenomena signal a revival of the sacred? Defenders of the "counter culture" such as Roszak, Reich, and Winter do not hesitate to answer this question affirmatively. In doing so they merely follow the lead of some eminent sociologists of religion who record the reappearance of what religion has traditionally featured most prominently: integrating symbols. The all-integrating character of the sacred is an undisputed fact. But does it entail a full identity of religion and symbolic integration, as Robert Bellah implies? "Religion, as that symbolic form through which man comes to terms with the antinomies of his being, has not declined, indeed, cannot decline unless man's nature ceases to be problematic to him.'' [13] If this interpretation is correct, the so-called secularity of the present age means nothing more than that the established faiths which integrated an entire society and externally controlled the whole conduct of its members are disappearing, while new movements, perhaps less doctrinal and certainly less universal, but no less religious, are gradually taking their place.

Personally I believe the secularist revolution to have effected a more radical change, one that has not been reversed by recent trends. Because the so-called return to the sacred itself stems from a totally secular attitude. In the introduction to his *Feast of Fools,* Harvey Cox characteristically presented his new work on the renewal of religious celebration as a companion piece to his earlier, unqualified dithyramb on the "secular city." Indeed, one might interpret the religious trend as a more radical (and more sophisticated) effort to be secular by expanding the immanent world view so as to include even the *religious experience.* Thus modern man would attempt to embellish by a sacred glow his basically secular existence. Perhaps it is significant that the first prophet of the new awareness, Ernst Bloch, was an atheist who attempted to give the closed *Weltanschauung* of historical materialism a greater openness toward the future. After man has ceased to take seriously the traditional expressions of the transcendent, he nevertheless continues to feel the need for that other dimension which neither enlightenment nor scientism nor even the new social activism can provide. So he endeavors to regain the experience which now lies buried in deserted cathedrals and forgotten civilizations. But he intends to do so at no cost to his secular life-style, that is, without accepting a commitment to the transcendent as to *another* reality. Instead of risking the leap into the great unknown which his ancestors so adventurously took, he cultivates self-expanding feelings. He may even share his religious enthusiasm with a privileged few and articulate it in symbols borrowed from ancient traditions. But by and large he is not committed to their content, and his concern remains primarily with his own states of mind. I can think of no more appropriate term than *progressive secularization* for a phenomenon so very like Marcuse's *progressive alienation,* which defeats the opposition by incorporating it within itself.

It is important to realize the precise import of the preceding critique. Much of what passes for a revival of the sacred in our age is only marginally religious, and the so-called sacred presence usually turns out to be no more than a romantic remembrance or an aesthetic imitation of past experiences. Yet despite this absence of a genuine sacred quality in modern life, many continue to possess a keen awareness of transcendence. To me this indicates that we must not tie transcendence indissolubly to the much more particular category of the sacred. At the same time the absence of any direct experience of the sacred cannot but cause a profound metamorphosis in our awareness of transcendence.

THE INWARD TURN

In tracing the source of all holiness to a transcendent God the Bible removes the sacred from direct experience to a transcendent realm. Henceforth the sacred would be approached more by trust than by direct experience. Christianity adopted the same priority. Faith consists primarily in obedience to the Word and in hope of things unseen. Neither intensity of feeling nor immediacy of perception equal the free acceptance of the revelation. Nevertheless, both Christians and Jews continued to be supported in their faith by the wealth of direct experience available in religious environments. Those have now largely disappeared. Whether and how a mature, educated American or European is religious depends almost exclusively on a personal decision. The choice is no longer made by others at the beginning of one's life. Nor can one's decision count on a supportive environment. To be sure, Christians continue to be baptized and Jews to be circumcised in infancy. But this symbolic incorporation in the religious community has greatly lost the binding power which it once exercised. Even the parents who subject their children to those rites often no longer regard them as certain and permanent commitments. To many they express no more than a vague intention on their part to introduce the child to a way of life which they have abandoned themselves (A chaplain at a European university recently described infant baptism as "pouring water over a child in order to christen the parents.")

A religious world view is no longer a stable, cultural complex transmitted to new members of a society by their elders. Nor does modern society support the exclusive claims of any single institution. Instead, the individual finds himself confronted with what has been called an assortment of religious representations from which the potential consumer may select themes of ultimate significance according to his private preference.[14] Religious institutions continue to be among the sources contributing to this assortment. But their very pluralism becomes, at root, a purely private affair often eclectically constructed and never objectively secured. What complicates the matter for traditional faiths is that their increasing "specialization," concomitant with the pluralism of modern life, constantly erodes their integrating powers. Global claims appear much less plausible as they are made by marginal communities issuing requirements which their members can fulfill on a part-time basis (such as attending church or accepting certain beliefs about the nature of God).[15] Thus, even for the traditional believer, the power of institutional norms and representations has become seriously weakened.

In all cases, then, the integrating synthesis of values—so essential to the religious attitude—appears to be left to the individual, who may or may not use for this purpose the religious institutions to which he or his ancestors traditionally belonged. A religious attitude, today more than ever before, requires the believer's personal decision, not only in general, but also for the acceptance of specific beliefs and norms. Once the believer has made this decision, a total integration of life in all its aspects becomes possible again, even though in the present situation it is rooted foremost in a personal act rather than in surrounding cultural and social structures.

Religion has become what it never was before: a private affair. In a secularized society the religious person has nowhere to turn but inward. There, and for the most part there alone, must he seek support for his religious attitude. Whether such a state of affairs gives rise to a transcendence more consistent with the biblical principle that God alone is holy or merely marks the end of traditional religion is a controversy we need not enter into. But in any event it introduces a new way of being religious to which the term *sacred* in the sense of direct, worldly experience of transcendence has become wholly inappropriate.

Nevertheless, many continue to refer to the modern awareness of transcendence as sacred. Some earlier definitions may lend some support to this subjectivist reinterpretation of the sacred. Did Rudolf Otto not describe it as a subjective a priori? Otto himself could invoke Schleiermacher's theory of religion. Yet I consider the new approach to transcendence too far removed from the traditional concept of the sacred (however vaguely defined) to justify a continued usage of the term. Undoubtedly, there exists an inner experience consonant with the earlier meaning of a direct awareness of transcendence on the basis of a specific objective area. Whosoever "hears" in conscience the voice of God, as Newman did, may claim as direct an experience of the sacred as any holy space or time ever provided. But that is not, or is not primarily, the content of the inner awareness today. For the latter possesses none of the specificity so characteristic of the traditional notion of the sacred, including the sacred voice of conscience. Most often it is not even sufficiently specific to be confidently identified with an awareness of the God of Christian or Jewish revelation. Antoine Vergote, who, to my surprise, persists in calling it "a sense of the sacred," describes it very aptly:

> After faith has lost its quasi-natural evidence, after objectification has taken the mystery out of the world, man finds himself more subjectively confronted with his singular desire for meaning and happiness. At this stage of a desacralized culture emerges the sense of the sacred. It consists in the memory of a divine presence the absence of which opens to the desire the subjective ways to a transcendent [*infini*]. Even if man has retained his faith in the living God, cultural desacralization obstructs his efforts to interiorize the revelation into his actual existence. With the God of faith man maintains no more than a broken bond. So he attempts to insert the words of revelation into that mediating experience which consists of the consciousness of the sacred as a quality of transcendence [*infini*] inherent in existence itself.[16]

My only disagreement with this discerning judgment is terminological. What to Vergote is "the prereligious sacred" of modern man is to me "desacralized religion" or, at least, "desacralized religiosity." The difference is important insofar as my terminology reflects the very real break with the traditional experience of transcendence which makes the term *sacred* altogether inadequate. This, of course, is not to deny that to many contemporaries, even educated ones, the traditional sacred may still be present. In fact, I suspect that on rare occasions the transcendent still manifests itself in the world to most believers. But such hierophanies are definitely not typical of the religious mentality of our age. We seldom encounter the sacred in an objectively given, universally attainable reality, as the miraculous statue or the rustling of leaves in an oak forest were to our ancestors. Our way leads through private reflection and personal decision. Almost nothing appears directly sacred to us. In this respect we find ourselves at the opposite extreme of archaic man, for whom at least in some sense everything is sacred. We no longer share a coherent, sacred universe with all other members of our society or our culture, as religions in the past did. Nor are particular times, places, or persons *experienced* as sacred, as they were until recently even in Christianity and Judaism. If anything is "sacred" to the modern believer, it is only because he *holds* it to be so by inner conviction and free decision, not because he passively *undergoes* its sacred impact. This mediated "sacred" substantially differs from the traditional meanings of the term; it is no longer a primary category of religion (as it was even in the Judeo-Christian tradition) and it lacks the essential trait of direct experience. What we are claiming, then, is not the disappearance of the category of the sacred altogether: we continue to give the name to persons and objects as we include them in our relation to ultimate transcendence. But since that transcendence itself is no longer *perceived as sacred,* the whole process of naming sacred, or holding sacred, is demoted from the primary level of experience to the secondary level of interpretation.

The center of human piety has moved inward where the self encounters its own transcendence. The modern believer sacralizes from within a world that no longer possesses a sacred voice of its own. His initial contact with transcendence occurs in an inner self that is neither sacred nor profane. While in the past nature, verbal revelation, and ecclesiastical institutions determined the inner experience, today it is mostly the inner experience which determines whether and to what extent outer symbols will be accepted.

NOTES

1. W. Robertson Smith, *Lectures on the Religion of the Semites* (1890; republished after the third edition by Ktav Publishing House, 1969), actually distinguishes the sacred from "the common," but it was this distinction which led Durkheim to the one between the sacred and the profane.

2. Émile Durkheim, *The Elementary Forms of the Religious Life,* trans. Joseph Ward Swain (New York: Free Press, 1965), p. 340.

3. According to Franz Steiner, *Taboo* (Baltimore: Penguin, 1956), pp. 87–88, taboo does not separate from the sacred but from the *common,* which can still be sacred.

4. E. Evans-Pritchard, *Theories of Primitive Religion* (New York: Oxford University Press, 1965), p. 65. The entire problem of the taboo as religious separation device was competently discussed in a recent publication by E. M. Zuesse, "Taboo and the Divine Order," *Journal of the American Academy of Religion* 42 (1974): 482–504. His conclusion is unambiguous. "The deeper function of taboo, in short, is to define the divine life. It is *not* to keep man protected from entering into the sacred form from his 'profane' existence, but it is rather to keep man *in* the sacred order in all his existence" (p. 492).

5. In an article devoted to Eliade's theory of myth Jonathan Z. Smith questions the opposition sacred/profane in one particular instance. The chaos is not profane in the sense of neutral, as Eliade claims, but sacred in a negative way ("The Wobbling Pivot," *Journal of Religion* 52 (1974: 143). I suspect that the same principle would apply to every instance of "the profane" in a primitive culture.

6. The transcendence is reflected in the usage of the root *q-d-sh.* The verbal adjective *qadosh* is used for God (exclusively) and for persons (mainly), while the participle (mostly used as abstract substantive) *qodesh* is primarily applied to inanimate beings.

7. Ex. 31:13; Lev. 20:8.

8. *Midrash Rabbah*, ed. H. Freedman, M. Simon, vol. *Exodus* (London: Soncino Press, 1939), p. 195.

9. Paul Mus, *Barabudur* (Hanoi, 1935), pp. 94–96.

10. H. Bouillard, "La catégorie du sacré dans la science des religions," in *Le sacré,* ed. Enrico Castelli (Paris: Aubier, 1974), p. 48.

11. J. Grandmaison, *Le monde et le sacré* (Paris: Les Éditions Ouvrières, 1966), 1:26. Emphasis and translation mine.

12. Sociologists of religion also attribute an important part to cultural dissatisfaction in their interpretation of the religious attitudes today. But their argument usually adopts a less absolute form. It goes often as follows: Dissatisfaction with their present life forces our contemporaries to pose, once again, the *question of transcendence,* and leads many eventually back to some religious world view. Cf. Robert Nisbet, *The Social Bond* (New York: Knopf, 1970), esp. pp. 239ff.; Andrew Greely, *Unsecular Man* (New York: Schocken, 1972); and, most interestingly because most qualifiedly, Peter Berger, *A Rumor of Angels* (Garden City: Doubleday, 1967).

13. Robert Bellah, *Beyond Belief: Essays on Religion in a Post-Traditional World* (New York: Harper & Row, 1970), p. 227. For an incisive critique of the symbolic integration theory, cf. Charles Hardwick, "The Counter Culture as Religion," *Soundings* (Fall, 1973): 287–311.

14. Thomas Luckman, *The Invisible Religion* (New York: Macmillan, 1967), p. 105.

15. Ibid., pp. 75, 85.

16. Antoine Vergote, "Equivoques et articulation du sacré," in *Le sacré,* pp. 490–91. My translation.

Chapter 4

THE PERSON GOD IS
Peter A. Bertocci

WHAT IS THE QUESTION OF GOD?

Since my childhood I have given up several conceptions of God. Each time there was quite a wrench, for, in my own limited way, I had been walking with my "living" God. In my philosophical and theological studies, I have been impressed by the fact that one deep-souled thinker found the living God of another "dead". And then I realized that a God is "living" or "dead" insofar as "He" answers questions that are vital to the given believer.

Every believer in God, I am suggesting, lives by some "model" of God that helps him to live with the practical and theoretical problems he faces from day to day as an actor and a thinker, or, if you will, as a thinker-actor. And he keeps that "model" of God frequently long after he has begun to realize that it conflicts with the vital evidence as he sees it. He will go on living by it until another view makes more sense to him as a thinker-actor. Sometimes he changes his thought and action with a wrench; sometimes he finds that gradually one view of God died as another came alive. Note, this does not mean that God, granted he exists, died; it means that a given view of God is first challenged by another and then rejected because the other now seems more illuminating. This change in views is no different from what happens every day in our thinking about the world. We are changing our ideas about the moon (and the possibility of life on it) to accord with better evidence.

But the same line of reasoning may be used with regard to the very existence of God. A person may find that any conception of God simply is incoherent with

From: Peter A. Bertocci, *The Person God Is* (New York: Humanities 1970), pp. 17–37, (London: Allen & Unwin, 1970).

the problems that arise out of his thinking-acting life. Then not only does *a* conception of God die, but the conception that any God at all exists dies. For, it is now held, belief in any God simply does not fit the evidence at hand.

Of course, this matter of what it means to fit the evidence, that is, what our standard of truth requires, is the crucial question. But we shall in this essay assume what has already been implied, that belief in God and belief in a specific kind of God is a person's thinking-acting response to a conception of God that seems to him more coherent, and that fits in better than any other conception with the evidence.

Any of us who has tried to keep alive to the history of even one great theological-philosophical tradition without losing our sensitivity to the intellectual, religious, and social developments of our own day realizes that a philosophical and theological *aggiornamento* must always be part of our task. Yet—and even here our criterion of truth begins to exert itself—*aggiornamento* must mean bringing the present into challenging relation to the past. The assumption that the "past" must be brought up to date is as questionable as the assumption that the "past" can learn nothing from "the present". Perhaps, as I think reflection will show, we can, *as thinkers,* forget the labels 'new' and 'old' and ask which idea, hypothesis, which view of God, best illumines the evidence at hand from every source.

If this be granted, then any real dialogue about the nature and existence of God must presuppose a willingness on the part of participants to realize that they cannot hold a fixed view of "what God must be like" regardless of what the evidence indicates. Great minds, alas, have said, "There is no God", when all that their arguments showed is that a certain view of God is untenable in the light of what they regarded as relevant considerations.

Spinoza, for example, argued (in part) that the Cartesian view of God as Creator was really not God. Why? Because a God who is a Creator is one who presumably would have somehow existed "in want" until he did create the world and man. This of course is nonsense, but only if the model of God guiding Spinoza is the real God! Again, Paul Tillich argued that God cannot be one being alongside, or among, other beings, for this would not really be God, but some sort of great, yet finite Being. Yet one who knows what Tillich means by truth, and how he believes we come to know it, will see that his view of unconditioned Being is related to the evidence he considers crucial. He may be correct, with Spinoza, but I cannot help wondering why a particular model of God is asserted to be the only being worthy of being called *God.* Obviously, each of us will believe, and should believe that the conception of God which fits the evidence is the true conception of God, but we cannot presuppose what the true God is and then fit the evidence to our view.

To come at last to my purpose here. I know that many have insisted that if God is not a Person he is dead. I see no good reason for such an adamant stand. But because I find it almost fashionable not to know *what considerations led thinkers* to believe that God is a Person, I should like to indicate what it means to say that God is a certain kind of Person. Obviously I cannot speak for all personalistic theists, or for a perspective called classical theism, but only for *a* way of expressing the meaning of God in relation to man and Nature.

IF NO PERSON-GOD, THEN NO UNITY AND UNIFORMITY OF NATURE

First, then, what is the essence of the view of person that serves as a guiding model? Any *person* is the kind of being who is a knowing-willing-caring unity in continuity. Let us limit ourselves first to the notion of a person as a unity-in-continuity. The inescapable model is myself as a person. I don't know how it happens, but I cannot escape the fact that I am self-identical as I change. It is as simple and as difficult as that! I, as a person, am not a fusion of, or collection of, parts; I am an initial unity which, though changing, nevertheless retains self-identity. Without self-identity there can be no knowing of change. But more, if there were nothing persisting in change, we should say not that a being changes, but that one being has been substituted for another (as one actor substitutes for another). This is not all there is to being a person, but it is essential.

Thus, using this model, to say that God is a Person is to assert a Being who, however related to all other beings, is not a unity *of* them; he is self-identical. The question that arises from some who seem to know already what God's nature *must* be, is whether God can, being God, change in any aspect. This view of a God who is unchanging Alpha and Omega may be correct. But we need to remind ourselves that to call God *person* is to insist only that God is Unity-Continuity and is unchanging in the unity of his essential being. As a Person he does not change, even if the particular content or quality of his being changes (as when he "rejoices" when the prodigal son returns).

But why claim that such a being exists at all? What does the Person-God as Unity-Continuity enable us to understand?

Human thought and action are grounded in the regularity and order in the events of the world. To speak of a *universe* is to presuppose beings and events united in such a way that what occurs at one place is connected in an understandable way with what takes place elsewhere. We may not now know how or why one part of the universe is related to the other, but we think and act as if it is not unknowable *in principle*. Order and regularity of some sort constitute "the way of things."

Now, such interrelated unity and continuity among the beings and events in the world are illuminated, says the personalistic *theist,* by supposing that there is a Unity-Continuity that creates and sustains all there is, in such a way that basic order, regularity, and connectivity is possible among all the parts.

There are personalistic *pantheists* or monists who would want to assure such ordered connectivity by maintaining that all the beings or events in the world are parts, modes, or centers, of one Absolute Person. Either personalist, theistic or monistic, takes one fundamental stand: no cosmic Unity-Continuant, then no ultimate Ground for the trust we all have in the order of things. (Unless further notice is given, I shall use the word *personalist* to mean personalistic theist—for whom God is transcendent of, yet immanent in, Nature.) Both pantheistic and theistic personalists argue that we can *reasonably* trust our ventures into the presently unknown only if we can reasonably believe that the unknown is basically continuous with the character of what we do know. And this leads us to the second characteristic of Person, knowing.

THE PERSON GOD IS: COSMIC KNOWER

Important as the emphasis on Unity-Continuity is, it is the insistence that Unity-Continuity is most coherent only as it is a knowing Person which gives the personalistic view its name. The personalist holds that the self-sufficient, cosmic Unity-Continuity is, like the finite person, a Knower, a Mind or Spirit.

The storm that has raged around this concept has been caused by the "model" that controlled the use of the word *person*. The pre-Socratic Xenophanes wryly exclaimed: The Ethiopians "make their gods black-haired and blue-eyed." What adolescent mind has not sooner or later smartly commented that, after all, men made God after their own image—as if this ended the matter once and for all! Yet, if the world is a universe, and if some Unity-Continuity can be postulated, our thought cannot rest without trying to conceive of what its nature "must" be in order to fit what we know. And the fundamental fact is that we, as persons, not only ask the questions, but also believe that our human logical questions when supported by human observations will not lead us astray in this universe. Can this universal unity be unlike ours *in principle?*

It is not unsuggestive that Xenophanes, who found no reason for holding that God had blue eyes, did nevertheless say that the nature of Ultimate Being was Thought! That God-intoxicated philosopher Spinoza deanthropomorphized God by saying that the One Substance was no more like a finite person than the celestial constellation the Dog Star was like a barking dog. But the same Spinoza insisted that, of the infinite number of attributes of Substance, *thought* as well as extension defines the essence of Substance. While Paul Tillich cannot define Unconditioned Being as person, he says: "The God who is *a* person is transcended by the God who is the Personal-Itself, the ground and abyss of every person."[1]

Any personalistic theist must be sympathetic with every attempt to keep before the believer the realization that no concept of the cosmic Unity will comprehend it completely, that all man's concepts will leak, if for no other reason than that man's knowledge is incomplete. He can also understand why it makes sense to say that no part of the universe, including the human, can, without qualification, describe the cosmic Unity. Yet he urges that it must remain a matter of live debate whether there is any "model" other than Mind, even as we know ourselves, that will be more helpful to us in defining the *kind* of unity, continuity, and order that will account for the fact that our minds, existing in this world, have been able to fathom its nature progressively.

After all, the basic drift of scientific and philosophical theorizing presupposes that what lies beyond man can be understood by the human mind. This is not to say that man will understand all, but it does mean that the schemes of Nature, however far-flung, are not intrinsically and in principle beyond disciplined human knowing. Indeed, when a person doubts concretely that a particular conclusion in science and philosophy is true, is he not using other considerations, which he believes to be true descriptions of the world, to support his doubting? In the last analysis, we do not believe that the segment of the world we do seem to know will be basically rejected by the rest of the universe we do not now know. The maps we now have will need revision, the models will be fashioned by the very minds that learn from their mistakes and yet press on in the faith that the next map, the next model, will be more illuminating for thought and action.

It is this kind of consideration that leads the personalist to find, expressed in the order of the world, a Mind that in its basic structure is not foreign to his own. If *our* map making, encouraged and discouraged by the terrain about us, if *our* models suggested by what we know and remodeled in the light of what we encounter, do get us on with the total business of understanding and living in both the microscopic and macroscopic realms, can it be that the total universe as we envision it and interact with it is alien to our being as persons? To change the figure, if the key "in our natures" can open the lock of the world to any extent, why is it farfetched to suppose that the key and the lock do not bespeak a common locksmith? It is easy to scoff at what I believe to be a *legitimate* anthropomorphism. Yet is not the scoffer boasting of his luck if he continues to urge that the way to know what is real is to think logically, observe thoroughly, hypothesize in the light of evidence at hand, and act on hypotheses with concerted further thought and action?

Whenever a personalist, then, hears someone say "but the universe is beyond anything the human mind can know," his rejoinder is insistent. "This is logically possible. But do you claim your mind can know *that?* If it can, and if your mind can *know* that, aren't you asserting that somehow your mind has the secret to its own impotence? It is one thing to assert that we don't know all: it is another to say that what we know in ourselves and in the world provides no good ground for supposing that our progress is helping us to identify the nature of a cosmic Mind."

Here the retort may readily be made: But do you mean that the word *know* is to be used for God in the same sense as it is used for man? The answer: Whatever the particular knowing processes in God are remains open for further discussion. A responsible philosophical theology must be as clear as it can be about the nature of this knowing. It will not evade such questions as: Is God's knowing intellectual in the sense in which our logic is syllogistic, or is it non-discursive and intuitive?

We might at least bear in mind, in passing, that God does not "speak" either in English or German, or use words—but neither do animals or the deaf and dumb express their level of awareness in such ways. More relevant is the suggestion that we seek analogies within the whole range of human *awareness,* inclusive of aesthetic, moral, and religious awareness. But the minimum intellective awareness is knowing similarity and differences in itself and everywhere else. In short, the essential personalistic contention is that, whatever the "infinity" of a cosmic Unity entails, we endanger the Unity if we deny that it is self-conscious and knows the difference between himself and his world, including persons.

Again, there is a basic problem here. When we stress the immensity of the universe, the unlimited majesty of God, the unconditioned nature of his Being, or what have you, do we mean that no link, no common bond, exists between man and God? Do we mean to say that what is logical to us would be nonlogical or illogical to that Being? The personalist, while he must speculate about the nature of the difference between man and God, insists on the essential continuity between the best in his own experience and in the universe, including God. Why court mystery here when we decry impalpable mystery elsewhere? In the name of modesty and humility we can urge that no human symbols are adequate, but if we take this seriously we belie the amount of success our symbolizing has had, and we tend to foster more skepticism than we intended. At the same time we have disqualified a particular view of God's nature by what are ultimately loaded views of God's ultimacy and perfection.

Again, what does it add to say that God is what we can know *and more?* For if the word *more* means "more of the same," it can be granted. But if the *more* means difference in kind, we simply cannot know what *that more* means even though we seem wise and modest in saying so. What would happen to the construction of computers if we said, for example, that, though the actual process be different, what goes on in the structure of a computer has *no* counterpart in the structure of man, even though, for example, the computer can solve problems it would take ages for man to solve? What would happen to our attempts to understand what goes on in lower animals and in plants if we let our realization that there is "more than we know in ourselves" stifle reasonable analogy?

Obviously, much needs to be added. It is not incidental, however, to remark that what tends to control thinking here is the model of the finite person we have in mind when we say that God is a Person. If I thought that the person is identical with his brain and body, I would not use the word *person* for God. In our day there are many who, unwittingly or wittingly, think of a person as some sort of body. But do these same individuals think that a person is a male or a female, or are they assigning *person* to a being, who, however his body is related to him, is *not identical* with that body? Ambiguity courts disaster at these points.

Once more, if, as many in our day hold, the person is a sociobiological phenomenon, then the denial that God is a person is understandable. For God's nature, if it is to fit our cosmological evidence, is not the product of learning in some environment (and I say this even though I myself hold that God in some respects does change in response to changes initiated by persons).[2] For the personalist, however, the word *person* identifies an agent capable of self-consciousness and of action in the light of rational and moral-aesthetic-religious ideals.

To summarize: in hypothesizing that the cosmic Unity is a Person we are carrying on the same kind of process, of moving from the unknown on the basis of what is known, that activates careful reflection in the other concrete areas of human investigation. If by careful observation, guided as far as possible by scientific method, we discover that our thought forms do engage us with the world beyond in such a way that one discovery leads to another, on what grounds, consistent with experiential procedures, can we argue that the Being manifest in our world is totally different from our mind form?

To say that Being or Unity is more than we are is, after all, to say something very innocuous theoretically. This dictum applies not only to God but to everything we know. But, as I suggest, in the actual course of argument, this "more" in God is often used to disqualify attempts, built on reasoning however inadequate, to see what seems reasonable granted given evidence at least. In every area, the theoretical problem is always one of defining what the nature of "the more" is. But do we dare move without the reasonably established faith that the more is not unlike what we already know? In a word, the faith of the personalist at this point is, minimally, an extension of the faith that guides all theoretical activity.

THE PERSON GOD IS: LOVING AGENT

We have argued that if God is conceived as a Person, as a unified Knower, then we can the better understand why our thought forms have succeeded in knowing the interconnected order of Nature. To think of God as a cosmic Person is not to indulge a human whim, but to ground more adequately all of our theoretical ventures, including the scientific. But is God good? Let us ask the same question we asked before. What problem would be solved by this conception?

In answer, we turn again to human experience and ask what the lasting basis of human goodness is. Many factors contribute to human existence and to the growth of quality in human experience. But if the personalist were to be limited to any other one factor, beyond knowing, which makes for *quality* in every area of *human experience in this world,* he would select *loving.* Thinking-loving gives support to thinking-acting; they are the creative matrix in which every other human good is strengthened. Without the other each falters. Accordingly, the personalist argues, thinking-loving is the clue to the best the universe makes possible, as far as we know.

To elaborate: When a person dedicates himself to the growth of other persons in full awareness of their mutual potential for growth, we say that he loves. And he loves unto forgiveness when he does all in his power to enable even those who have purposely abused his love to join the fellowship and community of love. And separation, as Ian Ramsey says, is hell[3]. In a word, in human experience there is no greater good than to be a responsive-responsible member in a community dedicated to mutual growth. This good we call love. Any being whose purposes include the growth of persons-in-community, and who does all in his power to realize this purpose, is loving. The Person God, says the personalist, is good; he is a loving agent. The grounds for this contention may be further elaborated in two steps.

First, is it not experientially sound to say that to the extent to which love is realized in an individual personality, in a family, and in a community, every other value that human beings find worthwhile is enhanced? For the ideal of love-unto-forgiveness. (I do not mean sentimentality) is not a dream. It is an actual description of how persons, in relation to other persons, can fulfill themselves in the world as they know it, within themselves, and beyond themselves. Persons are desperate when they feel alienated both from the best in themselves and the best in others. They are more likely to improve and grow if they feel the forgiveness that, looking beyond the harm they have done, draws them into a community of mutual concern. These are requirements for growth in self-fulfilment in community.

Man does not make up these requirements any more than he makes up the laws governing the growth of bodies or the changes in molecules. He finds them—not as he finds the stars or the law of gravitation, however. He finds them in the midst of his very attempt to know what he can best be-in-act. A loving man is a knowing-willing man developing dimensions of his own being and of other beings, dimensions that come into being *as* he loves. His *knowing in loving is a more comprehensive knowledge* which tells him about himself and his fellow men even as they both realize their potential and fulfill each other with a minimum of fruitless conflict.

To put this in a different way: What the personalist is calling to our attention is that men and Nature do not stand in an indifferent relation to each other; they are not juxtaposed. Men are facts about the total world that includes biological and physical beings; but they are also facts for each other in that larger world. For them to understand themselves is for them to become aware of their physical and social environment in such a way as to keep all of these in a responsive-creative relation to each other. Thus, when a man discovers that mutual respect for another's freedom is the best condition for their mutual personal growth, *he is discovering a fact that the total world, including himself, makes possible.* When he goes on to realize that such freedom—guided by knowledge of self, of others, of Nature—is supported and kept from self-destruction only as it is disciplined by loving, he is also discovering what his life-in-the-world can be.

This first step in the psycho-logic of love encourages a personalist to argue that the same universe which makes it possible for man to know, and to live by that knowledge, is the very universe which makes it impossible for man to perfect that knowledge unless he meets the conditions of love. He must learn to respect both "the structure and potential of things" for their own sake and the structure and potential of other persons for their own sakes. As long as a man lives in this world, he, given his nature, will not be able to fulfill himself simply for himself; he will not be able to treat either the world or others as if they were meant only for him. He will grow without fruitless conflict only as he grows *within* and *for* a community in which persons both respect each other and cooperate with each other in responsive-responsible growth. It is this fact about the world that best defines what it is and can be in relation to man. Thus, when the personalist says that God is a unity-in-continuity of knowing-willing-caring, he is asserting that the essential constitution of the world and the essential constitution of man are such that the highest good of man is realized in that kind of community in which persons respect and care for each other's growth.

A second step in the personalist's reasoning articulates the first by calling attention to what is involved in the human search for truth. As a matter of actual dynamics within the individual personality and within the community, knowledge grows not merely because the world is knowable. Knowledge grows apace only as it is put to use, and only as it is motivated by respect for other persons and by mutuality in the total venture of knowing. For, in their own way, the community of scholars, the growth of knowledge, the zest for the venture, grow apace as scholars know that their mistaken and misguided efforts will be sympathetically understood, that their errors will be rejected but their efforts encouraged. Thus, in the venture of acquiring and sharing knowledge, without which human existence is inconceivable, love is not an addendum which investigators may disregard.

This point is so simple that its very simplicity allows many to underestimate its importance and to be parasitic upon what makes for community in the knowledge venture. Again, the search for knowledge is encouraged by love for more than knowledge; it is sustained by mutual concern for the growth of persons as investigators who find and express themselves in sharing of insights.

Furthermore, truth-seekers in any one community must be free to respond to the lure of truth. But they will feel threatened in their efforts if they believe that the larger community upon which they depend will be intolerant especially when their discoveries challenge the status quo, or that the community will judge them only by their failures. Truth seekers themselves, of course, must be willing to suffer, especially before the intellectual conscience of man. But their courage to seek will be inspired if they can live in the assurance that they will not suffer vindictive punishment.

To summarize: Man, the lover-knower *in* the world, is the lover-knower not threatened by that world but nurtured, challenged, and supported by it as he grows within it. Love has no meaning without such challenge and support, whatever else it involves. Why not then hold that love is the broader principle involved in world-being as we know it? For man's justifiable hope for himself in his world is rooted in his daily discovery that, in disciplining himself by the norms of truth and love, he is part of "the drift" of things. In knowing-loving he enters into a fuller relationship with a universe that responds to him in his growth as inspired by truth and love. Why not then conceive of the Unity-Continuity of the cosmic Knower as a loving Person? This is the way to say that man's own joy in self-discovery and in mutual growth is no cosmic surprise, for it is grounded in a universe that responds to man's creative effort as knower and carer.

It should now be clear that a personal God is not one that human beings somehow add to their experience or their world. Personalists do not argue *that* there is a God and then add labels to that Being. They argue that, in the very attempt to discover what they are and can best become in their world, persons find a Person at work with them *in* and *through* their world. For the personalist, the God "up there" does not exist because he never did, as far as they know. He is always at work in the world and in relation to persons. But this takes us directly to the reasons for saying that God is the Creator of man and the world.

THE PERSON GOD IS: COSMIC CREATOR

The finite person, it has been argued, is dependent for his very being and sustenance on God. But finite as the person is, he is free to choose and to create within limits. In the context suggested above, each man, given basic cognitive and conative capacities, is free to choose, within the limits of these capacities, the knowledge ventures and the quality of caring he believes to be best. For this moral development man is himself so responsible that he is a creator.

Such a view of freedom is a minimal requirement for a personalistic view of the person; it is not argued here. But the consequences of this view are crucial for the personalist's thought about man's relation to God. As we have seen, a person is indeed related to his total environment, including God. But a person does not overlap with anything else in the world or with God. His being is his unity-in-continuity of knowing-willing-caring. God in turn, as a person, does not overlap with, or include, any other person.

This whole idea is not easy to conceive, let alone imagine. But it should be clear at the outset that it is the personalist's concern to protect the individuality of the person-man, and of the Person-God, that leads him to propose his doctrine of creation. Unless the context of the doctrine of creation is understood, this doctrine, mysterious enough at best, will be cast aside disdainfully as "impossible."

There are two other ways of conceiving God's relation to man and the world other than holding that God creates them "out of nothing" (*creatio ex nihilo*).

According to the first, which follows suggestions Plato made in the *Timaeus*, God may be likened to a sculptor who creates not "out of nothing" but out of the material or "stuff" at hand. This stuff is in itself relatively inchoate, and by itself would never take on any structure or order. While more than one specific order can be introduced into such inchoate being, no pervasive structure is to be found in its formless nature. Yet, because it is an eternal something rather than "nothing," it will "respond" to some forms of order better than to others. It may be of some help to think of clay or marble, which will conform to more than one "idea"; yet clay cannot become exactly what a block of marble can become.

Great philosophers have grappled with the problem of introducing any specific structure—regularity, order, form—into inchoate being which is something (not nothing) and yet in itself almost without any form. They have preferred to postulate some such formless matrix, or "womb of all becoming," rather than postulate what seemed preposterous—creation "*ex nihilo*," which they translated literally as *out of nothing*. Better to suppose that God is somehow coeternal with such "material for becoming"; better to hold that God did not create such being and that it could not create him. Better to hold that God and "matter" are two eternal Principles, two Kinds of Being, both needing each other if anything is to be developed in what is.

Such alternatives all sound so much more picturable and conceivable than "creation out of nothing" until we ask some other questions. Plato, for example, had to take one more step. For if God is the Sculptor, and the Material (the Receptacle) is that which takes on form, whence the Forms, whence the Ideas or Ideals, that guide the Sculptor in his creative work? There is reason to suppose that Plato believed that they too constituted a realm of their own, coeternal with "matter" and God. They are not dependent upon God or upon "matter" for their existence—in part because as Ideals they are to give form to both God and "matter." Hence Plato conceived of God as a cosmic Lover of Forms (Ideas or Ideals) that he did not create. Neither the forms nor the inchoate Being, then, are dependent upon each other. There results a coeternal trinity of beings in Plato's system at this point. And none of these beings, by definition, is related to the other.

Nevertheless, says Plato, this imperfect, but relatively orderly world can be explained by thinking of God as this cosmic Artist or Demiurge who, with his eye fixed on the coeternal Ideals,"persuades" the coeternal, inchoate being to take on as much form and order as possible. For Plato, the complex orderly world which man sees about him, and man's own capacity to know and interact with both the world and God, testify to the "creative" goodness of one member of the coeternal "trinity". Other thinkers decreased the difficulty to be mentioned by moving the Ideals into the mind of God, conceiving of them as the eternal Ideals guiding his will. For them God is still coeternal with Matter of some sort, and cosmic Trinity gives way to Duality. We need not stop to elaborate on this view, for our concern is to understand why either a coeternal Two or Three gave way to *creatio ex nihilo*.

It might be urged that any such one-of-two, or one-of-three, view of God was unacceptable to early Christians because it is unbiblical to make God finite. But this only skirts the real difficulty, which is the following. If there are two or three ultimate, coeternal Beings, is it not completely incomprehensible that they should be so complementary? Why should they find that they can interact in a way that does make this kind of orderly world possible? The mystery of mysteries, opaque to our human intelligence because it contravenes what we always assume in our known realms, stuns us. For, when beings are at all related to each other, we assume that, despite their differences, they are not separated by chasms as impassable as these coeternally different kinds of being must be by definition. Our minds demand that Creator, Ideas, and Stuff (or Creator and Stuff) have something in common if they are to interact at all. Indeed, the world as we know it, despite its dissonances and evils, is sufficiently good and sufficiently orderly to suggest that a better marriage actually took place than the one to be expected if both beings are completely independent of each other.

Once more, then, creation "out of nothing" may be mysterious. But on what grounds may we expect two eternally different principles to be able to interact in such a way as to produce the kind of orderly world we observe? If it offends religious sensitivity, on the one hand, to conceive of God as limited by some coeternal independent principle, then the theoretical reason cries out, on the other hand, against explaining the kind of orderly world we have by postulating two or three coeternal, different beings (if we take their independence seriously).

The personalist has no easy task in defending *creatio ex nihilo*. It is only when we become aware of difficulties in *absolute* monism and in *absolute* dualism or pluralism that we see why this difficult alternative became palatable to him. Accordingly, the personalist holds that God, the cosmic Person, *created* the world *ex nihilo*. But this "out of nothing" is the personalist's way of emphasizing his rejection of any coeternal, independent factor with which God has to deal. It is not simply that God is rendered finite if there is an independent noncreated matter; it is that we cannot account for the world's being an orderly world at all!

Difficult as *creatio ex nihilo* is, it is not so utterly indefensible once one fully understands what is at stake.

The personalist, accordingly, goes on to explain that God's knowledge of all the possibilities and compossibilities guided him in his care to create the orderly world in which persons are sustained. But, more important, the doctrine of *creatio ex nihilo* is also the personalist's way of saying that God is not identical with the world and with persons. Further still, God is not one "alongside" all the created beings, for they depend ultimately upon his will for whatever independence they have. Without his continuous creation and involvement in accordance with his own being and purpose there would be no "universe." The personalist in this doctrine, therefore, seeks to explain the order of the world in a way that preserves differences without endangering the autonomy and perfection of God.

Nevertheless, argue the critics of personalism, the cost of this doctrine is too high. They still find the notion of creation mysterious. The theist would agree that the doctrine is mysterious. But he urges that at worst this doctrine, *if* it is exemplified nowhere *in* our experience, nevertheless is not contradictory of anything we do find. Furthermore, every metaphysics and theology has some ultimate that is mysterious in that we cannot point to instances of it in the world. But the personalist does advance one other consideration to take the edge off this criticism.

Finally, *creatio ex nihilo* does not actually mean that God took "nothing" and made something out of it. The theist would agree that "from nothing" nothing can come. Neither God nor man can do what is not even thinkable, make nothing become something! But creation out of nothing does not mean that God "took nothing and made something out of it." "Out of" nothing, nothing comes, to be sure. But the personalist does not start with "nothing." He starts with God and says that this Person (far from being nothing himself) is the Creator-Ground of all.

In a word, to say that God creates is to say that beings now exist *that did not exist before*. Finite beings are not made "out of God" or "out of some coeternal being." They are made, produced, created. There is nothing contradictory in saying that a Creator brings into being what was nonexistent without the act of creation; to create means just that!

THE PERSON GOD IS: CREATOR OF COCREATORS

Yet before the personalistic theist can persist in this difficult theory of creation, he must explain why he does not find another great vision of God more palatable. Why not say that God is One with all there is, that nature and man are modes of God, or participants in his being who do not have any independent agency of their own?

We must not be casual about this concept of God as The One, for it is proposed by careful monists (Paul Tillich is fresh in mind). They are not saying that everything there is, collectively, is God. This simply renames things as they appear. Nor do such monists say that God is equally in all things that participate in his being. God is indeed the One who is manifest in the many, and the One would not be what he is apart from the many. God is to be found in his different manifestations in different degrees, just as a man is to be found in his varied utterances even though none of them express all that he is.

Again, The One may be said to have many centers of his being. However we express it, on this view the continuity and unity observed among the myriad things in the world manifest, at different levels or in different dimensions, the unity and continuity that God is. While significant exponents of this view—Plotinus, Eckhardt, Spinoza, Tillich—have tended to think of this One as supra-Personal in the sense indicated above, this being has been held to be Mind or Spirit, as in the thought of Hegel, Lotze, Bradley, Royce, and W. E. Hocking.[4]

With such a galaxy of stars gloriously arraigned against him, why does the theistic personalist still maintain his creationist stand? First, he would point out that the *how* of this One-in-many is essentially no clearer than is the how of creation "out of nothing." There is no contest here, for it is mysterious to know how the infinite can be both infinite and finite, perfect and imperfect. But there is less that is opaque in this mysterious relation than there is in the contention of the dualist and pluralist mentioned earlier. Indeed, many idealistic personalistic theists, such as B. P. Bowne and E. S. Brightman, would even argue that while persons have delegated freedom and independence, beings of a physical and biological nature are direct expressions of the cosmic Person. The main personalistic objection to monism, accordingly, is not that Nature is unified with One but that man is unified with the One. Why?

Persons are not only self-conscious unified beings; they feel themselves to be free, and there is good reason to suppose that this feeling is not a delusion. However, this freedom is not self-instituted nor is it without limits. The freedom of persons is the freedom to choose, within the margins of their own possibilities, in the world that surrounds them. But it is *their* freedom; it underlies their feeling of responsibility for much of what they do. If this is so, then they cannot be part of God, centers of his being. To express this crucial fact, the personalist calls for a doctrine of *creatio*.

It is important to emphasize here that the creationist theist will not allow any theory of the universe and of God to contradict or reduce to delusion the experience of free will. Human freedom, for good or ill, is limited, to be sure. But it is denied only at the cost of making human beings robots. To be sure, the exact scope of human freedom, and related matters, must be debated. But if man's actions are to be his, if they are to define his own individuality, he cannot be said to participate in God in any way that endangers this relative autonomy.

If a person is a mode or a center of another Being, *his* freedom, *his* individuality, is gone. Thus, *creatio ex nihilo* now becomes the personalistic theist's way of saying that every attempt to explain how persons can be free and still be *parts* of, or *centers* of, a larger controlling Whole will not do.

There are many who will insist that the doctrine of human freedom is mysterious enough, for they think that a free act simply must mean arbitrary action unlinked to anything else past or present. Why then extend such mystery to horrendous, cosmic proportions in a doctrine of divine creation of free persons?

The personalist stands firm and replies: If there is to be mystery in any world view, let this be where it is—namely, where it protects human finite unity and freedom, within limits to be determined in each instance. What is basically asserted in the doctrine of creation is that God can make what is not there before his act. This may be hard to imagine or picture, but it is defensible if theory is not to dictate to experienced personal unity and freedom.

Thus man is to be conceived of as a created cocreator. He has delegated responsibility for his own choices and subcreations in God's world. This means that God is transcendent, for he has a Being for himself. It also means that he is immanent not only by virture of the dependence of the natural world upon him, but by virtue of his relationship to free persons. For God has created persons endowed with freedom to choose within the limits of their own capacities and of the rest of the world as God made it. It also means that he will join man in creating what is not possible without God and man in mutual response.

Of course this doctrine of the cosmic Person as creator of free persons who, having a place in God's purpose, yet are not *in* or *as* his being, needs more defense. But since the monistic view of God is often defended on the grounds of the unity felt in mystical experience, one question may be raised here. What is love, or worship, if it does not involve the self-disciplined freedom of man to act in certain ways toward God and man? The personalist would argue that an adequate doctrine of sin, salvation, grace, prayer, worship, and immortality is not forthcoming unless persons are created, free, cocreators with God.

Finally, is God the Person-Creator in fact arbitrary? The personalist finds no arbitrariness. For (on other grounds) he believes that God in his creating expresses the purposes of love and reason that constitute his intrinsic nature. God, the Creator-Person, creates the finite creator-person in accordance with his purpose that men should be free to choose which way their souls shall go. God's own purpose, as the personalist sees it, calls for a community of responsive, responsible persons as the norm of creation and history. The kingdom of God, on earth and in heaven, is a community of persons, dedicating themselves to each other as persons. The "kingdom of heaven" is not the achievement of a benevolent despot; it is the qualitative growth of persons who find in their daily living that their freedom is most constructive and fruitful when it is expressed in creative and forgiving love.

The *Person God is*—he is the Lover-Creator who expresses his love in the order of Nature without which man could not even exist. But the *Person God is*—he is also the Lover-Creator who leaves man free to be a creator. The *Person God is*—he makes it clear in the foundations of Nature and Man that only in mutual love unto forgiveness is there self-fulfillment for God or man. Only in mutual love is there that fellowship-in-creativity-with-God that is God's highest goal for himself and for every man.[5]

NOTES

1. Paul Tillich, *Biblical Religion and the Search for the Ultimate Reality* (Chicago: University of Chicago Press, 1952).

2. Indeed, while much of this paper reflects the influence of F. R. Tennant, it is the influence of Edgar S. Brightman, Alfred N. Whitehead, H. Bergson, and Charles Hartshorne that has led me to conceive of change in God in ways similar to Hartshorne's view. At present my main hesitancy stems from the way in which the person is related to God in Whitehead, Bergson, and Hartshorne, for as I now see it the independence of the person is not adequately protected. For example, while the case for personal immortality must be argued, of course, I cannot accept the suggestion that there is wishful thinking and a false sense of values in the desire for personal immortality. On the contrary, if to be a person is to be a person-in-and-for-oneself, I fail to see why, in a universe that presumably conserves and increases value, it is an increase in value to preserve a memory, even in God (in Hartshorne's sense), while personhood ceases to be. Yet, I expect that the nature of creation and of personal continuity is the bone of contention.

3. See Chap. 13, "Hell," in *Talk of God,* ed. Royal Institute of Philosophy (New York: St. Martin, 1969).

4. An essay by Professor H. D. Lewis in *Talk of God* is an excellent presentation of the issue involved. At the same time Professor Lewis suggests a notion of "the elusive self" and of interpersonal relations that reinforces the view of personhood suggested here.

5. See "Free Will, the Creativity of God, and Order," in *Current Philosophical Issues* ed. F. C. Dommeyer, Essays in Honor of C. J. Ducasse (Springfield, Illinois: Thomas, 1966), chap. 14.

Chapter 5

THE ELEMENT OF MYSTERY IN THE CONCEPTION OF GOD
Kenneth L. Schmitz

BASING his remarks principally upon ancient Greek, Neoplatonic, and early Christian views, Hegel distinguishes the mystery of God (*Mysterium Gottes*) from the claim that God is unknowable. A mystery is a secret teaching know only to the devotees. If, as with the Eleusinian mysteries, a great many know them, they are still treated in a reverent manner and are not discussed in ordinary noncultic situations. The important point is that the secret is not in itself incomprehensible; on the contrary, it is essentially something known.[1] Nevertheless, Hegel cautions us not look to the Greek mystery cults for profound wisdom. Socrates knew better.[2] The Neoplatonists also used the word to designate the process of initiation into their own mystical speculative philosophy, and did not mean by it something unknowable.[3] So, too, the Christian mysteries are precisely the distinctive doctrines which communicate knowledge of God. Quite the contrary to their being secretive, they are manifestive.[4]

As essentially something known, the mystery is something reasonable. Now, what is reasonable is the work of speculative thought and will remain a mystery to sense and understanding. Both of these build up their representation of the meaning of revelation in terms of enclosed, selfsubsistent entities and their relation. In their representational field, unbridged difference is everywhere, and so everything is sculptured in an external manner which quite escapes, the interpenetration of opposites that characterizes speculative reason.[5] The under-

From: J. J. O'Malley et al. eds., *The Legacy of Hegel,* Proceedings of the Marquette Hegel Symposium, 1970 (The Hague: Nijhoff, 1971), pp. 125–136.

standing is governed by the fixity of simple self-identity, an identity which excludes all difference and opposition. For that reason that concrete process of selving and othering which constitutes speculative thought must remain mysterious to it. Conceptualization as the reconciliation of opposites appears to the understanding as something inconceivable; and so the speculative and the reasonable remain unthinkable to it. Moreover, if the speculative and reasonable comprise what is spiritual, and if God is spirit, then the true nature of God is indeed unknown and inconceivable to abstract thought.[6]

The true meaning of *religious* mystery, then, is to be found in the *speculative* capacity of religious revelation, and especially in the doctrine of the trinitarian God. The Trinity is the "mystery of Reason:"[7] "God is spirit, i.e., that which we call the triune God, a pure speculative content, i.e., the Mysterium of God. God is spirit, absolute activity, *actus purus*, i.e., subjectivity, infinite personality, infinite distinction of itself from itself."[8] The discussion of the coming of spirit to explicit manifestation and constitution in the Trinity is in terms of the elements of speculative thought [9] and these determine the nature of the opposition. It is not, therefore, the simple opposition of finite and infinite, but is rather the fixing and overcoming of differences which announce themselves at the level of sense and understanding as final and unbridgeable. In this sense, speculative thought is the very process of spirit by which contradictions are resolved; and this is the ultimate mystery.[10] Hegel's claim to the use of the term *mystery* is less artificial than it at first seems, for we are familiar with the religious use of the term as the *coincidentia oppositorum,* said of religious myths and dogmas. Hegel insists, too, that speculative thought seeks what religious mystery has always proclaimed: the union of all opposites, of man and God in the Incarnation, of mercy and sinner in religious forgiveness, and the like. For Hegel, the Trinity is the paradigm of such a union, for it is the "self-separating unity of absolute opposites," of infinite persons.[11] If specualtive thought can run through such a process of opposition and union, it can indeed claim to have caught up with its own presuppositions.[12]

Albert Chapelle takes very seriously Hegel's attribution of mystery to the Trinity, and seeks to understand the speculative truth of such an attribution. His defense is cathartic against any glib characterization of Hegel as a hard-shelled rationalist. His chief concern seems to be with those who would charge Hegel with reducing God to man, the infinite to the finite, and the knowledge of God to the knowledge of man.[13] In the energy and subtlety with which he pursues his defense, Chapelle seems to include a full sense of mystery within the Hegelian Absolute, a sense which in some way is not to do violence to the more traditional meanings of the term. He lodges the claim to mystery in the moment of negativity: "God is then for divine Reason the Mystery whose absolute presence does not exhaust the negativity of absence. God is not only Reason; he is negation of his knowledge and his revelation."[14] There are two characteristics of this alleged

Hegelian mystery of Reason which bear further comment. 1) It is a negative form of mystery, *a mystery of the absence of God* from himself. 2) It is a dialectical form of mystery, a mystery lodged in a moment of the final resolution, *a mystery of the moment.*

1) Since it is the speculative form of negativity, this mystery is unlike the other forms of negative mystery in two respects. First, it is a mystery of an absence which is sublated (aufgehoben) by the process of speculative recognition, whereas the previous forms of negative mystery were simple claims or confession of the unknowability of God. Second, it is a mystery of an absence which is absolute, since it is the moment of negativity within the Absolute. Now the moments of the Absolute must surely be themselves absolute, or the famous resolution is simply a patchwork job. Whereas the earlier forms of negative mystery were all relative and reducible to the finite, we are here confronted with the staggering thought of an absolute absence of an absolute presence from itself.[15] In the face of this infinite distance, the problem which seems to have been worrying Chapelle all along, the charge of confusing the divine and human, seems well taken care of! "The divine Logos is thus positively in theological Reason the Transparence of a total identity, at the same time as the Darkness proper to absolute Negativity verifies the divine nonidentity of the Mystery of God and of human certitudes."[16] 2) As a dialectical mystery of the moment, it is not simply a moment "within" the final resolution in the sense that it is a part or principle or factor in the resolution. That sort of thinking would make the resolution simply a totality of partial moments. We are far beyond the overcoming of the distinction of part and whole, for each moment is now the whole.[17] Nevertheless, unless speech is to lapse into an indeterminacy of nonsense or into silence, there must be interpretive meanings with which to differentiate the role of one moment from the other. In this sense, then, we can say that the whole Absolute is being "mystified" through the moment of its self-absence. Mystery arises in the capacity of the Absolute to be absent from itself. But now we must ask what it might mean for the Absolute to absent itself? And here we see two possible meanings. First, it might mean that it becomes finite, as in the Incarnation, so that when Jesus the Christ died, the Absolute died. This lodges mystery in the distance between finite and infinite, between God and man. However, it can also mean the absence of the Absolute from itself, that eternal process whereby the Absolute recognizes itself in each of its moments. To speak again of the Trinity, mystery would then mean that eternal process whereby each of the divine persons recognizes himself in the others, and recognizes his own otherness in them. It is even more, perhaps; it is that constitutive process whereby the divine persons in their own being pass over into the being of the others in the spiritual identity of their shared being.

This mystery of the negative moment is the mystery of identity-in-difference, of nonbeing in being, of untruth in truth. It is the farthest reaches of Reason, not because there is more which is inaccessible to it, but because Reason here exhausts all that can possibly be. It is in this sense, then, that the mystery of the negative moment is a dialectical work of speculative reason, *das Vernünftige*. It is the final statement of the Reasonable, and the first. For, I suggest, here in this absolute distance between God and himself, between the persons of the Trinity, the entire movement of the *Logic* can be cradled. So far can we go with Hegel, it seems to me. But to you, it may seem that we have gone by far too far.

Throughout most of this essay, and with our own emphasis, we have tried to reconstruct the sense of religious mystery according to Hegel. Towards the end, taking an insight from Albert Chapelle, we have developed a mystery of absolute absence. This is a turn which Hegel does not seem to have taken explicitly. His tone is usually confident and affirmative,[18] whereas the turn taken might appear to imperil the success of the Hegelian enterprise by raising the negative to so great a power that it threatens a new and absolute dualism. Such a threat is implicit in the conception of the Trinity itself. After all, a distinction of absolute persons is an absolute distinction, which must be neither wiped away into an indeterminate ground, nor advanced by the abstract understanding to three distinct gods.[19] Hegel thinks that he has met the threat by sublating the differences as moments of the concept. Where might we begin to probe the efficacy of Hegel's resolution?

The other as negative moment. If criticism is to be entered into, it might best begin by looking at the Hegelian "other," which is construed throughout his philosophy as a "moment" within a process of self-resolving moments. The characteristic movement of Hegel's thought is from the otherness implicit in a multiplicity to its explication in difference. With that explication, difference becomes opposition, that is, the difference of one with respect to another. The final moment in the hardening of conflict and the beginning of its resolution arrives with the self-contradiction inherent in explicit opposition. The original entity finds itself constituted through its opposition, and therefore through its other. With this realization, the conflict moves from an external rebuff of a separate other to an internal conflict within the original entity itself. The dialectic takes the form of exploring every possibility of resolution through the coconstitution of opposed entities until this develops the process of explicit spirituality described earlier. Here the self recognizes its essential being and destiny in its mutuality with the other. Self and other, then, become "moments" in a self-differentiating and self-resolving process.

A question of presence. Hegel called the speculative comprehension of this process of moments the *Mysterium* of God; and we have suggested that an absolute mystery of the negative moment is consonant with his philosophy. It remains to ask: Is there a mystery of presence?

Before we reply, it is necessary to establish the scope of the mystery to which the following remarks are taken to apply. A claim that Being is mysterious is distinct from the claim that God is mysterious. The mystery of Being is an intelligible and philosophical claim; the mystery of God is a metaphysical, theological, or religious claim to a mysterious being. Furthermore, the mystery of God may allege that God is mysterious only to man, or that he is also mysterious to himself. Throughout this essay we have directed our attention to the Trinitarian God as revealed in Christianity, and so in order to sketch out a possible mystery of divine presence, we wish to present a strong claim, the claim that God is mysterious not only to man but also in and to himself. To present a claim is not to prove it, of course, but is merely to suggest a line of reflection that might test the efficacy of Hegel's resolution.

A trans-Hegelian power of the negative? As negating the whole process the moment of absolute negativity poses a threefold option. First, if absolute negativity is understood to be a detailed reversal of all that absolute presence affirms, it can be safely tucked within the final resolution as a moment correlative to affirmation. Second, if absolute negativity is understood to be a collapse of the developed synthesis which spirit has labored to achieve, such a relapse into absolute indeterminacy will put us at the beginning of the *Logic* or the *Phenomenology,* so that we may begin the long climb again. Third, if, however, we understand by absolute negativity a stance of critical reflection which withdraws from the entire process of self-developing moments, then there arises out of the Hegelian dialectic the possibility of a nondialectical presence. Like the Phoenix from the ashes, so too from absolute negation a new presence may arise which may appropriate for itself other presuppositions than those which sustain the dialectical movement. This presence may bear traces of the dialectic, even as it stands free from it. The third option may seem like a *tour de force* turned against the Hegelian dialectic, but it is, after all, not unlike what has actually happened since Hegel. It is characteristic of the history of philosophy that it breaks free of its prior presuppositions and that it breaks the exclusive claim which a philosophy like Hegel's makes and thereby deabsolutizes it.

The question of indeterminacy. The Hegelian objection to such a "free" spirit, of course, is that it would be indifferent to man unless it were "run through" by him,[20] and that at best it would be externally related to him. For such a charge to be effective, however, we must accept the Hegelian interpretation of what it means to be related to something. The first step in acceptance is to permit Hegel to attribute to the negative a constituting power. Such an attribution already determines the character and possibilities of the other in a definite fashion, so that intelligible being is constituted of internally correlative moments. It follows, then that there can be no "other" which does not also fall under the necessity of constitutive correlation. The Trinity comes to be the paradigm of such correlation. The nature of conceptuality (*Begriff*) and the being of spirit (*Prozess*) is fixed. It is a version of the demand for reciprocity which defines the ultimate resolution as one of self-recovery and mutual constitution.

If for purposes of critical reflection we can put aside the Hegelian presuppositions, we might then recognize negation but not consider it as that which needs to be overcome in the form of self-recovery or self-identification. Suppose that spirit does not need to identify with *its* other? What, after all, is the force of the "its"? It seems that it is the bond of equals, or more exactly, of those which equally need each other. A more radical other, "free" from the burden of correlative constitution, would not be so related. It would be an Other so radical that its being would not be defined by its "otherness." Such an Other would be radically free and would not need to occupy its correlative in order to reconstitute and recover itself and its other.

The question of necessity. Nevertheless, the correlation of moments in the Hegelian system and their being "run through" *seriatim* was meant to secure necessity. Even the final negative mystery which appears in the Hegelian philosophy is a necessity of thought-thinking-being. Certainly, some sort of necessity seems to be the condition for any philosophical restatement of mystery, whether on Hegelian or non-Hegelian grounds. Mystery as contingent or arbitrary cannot be the foundation of being and knowledge. On the other hand, if mystery arises through the necessity of thought-thinking-being, it will have both epistemic and ontological authenticy. Now, if the Other is freed from the logic of moments, its necessity too will be of another order than dialectical necessity; and it remains to suggest what the character of that order might be.

Mystery as determinate actuality of another order. A pre-Hegelian model may serve to indicate a kind of absolute presence which might be recovered through the moment of absolute negation. To make the argument cogent, the third option would have to be reduced from a "maybe" to a "must." That is, the determinate character of mystery here suggested would have to be developed *out of* the absolute negation. One way would be to recapitulate the whole system in terms of a latent presence in it.

The history of some religions, to which Hegel also appealed, tells of the manifestation of the sacred as announcing itself in a way that bespeaks its compelling existence, a unique sort of necessity which is not incompatible with a certain appearance of arbitrariness that confirms the absolute status of its presence. Reflecting upon such experience, metaphysical theology among Jews, Christians, and Moslems came to attribute to the holy God a *mystery of excellence.* He was figured as too bright a light for clear sight, too precious a good to be measured or weighed. This central conviction characteristic of a certain classical understanding of these theistic faiths offers us a distinction between what I might call mystification and mystery. A state mystification rises out of the darkness of ignorance due to the weakness of our faculties, the poverty of the object, or the obscurity of the medium. Mystery, on the other hand, arises out of the light of knowledge in the presence of that which excels and outstrips every effort to "run it through," to define it in concepts or to embody it in words. The Hegelian dialectic may purge the presuppositions underlying the metaphysical theology associated with this sort of mystery, but that in itself does not invalidate its testimony to an extraordinary presence. Such a mode of mystery would point to a peak of actuality, seen not as the assertion of contingent particular existence from below, but as a transparency, a luminosity, a necessary existence from on high. Such a presence would not be apprehended as indeterminate in the Hegelian sense, but its determinacy would be of an order of actuality that stands free from all conceptual moments. Concepts would not comprehend it, but merely open out towards it.[21] God would exceed all predicates and outstrip all moments. Mystery, inseparable from his presence, would manifest itself as power, abundance, openness, apprehended either through a religious faith or through an intellectual reflection. As with the Hegelian spirit, so too with this mysterious God, his mystery would be both his act of revealing and his act of being, so that God would not be mysterious simply for us. "Mystery" would be the name of God and his way of being present to himself.

Mystery as transverbal, transconceptual presence-in-absence. When those who assent to the mysterious character of God say that he "exceeds" all dogmatic formulas, that he is "more" than Father, "more" than Love, this mysterious excess does not have an ordinary meaning. It is not a "more" that can be filled in by speech that is being held back from crossing an alleged limit. This "more" does not mean that speech about God is "less" than it might be or will sometime be. Just as color does not restrict flavor, so mystery does not restrict speech. Hegel, of course, might ask whether a spirit can settle for a speech that reaches "less" than total comprehension of all. Those who might uphold a mystery of excellence and defend it on the grounds of religious faith or of thought-thinking-being might reply as follows. Spirit (both in its divine and human forms) has access to the full mystery which is at least implicit in the apprehension of reality and of the sacred. The "more than speech" does not designate a simple lack, but rather a transverbal, transconceptual mode of presence. Speech is not thereby limited; everything that is sayable of God remains sayable. No propositional truths are withheld. It is, rather, to use Spinoza's term, that speech is infinite in its own order. It is not limited by anything else, and yet it is a determinate mode with its own possibilities. Transverbal presence is another determinate mode of being, the mode of silence. Now, this silence is not merely a correlative absence of the speech of the dialectic, for it manifests a meaning of its own.[22] Such a silence is not perspectival, but it is determinate and actual. The "more" is not simply negative as though lying out of reach of speech. It is, for example, the unsayable in the religious myth. Now, the unsayable is not a simple negative. The "beyond" which remains unsaid and unsayable in the saying of the myth is carefully determinate and carries its own meaning. That determination is not of the same order as the representational or conceptual elements but is even more actual. Indeed, it is the actualizing power of the myth. Whereas for Hegel the Logic is the thoroughly conceptual and comprehensible discourse of God, the negative in the unsayable announces itself as a transforming power and presence of the sacred.[23] Mystery is God's way of being present and a manifestation of a meaning that is transpropositional. The proponents of the mystery of excellence might reply that, like Hegel's spiritual process, the divine mystery is both the ontological foundation and the epistemic presupposition for all being, knowing, and speaking.

The negativity of the third option, through which we first suggested a mystery of excelling presence, is strikingly manifest in the religious myth. For what is there revealed is also hidden from conceptual thought and propositional speech. In revealing himself, God also "hides"—not because he withholds part of himself out of envy or fear, but because his revelation exceeds the capacity to be comprehended. The final word of his manifestation is that he is mysterious. Religious mystery is incomprehensible, because if it were comprehensible it could be "run through." To comprehend something is to "run through" it, to occupy it, to gather it, to gather it up into a totality. This is what Hegel's discourse does, moving ultimately to the absolute. Indeed, a moment is the "other" in the form of being able to be run through. Even Hegel's mystery is *in this sense* comprehensible; and is just *in this sense* that the mystery of excellence, presence and silence is not. According to the mystery of presence which we are sketching we cannot run through the divine nature to gather it up. This is not because it lies "beyond" a barrier in an unknowable darkness, but because it lies infinitely open. Now it is not only that *we* can't run through God's nature in order to gather it up, but that "gathering up" is always short of the "free" infinite. God cannot gather himself up. God is ultimately incomprehensible to God, not by a failure of knowing but by an excess of a kind of presence that is not a running through.

A *selective affinity between thought and images*. A philosophical reflection is an interplay between leading ideas and suggestive images, and so a philosophy draws towards itself those images towards which it is drawn. The mystery of presence sketched out above draws its own images towards it. Perhaps its most preferred images are those associated with a properly religious joy. This is not an ordinary happiness or pleasure. It is sometimes lived as sublime peace, but at others in the most trying anguish. It includes the joy of consolation which a community of believers suffer in the death of a person. It is, above all, in the feast—solemn and funereal, or alight with joy—that the mystery of presence is caught in flight. When Hegel speaks of the feast he speaks of the fruits of earth rising to a new possibility, that of being eaten in enjoyment by a self-conscious being; and the mystery resides in the revelation of the unity of earth and self in this act.[24] But, in truth, who surrenders to the feast is carried along, poured out into a festal freedom that has no goal—into a domain that is the play of the divine. The image of the feast seems to underly the Greek Fathers' understanding of the Trinity, and a sense of divine play.

Hegel's consideration of the Trinity differs considerably from previous traditional understandings, especially from those of the Greek Fathers.[25] The most significant difference, perhaps, is that Hegel describes the Trinity as a movement from the Father to its culmination in the Holy Spirit, a process which allows for the appropriate Hegelian function of the negative, and which allows a portrayal of the Trinity as a rational process of development and fulfillment. The Greek Fathers see it rather differently. Their stress is rather on the Father and his superabundance of ontological generosity, of which the other persons are the response.[26] Hegel's Trinity is somber and hardworking, a striving towards the goal which it appoints for itself. It is a marvelous goal, to be sure, but one which is arrived at by careful steps, and whose exact stages we can recount with precise, methodical conceptual clarity. There is everything here that some philosophers might want, and almost nothing that some religious persons might recognize. In the Greek Trinity, the Father, so to speak, finds himself with a family; in the Hegelian Trinity, he plans it. The Greek theologians celebrate the Father as generous source; Hegel ushers in the Holy Spirit as a primordial *telos* achieved. Nevertheless, he has taught us the power of the negative and made us realize that one-sided affirmative images and conceptions of presence have no exclusive role in teaching us of God, and that without the qualifying power of the negative they distort and corrupt. He has justified the images of absence and the thinking of "not" at the highest reaches of reflection. It is not accurate, I think, to say that Hegel has rationalized or secularized his Trinitarian paradigm. It is more accurate, perhaps, to say that he catches the more somber shadows of religion, and, above all, its relentless energy—but not its dalliance and pleasure. There is no ambrosia in the Hegelian synthesis, even as it foams forth its own eternal moments.

NOTES

1. The edition used throughout the essay is that of Georg Lasson, 1925, 1927: G. W. F. Hegel, *Vorlesungen über die Philosophie der Religion*, 2 vol. (Hamburg: F. Meiner, 1966). Hereafter *VPR*. For a discussion of the considerable textual problems see the Appendices. In recognition of them (g) will represent Hegel's own autograph text, (k) the students' notebooks and materials from earlier editions. The English translation from Bruno Bauer's unsatisfactory edition is by E. B. Spiers and J. B. Sanderson, (1895), *Hegel's Lectures on the Philosophy of Religion*, 3 vols. (New York: Humanities Press, 1968). Hereafter *LPR*. 2/2, 177 (g): "Geheimnis ist wesentlich etwas Gewusstes, aber nicht von allen, hier aber ein Gewusstes von allen, aber als geheim Behandeltes . . . bekannt, aber wovon man nicht spricht." Cf. *LPR* II, 257–58: "In this religion [of humanity] there is nothing incomprehensible, nothing which cannot be understood; there is no kind of content in the god which is not known to man." [Since

this article first appeared the relevant part of VPR has been translated from a more critical text: *G.W.F. Hegel: The Christian Religion. Lectures on the Philosophy of Religion, Part III: The Revelatory, Consummate, Absolute Religion*, ed. and trans. by Peter C. Hodgson. American Academy of Religion Texts and Translations Series, no. 2, Scholars Press, 1979. See also W. Jaeschke, "Hegel's Philosophy of Religion: The Quest for a Critical Edition," *The Owl of Minerva*, vol. 11, no. 3, March 1980, pp. 4–8.]

2. G. W. F. Hegel, *Philosophie der Geschichte*, ed. F. Frunstäd (Stuttgart: Reclam, 1961), p. 350: "Die Mysterien waren vielmehr alte Gottesdienste, und es ist ebenso ungeschichtlich als töricht, tiefe Philosopheme darin finde zu wollen."

3. *VPR* 2/3, 77 (k): "*Mysterion* nämlich ist das, was das Vernünftige ist; bei den Neuplatonikern heisst dieser Ausdruck auch schon nur spekulative Philosophie." G. W. F. Hegel, *Lectures on the History of Philosophy*, trans. Haldane and Simpson (London: Routledge 1968), II, 448: "Thus Proclus for example says . . .: 'Let us once more obtain initiation into the mysteries (*mystagogian*) of the one.' Mysticism is just this speculative consideration of Philosophy."

4. *VPR* 2/3, 77 (k): "Ein Geheimnis im gewöhnlichen Sinne ist die Natur Gottes nicht, in der christlichen Religion an wenigsten." Cf. Albert Chapelle, *Hegel et la religion* (Paris: Presses Universitaires de France, 1966), II, 66 (n. 102): "Comme chez les néoplatoniciens, le *mysterion* trinitaire est moins le secret interdit á l'histoire que l'intelligibilité spéculative de sa tradition, de sa mémoire." Hereafter *HR*.

5. *VPR* 2/3, 70: "Was für die Vernunft ist, ist für diese kein Geheimnis; in der christlichen Religion weiss man es. Geheim ist es nur für den Verstand und die sinnliche Denkungsweise. Da sind die Unterschiede unmittelbar, die sinnlichen Dinge gelten; es ist die Weise der Äusserlichkeit, Sobald aber Gott als Geist bestimmt ist, so ist die Äusserlichkeit aufgehoben. Doch ist es ein Mysterium für die Sinne . . .''

6. *VPR* 2/3, 79 (k): "Man nennt es unbegreiflich, aber was unbegreiflich scheint, ist eben der Begriff selbst, das Spekulative oder dies, dass das Vernünftige gedacht wird." *Cf.* G. W. F. Hegel, *Enzyklopädie der philosophischen Wissenschaften im Grundrisse*, eds. F. Nicolin and O. Pöggeler, (Hamburg: F. Meiner, 1959), #82, Zus. (Wallace trans.), p. 154.

7. *VPR* 2/3, 69 (k): "Die Dreieinigkeit heisst das Mysterium Gottes; der Inhalt ist mystisch, d.h. spekulativ." For the most extensive and serious consideration of the Hegelian Trinity in English, see the perceptive study of E. Fackenheim, *The Religious Dimension in Hegel's Thought* (Bloomington: Indiana University Press, 1968). See also J. Splett, *Die Trinitatslehre G. W. F. Hegels* (Freiburg: Karl Alber, 1965). For a critical view of the work of Chapelle, Bruaire, Splett, Wolf-Dieter Marsch and Traugott Koch, see the review article of H. Kimmerle, "Zur Hegels Religionsphilosophie," in *Philos. Rundschau*, 15 (1968), pp. 111-135.

8. *VPR* 2/3, 57 (g): "Gott ist Geist, d.i. das, was wir Dreieinigen Gott heissen, [ein] rein spekulativer Inhalt, d.i. [das] *Mysterium* Gottes."

9. *Cf.* Chapelle, HR II, 62ff., who notes that Hegel displaces the traditional theological terms of generation and procession for the dialectical ones of differentiation and partition.

10. Cf. *LHP* III, p. 152: "In Protestantism, on the contrary, the subjective religious principle has been separated from Philosophy, and it is only in Philosophy that it has arisen in its true form again. In this principle the religious content of the Christian Church is thus retained . . ." And p. 165: "Here [in modern as distinct form ancient philosophy] there is a consciousness of an opposition . . . [which] . . . is the main point of interest in the conception of the Christian religion. The bringing about in thought of the reconciliation which is accepted in belief now constitutes the whole interest of knowledge."

11. Said of Jacob Boehme's notion of God in *LHP* III, p. 198.

12. *VPR* 2/3, 22 (k): "Das Zeugnis des Geistes in seiner höchsten Weise ist die Weise der Philosophie, dass der Begriff rein als solcher aus sich ohne Voraussetzungen die Wahrheit entwickelt und enwichelnd erkennt und in und durch diese Entwickelung die Notwendigkeit der Wahrheit einsieht."

13. See his discussion in *HR* II, 75–76 and ns. 141–143. The chief point is that God is the true infinite who is the Measure but who is not himself subject to measure.

14. Chapelle *HR* II, 75: "Dieu est dès lors pour la Raison divine le Mystère dont la présence absolue n'épuise pas la négativité de l'absence. Dieu n'est pas que la Raison; il est négation de sa connaissance et de sa révélation."

15. This must be one of the strongest interpretations of the "ungeheure, fürchterliche Vorstellung," of the death of Christ: "Got ist gestorben, Gott *selbst* ist tot." 2/3 IV, 157–158 (g), italics mine.

16. Chapelle *HR* II, 79: "Le Logos divin est ainsi positivement dans la Raison théologique la Transparence d'une identité totale, en même temps que la Ténèbre propre à la Negativité absolue vérifie la non-identité divine du Mystère de Dieu et des certitudes humaines." It is clear from n. 146 that Chapelle takes this negative mystery to be harmonious with "the idealist conception of the absoluteness of the Absolute and of the negativity of mystical knowledge, [of] speculative knowledge, [which] reawakens the theological categories of Absence and of Distance from man, of the cloud of Unknowing."

17. G. W. F. Hegel, *Wissenschaft der Logik*, G. Lasson, ed., 2 vols. (Hamburg: F. Meiner, 1967), 2:/138ff. English: 1) *Hegel's Science of Logic,* trans. A. V. Miller (New York: Humanities Press, 1969), pp. 513ff.; 2) *Hegel's Science of Logic,* trans. W. H. Johnston and L. G. Struthers, 2 vols. (New York: Macmillan, 1951), 2:143ff.

18. Although see the closing pages of the Berlin lectures on the philosophy of religion. Each commentator on the *Logik* as well as on the Berlin lec-

tures has to comment upon the threat of a resurgent dualism at the apex of the system. See a discussion of the literature on this in Malcolm Clark, *Logic and System* (Louvain: Universitaire Werkgemeenschap, s.a.), especially touching Litt, Iljin, Coreth, Gregoire. See also Jan van der Meulen, *Die gebrochene Mitte* (Hamburg: F. Meiner, 1958), and the comments of E. Fackenheim, *op. cit.* concerning the closing pages of VPR.

19. *VPR* 2/3, 71 (k): "Da *scheint* der Widerspruch so weit getrieben, dass keine Auflösung, keine Verwischung der Person möglich ist." Italics mine. The *reality* is, of course, the resolution of this contradiction in the process of spirit, in the *Begriff.*

20. The phrase is meant to capture the methodical ratiocination required to follow the path of the dialectic from moment to moment, stage to stage, and to hold it together.

21. Obviously, an appropriate theory of meaning is required here.

22. A theory of religious language is needed here.

23. For this view of religious myth, see Kenneth L. Schmitz, chap. 1 of this volume.

24. *Phänomenologie des Geistes,* ed. J. Hoffmeister (Hamburg: F. Meiner), p. 503; English translation by J.B. Baillie, *Hegel's Phenomenology of Mind,* rev. 1931, (New York: Macmillan, 1955), p. 726; a new translation has since appeared by A. V. Miller, *Hegel's Phenomenology of Spirit* (Oxford: Oxford-Clarendon, 1977), p. 437.

25. For a good discussion of the differences, see Chapelle *HR* II, 55–109, including the discussions in the footnotes. See especially, p. 106: "La spéculation trinitaire de Hegel ne s'organise donc pas comme la théologie grecque selon un principe de génerosité communicative. . . . Le principe de la génerosité paternelle fait place à la négativité. . . ." And n. 321: "Le pôle extatique de la contemplation patristique grecque est le Père, Source abyssale de toute la divinité. Dans la spéculation hégelienne, les moments du Concept s'organisent en référence à leur finale en l'Espirit."

26. Cf. Hegel's comments on the *kenosis* in *Phänomenologie,* p. 534; *Hegel's Phenomenology,* p. 767.

PART TWO

Religious Reasoning: Proving God?

INTRODUCTION BY FREDERICK FERRÉ

T HIS section has two jobs to do. Or perhaps
a better description would be that it has a single
job with two aspects: first, to discuss whether genuine reasoning about God is possible at all (and if
so, how), and, second, to give three examples of
such reasoning.

The first two essays are both involved explicitly
with the epistemology of religion. James F. Ross
surveys the scene and finds, contrary to much recent received opinion, that there are no overwhelming impediments to religious "knowing" in a
straightforward, standard sense. His overall strategy is to shift the burden of proof to the skeptic
who challenges claims of religious knowledge in

principle. If the skeptic cannot make good his claim that there is some identifiable *infirmity* in religious discourse or religious believing or religious experience or religious subject matter (God) that makes religious knowledge claims inappropriate, then there is no reason to doubt the cognitive status of religious thinking. Ross moves systematically through these four areas, consequently, answering allegations of impediments and clearing the way for an uncompromising cognitivism in religion.

The following essay, by Frederick Ferré, focuses on just one of the four areas considered by Ross: that of religious discourse about God. Ross appeals to the legitimacy (and to the pervasive normality) of analogy in speech, and shows the similarities between theological discourse and other technical or "craft-bound" forms of speech and life. Ferré examines some traditional problems with making analogy work in the context of talk about God and concludes (1) that there are indeed serious impediments in the traditional metaphysical formulations of doctrines of analogy, but (2) that as a discipline for the use of language within a given form of speech, analogy may be clarifying and helpful. The logic of analogy is internal to what Wittgenstein called the "language game" of the religious form of life, and as such it is quite legitimate; but the whole "language game" cannot rest upon merely analogical foundations. For proper support of its internal logic, theological discourse as a whole needs external connections of a broader metaphysical sort.

The next three essays of this section are devoted to reasoning about this wider metaphysical task. They do not take the same point of view (they are not even discussing the same arguments), but they are all examples of what has been defended earlier as a viable possibility. James F. Ross, for example, formulates and defends what he calls a "modal" argument (from necessities and possibilities) for the existence of God. This argument, which is related to the more familiar family of Ontological and Cosmological Arguments, purports to show conclusively that God as the "unproducible and unpreventable" being must exist; but Ross is quick to point out that further argument would be needed to show that this being is also to be identified as the benevolent Lord of religious interest.

Louis Dupré is still more guarded about the Teleological Argument, which he finds intellectually uncompelling. While Ross sees his Modal Argument for God as philosophically strong but religiously unavailable without considerable supplementation, Dupré argues, contrastingly, that the Teleological Argument functions better as a pointer for the religious mind to a set of remarkable facts through which the transcendent may be confronted than as an exercise in philosophic logic.

Finally, Peter A. Bertocci advocates a Wider Teleological Argument through which, in his view, the probative power of philosophy and the inspiring influence of religion may come together. The basic contention of his essay is that the

Teleological is a reasonably acceptable argument if it is viewed as cumulative, broadened rather than "supplemented" by other arguments. This wider argument does not depend upon the ideal of perfection governing the classical Ontological Argument, nor upon the myriad specific adaptations of one organ to another, nor upon the surviving of organisms especially adapted to environments, nor upon the profound ethical and religious "intuitions" of the race. Its underlying theme is, as with other dependable beliefs (such as that in biological evolution), that while no one link in the argument justifies the conclusion, the available links can mutually reinforce each other and contribute to a reasonable belief.

Chapter 6

WAYS OF RELIGIOUS KNOWING
James Ross

"RELIGIOUS knowing" sounds like a contradiction in terms. One might say, "insofar as something is knowable, it is not religious." While many would accord *belief* status to some religious claims, they would deny *knowledge* status to any.

Where there *cannot* be knowledge, some *infirmity,* whether in us or in the subject of belief, must *prevent* it. So we look for the preventing factors in religion.

Is there some *infirmity* in religious discourse, some *infirmity* in religious believing, some *infirmity* in religious experience, some *infirmity* in the very subject of religion (God) itself, which *precludes* knowledge? If not, then there is no reason in principle to say that knowledge is less common about religious matters than it is about the other areas of life.

Moreover, when we examine the minimally acceptable accounts by "foundationalists" and "explanatory-coherence" theorists of human knowledge in general, we will find that religious belief fits naturally into the justification scheme, along with historical and other kinds of knowledge.

The characteristic anticognitivist philosophical position, of course, has maintained that there are infirmities that prevent religious knowledge: (1) the *discourse* in which religious convictions are expressed is unintelligible and its content inaccessible; (2) believing on *faith* is inherently incompatible with knowing; and (3) religious claims are neither establishable by proofs nor adequately confirmable in experience. In a word, knowledge of things religious is said to be precluded

---

"Ways of Religious Knowing" is published for the first time in this volume.

at every level: the linguistic, the nontheoretical level of experiential and testimonial knowledge, and the theoretical level of "the established" or "proved."

But reexamination of these matters suggests quite the opposite: that there is *no* infirmity about the discourse, the process of belief, the role of theoretical proof, or the role of experience which precludes religious knowledge, and, that the continuity of religious discourse, experience, and theoretical inquiry with other kinds of knowing suggests that religious believers may very well possess knowledge of what they affirm.

I shall summarize here what I think can be shown concerning each of those topics in order to sketch the outline of a positive theory of religious knowledge that I think adequate to the demands of contemporary thought. I defend:

- (a) the intelligibility of religious discourse (i) inherently (vs. the discontinuity hypothesis), (ii) accessibility (craft-bound discourse).
- (b) the compatibility of faith and knowledge (vs. the inherent opposition doctrine).
- (c) the limited role of proof or establishment (vs. the claim that nothing relevant can be established).
- (d) the role of nontheoretical, experiential, and testimonial knowledge (vs. the claim that nothing can be experientially known about God).
- (e) the privileged access to reality through religious faith (vs. the view that faith is an affective deformation of the world).

The object of this essay is to display the strategic steps in a comprehensive theory of religious knowledge which will not only suggest that religious knowledge is possible but will further suggest that reality is, in central features, incomprehensible, inaccessible, and *misconstrued* in experience without religious faith.

THE INTELLIGIBILITY OF RELIGIOUS DISCOURSE

A literate late-twentieth-century audience may not have an antecedent interest in disputes about whether sentences like "God loves all men" and "God will forgive the repentant man," are or are not without cognitive meaning. But from a theoretical point of view this question, which was hotly debated at the mid-century and was equally vehemently debated in the Middle Ages, is of cardinal importance. For if the expressions in religious discourse are without cognitive meaning, then there is nothing (religiously relevant) to believe or to disbelieve as a result of someone's uttering them. Where there is nothing to believe or to disbelieve, there is nothing to be known.

Nevertheless, in sketching a comprehensive answer to this dispute, there is no need for me to contend with the dinosaur of the verifiability-falsifility criterion of meaningfulness. Those critera died of overweight in the 1950s when it was established both that the criteria where not themselves verifiable or falsifiable and that any version of the criteria *strong* enough to cast doubt upon religious discourse would also cast doubt upon the heartland of science; and that any version *weak* enough to leave science unchallenged would permit religion, metaphysics, aesthetics, and all the forms of "effete" thought back into the theater of the meaningful.

In *Theology and Meaning* Raeburne S. Heimbeck[1] surveys the key literature in the verification debate and presents a very interesting "configuration" theory (not unlike the "perceptual-set" theory that I employ) to show how experience can yield confirmation of religious beliefs.

But still, a variant of an old problem remains: is there a *meaning-evacuating discontinuity* caused by meaning differentiation? If a given term takes on different senses in expressions concerned with suitably different sorts of things, then how do we know whether any *continuity* of meaning remains from one meaning-differentiated occurrence to another? That is a *general* problem about meaning, of which the religious applications are only particular instances. For instance how do we know whether expressions applied to God, like "loves," "forgives," and "creates" are *merely equivocal* with application to creatures?

To resolve that issue, we first examine religious discourse to see whether it suffers some peculiar infirmity in that its terms meaning-differentiate from context to context in ways which are not usual in intelligible discourse, and which evacuate the cognitive content from the expressions. *Secondly,* we discover what principles determine how a single expression *does* meaning-differentiate in intelligible discourse. Thirdly, we then show that the structure of meaning differentiation *within* religious discourse is exactly the same as that which obtains in the language in general, and that there is no evacuating factor present because each case of meaning-difference can be accounted for by principles which do not, in general, have a meaning-evacuating effect. A new analogy theory will answer the questions about the cognitive content of the religious discourse, at least until someone comes up with an entirely new account of cognitive evacuation.

Analogy: The next few pages are intended to provide an *initial* insight into the nature and strategic role of the analogy hypothesis.[2]

Same terms adapt in meaning to their contrasting contexts, sometimes *differentially*: that is meaning differentiation. For instance, the frame "the ——— charged the ———" completed by "the bank *charged* the account" and "the judge *charged* the jury." There are two kinds of meaning differentiation of same terms (e.g., "He wrote his name on the board"; "He wrote a book with a tape recorder"): *unrelated* (or merely equivocal), "pen," "pen," meanings; and *related*, or analogous meanings. Related, or analogous meanings are either denominatively analogous ("to plow," "a plow") or analogous by proportionality ("caught a cold" and "caught a thief"). Analogies by proportionality are either proper ("expected a raise," "expected a friend") or metaphorical, ("the maid washed the floor," "the wind washed the sky").

When we study the semantic regularities governing the way in which a given term adapts to its various contexts, taking on a meaning appropriate to each, we find that the principles of *semantic contagion*, of *semantic dominance*, by which dominating terms determine the meanings of context-indeterminate and determinable terms, are general throughout the language an are *lawlike*.

So, the fact that *wise, knows, forgives, loves,* and the like differ somewhat in meaning when applied in sentences about God is no more surprising than that *wants* differs in meaning in "The children want candy," "The cat wants to go outside," "The plant wants water" and, "That bearing wants oiling." In fact, if differences of meaning were *not* contracted by concatenating predicates with *God* rather than *Socrates, that* would demand explanation!

In some cases where terms meaning-differentiate in different applications there is a discernible *relatedness* of meaning, indicated by the overlap of applicable near synonyms, despite meaning adjustments to the contrasting completion expressions making up the sentences. In the pair "He expected a raise" and "He expected a defeat," *expected* has meaning-differentiated but not to *mere equivocation*; for, the common terms, *anticipated, was not surprised by, was not in great doubt about* apply in both; but *hoped for* does not apply in the second and *dreaded* does not apply in the first; *was resigned to* does not usually apply in the first but often does apply in the second. Those differences of meaning are contracted to *expected* from the semantic contrast of *a raise* and *defeat*.

Then should we be surprised that expressions like *loves, forgives, understands, wills, predetermines,* and *judges* also meaning-differentiate when concatenated with expressions like *God, The maker of the world, The necessary being,* in contrast to completions by *Socrates, The father of the family* and the like?

Once general principles describing the semantic contagion by which a term meaning-differentiates from one sentential context to another are identified and modeled, we find that what happens to terms in religious discourse is not a case of language "slipping its moorings" or language "going on a holiday" but is the effect of semantic regularities which are obeyed throughout our natural language, and probably throughout all natural languages.

The apparently *anomalous* meaning shift of terms applied to God, as compared with applications of the same terms to creatures, is in fact, merely an instance of semantic contagion, a phenomenon governed by general linguistic regularities, and is *not* an infirmity peculiar to religious discourse.

Of *course*, some predicates will have different meanings when applied to God, as compared with applications to creatures; but that is no longer surprising; it is a semantic necessity. And further reflection discloses that meaning-differentiation in what can loosely be called "categorically contrasting contexts" is not something that unties religious discourse from the eventual experiential moorings that all intelligible discourse requires. Quite to the contrary, the fact that the meaning-differentiation in religious discourse is generated according to synchronic regularities governing natural language *guarantees* that the experiential moorings remain unbroken, even throughout successive abstractions.[3] There is no identifiable *linguistic or semantic discontinuity* between religious discourse and the other kinds of discourse in natural language. So the dispute about the meaningfulness of religious discourse, logically, shifts ground. No longer can it be contended that the synactically well-formed expressions of religious discourse are semantically incoherent or otherwise *evacuated* of content that would form an appropriate object for an epistemic attitude (an attitude of belief, disbelief, doubt, or other cognitive attitude to which considerations of evidence or grounding are relevant) merely by being religious. Rather the new form of the discontinuity claim has to be that the *content* of otherwise meaningful religious discourse is inaccessible.

Access to the Content

The idea behind the "inaccessibility" attack is that religious discourse is to the intelligent non-believer the way jazz discourse is to the intelligent outsider: not that what is said is without a content appropriate for belief, etc., but that there is *no way into* the discourse by which the observer can satisfactorily discover what is to be believed, doubted, denied, etc.

But the fact that mere observers may be denied access to the discoursing community does not show anything of importance. For *usually* mere observers are without reliable access to the content of craft-bound discourse, e.g., of doctors, lawyers, philosophers, painters, and auto mechanics. And, of course, with religion sectarianized, there are many fragmentary discoursing communities for whom common terms have taken on community-oriented special meanings. For instance, *salvation* might mean one thing to a medieval Thomist and quite another to a contemporary fundamentalist. There is no antecedent reason to expect a mere observer to have a reliable grasp of the discourse.

Furthermore, religious discourse *is* craft-bound discourse, the kind of discourse which is not fully accessible to those who have taken up or at least seriously participated in the form of life for which the discourse serves as a communicating thought form. You can't really grasp the talk of lawyers or doctors or mechanics unless you can make the judgments they are competent to make, dispute in their terms, and, generally, behave indistinguishably in the craft roles.

Nevertheless, the possession of an analogous form of life may provide a partial but satisfying grasp of the discourse within another; for instance, a Mediterranean Christian may attempt to understand the religious discourse of committed Muslims and may, especially if instructed by a believer, to an extent succeed. But where the life forms are very far apart, transformations of single utterances in the one discourse into single utterances in the other may lead to great confusion; for instance, the translation of assertions of Buddhist believers as *negations* of Christian beliefs, or vice versa, may display the inadequacy of one's grasp of the religious discourse appropriate to a religious life at considerable cultural remove from one's own.

In principle, there is no greater difficulty in gaining access to the thought content of religious discourse than there is to the content of any other craft-bound discourse: farming discourse is just as difficult for the city dweller, and so is mountaineering discourse to a plains shepherd.

Full access can be gained only by one's learning to talk as a member of the community—to explain, defend, criticize, qualify, amplify and otherwise assert claims in a mode of speaking that would appear "native" to the dwellers of the belief system or craft.

The contrast between religious discourse and other kinds, e.g., backpacking discourse, has been impliedly exaggerated; the accessibility problem is the same: the more complex the life form involved, the more intricate the discourse of description, appraisal, qualification, amplification, explanation, and criticism, and so, the more extensive the scientific observation or participatory experience that will be required for confident comprehension and confident participation in the discourse.

I do not know of a serious philosopher who really holds that religious discourse, if it has cognitive content (as I have shown it must), is such that no one, not even the believers of the religion, can gain access to its content. But if anyone should be tempted to try to make such reasoning persuasive, he should remember that more than an accessibility *difficulty* will have to be demonstrated, because all craft-bound discourse presents a *difficulty of access;* a neophyte can come fully to understand the talk only by becoming competent in the form of life of the discoursing community and in the events which are the occasions for craft-bound talk.

There is, in principle, no more difficulty in comprehending religious discourse adequately than there is in participating in a sports-watching community with appropriate remarks, objections, observations, and appraisals.

It is quite misleading to suggest that access to the content of discourse may be vitiated by the fact that (for all the observer knows) there may be nothing that it is about; for similarly, discourse about Norse gods and the like is not vitiated and rendered inaccessible by the nonexistence of such beings.

Hence, the existence of an ontological dispute about the existence of God cannot defeat the accessibility of the content of religious discourse. The same holds for talk of ghosts, leprechauns, astrological influence, justice, and many other things.

Anyway, that position would defeat itself. One would, presumably, not be able to gain access to the utterance "God does *not* exist" unless the body of discourse were meaningful; and *that* would require that "God does not exist" be *false;* so, the odd conclusion would follow that unless God exists, the sentence "God does not exist" would have no accessible cognitive content. We should then be able to infer the existence of God from the manifestly accessible cognitive content of its negation. It is not really a central problem, concerned with religious knowledge, to discuss the *means* by which cognitive access to religious discourse may be obtained. Once we see that the access to religious discourse is an instance of access to craft-bound discourse, in general, no specially *religious* problem remains. It would, of course, be illuminating to carry out a more detailed investigation of the way experience and discourse operate to create one another, and we might come to know much more about the way religious experience and religious discourse are related, by comparing the two to discourse and experience of different sorts. But there simply is not a serious doubt that one can come to know what religious expressions mean provided one will seriously take part in the discourse of the community that employs it. The fact that the expressions may turn out to be disappointingly vague or ambiguously employed or even wholly equivocal in various applications should create no greater difficulty of access than we encounter frequently with discourse about subjects other than God, subjects as diverse as the interest paid by banks and the interests served by the government.

Access to Truth Value

But still, it may be contended, even if you come to know *what* the believer claims and even if what he claims is appropriate for belief, disbelief, doubt, etc., *still,* you can never *know* whether or not what has been said is *true* or *false,* hence, there still is no religious knowledge. The *content* of the assertions may be accessible to belief. But the *truth* values are not cognitively accessible.

Two sorts of reasons may be offered: that the best that is possible in religious matters is faith and faith is the very antithesis of knowledge, being always a belief that goes beyond the evidence; and secondly, that knowledge in religious matters is excluded (a) because nothing religiously substantive can be proved, demonstrated, or established; and (b) experience can provide no knowledge of God because God is a transcendent being that cannot be experienced. Since theoretical proof and sensible experience are the only sources of knowledge, there cannot therefore be any knowledge of matters substantively religious.

When one replies, "What of knowledge through testimony," the rejoinder is that testimony is merely a form of faith and cannot ever provide knowledge.

Unless these positions can be defeated, religious claims (and their negations) will exhibit an infirmity that precludes their being *known* to be true or false. But these skeptical positions are riddled with confusions and errors.

THE COMPATIBILITY OF FAITH AND KNOWLEDGE

The opposition of faith and reason has been exaggerated from the Middle Ages onward. An exaggerated contrasting of "faith" and "science" is at the root of the confusion.

We must not regard the words *faith* and *reason* as naming the products of diverse processes, so that nothing which is ever the outcome of the one is an outcome of the other. Rather, consider the terms *faith* and *reason* to be names for generic kinds of inquiry whose *outputs* need not be different and whose constitutive elements need not be entirely different either. To put the matters simply, as was done in chapter 2 of *Introduction to the Philosophy of Religion,*[4] contrast "finding out for oneself" with "taking someone's word for it." Contrast these, not as if they had no features in common, but as opposed descriptions of the process which *predominates* in a particular inquiry which is undertaken to arrive at belief.

We can thus contrast faith and reason as *modes of inquiry capable of yielding knowledge*. The crucial step in making this conclusion plausible is that I should convince you that "taking someone's word for it" really is a means of arriving at belief which satisfies all the conditions for knowledge.[5]

If "faith" is as much a vehicle of knowledge as is "reason," then the "faith" oriented belief system of a religious community need not be incompetent as a source for knowledge about God, especially if certain conditions for critique of belief, formulation of common belief, certain conventions of discourse, are found to obtain within a believing community, just as they do in the more rigorously structured scientific discourse.

And, of course, once we establish that the scientific community is as thickly textured with a fabric of belief based on testimony as is the religious community, then the extremes of the contrast (between faith and science) will have disintegrated, leaving it clear that the difference between scientific and religious belief lies not in the presence of knowledge as product of the one, and unfounded belief as product of the other, but rather in the fact that in the scientific community, the object of the inquiry is *establishment,* whereas in the religious community the object of the inquiry is *discovery* (of truth, understanding, or the like). That is, religious inquiry ends in discovery or enlightenment; scientific inquiry (and that sometimes includes philosophy and theology, too) must attempt establishment; for the very method by which the "knowledge status" of what is discovered in science is validated is the method of proof or establishment in a public domain.

Faith as a Means of Knowledge. Nothing beyond the most primitive knowledge is possible without a community of belief and communication. We tend to think too restrictively of knowledge in its experiential modes. At the one extreme there is "science," the abstract and ideal achievement of disinterested understanding yielding "established" truth. At the other extreme there is the knowledge of the directly evident: here, while philosophers primarily disagree as to its objects, there is relatively little disagreement among them as to its actuality, though Keith Lehrer's "explanatory coherence" theory attempts to get along without propositions that are "directly evident," as do other recent theories.

We do have knowledge by acquaintance with some things. Disputes center upon what things and why. The way some philosophers talk, the knowledge of encounter is the same thing as the knowledge of acquaintance, so that whatever I can be said to know by direct encounter, I can be said to know by acquaintance; and others say that acquaintance is a technical notion, more or less of the sort that Bertrand Russell had in mind, a notion not to be confused with the non-propositional knowledge of persons and other minds by encounter. We need not attempt to settle whether the foundation of our knowledge rests upon the directly evident or whether there is nothing that is directly evident. One thing is certain, if anything is directly evident, it belongs to a small part of what we know.

Between the extremes of the directly evident and the scientifically established lies the bulk of human knowledge. The bulk of human knowledge is a mixture of one's finding-it-out-for-oneself and one's-taking-someone's-word-for-it. There is probably very little that we know which fully satisfies either the extreme of acquaintance or of science. Rather, most of what we actually understand and really know falls in between.

I do not think that there is anyone who seriously doubts that one can come to know some things through taking another person's word for it (in the right sort of circumstances), and that this is a very common source of knowledge (as both Aquinas and Cicero felt compelled to remark). Moreover, there are some things which *cannot* be known unless we can rely upon someones's "word for it": e.g., that you are in the United States of America, 1982, etc. Such truths are *constituted* by a pattern of belief and behavior and cover a wide spectrum of human knowledge.

The question of whether faith yields knowledge usually arises in the context of a generally negative attitude toward religion; faith is thought to be the equivalent of unjustified belief and therefore the antithesis of knowledge or reason: what a person takes on faith may be true, but the belief will be unjustified.

But this is incorrect. I want to emphasize that believing someone else is not only a normal, indeed a usual way of finding things out; it is, in fact, indispensible (psychologically and physically) for the existence of the body of information we have and can develop; and it is logically necessary for some kinds of knowledge (e.g., where you are) and psychologically necessary for most kinds of knowledge.

Faith and Knowledge. We all know that no matter how much information you have at a given moment in making a given perceptual judgment, it is possible that you should have been mistaken, regardless of whether you were in fact mistaken. This does not justify us in saying that no one ever has perceptual knowledge at all because of the logical possibility of the mistakes which do not in fact occur. It would, then, be equally absurd to argue that we can never come to know anything by taking someone's word for it, because it is always possible that the other person is mistaken or lying or misstates his belief or that we misunderstand him. It *is* always possible that that is what happened; but it is not always true that that is what happened.

The tableware that says "made in U.S.A., U.S. Steel" may be counterfeit, it may not have been made by U.S. Steel or in the United States of America.

But if it was, and if I believe the inscription and have no reason to doubt that inscription and it was imprinted with purpose to inform, etc., then I *know* the tableware was manufactured in the United States of America.

And no matter how many errors might have been made in communicating to you that you are "so-and-so," in fact those errors did not occur. The argument from the possibility of error is no better founded or more persuasive with regard to testimony as a means of knowledge than it is with regard to sensation as a means to perceptual knowledge. The reasoning concerning the possibility of error applies equally to both and supports skepticism equally poorly in both cases.

Most of what you know, you know by way of taking someone's word for it, either directly or indirectly. Were it not so, that we gain knowledge by taking a person's word under suitable circumstances, there are things that we would be unable to find out for ourselves at all because we cannot reproduce the efforts of the other persons in time. For instance, if I am a bird watcher and I identify a certain bird on the basis of a classification found in some published authority, I may thereby come to know that the "N-type Warbler" has appeared north of Philadelphia. But if I insist upon establishing the classification of bird types for myself, before I identify birds as satisfying it, then I would not have completed my work before my evidence flew south for the winter.

Knowledge acquired by taking someone's word for it is frequently the indispensable framework for the possibility of further knowledge. This is especially true in scientific matters where the very identification of the observations on instruments will depend upon a consensus of belief.

How do you know that the scale you use to measure something is really twelve inches? How do you know the beaker holds one pint? You may look into the catalogue to see. How do you know the catalogue is not a pack of lies? The entire fabric of knowledge is made by the woof of sensation and the warp of taking someone's word for it.

In fact the background condition of the possibility of the sort of sophisticated knowledge one is expected to have in later life is the testimonial knowledge conveyed by one's teachers. What else do we send students to college for but to be told what is so or to be told how to find out? Why don't we give students a spoon and a microscope, a pencil and a pad and say "Go find out"? Because you *can't* find out without the background of testified belief. For most people most of the time the background of belief within which the person finds out for himself was acquired by his being told.

Even if it be conceded that faith *is* a source of knowledge and indeed even a prerequisite in some sorts of situations for the exercise of reason as an effective means of inquiry, we still have to see how that will show that religious knowledge is possible. Yet, our discovery that *faith* can be a means to the acquisition of knowledge is an important step forward.

Testimonial knowledge has no more pervasive a role in religious life than it does in the rest of practical living. Faith even extends intimately into the fabric of belief upon which we stitch the design of science. And that *tells us that the mere fact that the sources of present religious belief are frequently and predominately testimonial does not by itself diminish the likelihood that the beliefs so acquired have the status of knowledge.* We have then to look at the *experience* from which the chain of testimony developed in the first place. But up to now, we can see that the time-honored contrast of faith and reason as resulting respectively in knowledge and unjustified belief is false and misleading. Before inquiring about the infirmities of experience, a word about proof is in order.

THE REALM OF PROOF OR ESTABLISHMENT

Faith, which is simply "taking someone's word for it" can and indeed must, at least sometimes, lead to knowledge. But the things believed on faith might be both indemonstrable and unknowable through experience; in that case, there would be no way for the chain of "taking someone's word for it" to be anchored in demonstrations. As a matter of fact, there is no reason to suppose that it is actually so anchored. Therefore, the existence of demonstrations of religious truth is really irrelevant to the justification of the chain of testimony by which most believers have acquired their faith and cannot determine whether those beliefs represent prior *knowledge* or not.

Moreover, it is psychologically naive to suppose that demonstrations which meet philosophical standards of completeness and explicitness (even if there are any) are in fact the basis of anyone's taking up or abandoning belief in such important matters as whether God exists or whether there is personal survival after death. Persons simply do not give up or take up beliefs which involve an evaluation of the meaning of the universe for them on the basis of philosophical arguments or any other arguments at all. An argument, whether good or bad, may happen to tip the psychological balance; but that is not the *function* of arguments.

Demonstration is neither the same as "convincing everyone" nor is it merely a valid argument with true premises. There is no argument for anything which is convincing to everyone; and, as I have elsewhere argued,[6] there is no true proposition for which a sound argument cannot be constructed; hence, if the propositions of religion are true, a sound argument can be constructed for each, and if "sound argument" and "proof" or "demonstration" were the same thing, then each true religious proposition could be proved. That, of course, is ridiculous.

Demonstrations must be sound arguments; but soundness is not enough. What else is required (and theories about that vary) determines what can be proved.

If nothing else is required, every true proposition can be demonstrated; if "convincing everyone in the world" or "convincing everyone who understands the argument" is required, probably nothing can be proved at all. If "satisfying the prevailing standards of interpersonal objectivity of knowledge'' is what is required, a great deal can be proved, but *what* can be proved will vary from epoch to epoch, depending upon the prevailing standards of objective interpersonal knowledge. Thus, in the days of Saint Anselm, the believing community regarded certain *religious* truths as being within the body of objective and interpersonal knowledge and as being appropriate as premises in demonstrative argument; that is why Anselm could pretend to demonstrate the truth and necessity of the Incarnation. The fact that we do not so regard his premises nowadays may tell us very little, because fashions change and a millenium hence such premises may again enjoy the status of agreed-upon objective truth.

What can be proved among one's religious beliefs depends upon two things: what is *true* and what, in addition to soundness of argument, is required for proof.

No one is quite sure what conditions of objectivity and interpersonalness proofs in the hard sciences actually meet; but it appears to a number to philosophers now, e.g., Hartshorne, Plantinga, myself, and even Gödel, that the existence of God can be established with a certitude that approximates that of contemporary science, in fact, with a certitude approximating that of mathematics.

Now of course there are various debates concerning that matter. But a startling charcteristic of this quarter century is that a number of philosophers familiar with contemporary logic are persuaded that one or another form of what is called a modal argument—an argument from the possibility of the existence of God to the actual existence of God based upon the contradictoriness of the claim that God exists contingently—is *evidently* sound.

There are, of course, many areas of undeniable utility for demonstration in matters religious, though none so dramatic as the existence of God. For instance, there is plenty of room for demonstrations that if one holds God to be omnipotent (under a certain definition), God could not have begun to be; that if one holds that "goodness" means a certain thing, then one cannot infer from the structure of the world that God is not good; that if one holds that God has foreknowledge and predetermines human events, it does not follow that man fails to have effective free will; that if you hold that God has a purpose for creating the world, it does not follow that he had that purpose by nature and does follow that he had some purpose for the having of which he did not have a purpose.[7]

Different sciences have different standards for establishment; the kind of argument that is taken to establish a point in sociology or anthropology would often not be acceptable in chemistry or physics. As a result, the question "Can religious truths be proved or established?" is ambiguous. Some such truths (the existence of a necessary being, for instance) can most likely be proved with a quasi-mathematical deductive rigor. Some can be established with the reliability available in the social and behavioral sciences: for instance, that Jesus really was crucified and buried and that he did found a religion and that he did claim a messianic role.

Differences of standards of establishment should not generate skepticism about what can be established any more than such differences generate skepticism about science. I do not suggest that Anselm's project in *Cur Deus Homo* will or should ever be entertained again: where philosophical demonstration (which was in his day considered the paradigm of science) was supposed to *establish* the central truths of religion, like the Incarnation. For, to the contrary, even the modest expectations of Aquinas probably cannot be met, for instance, to establish personal immortality and the freedom of the will. The freedom of the will still seems a reasonable candidate for demonstration; but the immortality issue appears to defy decisive settlement. But, perhaps, that conjecture of mine merely reflects a pessimism peculiar to our time. In any case, establishment may not be available for all the *preambula fidei*, as Aquinas thought, but it is surely not confined to the nonsubstantive elements of the religion, and it can in principle extend to a resolution of disputes concerning the nature of personal resurrection, the nature of sin, and the like.

The function of demonstration is not to create belief among the unbelieving; experience and our knowledge of human psychology display the futility of such pretensions. It is to provide, within a theoretical world view, a public, objective place among the assuredly known truths for its conclusions. Demonstration is not the product of discovery (though one can discover *how* to demonstrate something); it is the *product* of science, whether philosophical, mathematical, or empirical. That there can be and is some demonstrative knowledge about matters religious may be comforting to the religious believer and discomforting to his opponents; but it simply does not *function* as the reason for taking up or the reason for rejecting religious or antireligious attitudes. The function of demonstration is theoretical; it is not a form of persuasion or of enchantment. Demonstrative knowledge of religious matters is theoretical and probably commands at most what Newman called "notional assent" rather than "real assent" unless existentially reinforced by knowledge through faith.

This conclusion about the limited psychological force of demonstration runs counter to common belief, which expects too much of the demonstration and tends to confuse the effectively persuasive with the demonstrative. But, I suggest, reflection will convince you that demonstration is *not* a source of conviction by itself, and demonstration, without a fabric of real assent acquired from other sources of knowledge or belief, is simply sterile on *any* important matter whatever, whether religious or scientific. This suggests that demonstration may provide knowledge for the believing person who is also theoretically inclined and that demonstrations may function instrumentally (as objects taken on faith) for persons who do not even understand them, but demonstrations are not themselves the source of conviction (either pro or con) about religious hypotheses.

But no matter what the success of demonstration, the largest part of substantive religious belief will never be demonstrated even if it is true; and even if faith is a vehicle of knowledge, and even if analysis of the structure of the testimonial chain leading back to the apostles, the evangelists, and the Old Testament prophets does confirm its essential trustworthiness, the question will still arise as to whether the *experiences* of the apostles, evangelists, and prophets *could* have provided a *knowledge* base for the transmission of religious knowledge.

EXPERIENTIAL AND TESTIMONIAL KNOWLEDGE OF GOD

Where there is a chain of testimony over several generations, we can speak of a tradition. And by comparing the methods adopted in different societies for the protection of oral and written traditions, for instance, the tradition of property ownership in primitive societies, the preservation of ancient Eastern religious texts, and even the property-*recording* customs and laws in our own society, we come to know that a chain of testimony, a tradition, can be effectively protected and guaranteed basic reliability through the imposition of social sanctions for its protection. Passing over, for now, the empirical question as to the integrity of the Western religious tradition and the social sanctions that existed to preserve its content, and assuming that there were in fact pragmatically effective interests and social sanctions which operated to assure its core integrity (not necessarily purely linearly in time), the central epistemological question concerns whether the originating experiences (of prophets, apostles, and disciples) were evidentially *insufficient,* somehow epistemically *infirm,* so as to be unable, even if veridical, to have provided even those who participated in the salvation events with knowledge of their divine origin and authorship.

By making that issue central, I do not mean to derogate the equally interesting question of whether persons who have religious experiences *now* may also acquire, without accepting the testimony of other believers as to their authenticity, knowledge of past salvation events. Nor do I intend to derogate the authority of *present* belief as the final available authority to authenticate claims as to what belongs to the faith and, indeed, which elements of the tradition belong to its integral core.

Rather, if the originating believers *could not* have known whereof they spoke, there would be no knowledge of that sort for present-day believers to acquire, whether through testimony or through present religious experience. That is, an essential element of Western religious faith seems to be that the apostles and some disciples of Jesus participated in and came to understand, at least approximately, the nature of the realities that constituted redemption and that their interpretation of these events is faithfully transmitted in preaching. So, the central question here is whether the originating experiences *could* have been *knowledge* makers. Were they capable of conveying to the human mind information of the sort which was thought to be extracted?

Experience: The notion of experience has to be expanded, as compared with the notion epistemologists sometimes have in mind: sense data or impressions, uninterpreted: "the given," no matter what its particular description. The objects of experience must not be restricted to sense data or sensings, or the like, or to any form of "the directly evident." In fact, the notion of experience employed includes all perception by which we understand what someone else says. "Experience" includes linguistic perception, as well as sensory perception. And this broader conception of experience makes us notice (1) how indispensable are a person's perceptual sets and his broader expectations as "forms" of his experience; (2) how significant *disclosure situations* are in making certain kinds of perception possible; and (3) how the belief and discourse tendencies in one's community affect both the perceptual sets and the disclosure situations through which experience is made possible.[8]

In the end, the means of access to the content of what is claimed becomes the mode of ascertainment, or certification of the truth that is claimed. Membership in the discoursing community opens one's mind to the perceptual sets and cognitive expectations which are necessary even to collect the data into *patterns* which stand in evidential relationships to substantive religious claims. Participation in the religious community is a psychological prerequisite to understanding the discourse fully and to acquiring the conceptual sets necessary for facts to *stand,* evidentially, for religious beliefs.

Linguistic experience, talking a certain way, and *belief experience,* belonging to a group that believes a certain way, interact, on the one hand, to determine the *intelligibility* of some expressions which are peculiar to the group, and, on the other hand, to create both the *perceptual sets* and *disclosure situations* which give members of the community access to empirical evidence that confirms or makes evident certain religious states of affairs.

As one enlarges the number of elements which he takes to be fundamental to human perceptual experience and elaborates the interrelationships of sensations, appearance, expectations, and language skills of the perceiver, it becomes more plausible to say that religious experience may be a source of knowledge; for religious experience emerges as "situated" in life and thought in a manner comparable to "family" experience, "professional" experience, and other broad kinds of experience (e.g., "musical" experience, etc.).

These changes in the conceptual background for thinking about perceptual knowledge have to be made *not* only on grounds that the impoverished conception of experience discords with various scientific achievements; it also ignores what we introspectively know about our own perceptual states and has yielded a ludicrously oversimplified conception of human knowledge. When those changes are made, then it becomes much more plausible to consider religious experiences as candidates for knowledge-generating situations.

The changes to be made in the conception of experience are these: to acknowledge that perception does not occur in the absence of perceptual sets; that our linguistic skills and proclivities affect the sets both in their formation and in their relative influence; that perceptual sets create perceptual expectations; that perceptual sets reveal meaning in things; that linguistic proclivities and community beliefs precondition disclosure situations.

Disclosure situations are vehicles to understanding objective meaning. Among originating religious experiences, such events are broadly revelatory events. Disclosure is a *sudden and dramatic* seeing *x* to *be* something, something other than what you took *x* to be or would have taken *x* to be without the perceptual set that controls the perceptual judgment. The total meaning of familiar events may be changed for us on the basis of clues which are subliminal (either not consciously distinguished among the items perceived or not even of enough sensory intensity to give rise to a conscious judgment). (The transfiguration of events is being explained here by analogy to the event of Transfiguration). Whole lives are changed by the sudden recognition of meaning in events, objective meaning. The *meaning in a thing or event* is the accessible information contained in it about a thing or event which is logically distinct from it. And we can, of course, imagine a Shannon-type "bit" or "unit" of meaning: the least amount of information in a thing which is needed to reduce one's uncertainty about some logically distinct thing in some respect by one-half.

Disclosure situations are created through perceptual sets. We know that persons see what they expect to see, that where the background signals (e.g., noise) resemble certain person-seeing situations, you will perceive in those clues a whole person, perceptually constructed.

I think we can make explanatory progress in considering religious experience as a source of knowledge, provided we regard all perception as a constructive process. I mean that the information presented to consciousness in any short time interval of perceptual experience not only is logically insufficient to imply the truth of what is believed about object states, but is only loosely connected (by lawlike or probabilistic regularities) to what is believed. That is, the formation of the "present" total perceptual experience does not proceed from the momentary sensory stimulations by logical entailment, by nomological implication under psychological laws, or even by broader probabilistic implications, but rather by way of subjective regularities (which the person, of course, usually shares with many others) that are *regularities of signification,* of meaning. The disclosure situation is simply one in which an important new meaning is revealed to a perceiver. And the perceptual sets and linguistic sets are, along with prior belief, the determinants of the readiness for disclosure. This means, in effect, that it is no more difficult for God to be encountered by Moses, who sees a burning bush that the fire does not consume, than it is for me to encounter the president of the United States: the perceiver must have certain expectations that turn the data into *configurations of evidence.*[9]

Meaning, in this context, is information contained in one event and available to a perceiver, concerning some other event(s).

There is *objective meaning in events* when the information contained in the event is available to a public and is interpersonally decidable by experiences (even though it is not available to everyone). So, as you travel with a guide along a trail, he can tell you from its appearance when the last large animal passed and how large it was: you cannot do that, though the same objective information is there for both of you and light from the same general areas strikes your retina as well as the guide's.

Though a meaning is objective, it is not available to you if you lack certain sets, expectations, and critical skills. And the perceptual sets are as much the result of community attitude and reinforcement as they are the results of information the individual acquired for himself. The keys to objective experience are given to the individual by the community in which the individual matures, both in converse and in critical belief. I am not here worried about exceptional cases, e.g., great scientists like Galileo and great artists for whom the discernment of objective meaning is specially developed far beyond the skills and habits of the community. Community-reinforced attitudes, skills, and expectations result in *perceptual* sets which, in turn, become the vehicles for disclosure situations and for those *transformations of the appearance of reality* which are peculiar, for instance, to the experiences of the apostles in dealing with Jesus.

Perceptual sets have two functions: (a) to *cause* disclosure situations to occur and (b) to be means for the continual revival of meaning perceived. This applies to religious knowledge as follows. It is likely that among ancient peoples the recitation of the tribal myths concerning God filled with symbols and assigning meaning relationships to various natural events (like storms, illness, good fortune, etc.) created in some extraordinary men both the desire to encounter God and a propensity to find in events indications of the presence of God, so that a perceptual set (or family of them) was generated in some individuals which both (1) realized community expectations as to the description of God and (2) disposed the individuals to have experiences in which the divine was revealed to them in the transfiguration of the normal: thus, the appearance of God in a burning bush.[10]

That is, experience of God, the objective experience of God which is relived in accidentally differing forms by many prophets, is made possible because of the interaction of community influence and individual psychological disposition through the generation of perceptual sets and their resultant creation of disclosure situations: the community "prepares" the individual in the *expectation* of theophany, in *what* emotively and associatively theophany will be like, and in the expectation that theophany occurs through manifestation in nature.

Of course, all this could be taken as an elaborate rationalization leading to the consequence that no one can ever know whether he has experienced God or whether his experience is just a projection of the tribal aspirations as funneled through his own desires and expectations.[11] But that is nonsensical. The fact that I might have been deceived about the presence before me of the piece of paper upon which these words are inscribed is no reason whatever to think that there is not in fact before me such a piece of paper, as indeed there is.

The fact that we can adequately and independently (by anthropological and psychological hypotheses) account for the generation of the originating religious experiences, far from being evidence that the experiences did not occur or are not veridical, *warrants neither conclusion*, but rather indicates the degree to which these experiences resemble the main features of human perceptual experience.

Most people no longer have perceptual confrontations with the world in which it is a matter of life and death that the perceptual judgment shall be correct despite its being based upon very limited sensory data: a ting sound, the slither of a snake, the click of a gun, the flash of a wing in the moonlight. As a result we do not live in the lively awareness of the *active*, interpretative, and constructive elements of perception which one may identify in the experience of the hunter, the warrior, the trainman, the pilot, and others whose careers and lives depend upon sensory perception.

It seems clear enough that if God's presence can be manifested through physical events, individuals *can* be in the psychologically disposed situation to experience that presence. A reason that some people *have* the experiences and others, similarly disposed, do not, is sometimes to be found in the liveliness of their expectation, which may be a manifestation of their individual absorption within the ideals of the community. There is no epistemic infirmity in the idea of originating religious experiences of the sort that characterizes Western religion.

If the burning bush really is a theophany, if God really is present and Moses encounters him, then the long chain of testimony is suitably rooted in experience, and knowledge is available to those who listen to those who believe.

The chain of testimony must end in religious experience. And to analyze that experience, one considers the elements of ordinary experience which one might not have thought about otherwise, but which we see are *necessary* to manifest the meaning of events to a perceiver. Particularly, I think the interaction of linguistic factors, community belief, and personal motivation in the creation of perceptual sets and of interest, motivation, and sensation to produce perceptual experiences, some of which are disclosure situations, is sufficient to show that the originating experiences are structurally on a par with experience in general and *would* be knowledge-bearing if, in fact, they *were* true.

There is, of course, no *independent* way to show that they were veridical experiences—but they *could* have been and, thus, knowledge through faith is possible *now*.

FAITH OVERCOMES THE WORLD

When Saint Augustine said that Christianity is the one true philosophy, *una vera philosophia*, he meant not only that the faith is the only genuine wisdom, the only adequate version of what the ultimate realities of human life consist in and the only adequate way in which the human condition is to be described, assessed, and overcome. He meant also that *without* that faith, the basic reality of the world is inaccessible either for living or for rational reflection.

He saw his faith as a competitor of all pagan philosophies, not merely as a competing ethic and value theory, but also as a competing account of what utlimate reality consists in.

Now if faith is, as I suggested, at least potentially a source of knowledge about basic truths (the origin of the world, the structure of human history, the destiny of individual human life), and if the things known by faith create correct fundamental evaluatory schemes in which life as a whole is lived, then, faith might, in addition, be the *only* avenue to the full reality of the world. The world is not in opposition to religion; the world is *overcome* by it, *ingested, incorporated, transfigured, transsignified,* and made part of an integrated reality which is, objectively, independent of an individual's thought but accessible through his faith.

Augustine's two-cities analogy helps: the inhabitant of the secular city mistakes himself for a realist, the man without illusions; but the religious man knows the inhabitants of the secular city are color blind and without stereoscopic vision— they experience neither the shades nor the depth of reality. Theirs is not the *real* world, but only a black and white reproduction of it. Faith overcomes the secular city by transforming it, transfiguring it, discovering and disclosing the meaning, the internal relationships in the world which are not even perceptible to its unbelieving benighted inhabitants. The secular city is simply a fantasy of despair.

This is the epistemological correlate of Saint John's teaching that "this is the victory over the world—our faith" (1 Jn. 5:4). Once having faith, a person, like a child who has acquired the skill of tuning a violin, can make perceptions and appraisals that are totally beyond the experience of the person without that cognitive ability. How absolutely irrelevant would be the claim of the untutored person that he *cannot* hear the differences of sound the trained child discriminates. If faith functions to *disclose* reality, its products *cannot* be disconfirmed by the failure of those without faith to share the experiences.

CONCLUSION

The cognitivity problems of religion appear to yield to the following considerations: (a) The intelligibility of religious discourse is assured as to *content* by the analogy theory of meaning (which accounts for the meaning continuity of the expressions employed with other realms of discourse which have unchallengeable cognitive content); and as to *accessibility,* by application of what we know of the means for acquiring *any* craft-bound discourse, namely, participation in the form of life for which the discourse is fashioned (a doctrine that we see, even now, becoming prominent in anthropology, linguistics, and even political science). (b) The access to *knowledge* of religious truth is supported (1) by our recognizing the role of faith as an indispensable means to knowledge, even in science, and of the indispensability of testimonial knowledge; (2) by our recognizing the limited, ancillary, but occasionally helpful role of demonstration to provide theoretical knowledge of religious matters; and (3), finally, the indispensable and appropriate role of experience in the generation of religious knowledge, and the futility of arguments ranging from the transcendence of God to the conclusion that God cannot be experientially apprehended. Lastly, the believer and the unbeliever are not to be distinguished by their difference of belief alone, but by what their experienced *reality* consists of. They live in different worlds. And just as a paranoiac and a therapist could agree on certain features of the world (e.g., that there are persons capable of doing harm as well as persons capable of doing good), the essential features of *meaning*, the significance of gestures (threatening to the paranoiac and helpful in the appraisal of the therapist) are different; the world of the paranoiac is not the real world, however real it is to him. The invitation to faith is threatening too; it is the invitation to place one's values, one's appraisals of what is *real,* in the hands of someone else who promises to transform one's experienced world. I suppose that there is some unhappiness, incompleteness, derangement, or incapacity in the spiritual realm which parallels the discomfort in the psychological realm that triggers a person to trust a therapist in the reality-transforming process of anlysis; so too, with religious faith.

Faith discloses rather than distorts reality. It is not an affective deformation of reality but a disclosing insight into the world. And nothing in the history of philosophy provides even a reasonable ground for our believing otherwise. No one has succeeded in diagnosing any inherent infirmity in religious discourse as a means of communication, in religious faith as a source of knowledge, or in religious experience as basic to an understanding of the world. Every effort at discrediting has had the happy result of leading us to a better understanding of language, knowledge, and the world, and to a consequent reinforcement of the reasonableness of religious belief.

NOTES

1. Raeburne S. Heimbeck, *Theology and Meaning* (Stanford: University of California Press, 1969).

2. A detailed account of analogy of meaning is completed and will appear under the title *Portraying Analogy,* Cambridge University Press, 1982.

3. This, no doubt, needs further explanation, which will be offered in *Portraying Analogy.*

4. James F. Ross, *Introduction to the Philosophy of Religion* (New York: Macmillan, 1970).

5. See my "Testimonial Evidence," in Keith Lehrer, ed., *Analysis and Metaphysics* (Dordrecht: Reidel, 1975), pp. 35–55, where a detailed argument based upon Chisholm's principles of indirect evidence is presented to establish the position. See also "Aquinas on Faith and Knowledge" (Aquinas Centennial Lecture, 1974), which shows that Aquinas himself knew that faith is a source of knowledge and, in fact, that acts of faith are basic to the structure of empirical knowledge.

6. James F. Ross, *Philosophical Theology* (Indianapolis: Bobbs-Merrill, 1969; Hackett, 1980), chap. 1; "On Proofs for the Existence of God," in *The Monist* 54(1970), 201–217, reprinted in this volume as chap. 8. See also George I. Mavrodes, *Belief in God* (New York: Harper and Row, 1972).

7. See Ross, *Philosophical Theology*.

8. For no. 1 above, see Jerome S. Bruner, *Beyond the Information Given,* ed. J. M. Anglin, (New York: Norton, 1973), chaps. I and II; concerning no. 3, see N. Goodman's *Languages of Art* (Indianapolis: Bobbs, 1976): "reality is the product of art and discourse."

9. Cf. a similar idea in Heimbeck's *Theology and Meaning*.

10. See Heimbeck's *Theology and Meaning* for the "God configuration" correlate of this idea.

11. It is worth considering G. Mavrodes, *Belief in God*, which argues that all experiences of God *must* be veridical because of God's universal causality.

Chapter 7

THE LOGIC OF ANALOGY
Frederick Ferré

T HE fundamental problem for users of theo-
logical language, as seen by one theological tradition, is the avoidance, on the
one hand, of anthropomorphism and, on the other, of agnosticism. Let us examine
the problem as it is visualized by these theologians.

ONE

Human language, all admit, is best suited for deal-
ing with familiar objects, qualities, and relations. The very meanings of the
terms in our speech—as illustrated by the paradigm case technique—have grown
up through the needs and experiences of ordinary life. Since our language is
thus firmly rooted in human purpose, it would seem inevitable that wherever it
is applied it must express its ancestry by imposing human categories of thought
on everything it touches. But if human speech brings with its use unavoidable
anthropocentric distortion, how is anthropomorphism to be avoided in theological
discourse?

God is traditionally held to be ''infinite,'' of course, and lip service is paid
to his ''transcendent and unimaginable glory''; but despite these verbal bows in
the direction of God's ''otherness,'' language developed to deal with finite
objects is used to describe him—and at times to do so in considerable detail!
The inexorable pressures of language would seem to prevent anyone from speaking about the infinite or the transcendent, but rather to force one to speak—
despite oneself—less of infinite God than of superlative man.

From: Frederick Ferré, *Language, Logic and God* (New York: Harper & Row, 1961).

Let one speak of God as "the All-Wise One," for example, and his language compels him to understand the "wisdom" of God in the same sense that human wisdom is understood (though greatly magnified, no doubt), *if he is to understand anything at all* by these words; this is the only sense of the word that human beings can know. Even the traditional recourse to the "theistic proofs," if looked to as providing words which are straightforwardly applicable to God, must fail, since (even if the proofs were valid) to prove God a "first cause" or an "unmoved mover" or "sum of perfections" or "self-existing being" is either to deal in human language and in human meanings, or not. On the first alternative, "God" becomes merely a part of the natural order, "for clearly causes and effects are terms in a single series and belong to the same order of reality," and God's perfections are reduced to the level delimited by human imagination. On the second alternative, *cause, mover, perfection, existing, being,* and the like are emptied of meaning when predicated of God.

> You are in fact in an insoluble dilemma. If you assert existence and causality of God in the same sense in which you assert them of finite beings, you are rendering God incapable of fulfilling the very function for whose performance you alleged him to be necessary. But if you assert existence and causality of God in an altogether different sense from that in which you assert them of finite beings, you are making statements about God to which you can, *ex hypothesi*, assign no intelligible content. God therefore is either useless or unthinkable; this would seem to be the conclusion of the matter.[1]

The theist is caught in a cross fire. Either human language is allowed to retain its meaning, drawn from human experience of the finite, in which case it cannot be about the God of theism, who is not supposed either to be finite or to be properly describable in finite terms; or language, "purified" of its anthropocentric roots, is emptied of meaning for human beings, in which case it can be neither human language nor—for us—"about" God. Put more technically, the theist would seem compelled to choose between *univocal* language, which makes the object of his talk no longer "God" because merely comparable to the rest of his experience, and *equivocal* language, which "cleanses" the terms used in describing God entirely of any anthropomorphism they might ordinarily possess but thereby forces the theist into a position of total agnosticism, capable of knowing nothing as to the *meaning* of his words about God—not even knowing whether *existence* when applied to "God" has any relationship to its ordinary human use. From the standpoint of logic, the theist who chooses to speak in equivocal terms is only punning on the English language when he calls God "good" or "loving" or "wise." Apart from sheerly emotional factors, he should have no objection, from this position, to speaking of God as "pink" (in a "completely different sense") or "multicellular" or "washable" (in senses "wholly uncontaminated by their ordinary meanings").

There seems no escape. If univocal, then language falls into anthropomorphism and cannot be about *God;* if equivocal, then language bereft of its meaning leads to agnosticism and cannot for us be *about* God. But at this point it is the contention of a major theological tradition that between the univocal and the equivocal lies a third logically important employment of language which can provide theological discourse with a live alternative to both anthropomorphism and agnosticism. This "middle way" is the logic of analogy.

TWO

"Analogy is a relation between objects," says Austin Farrer, "capable of being classed as a species of 'likeness.' " The sort of "likeness" on which any analogy depends, he continues, is that which is "reducible to the presence in the similars of an identical abstractible characteristic."[2] If this is the case, then subscribing to the logic of analogy concerning statements about God would entail our accepting the proposition that there is at least one abstractable characteristic which God, in some legitimate sense, can be said to share with finite being. The function of a theory of analogy on this interpretation must be to explain in *what* "legitimate sense" or senses such a characteristic would be predicated of God. We shall have occasion later to question the objectivist view of analogy which is offered here, but since the traditional account given of this logic has been in terms of a "theological object language" it will be useful to follow the exposition of this viewpoint in traditional terms.

Two kinds of analogies are distinguished as relevant to theism. The first, usually called the "analogy of attribution," relates two analogates which may in many respects differ widely from each other. One of the analogates (the prime analogate) possesses the characteristic predicated of it in a "formal" manner, that is, in a wholly proper (univocal) and actual sense, while the other analogate has predicated of it a "like" characteristic in a relative or derivative sense. Some example like the following is often chosen to illustrate this variety of analogy: we may call both men and mountain resorts "healthy." The place may be called "healthy" in a derivative sense thanks to its tendency to cause the men who live there (the prime analogates in this case) to be called "healthy" in a formal sense. This is a good example since it shows not only what is meant by "formal" and "derivative" predication in the terminology of the classical doctrine of analogy but also the importance for the very possibility of the analogy of the *real relation* in which the analogates stand. No analogy of attribution can be manufactured out of thin air; there must be some prior relationship between the terms on the basis of which common attribution is possible. Nor does the theological use of the analogy of attribution admit exception to this rule. "In its theological application, where the analogates concerned are God and a creature, the relation upon which the analogy is based will be that of creative causality; creatures are related to God as his effects. . . ."[3] Once it is made clear that the theist bases his language about God on the understanding that God is the creative cause of finite things (it is held), there should be no obstacle to admitting that theological language founded on this actual relation is fully meaningful by virtue of the analogy of attribution.

In addition to the analogy of attribution there may be distinguished another theologically useful kind of analogy traditionally called the "analogy of proportionality." While the analogates composing an analogy of attribution are "unequal," that is, only one of the two really deserving to have predicated of it the common abstractable characteristic (the "analogue") in a *formal* sense, both the terms in an analogy of proportionality posses the analogue in a literal and unmetaphorical sense. But each possesses it only *proportionately to the nature* of the analogates concerned.

If, on the one hand, one were to speak of himself as "feeling blue" or of the air as "blue" with invective, he would (strictly speaking) be equivocating. The analogy of proportionality would stand closer to univocal speech than this. If, on the other hand, one were to call identically colored wallpaper in different rooms "blue," language here would be used univocally. Analogy must insert itself between the two. By means of an analogy of proportionality, to continue the illustration, I might call the sky "blue" and my wife's eyes "blue"; here both terms possess the common characteristic *formally, but in the way appropriate to their distinctive natures.* My wife's eyes are blue with a "blueness" literally appropriate to human eyes and not to the sky; the sky is blue with a "blueness" literally appropriate to an August day and not to a human eye. In this way analogy, we are told, is able to strike a middle way between univocal and equivocal language. "In the strict sense, an analogy of proportionality implies that the analogue under discussion is found formally in each of the analogates but in a mode that is determined by the nature of the analogate itself."[4]

The application of analogy of proportionality to theological discourse is straightforward: a term predicated of God belongs properly to *his* nature, in a way proportionate to his nature, in the same way that a term predicated of one of his creatures belongs properly to *its* nature, in a way proportionate to its nature. Man is "good" in a way literally appropriate to man's finite nature. Thus, the classical doctrine concludes, "God's goodness" is neither something unrelated to "man's goodness" nor merely identical to human virtue. A similar analogy of proportionality would be found to hold between each of the qualities and attributes which could be predicated of divinity. In this sense: ". . . while there cannot be a proportion of the finite to the infinite, there can be within both the finite and the infinite proportions which are similar. Thus the divine goodness is to God as human goodness is to man, and the divine wisdom is to God as human wisdom is to man, and, in general, the divine attributes are to God as the analogous finite qualities are to finite things.''[5]

THREE

This means of avoiding the dilemma confronting theological discourse through a "middle way" can, with proper interpretation, be of value to modern students of theological language; but a recognition of the many shortcomings of the approach must precede any genuine appreciation of the logic of analogy.

First, the analogy of proportionality suffers from serious difficulties. Superficially it seems that true proportionality is affirmed for the analogates, but, as E. L. Mascall points out, at no point may an unambiguous "equals" sign be placed between the terms of the pseudoproportion. Mascall illustrates this difficulty in terms of an analogy of proportionality between the "life" of cabbages and the "life" of men (here assuming "life" not to be a univocal term). At first, he says, a univocal sense is denied to the meaning of "life" when predicated of men and cabbages in favor of what appears to be a straightforward proportion: the "life" of a cabbage is to the nature of the cabbage as the "life" of a man is to his human nature. But, again, this seeming proportion must be denied in its simple form because the nature of the cabbage will determine not only what "life" will be for a cabbage but also *how it will determine* how it determines what "life" means in a cabbage. And once the process of determinations is begun there is no stopping it! The nature of the cabbage (or the man) must forever be allowed to determine how it will determine how it will determine . . . whatever it is determining, each stage further removed from any approach to univocal meaning, each stage finding the analogates separated by greater and greater distances from each other. At this point the bewildered thinker despairs! "For the fact remains that we have denied that our equal signs really stand for equality and we have not indicated anything definite that they do stand for.''[6]

A still more serious objection to the theological application of the analogy of proportionality is that the peculiarities of the theistic problems make this form of analogy able to "deliver" far less than it would seem to promise. We are offered what looks like a simple calculation to be worked out (although we have seen that it cannot be expected to be worked out as a mathematical problem might be): but if we try actually to employ the steps which it seems to recommend in order to learn the literal meaning of words predicated of God, we discover that the "proportion" is irreducible, since there are *two,* not one, "unknowns." "The quality x_1 is to man's nature in man in the same respect that this quality x_2 is to God's nature in God," we are informed. But though we have a fair idea as to what is meant by "man's nature" and what might be literally "appropriate" or "proportional" to it, we stumble in the dark when we try to conceive "God's nature" in the same way in order to have an idea of what could be "literally appropriate" to *it*. In place of "God's nature"—infinitely different, we are told, from all his finite effects—we might equally well substitute another letter symbolizing a second "unknown" in what already has proved a pseudoequation: "x_1 is to man's nature in much the same way as x_2 is to y." What has happened to our "middle way" of analogy? The "proportion" which was to throw light on the meaning of our terms has been exposed as unworkable; worse, if taken seriously it would appear to license the wildest equivocation on the basis of the infinite gap which yawns between the analogates. The only way this consequence could be avoided, it appears, would be to discover some literal truth about the "nature of God," as many have hoped to do through the "theistic proofs," whereby the pseudoproposition could be "worked." But this literal sort of knowledge, as we have seen, is unattainable.

Analogies of attribution, we may be told, sometimes span great diversity between analogates: but even this capacity is unable to establish theological discourse on firm logical ground. Analogies of attribution, unlike those of proportionality, are unconcerned with the formal or proper character of more than one of their analogates. They are content merely to state that the analogue is predicated of the secondary analogate in a "derived" sense based on a real relation. If the relation between the analogates is that of cause and effect, for example, then the analogy of attribution allows us to apply the name of the characteristic possessed formally in the prime analogate to the secondary analogate solely because of the latter's power to *cause* the predicated characteristic. A mountain resort is called "healthy" not because it possesses that particular predicate formally but simply because of its ability to *produce* health (literally understood) in men. Thus, in scholastic terminology, the mountain resort is "virtually" rather than formally healthy.

But this means that the analogy of attribution allows us to remain in ignorance of the formal nature of one of the analogates; our aim, on the contrary, was to speak of these very formal characteristics of God and somehow to justify our language about them. The analogy of attribution tells us nothing we did not know before: it merely tells us that whatever is capable of producing an effect may have applied to it ("virtually") the term properly signifying that effect thanks solely to the fact that it is able to produce that effect. In other words, whatever can produce an effect can produce an effect! Such an analogy can tell us nothing concerning God which theists had not accepted beforehand—that he is the *cause* of finite phenomena.

Thus, when we say that God and Mr. Jones are both good or that they are both beings, remembering that the content which the word *good* or *being* has for us is derived from our experience of the goodness and the being of creatures, we are, so far as analogy of attribution is concerned, saying no more than that God has goodness or being in whatever way is necessary if he is to be able to produce goodness and being in his creatures. This would not seem necessarily to indicate anything more than that the perfections which are found formally in various finite modes in creatures exist *virtually* in God, that is to say, that he is able to produce them in the creatures; it does not seem to necessitate that God possesses them formally himself.[7]

The analogy of attribution seems entirely redundant if its true purpose is to inform us as to the meaning of words referring to real properties possessed by God, since, as Dorothy Emmet points out, "the appropriateness of the analogy depends on the reality of the relation which it exemplifies. The existence of the relation cannot be established by analogical argument; but if there are independent grounds for asserting it, it can be described analogically."[8]

Analogies of attribution are not only redundant, however; they are also, even more damagingly, excessively permissive. Far *too many* predicates may be applied to God. If to be the cause of something is "virtually" to be characterizable by that predicate, then, if God is the cause of all things, theists should be willing to apply *all conceivable predicates* to him in this "virtual" sense. As the cause of the physical universe he must be (virtually) hot, heavy, multicolored, and so on. The analogy of attribution admits of no control. If some, but not all, of the predicates claimed by this type of analogy are held to be formally as well as virtually applicable to God, then what is to distinguish them? Can the theist be content to admit a method of talking which would seem to make God "sweet tasting" as well as "good," "finely powdered" as well as "wise"?

To answer this objection a theist might insist that some of God's "perfections" are formally appropriate to his nature while others are only virtually appropriate. He might try to deduce from "God's nature" which perfection would fall into which class.[9] But to make such deductions, some prior understanding of the words describing "God's nature" is demanded. Once again we find ourselves within a circle from which there appears to be no ready exit.

Does the logic of analogy provide us with a genuine "middle way"? Its original purpose was to mediate between univocality and equivocality, but the results of our inquiry thus far make us wonder whether Aristotle was not correct in classifying analogy as a form of equivocation. More accurately, perhaps, the logic of analogy as we have seen it is a combination of—or a running back and forth between—the two unacceptable extremes. F. C. Copleston acknowledges this point.

It would appear. . . that the theistic philosopher is faced with a dilemma. If he pursues excusively the negative way, he ends in sheer agnosticism, for he whittles away the positive meaning which a term originally had for him until nothing is left. If, however, he pursues exclusively the affirmative way, he lands in anthropomorphism. But if he attempts to combine the two ways, as indeed he must if he is to avoid both extremes, his mind appears to oscillate between anthropomorphism and agnosticism.[10]

If such oscillation is the inescapable fate of theological language, suspicion is thrown on the logical status of analogy as an independent logical alternative. Can it be that the theist it merely confused and undecided as to which horn of the dilemma he would prefer to be impaled upon?

Not only the conceptual fruits but also the ontological presuppositions of the logic of analogy on its traditional interpretation are vulnerable to criticism. Analogy, on the view expressed earlier by Farrer, depends on there being an identical abstractable characteristic "present in" two beings; but wholly aside from the difficulties inherent in the "theory of universals" which seems to be implicit here, the assumption that God possesses abstractable characteristics identical to some also possessed by men is radically questionable. On the theological level, this assumption has been vigorously rebutted by neoorthodox and reformed traditions which stress the complete alienation of sinful man from holy God through man's corruption. The depravity of man's very being, in this view, rules out any possibility of the "analogy of being" which must undergird the logic of analogy. And, on the philosophical level, the supposition that any identity of characteristic can hold between God and man is incompatible with the fundamental theistic assumption that God is infinite. It would appear impossible in principle that any finite characteristic could be identical with an infinite characteristic. If there is to be the relation of identity of abstractable characteristic between man and God, either man's finitude or God's infinitude is sure to be violated. To maintain these essentials of the theistic view the ontological foundations on which the logic of analogy rest must be abandoned.

It is no longer possible, I believe, to hold that the logic of analogy, as it has normally been interpreted, is cogent. Is there then no value in this traditional approach to theological discourse? To determine the answer to this question we must decide whether or not to allow any interpretation but the traditional, metaphysically oriented view of analogy to be heard. If we insist on the use of the "material mode" of speech, requiring analogy to provide us with information about real properties of supernatural entities, little can be salvaged. But if we allow ourselves to examine the logic of analogy as *one means of providing criteria for the disciplined use of ordinary language in theological contexts,* looking for its value on the "formal" rather than the "material" mode of speech, much that may be of interest to us remains.

Put in the "formal" mode, then, the essential problem posed for the logic of analogy is how human language, despite its anthropocentric nature, may be *given a use* within a theological context while escaping both the univocality which gives rise to anthropomorphism and the sheer undisciplined meaninglessness of equivocality. Analogy meets this problem by explicating *rules* limiting the use of words drawn from ordinary nontheological contexts in formulas containing the word *God* (where *God* entails such words as *infinite* and *transcendent*). The presence of these rules makes clear to the user that ordinary speech, if taken without qualification into the language of theology, will violate the latter entailments; at the same time, the rules license the use of certain words, properly at home elsewhere, in theological contexts.

Seen thus, the analogy of attribution states the rule: a word from a secular context may be used theologically *where there is already a ground* in the theological "universe of discourse" (authoritative doctrine, dogma, creed, or proposition entailed by one of these) for holding that this quality is derived from God's uniquely characteristic activity. But this rule also warns that the quality disignated by the word in question is not to be assumed "formally" applicable to God but only "virtually," as a reminder that within the theological conceptual schema God is taken to be its ultimate source.

The analogy of proportionality, in the formal mode, offers the rule: a word may be borrowed from ordinary speech for use in theological discourse only if it is constantly borne in mind that the word can apply to "God" exclusively in the manner (unimaginable to us) permitted by the fundamental axioms and entailment rules governing the entire system of theistic talk about "God."

So interpreted, the logic of analogy rests upon no ontological assumption of identity between God and man. It is not vulnerable to criticism from theologians who denounce the *analogia entis* as blasphemy or from philosophers who must insist on the qualitative distinctness of finite and infinite. It is not wounded by reproof for its failure to be informative, because its function is not to inform, but rather to limit the proper employment of language within the framework of theistic systematic assumptions. To interpret the logic of analogy in this way is to depart from tradition and to abandon much of what metaphysically minded theologians have sought in these doctrines, but the metaphysical value of analogy has in any case been shown to be wanting, while its usefulness for the understanding of the syntactic dimension of theological language may prove to be considerable.

NOTES

1. E. L. Mascall, *Existence and Analogy* (London: Longmans, Green and Co., 1949), p. 87.

2. Austin Farrer, *Finite and Infinite* (Westminster: Dacre Press, 1943), p. 88.

3. Mascall, *Existence,* p. 102.

4. Ibid., p. 104.

5. D. J. B. Hawkins, *Essentials of Theism* (London: Sheed and Ward, 1949), p. 95.

6. Mascall, *Existence,* p. 108.

7. Ibid., p. 102.

8. Dorothy M. Emmet, *The Nature of Metaphysical Thinking* (London: Macmillan, 1945), p. 180.

9. Cf. Hawkins, *Essentials.*, especially chap. 6.

10. F. C. Copleston, "The Meaning of the Terms Predicated of God," in *Contemporary Philosophy* (London: Burns and Oates, 1956), p. 96.

Chapter 8

ON PROOFS FOR THE EXISTENCE OF GOD

James Ross

INTRODUCTION

First, I shall summarize a few points which have been explained and defended elsewhere.[1] Some may find these assumptions unacceptable; but it seems otiose to repeat arguments I cannot at present improve.

1. Proofs for the existence of God cannot be characterized usefully in terms of whether they are convincing, persuasive, cogent, etc.; those predicates are person-relative and are circumstance-relative as well.

There are no arguments for any conclusion which could reasonably be expected to be convincing, persuasive, or cogent for everyone or even anyone, regardless of the circumstances in which they are encountered. An argument will prove its conclusion if it is sound, epistemologically straightforward (with premises epistemically prior to the conclusion), and has premises which are affirmatively decidable through philosophical analysis. Whether a given argument constitutes a proof or not can vary from time to time, depending upon the state of what is known by the community of scholars. So we are not able to give a useful analysis of what it is for an argument to prove its conclusion; though we do know what it is for an argument to prove its conclusion to *so and so;* but "being a proof," in general, is not a function of the number of persons for which an argument serves as a proof. It appears rather that, whether a sound argument is a proof or not depends primarily upon the status its premises hold within the body of human "scientific" knowledge at the time.

From: *The Monist* 54(1970): 201–17.

2. When we talk about proving the existence of God, we ought to be aware of the pragmatic inconsequentiality of good over bad arguments. In general, arguments have little or no effect on whether a person takes up, gives up, or continues his belief or disbelief in the existence of God; but insofar as they do have some effect, they have it not in virtue of their soundness or their objective goodness, but in virtue of their persuasive attractiveness, which may be quite independent of their objective merits or defects when considered from the point of view of theoretical inquiry.[2] Knowing that, we shall restrict our critical consideration of proofs for the existence of God to a theoretical context: What are the conditions which a chain of reasoning must satisfy in order successfully to incorporate the existence of God among the body of things known by way of theoretical inquiry? We will require that it be sound, logically and epistemologically straightforward, and that it should survive philosophical scrutiny— not that every philosopher must accept its premises as true or that none may claim to have found them false—only that none shall have succeeded in showing the premises to be false or that the premises are inaccessible to our decision or that they are epistemically inaccessible to anyone who does not have prior knowledge of the conclusion.

3. I think we can take it as quite probable that the standard arguments from design, causality, motion, moral objectivity, and perfection have been found not to be proofs of the existence of God; not as they stand in the classical theological texts and not as they have been reformulated so far.

4. There is a difference between the *considerations* to which it is reasonable to attend when one is seeking to find out whether God exists or not (for instance, the origins of being, change, contingent things, the apparent hierarchy of perfections, and the orderliness and purposiveness of things in nature) and the *arguments* which have been formulated employing generalizations about these matters as premises and the existence of God as a conclusion. Such arguments have been variously criticized: as having false premises, as being invalid, as having premises which are epistemically posterior to the conclusion, etc. But the criticism of specific arguments will not preclude the formulation of new ones which begin with generalizations about those same considerations and argue that those generalizations could not be true if God did not exist. There is no a priori reason why such a new argument will not be discovered at any time. We shall, therefore, concede neither that cosmological, ontological, or teleological considerations are irrelevant to proving the existence of God, nor that all arguments based upon such considerations have been found to be unsatisfactory; rather, only a few have been considered and rejected.[3]

5. We need to distinguish an argument from a given formulation of it. For instance, there have been many formulations of the argument from design or the argument for a first uncaused cause of motion, etc.[4] Formulations are classified as formulations of the same argument if they rest upon the same basic consid-

eration (e.g., "that things acting purposefully but themselves incapable of knowledge must be directed by an intelligent agent," or, "that motion arises from an external agent and that the chain of such causes cannot be without a beginning," etc.). The argument does not exist apart from its formualtions, but is not identical with any of them. However, the argument is sound if any of its formulations is sound, unsound if none of them is, and is demonstrative if in at least one of its formulations the argument satisfies the conditions for proving its conclusion.

Thus, to show that in one or another formulation a given argument is unsound is not to show that the argument is unsound; there must be additional evidence that no formulation which does not alter the argument (by changing the central considerations) will be sound. Thus, refutation requires that we show the central consideration (which threads the different formulations together as formulations of one argument rather than as different but similar arguments) to be incorrect, cognitively inaccessible, or so related to the desired conclusion that no formulation will be valid and consistent.

The reason that I emphasize the distinction between an argument and its particular formulation is that not all the arguments called "modal arguments for the existence of God" have the same logical form or have the same semantical difficulties; some are better than others. Yet all seem to rest upon a common consideration: that whatever kind of thing God is, he is the sort of thing whose existing is consistent and whose nonexisting is excluded by the sort of thing he is. There is a further common consideration among the modal arguments: that the proper procedure is to offer some definition or characterization of God which, combined with the assumption that God does not exist, will yield a contradiction. The modal arguments which I employ depend upon the concept of explicability (the consistency of saying that there is an explanation for such and such), whereas some of Charles Harthsorne's versions rest upon the concept of a perfect being; but these are preludes to different characterizations of God and do not, I think, essentially differentiate the arguments.

Insofar as two or more proofs are known to share their central considerations, it seems reasonable to regard them as diverse formulations of the same argument; thus, criticism tends to focus directly upon showing that upon *these* central considerations no argument at all can be constructed which will yield the conclusion desired while satisfying the requirement of soundness, noncircularity, epistemic straightforwardness, public accessibility of the premises, and analytic (or observational) decidability for its premises. Of course, according to this high standard of refutation, none of the traditional arguments for the existence of God has been refuted.

6. The modal arguments which occur in different forms in Hartshorne's works and in my own do, in my opinion, establish the conclusion that there is a being which exists necessarily and exists in virtue of what sort of thing it is (this point will be supported by a specific argument below). Some of the presuppositions of these arguments are interesting and worthy of further examination.

AN ARGUMENT

The question at issue is whether there can be a good a priori argument that God exists. I offer here a simplified formulation of an a priori argument which is presented more elaborately elsewhere.[5] The purpose of my stating the argument simply is not to persuade anyone that it actually establishes its conclusion or to excuse its defects by appeal to its simplicity, but to facilitate discussion of some ideas which are relevant to appraising whether it (in this formulation or in more elaborate logical form) establishes its conclusion. Simple statements, like the one to be offered, are, like the arguments of Aquinas in 1, 2, 3, to be regarded as schemata, as descriptions designed to communicate the basic idea and form, but not necessarily the detailed content and most efficient logical formulation of the argument mentioned. We are substituting a line drawing for a photograph because the latter is inconveniently large and the point at issue does not depend upon the missing details.

Two preliminaries. First, the argument mentioned does not purport to establish that there is some thing which has all the divine attributes (the attributes that God actually has) but only that there is something which has certain of the divine attributes. That is the same as saying that is establishes that the being-which-is-God exists, but does not pretend to establish *that* it is God—not in a simple step. This is like establishing that the x which is president of the United States exists, but not that x *is* the president of the United States: such a thing could happen only if x is legitimately considered under some description which is not synonymous with "the president of the United States", but which is compatible with it.[6]

Secondly, the selection of that description is important; for while compatible with all the divine attributes, it will not be synonymous with them or their conjunction; yet it will have to represent a central element in our conception (both religiously and theoretically) of God, otherwise there will be no reason to regard a proof in which it figures as a proof of the existence of the being-which-is-God, rather than of some other being. The description I propose to use is this: "a being which is unproducible and unpreventable." Such a description logically implies that any such being has other attributes and that those other attributes logically exclude a cause of or external agent for the existence or nonexistence of such a being. In the case of God, there are a number of such attributes; I mention omnipotence only as an example. If a being, S, is omnipotent, then (by definition) for any logically contingent state of affairs p, "p is the case" is logically equivalent to "$SsWp$" (S effectively wills that p). If there is a being which is onmipotent (as the term is defined), then there cannot be anything else capable of causing it to be or preventing it from being. For if there were such a causing or preventing thing, the proposition that S exists would have to be inconsistent or contingent. We can assume that it is not inconsistent; if it is contingent, then its negation is contingent too; but if something prevented S from existing, it would (by the definition) have to be true that S willed that S did not exist; for we can substitute "S did not exist" for "p". If S were prevented from ever existing, the condition would still hold that if it is contingent, S would have to will it—with the result that a contradiction is yielded: for if "S" never existed" were contingently true, it would have to be true that S willed that S never existed; but "S wills p" entails that S exists; hence the *falsity* of "S existed sometime" has as a necessary condition that S existed sometime. Thus, all omnipotent beings (as the property is defined above) are uncausable and un-preventable. (It is, of course, also true that all omnipotent beings exist and exist necessarily.) The point here is that the properties involved in our description of the being whose existence is to be proved are themselves logically consequences of the traditional "divine attributes," and while all the traditional attributes are not connoted by the description, it is the being to which all those attributes were traditionally assigned whose existence is in question and whose existence is to be proved.

The summary of the argument is as follows:

1. Every logically contingent state of affairs is heteroexplicable.
2. That there exists an uncausable and unpreventable being is not heteroexplicable.
3. Therefore, it is not a contingent state of affairs.
4. But it is a logically consistent state of affairs that there exists an un-producible and unpreventable being
5. Whatever state of affairs is consistent but not contingent is logically necessary.
6. Hence it is a logically necessary state of affairs that there exists an uncausable and unpreventable being.
7. What is logically necessary is actually so; therefore, there exists an unproducible and unpreventable being.

This is an a priori argument based upon the exclusive disjunction of all states of affairs as necessary, impossible, or contingent. It is assumed that what is in question is not impossible, and it is demonstrated that it is not contingent; from which it follows that it is necessary. Apart from the assumption that it is consistent to say that some thing which exists is unproducible and unpreventable, the two key assumptions of the argument are (1) that every contingent state of affairs is heteroexplicable and (2) that whether there exists an unproducible and un-preventable being is not heteroexplicable. We shall, therefore, consider each of these.

Heteroexplicability

Just as the concept attached to the name *God* is distilled from a consideration of the way the name has been used in the teaching and practice of Western Judeo-Christian religion and in the theoretical commentaries on such teaching and practice which we find among philosophers and theologians, so too, the claim that all contingent states of affairs are heteroexplicable is justified by consideration of the way human inquiry is carried out and by attending to the commentaries upon the process of and nature of inquiry which we find among philosophers and scientists.

Take anything which might have been otherwise than the way it is; for example, that a railroad train does not leave Philadelphia for New York as scheduled on a certain day. If we inquire into that fact and are told that there is nothing whatever which accounts for its being so, we may be incredulous or skeptical; but we will not react with the same rebellion as when told "that the train did not leave on schedule is not only unexplained, it *could not* have been explained." Such a reply is utterly without foundation in any human experience; there is nothing about any contingent state of affairs which could ever be evidence that it is inexplicable; there is something about every contingent state of affairs which is evidence to the contrary: namely, that it is *consistent* to say of that state of affairs (however complete its description in terms of observable and inferable properties may be) that there could have been an explanation for its being the case—an explanation in some logically independent and logically distinct contingent state of affairs which involves an existent. The train could (logically) have been prevented from leaving by the choice of some human, by the advent of conditions making its leaving physically impossible, or by the caprice of its engineer, etc. It is simply inconsistent to say of any logically contingent state of affairs that some other state of affairs could not have occurred which would serve as its explanation. Were the world weird enough, anything (involving an existent) could explain the occurrence or the prevention of anything else. Contingency entails explicability. This can be generally proved in the following way: let p be any contingent state of affairs at all; let q be any other logically independent state of affairs distinct from p and involving the existence of something or another; then there is a logically contingent lawlike universal of the form "if p then q" which is logically independent of the conjunction of p and q. (That is, the corresponding universal statement could be true if both p and q were false, or if q were true and p false, though not, of course if p were true and q false). The state of affairs, q, is hypothetically-deductively heteroexplicable by way of the conjunction of p and the contingent natural law represented in the lawlike universal statement "if p then q." If both the law and p were the actual and contingent states of the world, then there would be an explanation for q's occurring, a heteroexplanation, an explanation by way of an independent state of affairs. Since p and q can be any two logically independent contingent states of affairs, it follows that every contingent state of affairs is heteroexplicable.

Notice that we are not claiming that there *is* actually a state of affairs involving an existent which can consistently be said to be the explanation of all contingent states of affairs—that would be inconsistent. We merely state that for any contingent but actual state of affairs it is logically consistent to say that there is some other state of affairs involving an existent, which is its explanation.

Again, all hypothetico-deductive explanations of contingent states of affairs are examples of heteroexplanation; since any contingent state of affairs is hypothetically-deductively explicable (provided we will make wild enough lawlike assumptions), it follows that every contingent state of affairs is heteroexplicable.

We therefore have two reasons, at least, for asserting our first premise of the argument-schema: (a) that logical considerations disclose that it is a priori true; (b) that both the linguistic structure of discourse during and about inquiry and the way we think about contingent states of affairs require that we regard heteroexplicability as a logical consequence of contingency.

Unproducibility and Heteroexplicability

We can now turn to whether the fact that something, in virtue of *what* it is, has attributes which render its existence unproducible and unpreventable also excludes its existence from being heteroexplicable.

(1) Further examination of the assumption that *what* a thing is may render it unproducible and unpreventable, seems useful. The way I imagined the relation was illustrated with the example of omnipotence—but this is only an example. For even though an entity may exist whose omnipotence excludes its being producible or preventable, omnipotence is not a first-level property (a property which does not logically presuppose other properties or characteristics of the thing). Both "unproducibility" and "omnipotence" are *propria* in the technical sense of early logicians: they follow necessarily from the properties which are essential to the being that has them, but they are not its essence, nor, strictly speaking, of-the-essence; for instance, the capacity to laugh (risibility) was called a *proprium* of man because, although it follows necessarily from man's being a rational animal, and although there cannot be a man who does not have the property, it is not essential: an essential property or attribute is *both* necessary and *constitutive* of the thing. The essence, as Aquinas says, is that *a parte rei* which is signified by the definition. But not all necessary properties of a thing are given in its definition, only the attributes which are constitutive. A divine being is not constituted to be divine by its omnipotence, rather, its omnipotence is a consequence of its divinity.

This may be part of the reason some philosophers, like Aquinas, looked for a description of God which presupposed no other property to be attributed to God and entailed every other property which God is said to have by nature or necessarily. For instance, Saint Thomas's description of God as *actus purus* and as *ipsum esse subsistens* (which are the same thing) was an attempt to describe (in a metaphysically general way) the first-level attribute of God which, if understood, would explain how God had by nature all and only the properties usually ascribed to him.

A brief reconstruction of Saint Thomas's reasoning may assist a reader unfamiliar with medieval metaphysics in grasping this idea, which I also share but can explicate here only with such examples.

For Aquinas, act was contrasted with potency; act is the principle (or "origin") of nonlimitation, of realization, actuality, exercise, etc. with respect to a capacity; potency is the principle (or "origin") of limitation, of capacity (both passive and active), and relative nonbeing in comparison to act. Act is logically prior to potency: there can be no potency except in that which is otherwise in act and no potency can be "reduced" to act (no capacity fulfilled or exercised) except through an agent in act. Act is also the principle (or "origin") of perfection; in fact *act* and *perfection* are logically equivalent (though not synonymous), just as *potency* and *imperfection* are equivalent.[7]

The positive attributes of things are called perfections. There are two kinds of perfections: those attributes which presuppose that the subject has some unfulfilled capacity or unexercised ability or some dependence upon external causes; these are limited or mixed perfections and are contrasted with the pure perfections. Pure perfections do not entail that the subject has an unfulfilled capacity, an unexercised ability, or any passive disposition at all to undergo alteration and do not exclude any other attribute which satisfies those conditions; examples of pure perfections are: to be, to live, to know, to will, to be simple, to be eternal, to be omnipotent, to be omniscient, benevolent, omnipresent, good, etc.

A being in pure act (*actus purus*) is in no way in potency, having neither unfulfilled capacities to be or to become, nor unexercised abilities or passive dispositions of any sort. It can have no predicate, therefore, which is not a pure perfection; for if it had a limited perfection, it would be in potentiality in some respect and, therefore, would not be wholly in act. Moreover, a being in pure act must have every pure perfection. This can be seen by our assuming that there is a being in pure act and that it lacks one or more pure perfections; we then derive a contradiction from those premises.

Assume that there is something *a* which is in pure act and has the pure perfections A through H but lacks K and L, which are also pure perfections. Why does *a* lack K and L? It cannot be because of what *a* is, because pure perfections do not exclude one another; A–H does not exclude K and L. It cannot be that *a* lacks K and L because some external cause prevents *a*'s having K and L; for a being in pure act has no unfulfilled capacity to be or to become, and to be *prevented* externally from having K or L would require that *a* be in potentiality to K or L. Hence, if *a* should lack K or L, that state of affairs would be inexplicable by appeal to *what a* is and would be equally inexplicable by our postulating a preventing external cause. But any consistent state of affairs is, in principle at least, explicable. Hence, it is not a consistent state of affairs that *a* would lack K or L. So, a being in pure act has all pure perfections—and it has them in virtue of its being in pure act, which is its "first-level" property, a property logically prior to and entailing each of its properties.

To determine which properties *a* has, one conducts a conceptual analysis of the predicates we ascribe to things in order to determine which satisfy the conditions for a pure perfection: they are all to be attributed to the being in pure act. That is how the elaborate list of divine predicates that we find in *Summa Theologica* can be derived from the metaphysicians' most general description of God; it is how the apparent non sequitur of Saint Thomas's saying "and this is what everyone calls God" is shown to be justified.

Within Aquinas's metaphysical scheme a first-level property of God can be described from which the *propria* of God can be derived logically; that provides a way one can come to know *that* the *actus purus* is God. Moreover the unproducibility and unpreventability of God can be derived directly from that first-level property: *actus purus*. A being in pure act cannot be potential with respect to any other thing. It cannot have external causes because only composites, things with unfulfilled capacities, unexercised abilities, or passive dispositions can be externally caused to be or become; God cannot satisfy any of those conditions; therefore the being of God must be unproducible and unpreventable.

This discussion of Aquinas is not intended to persuade one that Aquinas was right or even satisfactory in his account of the being and nature of God, but only to illustrate what I mean by asserting that unproducibility and unpreventability are not first-level properties of a divine being but are the logical consequences of its essential (necessary *and* constitutive) attributes.

Moreover, this discussion of Aquinas should make clear that one does not have to rest much upon my example of omnipotence as a property which logically generates the unproducibility and unpreventability, because there are other attributes which will serve the same end. I do not pretend to have found a substitute for the family of basic metaphysical concepts which makes this derivation so easy within Saint Thomas's terms; but one does not need a full-scale system of metaphysical discourse within which we can characterize the essence of God in order to make it plausible that unproducibility and unpreventability are not first-level properties but are derived and suitably characteristic properties of the being which is God. It appears that we have good prima facie evidence for accepting the assumption that *what* a thing is can account for its being unproducible and unpreventable: that is, an entity, x, can be, because of *what x* it is, such that any statement of the form "There is a y ($y \neq x$) such that y produces x or prevents x from existing" is self-contradictory.

Reflection upon the theological metaphysics of Aquinas discloses that within his theoretical system unproducibility and unpreventability are logical consequences of his description of the divine nature. This theoretical system is just one example of the plentiful evidence within the theoretical discourse of Western religious speculation that God is to be regarded as a being which is unproducible and unpreventable through any agent or cause.

This view of the divine attributes is supported also by appeal to the ordinary religious discourse of religious believers, who are taught to regard the question "What produced God" as an absurdity which discloses that its utterer is either not serious or is deficient in a grasp of *what* God is. When you ask a believer the more unfamiliar question, "Do you think, granting that God does exist, that it *might* have happened that He did not?" he has difficulty grasping what you are asking; for he sees that, as he understands what God is, nothing could account for God's not existing; as a result, he can't imagine the situation you inquire about. Appeals to ordinary discourse are, of course, only auxiliary in such cases as this and serve only to reinforce the theoretical and historical evidence which indicates that it is appropriate to regard a divine being as a being which is unproducible and unpreventable and as a being which has prior properties from which those attributes are logical consequences. It is still a long step to justifying the claim that any unproducible and unpreventable being may be regarded as identical with God; it is not pretended that we shall do this and it is not necessary for one who sets out to show that the being which God is exists.

(2) Now we can return to the question as to whether unproducibility and unpreventability exclude heteroexplicability. That this is so can be concluded from the fact that if a being is produced it is produced by another, and if it is prevented from being, it is prevented by another; and if it is heteroexplicable, it must be producible or preventable.

It is more convenient, perhaps, to regard production and prevention as relations among states of affairs; thus we speak of "its being produced or prevented that there is a being of a certain sort"; in this case, "that there is a being that has attributes which logically entail that its existing is unproducible and unpreventable." The contradiction inherent in the claim that such a state of affairs can be produced or prevented is evident.

When what is to be heteroexplained is the existence or nonexistence of something, there can be no other forms of explanation but prevention or production. How could some logically independent state of affairs, p, account for the actuality or nonactuality of some state of affairs q which *is* the state of affairs that a exists, unless p's being actual either brings it about or prevents its being so that q is actual? The existence or nonexistence of a thing is heteroexplicable only through states of affairs which cause or prevent it. It is therefore analytic that any state of affairs which is unproducible and unpreventable is not heteroexplicable.

C. The Possibility of the Unproducible and Unpreventable

Unfortunately, we cannot claim to have demonstrated step four of the argument. Some progress towards making the truth of the claim evident can be achieved, but the premise cannot be demonstrated because proofs of consistency are always relative to something which is presumed to be consistent and which can be questioned just on the ground that it leads to a proposition whose consistency is doubted. For example, the consistency of the proposition that there exists an unproducible and unpreventable being can be demonstrated if we are permitted to assume that it is consistant to say there exists a being in pure act. But for a philosopher who doubts the fourth premise, the additional assumption will be even more suspect when it is found to yield the doubted fourth premise as a logical consequence. When we cannot prove the consistency of a proposition by producing the state of affairs it describes or confronting that state of affairs in experience, we have to acknowledge that there is no inherent terminus to a dispute about the consistency of the propositions in question.

Strategically, however, one can appeal to two other factors: (a) that centuries of discussion of the existence of God in terms closely resembling these have not resulted in the discovery of an inconsistency in the supposition that such a being exists; (b) that, as Duns Scotus pointed out, the propositions (i) every producer is produced; (ii) every chain of producers is infinite and (iii) every producer is producible, are not thought to be necessarily true, are not thought to have self-contradictory negations; therefore, the hypothesis that there is a first unproducible producer is consistent.

"HOC EST QUOD OMNES VOCANT DEUM"?

Many philosophers, even those sympathetic to religion, think proofs for the existence of God will, no matter how carefully conceived and executed, inevitably founder, not necessarily upon the first and existential step, but upon the identificatory step; especially, they believe that it is a long and logically unassisted leap from the existence of some unproducible and unpreventable being (which might be the world as a whole or some evil demon, for all that has been shown) to saying *"hoc est quod omnes vocant Deum."* The predicates involved in our ordinary concept of God exceed in logical content those predicates which are employed in the proof of existence, whether it be one of the classical arguments or a modal argument. In fact, if an a priori argument of the Hartshorne variety is employed, using a predicate like "a perfect being," and if certain assumptions about the necessity that such a being should be in process are attached to that notion, then a great number of religious believers will deny that the existence of God has been proved or even that the existence of the being which is God has been proved—because the description in terms of which the proof is constructed is imcompatible with what these believers take God to be.

Metaphorically, we can say that the description of God is the "middle term" of the demonstration, it is that upon which the claim that it is God whose existence has been proved, pivots. (1) If the description is too thin, too limited in the list of predicates involved, there will be no ground for concluding that it is God whose existence has been proved, but only for saying that the existence of some being has been proved, and that this being could, for all that is known so far, be God. (2) If the description is too rich (and, some would think, Hartshorne's metaphysically baggaged concept of perfection is), it will be denied that it is a proof of God's existence, because what it claims to exist is something with quite different properties, properties which exclude the existence of God as God has traditionally been conceived.

Moreover, when the description is "rich," it is important to determine whether the intermediary premises and logical form of the argument justify one's allowing the entire description to appear in the conclusion. For instance, if I began the brief modal argument stated above with a description of the form "God is an uncausable, unpreventable, omniscient, omnipotent, benevolent, eternal being" and then in the conclusion asserted that God exists, it could rightly be objected that while I had proved the existence of something uncausable and unpreventable, I had not proved the existence of such a being *and* that it is also omniscient, omnipotent, benevolent, and eternal; it therefore remains an open question as to whether the existence of a being *which* is uncausable, unpreventable, omniscient, omnipotent, benevolent, and eternal has been proved. That question cannot be settled without an additional argument which will show that if a being is uncausable and unpreventable it has those other properties.

The identificatory stage of proof of the existence of God encounters difficulty in relation to the elaborateness of one's metaphysical system. For instance, as I showed above, it was very easy for Saint Thomas to go from the assertion that there exists a being which is in pure act to the conclusion that there is a being which, without any limitation at all, exists, lives, thinks, loves, chooses, and is therefore simple, eternal, good, omniscient, omnipotent, etc.

Without a metaphysical system to allow me to pass from the narrow group of predicates used in the proof of existence to the wider group used in the identification with God, it is very difficult to justify claiming that one has proved the existence of God (no matter how good the existential argument actually given may be); it is more nearly correct to say that one has established the existence of a being which may be God and, unless the world is quite different from the way we have imagined it, can only be God.

Even with a metaphysical system to allow one to pass from the existential to the identificatory stages of proof, strange things can happen which result in the falsity of the principle "but this is what everyone calls God." For instance, if one accepts Hartshorne's basic metaphysics of process, omnipotence is not power over all contingent states of affairs, exercised immediately and entirely (as I described it above). It is power over all beings and power to have all things as objects of knowledge. In this system it will turn out that omnipotence is not what it is in the modernized Scotist framework I employed above; yet both interpretations of the predicate will be compatible with the orthodox Christian religious talk about God as almighty. Still, one of us must be mistaken; there certainly cannot be two Gods, one as I describe him and one as Hartshorne does. The disagreement arises from the way we understand and define different divine attributes in relation to the overall metaphysical framework in which we speak of necessity, contingency, explanation, perfection, power, knowledge, and goodness. The difference about God can be traced to differences which are more general.

Furthermore, in order to identify the being whose existence is established with God, the various predicates to be attributed to it must be analyzed. That process requires that what is indefinite in ordinary religious discourse concerning God's knowledge, power, will, and moral quality must be made determinate by way of theoretical considerations, some of them, as in Hartshorne's case, being the result of very general metaphysical hypotheses about the whole universe. (This was true of Aquinas too, of course.) A religious believer may be quite surprised when he finds out what is involved in the attributes which are predicated of the basic existent in order to justify calling it God. Moreover, since the ordinary religious concept set is incomplete and indeterminate, a theoretical establishment of the existence of God cannot escape a certain amount of legislation; with the result that there can be competing "proofs" of the existence of God which differ radically at the identificatory stage in their conceptions of the divine attributes. (I would imagine that this difference would be quite obvious between Hartshorne's theory and mine.)

Now if my assumption is correct that one cannot pass from the existential to the identificatory phase of proving the existence of God without employing background metaphysical concepts, then the identification of a being whose existence has been proved with God will not itself be an object of demonstration, but will also presuppose the justification of the metaphysical system as a whole. This suggests that because of the uneliminable element of legislation involved, we shall have to say that there cannot be a proof that any given existent is God; at best there can be a probable argument. That there can be a proof of the existence of a being which is God, I have no doubt; that we can *show* that such a being is God does not seem likely when it is God as conceived by religious believers (rather than metaphysicians) who is to be identified.

NOTES

1. Cf. my *Philosophical Theology* (Indianapolis: Bobbs-Merrill, 1969, Hackett 1980), chap. 1, where these matters are argued in detail.

2. These points and a number of related points have, I think, been successfully argued by George I. Mavrodes in *The Concept of a Direct Experience of God* [a University of Michigan Ph.D. thesis, 1966] (Ann Arbor, Michigan: University Microfilms, 1962).

3. There is nothing wrong with our speaking of the various proofs *for* the existence of God and denying that they are proofs of the existence of God. For to say of A, "A is a proof for *p*," is to say that A purports to be a proof *that* *p* or a proof of "*p*." The standard arguments do not succeed in establishing their conclusions, though that is surely what they are *for*.

4. For instance, St. Thomas uses the argument from order in the world *ten* times (in slightly different formulations). They are (as determined by Fr. Jules Baisnée, see reference below):

"*In II Sent.;* D.I., q.l, ar. l; *De Veritate,*q V, a 2; *Contra Gentiles,* I, 13, and 44; II, 43; *De Potentia Dei,* q. III, a.6: *Summa Theologica,* I, q. 2, a 3, In *12 Metaphysicorum,* lect. 12; In *Evangelium S. Joannis, Prologus; Super Symbolorum Apostolorum,* a 1.*"* St. Thomas offers seven formulations of the argument based upon motion, five formulations of the argument *"ex gradibus perfectionis,"* four formulations of the contingency argument, three versions of the argument from the plurality of things, etc. A great deal of additional information on the various formulations of the arguments and their correlation with various periods of St. Thomas's life is to be found in the paper "St. Thomas Aquinas', Proofs of the Existence of God Presented in Their Chronological Order" by Jules A. Baisnée, S. S., in *Philosophical Studies in Honor of Ignatius Smith,* ed. John K. Ryan (Westminster, Md. : Newman Press, 1952).

5. Cf. Ross, *Philosophical Theology,* chap. 3.

6. This is developed further (below) under the heading *"Hoc est quod omnes vocant Deum"?*

7. The pairs of terms are not synonymous because the members have partly different connotations which derive from the nontheoretical contexts from which the terms were extended to their theoretical uses.

Chapter 9

THE TELEOLOGICAL ARGUMENT
Louis Dupré

T HE argument of design is not a single, homogeneous structure. Kant, who was familiar only with a modern version, referred to it as the oldest proof for the existence of God. Old it is indeed, even though we do not have evidence of its use as a "proof" until Philo. Although Aristotle was the one who developed the very concept of teleology on which all later arguments would be based, he himself used the argument in none of his extant works: the process of adaptation is a work of nature rather than of God.[1] Even to the Stoics the idea of an ordered cosmos ruled by a divine Providence was more a theological conclusion than a philosophical premise. Instead of "proving" the presence of a divine Logos in the world, they rather attempted to justify this assumed presence in the face of objections of disorder. Today we would not term such an attempt natural theology but theodicy. Philo, from all appearances, based his argument on Aristotle's lost dialogue.[2] The argument as he uses it places most of the emphasis on the harmony in the universe. Later Aristotle's teleological considerations also would be developed into a full-fledged argument. Occasionally the two would run parallel, at other times they would merge. Since this article does not intend to be historical, I omit here the complex development of the two forms and merely take an example of each from Aquinas, who gave both their distinct expressions for many centuries. However, since I intend to deal primarily with the contemporary discussion, I shall not restrict myself to that early expression or concern myself with its historical circumstances. First, I shall consider the proof based on the existence of ends, then the one based on the order in the universe.

From: Louis Dupré, *A Dubious Heritage: Studies in the Philosophy of Religion After Kant* (New York: Paulist Press, 1977), pp. 152–65.

128

THE TELEOLOGICAL ARGUMENT

In the *Summa Theologiae* Thomas writes:

We see that things which lack knowledge, such as natural bodies, act for an end, and this is evident from their acting always, or nearly always, in the same way, so as to obtain the best result. Hence it is plain that they achieve their end, not fortuitously, but designedly. Now whatever lacks knowledge cannot move toward an end, unless it be directed by some being endowed with knowledge and intelligence; as the arrow is directed by the archer. Therefore some intelligent being exists by whom all natural things are directed to their end: and this being we call God.[3]

Two things are affirmed here. One, the constancy of relations and the general direction indicate the presence of a teleological directedness in nature. Two, such a directedness must be the work of a mind. Obviously the term *end* is to be understood here as the purpose which motivates the development, not as the actual outcome of a process. Yet the difficulty consists in detecting the presence of a purpose when we only have direct access to the outcome. We are clearly not justified to conclude to the former merely because we find some meaning in the latter. For as every conceivable state of affairs, even one resulting from the merest fortuitous coincidence, may be interpreted as a meaningful outcome, one could attribute purpose to every process.

Nor do repetition and regularity necessarily indicate the presence of purpose, since a particular system may perpetuate itself if the factor which disturbs it entails an element that will restore the original state. Predictability, then, is no indication of teleological directedness. Neither is the mere fact that certain events condition the occurrence of other events. The ecological cycle of nature appears to be a marvelously coherent system. But must we regard it as a teleological process? Not necessarily, for the outcome in this case may not be more than the balance finally attained among conflicting elements. Moreover, which state would be the "end" of the system?

Can we ever conclude from the nature of the outcome and the development of the process to the presence of a purpose? Rigorist interpreters would claim that only acts of beings that are capable of belief and desire may safely be termed purposive.[4] If correct, this conclusion would deprive the argument of all its power, since the existence of such a being is precisely what must be proven. Others, such as C. A. Mace, have been more optimistic about the possibility of detecting teleological characteristics in the process itself.[5] Yet then the second question emerges: Must such a process necessarily be the work of a mind? Mace believes that it is at least highly probable that a teleological process defined in his terms occurs only where a mind is operative. In any event, the attribution of a teleological directedness to beings other than man and perhaps some higher animals cannot be fully verified. At best a teleological explanation of certain types of behavior may be empirically more satisfactory than a nonteleological.[6]

The advent of Darwin's theory has, of course, considerably contributed to the demise of teleological speculations. Yet in the final analysis, Darwinism neither adds to, nor subtracts from, the essence of the original teleological argument. Its strength and weakness fall entirely outside its scope. Nevertheless, a frequent presentation of the argument from the seventeenth century onward is very much open to Darwin's attacks. For any adaptation of a particular animal to its environment or of an organ to a particular function may be the outcome of an elimination process rather than of a teleological development. This applies to William Paley's famous description of the functioning of the eye[7] and to Hume's argument based on the complementarity of male and female for generative purposes in anatomy, passion, and instinct. Those arguments lose their power once the adaption is no longer conceived as an instant fact but as the outcome of a long and often devious evolutionary process. Darwin clearly anticipated the catastrophic impact which his theory would have on the traditional argument. "The old argument of design in nature, as given by Paley, which formerly seemed to me so conclusive, fails, now that the law of natural selection has been discovered. We can no longer argue that, for instance, the beautiful hinge of a bivalve shell must have been made by an intelligent being, like the hinge of a door by man."[8] The relation between the final outcome of an evolutionary process and the various stages leading to it is quite different from the one between end and means in the production of an artifact. Out of a number of mutations only those are preserved which enhance the individual's chances for survival in a particular environment. There is natural selection but no evidence of choice.[9]

Paradoxically, Darwin and his followers continue to use teleological models of interpretation. The very term *natural selection,* derived from cattle breeding, connotes a preexisting design as well as certain principles of economy in the execution of this design. Susanne Langer has rightly criticized this terminology. "So all the considerations of economy, time-saving, margins of safety, reserves of material, storage and deployment of power, and the principles of coordination and communication governing our industry are read into the organic forms and functions that have taken shape in the course of evolution."[10] The problems are increased by the fact that selection strongly evokes the idea of an intelligent agent. Darwin and his successors no longer refer to God as the supreme planner but they ascribe to "Nature" or "Evolution" pretty much the same function.

This is much more than a matter of linguistic accuracy, for the teleological implications may lead us to anticipate developments which are not borne out by the facts. Thus, on the basis of a teleological interpretation one would expect only those variations (mutations in Neo-Darwinism) to become permanent which contribute to the species' survival. But no evidence at all supports such a Leibnizian economy of perfection. A number of mutations are retained which fulfill no function whatever. The question clearly is not what "Nature" requires for its future perfection, but what the present situation allows. This situation displays neither design nor perfection, except perhaps in the highly qualified sense which I shall discuss later in this essay. Instead of a preexisting plan which tolerates no deviation, we only find undetermined impulses which are able or unable to assert themselves in a given environment. Such a view of evolution differs substantially from the common one, which appears to be guided by what one critic has called "the myth of the maximum," according to which the promotion of the ultimate end must be maximized. That only those acts which will yield a higher production than their alternatives will be chosen, may be validly assumed in economy. But nothing in the evolutionary process justifies the assumption that the fitness standard will be maximized. What remains is "not the best, but only the better, the good enough, the temporary expedient."[11] The "economic" teleology holds no basis in fact but only in an anthropomorphic, teleological model. In a complex system of agents various forms of interplay lead to different results, and only those results will be preserved which are not neutralized by opposite components. Thus, compared to its antecedents, the outcome "makes sense" and our tendency to give it a teleological interpretation becomes understandable enough.

Yet the evolution theory has not necessarily eliminated the possibility of a teleological world view. For as long as no purposive intervention is required for any particular adaptation the argument still stands. As Anthony Kenny remarks, "The argument was only that the ultimate explanation of such adaptation must be found in intelligence; and if the argument was correct, then any Darwinian success merely inserts an extra step between the phenomena to be explained and their ultimate explanation."[12]

Indeed, far from diminishing the possibility of a teleological world order, one might claim with Anthony Flew that the evolution theory has brought just so much more grist to the mill of the teleologist.[13] In the new context the object of teleological speculation will be the consistent, one dimensional trend of a development which, for all we know, is not the only possible one: an evolution toward ever greater complexity and deeper inwardness ultimately resulting in the improbable event of life. The development has continued to move toward the most complex forms of life, and from all appearances it still has not completed its course. Why, out of an infinite number of possibilities, were just the conditions of life fulfilled, and fulfilled almost at once?[14] Their fulfillment cannot be explained by a biological struggle for survival.[15] Everything seems to have been "arranged" toward the development of consciousness, although an almost infinite number of complex factors were needed for this *involution*. Individually all these steps can be explained without invoking teleology. But considering the steady development of the process toward greater complexity, the observer inevitably receives the impression that the evolution moves toward a specific goal. Still, no empirical evidence can ever establish more than a more or less steady development in one direction. Whether this directedness be interpreted in a teleological sense or not depends on the philosophical inclinations of the observer, but it can never be considered a strictly scientific conclusion. From the same facts and even theories which led Teilhard de Chardin and Lecomte du Nouy to a teleological interpretation, Monod and Rostand conclude to a purely deterministic, nonteleological one.

Even if a compelling case could be made for the teleological view, the existence of a perfect designer would not necessarily follow. For to warrant such a conclusion the evolutionary process would have to appear *evidently* good. But who could claim this for a development in which individuals and entire species are sacrificed? The end result is the outcome of a long and cruel struggle which left most of the participants dead by the roadside. From the victims' point of view at least there would be little perfection in the alleged ends-means relation of the present arrangement. That man, who came out as the winner of this contest, considers himself the goal of the development and imposes his own purposes upon all of organic and inorganic nature, is understandable enough. In one sense such a view is also correct, for only a person can conceive of himself as a purpose, and once he has started doing so is no longer able to see himself as subordinate to any other part of nature. But does the ultimacy of man's position indicate the existence of a perfect design? Could mind itself not be an abortive attempt, a terminus of the evolutionary drive, that is doomed to extinction? Behavioral scientists wonder more and more whether man will be able to survive his built-in problems.[16] Not only psychologists but also biologists (e.g., Paul Maclean) begin to question how man can continue to live with the schizoid nature that is his. Without considering these pessimistic forecasts, we may still wonder whether the record of his actual achievements, past and present, justifies the assumption of a vast and complex creation by an all-wise God. The unprejudiced mind finds it difficult to detect a divine purpose in man's accomplishments. Even Hegel, so incorrigibly optimistic in his philosophy of history, wrote at the end of his life:

> We see the earth covered with ruins, with remains of the splendid edifices and works left by the finest nations whose ends we recognize as having a substantial value. Great national objects and human works do indeed endure and defy time, but all that splendid national life has irrecoverably perished. We thus see how, on the one hand, petty, subordinate, even despicable designs are fulfilled; and, on the other hand, how those which are recognized as having substantial value are frustrated.[17]

Yet, one might object with Kant, even if man would never accomplish anyting else, he could still be the *moral* purpose of the universe. In his *Critique of Judgment* Kant claims that the universe finds its ultimate purpose not in man's cognitive or technical needs or in his pleasure, but in his moral will, which alone is an unconditioned end.[18] Only the moral will of man could give a Supreme

Being a sufficient reason for creating a world. Kant is not disturbed by man's apparent wickedness, for morality, being purely internal, need not be an external success. Nevertheless, Kant himself had to postulate an afterlife in order to give the will the holiness which it is unable to attain in this life and which alone makes man a worthy purpose of the universe. Thus, teleological considerations determine the meaning of the ethical postulate of the existence of God. But they were never adequate to become an argument.

In summary, I do not see how any teleological speculations could provide us with an "argument" for the existence of a perfect Designer. A person may draw his own conclusions from whatever private insights he has in this domain, but none of those can claim the universality of a compelling reason.

THE ARGUMENT OF ORDER

Let us now turn toward the concept of *order*. In the *Summa contra gentiles* Thomas writes: "In the world we find that things of diverse natures come together under one order, and this not rarely or by chance, but always or for the most part. There must therefore be some being by whose providence the world is governed."[19] The preceding concept of "end" is closely connected with the concept of "order" because a coordination of ends and means always presupposes some order among things. Yet order could conceivably exist without end-means relations. Moreoover, when teleological relations do obtain within the universe, the universe itself cannot simply be conceived in terms of end and means. I even suspect that teleological considerations become meaningless when applied to entire organisms within the universe. What could possibly be the "purpose" of a plant or an animal? To refer to them in such a manner is merely a crudely anthropomorphic way of saying that man uses them for his own benefit. At any rate, the term *purpose* does not apply to the universe as a whole, certainly not in the way in which end-means relations obtain *within* the world.

Another reason for distinguishing order from teleology is that the former appears to escape the specific criticisms to which the latter is subject. There is no question here of the adaptation of individual means to individual ends, or even of an ultimate purpose of all processes. The basic observation is that the impression of order is not restricted to the production of life from inorganic matter. Even in its static appearance the world seems to be an organized whole rather than a random collection of diverse and unrelated beings.

The concept of order refers to any disposition of elements which allows the mind to recognize the totality of them as an intelligible, aesthetic, or moral unity. Man has always perceived the world as a *cosmos,* to which the structures of the mind can be applied. But what is the significance of this fact? Does the coordination of physical phenomena and mental structures imply that the universe was "designed" by a mind similar to our own? Hardly. Structures are invented by the mind in accordance with its need to comprehend the universe as it in fact appears to us. Mathematical concepts apply to the world not because of a preestablished divine harmony between the mind and the world, but because that particular kind of symbolization was developed which proved most useful to understand the given world. Still, one might insist, the applicability of rational models presupposes the existence of a certain amount of coordination in the *real* world. This I fully concede, but, then, a universe without some degree of coordination would not only be unintelligible, it would also be impossible. If a universe exists at all, it must exist in some sort of order. Order is not an additional element, a distinctive ornament of one of the many possible worlds. It is the very condition of existence of a complex totality. We need no different justification for the order in the world than for the existence of the world. In whatever fashion the universe may have originated, a minimum of order had to be present instantly if it was to survive at all. The impossibility of absolute disorder, then, turns out to be the Achilles heel of the argument. For if order is a necessary condition of existence, its presence yields no indication of its origin.

Note well, the dilemma here is not between order and pure chance, as the argument's advocates claim, but between an order imposed from without and one emerging from within. The argument gratuitously assumes that the only possible alternative to blind chance is a transcendent design. The arrangement of diverse things into an orderly pattern cannot result from their own divergent natures, Aquinas claims.[20] But does the arrangement become more intelligible by assuming an orderly principle *above* the universe? Could rationality not have its source *in* the universe? If we accept a universe without beginning, as most Greeks did and as Aquinas himself considered to be irrefutably possible, could the arrangement not be inherent in the totality?

To be sure, the order in the universe impresses us *as if* it had been designed, because in manufactured products order results from design. But for the order of the universe no trace of an actual designer can ever be found, and we may be tempted to agree with the skeptic in John Wisdom's "Gods," that no gardener is responsible for the garden.[21] What ultimately justifies this skepticism is the well-known difficulty involved in transferring what we know about the origin of an artifact to the origin of the universe. To counter Hume's objection of our inexperience with regard to the origins of worlds, it is insufficient to reply that a perfect analogy exists nowhere and that all reasoning goes beyond actual experience. For the universe is unique in a different way: while all other things are part of it, here the whole, as such, is the very issue.

I repeat, the problem is not whether the existence of order requires an explanation, but whether this explanation must come from within the universe. The principle of an immanent Logos becomes absurd only if one previously *assumes* that the universe cannot be intrinsically rational or even divine by itself—as it was for the Greeks. But such an assumption already presupposes the acceptance of the very theism one wants to prove.

However, granting the existence of a designed (i.e., transcendently imposed) order, does the order which actually obtains require a *divine* designer? Certainly not if only a *perfect* order requires a perfect designer. Even if we are willing to assume that an imperfect order might have been designed by a perfect God, it is difficult to conceive how such an imperfect order could provide evidence of a perfect creator unless his existence was already known from other sources. What can we conclude about the nature of the designer on the basis of astral collisions in distant galaxies, natural disasters on a life-bearing planet, the extinction of entire species for lack of a proper environment, the births of monsters and defective individuals, and, among conscious beings, the inestimable amounts of suffering and pain? To be sure, one may still *assume* that the present order is the best possible, as Leibniz did, but there clearly is no evidence that such must be the case. Indeed, the apparent absence of due order has become as much an objection against the acceptance of a perfect creator as the presence of order is an argument in its favor. The basic question, then, is: Is the imperfect order of the actual universe sufficient to prove the existence of a perfect designer? Could a Being of absolute wisdom and almighty power not have prevented some of the disorder? Or, as Bertrand Russell somewhat maliciously put it, do you think that, if you were granted omnipotence and omniscience and millions of years in which to perfect your world, you could produce nothing better than the Ku Klux Klan or the Fascists?[22] The simple answer to this question is that we do not know, because we ignore how much evil *could* have been avoided and how much goodness *could* have been added. But as long as we remain in the dark on those issues, the argument misses a basic premise. We are stranded with the dilemma of a world that is too good for not having been designed at all, and too bad for having obviously been designed by a wise, omnipotent God. Or, as William E. Hocking aptly expressed it: "From the standpoint of naturalism, the world is surprisingly good; from the standpoint of religion, it is surprisingly bad; for naturalism, there is no problem of evil; there is no problem of good—and this problem is the substance of the teleological argument. But from the standpoint of religion, there is a problem of evil; and this problem is the burden of objection to the force of the proof."[23]

CONCLUSION

It may be appropriate to conclude this critique with a few remarks on its limitation. I have attempted to show that the argument of design independently of the religious experience is unable to prove the existence of God. Is the man who sees the hand of God in the workings of this universe therefore subject to an illusion? Such a conclusion does not follow from the preceding critique. What was an illusion is the "purely philosophical" status of the teleological argument. But the real thrust of teleological considerations in the religious vision does not lie in their probative power. *If man is religious* he cannot but see order as God's order, and he expresses this in a teleological theology. To him the order of the world, its beauty, its service to man, cease to be gratuitous. All these qualities, whatever their possible explanations may be, find their ultimate resting point in his faith. In this respect the attitude of faith differs substantially from that of philosophy, which can make no assumptions that it is unable to justify by logical reflection upon experience. Usually the so-called arguments merely allow the believer to understand what he antecedently believed.[24] In the words of Norman Kemp Smith: "In and through their religious experience of fellowship with God, they have belief in God, and coming to nature and history with this belief in their minds, they interpret nature and history freely in accordance therewith. They do not observe order and design, and *therefore* infer a Designer: they argue that order and design must be present even when they are not apparent because all existences other than God have their source in him."[25]

The argument of design draws attention to a specific set of facts in which the religious mind confronts the transcendent.[26] Order and disorder force both believer and nonbeliever beyond the mere acceptance of empirical facts. To religious man, the detection of harmony and purpose becomes an occasion of faith and joy, just as the inability to explain disorder induces religious doubt. (The Psalms and the Book of Job are eloquent witnesses of both attitudes.) He feels that the nonbeliever is also puzzled by order and disorder, and he wants to communicate his own world view. If he does this by attempting to educe the notion of Supreme Being from the idea of order, he merely commits a logical error. But often he is aware of the restrictions imposed by his particular universe of discourse. Even the much-criticized Paley did not think of himself as "proving" God to someone who had never heard of him, for he admitted that the recognition of divine purpose might require "some previous knowledge of the subject."

NOTES

1. Two rare instance where God is declared to be responsible for the adaptation are *De Coelo* 271ª33 and *De Generatione et Corruptione* 336ᵇ32. W. D. Ross interprets these passages as "a literary device and a concession to ordinary ways of thinking" incompatible with Aristotle's nonintervention theology. See W. D. Ross, *Aristotle* (Boston: Meridian 1959), pp. 81, 176. Yet in Aristotle's lost early work, *On Philosophy*, he clearly introduced the teleological argument. See Werner Jaeger, *Aristotle: Fundamentals of the History of His Development*, trans. R. Robinson (Oxford: Clarendon Press, 1948), pp. 159–161; and Anton

Hermann Chroust, "A Cosmological Proof for the Existence of God in Aristotle's Lost Dialogue, *On Philosophy*," *New Scholasticism* 40 (1966): 447–463.

2. *Legum Allegoriarum Libri Tres* III, 32. 97–99; *De Praemiis et Poenis* VII, 41–43.

3. S.T. 1, 2, 3. Translated as *Basic Writings of St. Thomas*, ed. Anton Pegis (New York: Random 1945).

4. C. J. Ducasse, "Explanation, Mechanism and Teleology," *Journal of Philosophy* 23(1926). Reprinted in *Readings in Philosophical Analysis*, ed. H. Feigl and Wilfred Sellars (New York: Appleton-Century-Crofts, 1949), pp. 540–544.

5. C. A. Mace describes as teleological a process by which a negative condition is counteracted by a contrasting condition in such a way that all action which increases the degree of the latter tends to be continued or repeated, while any action which decreases that degree tends to be discontinued, and that, with repetition of the process, the process as a whole approximates to a set of component actions which performed in that order and only in that order are sufficient to produce the second condition ("Mechanical and Teleological Causation," *Readings in Philosophical Analysis*, pp. 535–536).

6. This is the line of reasoning taken by Charles Taylor, *The Explanation of Behavior* (New York: Humanities 1964).

7. William Paley, *Natural Theology*, ed. Frederick Ferré (Indianapolis: Bobbs-Merrill, 1963), pp. 13–19.

8. Charles Darwin, *Autobiography* (London: Collins, 1958), p. 87.

9. Norman Kemp Smith comments on Darwin's text. "The hinge of a door affords conclusive proof of the existence of an artificer; the hinge of the bivalve shell, though incomparably superior as a hinge, affords no such proof; it is as natural in its origin as anything in physical nature can be known to be" ("Is Divine Existence Credible?" in *The Credibility of Divine Existence* [New York: St. Martin, 1967], p. 139).

10. Susanne Langer, *Mind: An Essay on Human Feeling* (Baltimore: Johns Hopkins University Press, 1967), p. 360.

11. William C. Wimsatt, "The Machine in the Ghost" (paper read at the annual meeting of the American Metaphysical Society, Washington, D.C., 1972).

12. Anthony Kenny, *The Five Ways* (London: Routledge 1969).

13. *God and Philosophy* (New York: Harcourt, Brace & World, 1966), p. 60.

14. The appearance of a single molecule of dissymmetry such as those of living organisms is difficult to explain by chance. The appearance of hundreds of millions of them becomes almost impossible.

15. F. R. Tennant made the point well: "Of a struggle for existence between rival worlds, out of which ours has survived as the fittest, we have no knowledge upon which to draw. Natural selection cannot here be invoked; and if the term

evolution be applicable at all to the whole world-process, it must have a different meaning from that which it bears in Darwinian biology. Presumably the world is comparable with a single throw of dice. And common sense is not foolish in suspecting the dice to have been loaded" *(Philosophical Theology,* 2 vols. [London: Cambridge University Press, 1935] 2: 87).

16. A popular expression of this doubt, which synthesizes a number of scientific conclusions, may be found in Arthur Koestler's *The Ghost in the Machine* (New York: Macmillan, 1967).

17. *Vorlesungen über die Beweise vom Dasein Gottes* (Berlin, 1966), p. 170; translated in *Lectures on the Philosophy of Religion,* trans. E. B. Speirs and Burdon Sanderson, 3 vols. (London: Kegan Paul, Trench, & Trübner, 1895), 3: 344.

18. *Critique of Judgment,* n. 86, trans. James Merideth (Oxford: Clarendon Press, 1952), p. 110.

19. *Summa contra gentiles,* trans. Anton Pegis (Garden City: Doubleday, 1966), Book I, chap. 13, p. 96.

20. *Summa contra gentiles,* Book I, chap. 42.

21. *Logic and Language,* ed. Anthony Flew (Garden City: Doubleday, 1965), p. 201.

22. Bertrand Russell, *Why I Am Not a Christian* (New York: Simon & Schuster, 1957), p. 10.

23. Unpublished lectures, Manuscript VII, C-6-6.

24. Cf. H. H. Price's statement that the traditional proofs are not arguments which "would follow logically from premises which every reasonable man is bound to accept."

25. *The Credibility of Divine Existence,* p. 390. By using the term *credibility* Norman Kemp Smith hoped to emphasize that he was not advancing one more argument for the existence of God, but rather an inquiry into the source and status of belief. Cf. introduction, p. 45.

26. J. J. C. Smart describes it as a "potent instrument in heightening religious emotions" ("The Existence of God," in *New Essays in Philosophical Theology.* ed. Anthony Flew and Alasdair MacIntyre [New York: Macmillan, 1968], p. 45).

Chapter 10

THE WIDER TELEOLOGICAL ARGUMENT FOR A PERSONAL GOD
Peter A. Bertocci

T HE cosmological argument, focusing as it does on the most reasonable way of understanding the dependable order of contingent beings and events, does not support the full-orbed conception of God, changelessly perfect, but opens the way to a conception of a contemporaneous Creator-Ground. Now, when attention shifts from the ultimate collocation of things to the orderly events and beings that fit into a broad, governing purpose, prior intimations both of an Intelligent Creator-Ground and of a cosmic purpose uniting the interlocking being-events are strengthened. Attention focuses on the instances of goal-fulfilling beings in the biological realm whose natures, on the whole, so dovetail into the order of the physical world that the line of least theoretical resistance is to propose that these creatures are specifically designed for a physical environment serving their goals.

Proponents of what we may call this "narrower" teleological argument[1] were wont to insist that a designing Mind was required to account for the many amazing adaptations of animals to the environment. Even as an architect guides the building of a house from plans already worked out to meet the requirements of the tenant's furniture, so God designed the physical and biological world with the specific needs of man in mind. Thus the world was made to fit man's nature, and man's nature was made to fit the world. It was such an argument, from specific, prearranged adaptations, which was undermined by the doctrine of

From: Peter A. Bertocci, *Introduction to the Philosophy of Religion* (Englewood Cliffs, N.J.: Prentice-Hall, 1951), pp. 329–383.

evolution. For now the adaptations, far from being specifically planned, were the result of chance variations which enabled certain living things to survive in the struggle with other animals and the environment. It consequently became no longer necessary to postulate specific actions of a Creator to account for the harmonious interplay between the abilities and needs of living things and their environment.

For many minds the theory of evolution put an end to the validity of any teleological argument for God. Many philosophical theologians therefore turned to the reevaluation of other approaches to the problem; in the main they turned to the moral argument for God, and to the argument for God from religious experience, or to more adequate statements of the ontological argument.

Others, and most notably Dr. F. R. Tennant, to whom our own exposition is heavily indebted,[2] set to work reconstructing the teleological argument for God in the conviction that this approach, moving closely to the empirical data of science, reflective thought, and moral experience, still could yield the most valid argument for God. The *wider teleological argument* for God, then, rests properly not on the specific restricted evidence of design and fruitful adaptation, but on the interconnectedness of physical nature, life, and human experience. This argument is content to rest its case not on the surface harmonies, but on the ultimate conditions which make harmonies possible. It stresses not the mere fact of survival of the fit, but it points to the *arrival* of the fit (or fit-able) in the first place.

The broader teleological argument for God as here presented will consist of seven links. These links, each aimed at resolving a problem, may be set out in topical form as follows:

Link One: The Purposive Interrelation of Matter and Life.

Link Two: The Relevance of Thought to Reality.

Link Three: The Interrelation of Moral Effort and the Order of Nature.

Link Four: The Interrelation between Value and Nature.

Link Five: The World as Good for Man.

Link Six: The Significance of Aesthetic Experience.

Link Seven: Religious Experience as Confirmatory.

However, Tennant did not articulate what I have advanced as the "essence" of the cosmological argument, and that I hold is the pervasive ground on which in fact the "wider" teleological argument builds as it provides more concrete interpretations of the physical, the biological, and the human realm (inclusive of value experience and appraisal). Link One, interpreting the relation of the physical to the organic world as purposeful, begins the process of indicating (as I would argue) that the cosmological argument is given "flesh and blood" as the "causal order" becomes the means of working out the ends that give fuller meaning and intelligibility to any specific contingent order.

Hence I would prefer to call the wider teleological argument "the cosmo-teleological-ethical argument," since the links do form a cumulative chain, in which the relationships between the physical, the biological, and the realm of values reasonably support a view of the Creator-Person that Tennant and classical theists would find objectionable.

LINK ONE: THE PURPOSIVE INTERRELATION OF MATTER AND LIFE

Life as dependent on, but not reducible to, matter. The account as given by the physical and biological sciences, of evolution and of the relation of the physical universe to life does not lend itself conclusively to any one interpretation. Yet the main issue is not about facts but about the ideal of explanation. There is no doubt about the fact that the conditions favorable to the appearance and survival of life on this globe were unique. It seems unreasonable to reduce the characteristic functions of living organisms (such as their selectivity, their ability to maintain their own equilibrium in interaction with the environment, and their capacity for reproduction) to the unselective and nonreproductive activities of chemical substances. Reduction does not account for both the appearance and the survival of living things.

Still, there are those who believe that science must insist on the possibility of reducing purposive living processes to nonpurposive chemical interactions. In this debate it should be clear that no basic prerequisite of science is at stake, but only a conviction of some who think that science cannot admit that goals of any sort are among the determinants of events. For them the effects of the present field and the past antecedents are the sole "causes" of anything that happens.

But the fact is that the scientist—as distinguished from the scientist become philosopher—needs to assume only that there is order among events when and where they appear. There is no intellectual necessity for reducing facts of one order to those of another *unless* this can be done without forcing the data. The biologist finds processes at work within living beings—such as healing and reproduction—which force him to develop descriptive terms that make no sense—unless distorted—in the field of chemistry and physics. Nonpurposive physical and chemical processes are involved in living processes. But chemical processes *in* living beings are very difficult to explain if goals for survival are not considered. There is simply no denying the amazing *inter*relationship of living beings and purely chemical beings. Developments in biochemistry underscore this intimate interrelation. But they do not prove the conclusion that life is reducible to the interaction of chemicals. The fact still remains that when life appeared, *life* appeared. If life crept in gradually in the reproductive capacity of some colloids, for example, the point is that however modestly it put in its appearance, it was *life* that appeared in addition to chemical activity. And the fact still remains that life's activities are situated in a world which supports them.

This collocation of events, this close interrelation of living and nonliving beings, is an opaque fact unless we postulate a purpose which uses one order as an aid to the continuance of another. Obviously this appeal to a broader purpose will not explain *how* the food that enters the stomach becomes part of the living blood, bone, nerve, and brain. Any biochemist can give us the sequence, but he is as silent before this fact of transmutation as we are. However, we are not trying to introduce a Purposer to describe what science has not so far described; here we seek to explain *the harmony between two orders of being,* the harmony between two differing and interacting qualities of existence. We are seeking a view which, far from denying established scientific facts, will allow them to fit into a broader scheme which decreases the mystery. What mystery? The fact that living beings should appear and be so closely interconnected with nonliving beings—especially if all there was to begin with was the nonpurposeful, nonliving, nonthinking hustle and bustle of units of energy.

True, this interrelation between life and matter may not seem to tell us much about the purposes or the Purposer. We must stop to think of what this means concretely. But as we reflect upon the preparation of the universe for life and the constant interaction of myriads of living things upon each other and the physical order, it becomes increasingly difficult not to see an intelligent Purposer at work. And the evidence for such intelligence multiplies as we recall the climb from lower forms of life to the possibilities in man, who uses lower forms of life and the physical order as a basis for his own

Our interest here is to emphasize the greater coherence which comes into our thinking if we consider the interrelation of the physical universe and life and the developing evolution of species as the handiwork of a creative Intelligence intent on producing a world rich in life, and, in the existence of man, rich in mind and value. *The evidence so far adduced enables us to envisage a Mind which is responsible not only for the ultimate physical preparations for life but for the first appearance of life in its many forms and for the additional mutations and variations discovered by our scientists.*

We must point out that the evidence so far reviewed has not been used to establish the existence of a morally good and an omnipotent Intelligence. The evidence thus far does indicate the presence of an Intelligence at work in the order of the world—even decay is an orderly process. It also suggests that the creative Intelligence does not, or cannot, succeed in all his undertakings. If there were no other evidence and no other factors to be considered, the author would still find it more coherent to believe in a universe largely governed by Intelligence than in a universe in which mindless, purposeless units of energy *somehow* fathered and protected living things and their evolution.

But we shall have to take the whole human enterprise into account before we can complete the conception of God or can deal with the difficulties suggested by suffering and tragedy.

LINK TWO: THE RELEVANCE OF THOUGHT TO REALITY

Knowledge as a joint-product of man's interaction with nature. Our minds do make many and serious mistakes in interpreting the world. However, we would not be making mistakes very long were it not for the fact that what goes on in our knowing minds and what goes on in nature are *relevant*. The word *relevant* is used in order to avoid the suggestion that our minds ever copy or mirror the world.

If any reader should think that in knowing our minds do mirror the world, it would not matter here. The important point is that our knowing, in order for that knowing to be trustworthy, need not mirror reality. Our knowledge must, however, be relevant, in the same way, for example, as a roadmap is relevant to the nature of the road situation. The map is certainly not the road; nor is it a copy of the road. It represents the geographical relations between roads in a manner capable of guiding human beings. If the map is accurate, the individual will be able to make his way from any one road to his destination. The map can be added to, and subtracted from, as changes in the human experience of the road actually occur and are recorded.

Knowledge, we may safely say, is a joint product of what is in the world and in the nature of human faculties. Man does not create his knowledge out of nothing; nor is it simply implanted in him by the events which occur. His is the *kind* of mind which can *think about* relationships and develop hypotheses to guide him in his interaction with the world. As we have seen, man has been able to develop scientific and philosophical methods which facilitate his understanding of the world and then lead him into satisfying relations with that world. Man knows very little, but the *fact that he can know, that operations in him are not hopelessly unconnected with the operations in things* is, in a sense, the most important fact about human experience and about the world.

In other words, the order of mind and the order of things have a correlation which in itself promises well for human adjustment.

LINK THREE: THE INTERRELATION OF MORAL EFFORT AND THE ORDER OF NATURE

MAN is free to will, within limits, those goals which he deems worthwhile and to which he feels morally obligated. Man's cognitive capacities, in the main, prepare him for the high drama of life, that of understanding his own abilities, needs, and wants, and of relating himself reasonably to others in the environment he shares with them. Unless man is free, there is no real point to moral effort. But moral freedom is not enough. For moral freedom in a creature with insufficient ability to control himself in his world would be cruel mockery. Still other conditions are required, however, if enduring moral effort is to be justified. What are they?

First, there must be limits to what moral beings can do, and these limits cannot be altered too radically or abruptly. Choices must have limited consequences and predictable consequences (though not completely predictable). If some human being could alter the sequences of physical nature, or if he could alter the basic laws of human nature—of thinking, remembering, and wanting, for example—laws upon which persons depend as they make their choices, any ethical order would be endangered. For his so-called freedom to change "at will" the basic structure of his own nature or of the world in any way might well create havoc. There would then be no order other than that which he would impose upon himself. If, for instance, a man labors in imagination to build a house for his children, and another man could alter the laws of physics upon which the builder was planning, nay, if all human beings could do what they wanted without conforming to some dependable structure imposed upon them, there would be no reason to work for ideals. Fortunately, then, man is not free without limitations. He acts within the limits of the natural world into which his own restricted nature is born. He may act freely within these limits, but *he* does not determine the limits. He can select and sow his seeds, but he cannot make the seeds or provide the laws of growth. He may follow impulse rather than thought, but, if he does, there are consequences he cannot avoid. The first condition of *any* ethical universe, therefore, is that controls exist within which freedom may operate creatively.

The second condition extends the first one. Man must be able to depend upon his own structure and that of nature to preserve what he has done, good and bad. If he builds an automobile after having disciplined himself to understand and use the laws of chemistry and physics, he must be able to depend upon the continuance of those laws. What would happen if gasoline ceased to ignite under the same conditions which prevailed in the past? So, also, if man trains his body and mind to perform certain tasks, good or bad, he must be able to depend upon their doing so in the future. The universe must not go back on its promise to him. A certain amount of contingency and "chance" might add challenge and variety to his effort, but the moment the laws of physiological or psychological nature became so undependable that he really could not know how to train his children (because he could not know what to predict), moral effort would be unreasonable even if possible. Man could no longer guide himself by past experience.

This point cannot be emphasized enough, for it enters into the consideration of the problem of miracles. If by *miracle* we mean the intervention of some power into the actions of nature so that what man had learned to expect from the past could not in fact be expected, then those persons depending upon the laws to work as usual would be sadly disappointed and their planning might well be discouraged. Nature, or the power behind it, had not kept her word. She had promised that rain would follow thunder, that suspicion would follow hate, that trust would follow love, but, lo, this did not happen as persons were led to expect from past experience. The so-called scientific objection to miracle is more than ''scientific'': it rises from the realization that unpredictable miracles would play havoc with the moral effort (and with faith in a reliable God).

To sum up: if there is to be a universe in which any consistent moral effort is justified, there must be freedom within limits *and* a world in which the consequences, good and evil, are allowed to stand until man himself does something to change them. If some power beyond man unpredictably interferes, or if there is not enough order in the universe to sustain the expectancies developed from studying it, the moral life is to that extent discouraged.

This is *not* to assert that moral effort requires a broad margin of safety everywhere or a universe in which there are no chances to be taken. But it is to insist that unless a dependable relation exists between man's abilities and the biological and physical orders upon which he depends for the embodiment of his values, then the quest for increase in values is a hopeless one. True, a man can always will; he can always try. But the moral agent has to be sustained, and if there is no assurance of reasonable success in preserving and increasing his values, there is no point to the moral life. What the right amount of assurance is cannot be measured in detail. Suffice it to say that, as a minimum, at any one time there must be a challenge reasonably commensurate with a man's ability to realize a balance of true values over disvalues.

LINK FOUR: THE INTERRELATION BETWEEN VALUE AND NATURE

Human values as not man-made. Fortunately, the nature of man's experience with value further corroborates our thesis that man's moral effort is not being carried out in a cuckooland. Not only does man's own nature make moral choice and effort possible, but his past ventures in the realization of ideals indicate that his world makes possible a wide range of values, more than enough, certainly, to whet his appetites and spur his efforts. Let us see what is involved here.

In our discussion of the nature of values, we concluded that a value is a joint product of man's nature and of the world in which he lives. There are no values independent of man, but there are value possibilities in his nature and in the world whose realization awaits his criticized and marshaled efforts. Man does not make his own basic nature, and he is not responsible for the possibilities of value in the world beyond him. The values he does approve and realize must, therefore, be taken as testimony to the fact that man's criticized wants and the constitution of the world do not work at cross-purposes.

To expand this point: man's wants lead him to seek satisfaction of many sorts, and his abilities enable him to discover the ways of satisfying these wants within his environment. Thus, were the structure of atoms, animals, and other persons unsuited to the demands of his own growth, he would die. Were he to die the world would remain with its value possibilities: a fertile realm with no being to bring forth and enjoy those possibilities. To the extent that man wants, criticizes his wants, and develops into a creature sensitive in appreciation and dependable in his creations, the whole world is the better. When man, feeling the imperative of duty, thrusts every effort into the realization of value, he does not find a constant rebuff in his own nature or the world's. *Accordingly, in man's desire and will to values, in nature's response to his efforts, a new realm of quality becomes reality; we may say that "Nature" reaches a "new high," a new range of fruition as life labors for and enjoys the values possible in it.*

Human values as revealing what nature can be. The reader must be alert to the particular theory of value advocated here. Man's dependable values represent coherent generalizations about his own experience in a world he did not create. These values tell us what nature *can be,* but they also tell us what man in and through nature, what nature in and through man *can* be—and *has* been. Man does not simply intuit values (be they in a Platonic realm or in the mind of God), which may or may not be *relevant to his nature in this world.* The values he knows are the consequences of the experimentation of some human being, some family, some society. Man has not known what would really satisfy his nature before experimentation with his own life, with the nature of others, and with the physical world.

Fortunately, the race of men has been blessed with members whose lives were unusually productive in the search for values. (Were they mere accidents in a churn of atoms?) These men pioneered in new areas when their more conservative and shortsighted brothers would not "take the chance." A host of prophets in all lands, sensitive to the suffering and sins of the dispossessed and the privileged alike, have refused to follow the value routes of other men.

And there have been those evildoers whose experiments with values have shocked men into the realization of the horrible potentialities of human nature— all those human beings, small and great, whose nasty little schemes or grandiose dreams have sought to prostitute the energies of others. These too, at great cost to themselves, and at great cost to those tortured and enslaved—these too have taught human beings where their truer values did lie.

Gradually, so frequently painfully, the human race extended itself in the search for values. But, again, every new success meant a new realization of what man could create in the universe and what the universe could create in man. In this way, as nature "extended" man by challenging him to new achievements, man "extended" nature by seeing and realizing new possibilities.

Human values as supported and guided by the nature of things. Civilization may be said, then, to represent certain broad patterns of behavior and certain ideals which have eventuated from the interaction of nature and man. Man has discovered that some of his value claims were so irrelevant to the world that they were indeed "subjective," sheer fancies finding no steady support either in his own nature or in the structure of events beyond him. Other value claims, he found, not only took root in his own nature, but also encouraged the realization of other values. By coherently organizing his value ventures, by devoted efforts in actualizing them, man has been able and is able, not to avoid frustration, but to decrease the amount of fruitless frustration and waste. He can achieve much if he is wise, circumspect, and adventurous; but reality, if it does not yield itself richly to the timid and imaginative, seems to abhor the undisciplined, the thoughtless, and the foolhardy. "Nature" will obey man's commands up to a point, but she will also visit him with physical and mental illness and death if he seeks to do "anything he wants when he wants it." All the way along, from the time she gives him physical birth to the time that he develops intellectual and aesthetic responsiveness, nature (including his own endowment) is the bank from which man draws, the project in which he invests his capital, and the source of the interest his venture earns. Surely there is basis for Tennant's conclusion: "The world is thus instrumental to the emergence, maintenance, and progressiveness of morality."[4]

It is time to summarize and reassess the whole argument thus far before adding a new link to our reasoning. We have held that man's cognitive enterprises are supported by nature; that his freedom to will is not unbounded (and yet not predetermined in efficiency); that the values he achieves represent what he can do with the nature given him and with the environment he lives in. His physical home, we have seen, is uniquely prepared for the survival of living creatures, and its lawful structure is a necessary support for his adventures in the realization of truth and goodness.

LINK FIVE: THIS WORLD AS GOOD FOR MAN

What constitutes a world good? Man, we have argued, is a moral agent whose search for truth and goodness finds considerable support in the ultimate collocation of things. Man and the world participate in the creation of values and disvalues. But were one to ask the question: Is this the best of all possible universes for man? we should, indeed, be doubtful. The limitations of man's innate constitution, the tragedies in which the upheavals of nature have destroyed the works of man, the struggle for value against tremendous odds, and man's inhumanity to man would indeed give us pause in framing a careful answer to this question. But we cannot move very far until we stop to consider what a best possible universe *for man* would be. Let the reader note the addition of the italicized words, for they are important. Any question about the "best possible" forces us to ask "for whom or what?" And it should be clear that the only question worth considering here is whether the world which man inhabits is the best possible for him. If man's happiness depended upon a surplus of pleasures as such over pains, and if a universe which insured such a surplus were considered the best possible, then one might well claim that the cosmic Mind had little if any interest in man's happiness. How many lives in the history of mankind could claim a balance of pleasure over pain? But do we really care about a balance of *any* pleasures over any pains? Would we not prefer certain kinds of tensions, uncertainty, and pain to a life of pleasure without them?

At this point each one of us needs to put the question to himself: Agreeing that as a human being I can undergo such excruciating pain and mortal anguish as even animals are incapable of, would I be willing to exchange the pleasures of love and friendship, the joy of music, the satisfaction of intellectual pursuits, and, further, *the very struggle to achieve these,* for the sake of a life in which all of these were forfeited but in which pain was impossible? Any person who finds it possible to reply in the affirmative will find the rest of this book inadequate. For we assume that the quality of friendship, aesthetic delight, intellectual satisfaction, and moral achievement are of primary importance to human beings. We assume that the *quality* of pleasures and pains and not the quantity is the determining factor in evaluating the status of human beings in the world.

Indeed, as we reflect upon the facts of existence, we realize that the emphasis actually seems to have been placed on the *kind* of struggle and on the *kind* of achievement as more significant than achievement as such! The process of achievement seems to be as important as the achievements in themselves. Man, we have seen, is free, in a limited sense, to help in creation of values. Indeed, is it not true that his deepest joys and his profoundest satisfactions reside in the very process of creating the values he enjoys? Let our thesis be firmly stated. The deepest values in human experience are never those which, as it were, another implants in us. They are those we have a share in developing. Whatever other interests the cosmic Mind may have in the creation of value, at the human level the values he has in mind *must* include the *co*creating of values by human beings. Again, that human beings should be cocreating values in his universe is *the* value attending all other values. For there is no human value which is not enhanced by the creative effort to appreciate or realize it. (God, on this view, is superior to man in enjoyment and accomplishment because he creates and cocreates so much more.)

This point is so important to our whole thesis that we rephrase it. The value possibilities (and the disvalue possibilities) are there in the world and in the potentialities of man. Man's task is to transform potentiality of value into actuality. The creative adventure of finding truth, developing imaginative disinterest, honesty, courage; the activity of creating a society where human beings may better realize their potentialities in mutual sympathy, forgiveness, and loyalty; the very process of enjoying beauty and creating works which express man's yearning for beauty—these experiences, we *know*, are the growing centers of human existence. In the attitudes a human being develops, in the setting of his will to the realization of some plan, in his determination to cocreate values— here we find not only the growing point of human experience, but also the value of values: the factor without which all the values of human life would be less valuable. Since what a man is willing to do with opportunities expresses his *character*, we may well say that *the value of values is character.* Character is not the only value. Indeed, its worth to a human being depends also on the other values it enables him and others to realize. But it represents the joy and struggle the person has undergone to cocreate values which his reason approved. The distinctive fact about the human level of existence—the fact which differentiates human existence from all other types—is this very fact that the *quality* of persons is in the making and not ready-made.

The cosmic Mind, we might suppose, could have created puppets which would execute his purposes as readily as do atoms or ants. Our thesis would be that had he done so, or had he approved a universe without cocreators in value, he would have done less than the best. In any case, here is man and here are his deepest and most valuable experiences. They cannot be left out in a reasonable account of the universe as we know it. The cosmic Mind did not rest short of man, and we may therefore well postulate with Keats that this universe is a "vale of soulmaking." Persons, we find, help to create values, and values determine the quality of persons.

Let us ask again: Is this the best of all possible universes for man? Since we deem it the highest value that man should be able to create his own character, and should thereby participate in the creation of other values, our own answer must be affirmative. The cosmic Person would not have been good to us had he created us puppets rather than cocreators with him in the development of the quality of our own lives.

What a "vale of soul-making" involves. But from the fact that man is related to God as cocreator there follow serious consequences both for the cosmic Person and for us. Had he made us puppets, he could be sure that his will would be unfailingly done. As it is, much that *he* would use for goodness only, *we* may use for evil ends. Thus, the power in explosives might be used to dynamite the way through mountains. God cannot stop us—if we are to be cocreators—when we use explosives to destroy each other. We may build battleships and slums when he would prefer schools and homes. The Creator must have known this could be, if he knew at all what human beings would be able to do. He preferred to suffer as his cocreator created evil, rather than to be sure his will would be done at the expense of human freedom and responsibility.

True, when one contemplates the horror and tragedy in human lives perpetrated by the hateful and selfish deeds of responsible human beings, he might wonder whether this were not a cruel joke: a vast arena of history in which human beings pit themselves against each other while the King looks on the "sport!" But this is to underestimate the quality of mind a cosmos-Maker would possess. Does the sensitive human mind have "fun" in seeing human beings, or animals, tear each other apart? No more would God! More needs to be said on this question, but taking their own deepest moral experiences as an analogy, the suffering of man has been deemed by many, and not only in the Christian tradition, to be a veritable cross to God—though gladly borne for the sake of the human values insured thereby.

God's experience, indeed, illustrates the full meaning of the tragic in existence, namely, the acceptance of undeserved suffering in the effort to realize the best. Let a child be tortured by a cruel parent and the Creator suffers in the cruelty of the parents, the cry of the child, and the abuse of physical and psychophysiological laws which make punishment possible. The creator-creating God accepts the suffering involved if finite persons are to be cocreators of value. His will may be crucified and scorned by the persons he would aid and by the abuse of the world of law he makes possible. But—and this is the crucial point—what greater aim could inspire the cosmic Mind than this creation of persons who are to decide for themselves, within limits, what paths their souls shall take?

The continuation of values as the ground for believing God to be good. Assuming that the fact of moral choice is a real blessing, and that the will to goodness, to rephrase Kant's memorable expression, shines like a jewel among all the values possible in life, are we justified in considering the cosmic Mind good just because it has made character possible? After all, we might say, even in the midst of excruciating suffering and *useless* hardship, it would be possible to do one's best to fight evil and to realize good. But would that by itself be an adequate justification for existence? If nature be so niggardly as to make life all but unendurable, and if moral achievements are not encouraged and preserved, we might well decide that the cosmic Mind is not interested in more than an endless struggle for character.

As we reflect upon this problem we observe what might be called a "continuation of values." Human beings do live in a world where a wide range and variety of values is possible; man can realize bodily, economic, recreational, social, aesthetic, intellectual, religious, and character values of many kinds. Indeed, to live for any amount of time is to enjoy some of these values. Furthermore, the values we enjoy we seek not merely to conserve but to increase both in our own lives and in the lives of others. Values are not dead, inert things which we can treasure under lock and key; they are the blossoming of life and mind in nature. Once human beings start realizing and enjoying values, man can preserve them and increase them in his manners and customs, in his laws, and in his institutions. He can, for example, make education and understanding more available to his children and to his neighbors, and in so doing he encourages mutuality in the extension of these values and the creation of new values, such as mutual trust and forgiveness. True, the nature of things may seem hard at times; disease germs and our native limitations, cyclone and earthquake, may impair or may destroy our networks of value; but one fact we must never forget: in the main, the Mind which made these values possible to begin with has *continued* to make them and others possible.

There have been dark days followed, however, by renaissance and reformation. One civilization falls, another arises. There is war, but coexistent are enough areas of peace to make waging war possible. Total evil is self-destructive. Fatigue and weariness come, but so do sleep and the next morning. Illness is often succeeded by recovery. Mental maladjustment there may be, but enough mental strength is left to allow healing and readjustment. There is hate, but there is also the love which hate offends and then succumbs to.

The cosmic Mind is not only the creator of value possibilities, but he is also their Continuer. The problem of evil must not be minimized, but the problem would not be so striking unless a fair inventory of the human situation served to show that values do in the main continue when man so wills. Even when any individual or nation fails, the opportunity for the realization of values goes on by another route; values crushed to earth rise again.[5]

The moral conditions of human fulfillment. Indeed, we must not discount the significance of a fact about our universe revealed by our abuses of the possible good. Human beings cannot escape conditions to which their ventures in value are subject. They are free to choose among the laws by which they will live (but laws that they cannot make or consequences they cannot escape). If they choose the ways of justice, certain consequences follow within their very natures and in their interactions with others, just as surely as health and vitality follow upon the use of proper food, rest, and exercise. They may choose justice, but they cannot change the consequences flowing from injustice any more than they can avoid fatigue and illness after they have abused their physical energies. The fact is that men cannot play fast and loose with their own lives and their universe. Men live in a universe in which there is a moral structure as well as a physical structure. If they defy the moral structure, their defiance illustrates it.

But while most human beings come to realize that there are physical and biological laws by which they must abide if they would exist and be healthy, they sometimes never quite recognize the *moral conditions*, or moral laws, which need to be observed if men are to realize the best which is possible in their lives. They come to see that if they disobey a physical law (such as exceeding a certain speed on the highway, or working harder than the body allows), they "can't get away with it." But they suspect that they can be selfish, merciless, cowardly, prejudiced, lazy, and irresponsible; and they think that they do "get away with it" because they go on living physically and biologically.

Some readers will have read the classic exposition of this theory of morality in the first and second books of Plato's *Republic*. There are many in our day who would agree with the comment that Plato's Glaucon made in his day about what a man would do if he were given a magic ring that could make him invisible.

No one, it is commonly believed, would have such iron strength of mind as to stand fast in doing right or keep his hands off other men's goods, when he could go into the marketplace and fearlessly help himself to anything he wanted, enter houses and sleep with any woman he chose, set prisoners free and kill men at his pleasure, and in a word go about men with the powers of a god. . . . Every man believes that wrongdoing pays him personally much better, and, according to this theory, that is the truth. Granted full license to do as he liked, people would think him a miserable fool if they found him refusing to wrong his neighbors or to touch their belongings, though in public they would keep up a pretence of praising his conduct, for fear of being wronged themselves.[6]

Much of the story of mankind is told in these words, is it not? The man who would rather suffer than cause unnecessary suffering to others, the man who is humbler, kind, industrious, frugal, gracious, courageous, meek, honest, tolerant, cooperative, generous, and forgiving—such a man, it is said, always ends up crucified and buried, with no hope of resurrection.

But we have no sooner uttered these words than we begin to see that these traits of human beings, if realized in more lives, would immediately dispel the major part of human suffering and evil. To be sure, these traits need to be accompanied by a deeper and broader understanding of human nature and the world in which we live; kindness and courage without intelligent understanding of the individual or the cause for which they are expended can, like Don Quixote, create so much havoc in the world. Yet, let human beings who exemplify such traits be the fathers and mothers, the laborers, employers, teachers, doctors, artists, lawyers, pastors, scientists, merchants—let these persons make and support social laws and institutions, and our society becomes transformed not, to be sure, into a hedonist's paradise, but into a culture in which human beings may grow and confidently cooperate in the realization of the best which human nature and Nature makes possible.

The universe in which we live does, then, lay down conditions which encourage or discourage human growth and the increase of values. Human beings are not forced to take one path in value realization rather than another, but if they take the low road, they are forced to live a makeshift existence, unblessed by self-confidence or the trust of others.

The nature of moral law. The reader has no doubt been ready for some time to ask: Do you mean that there is one basic moral direction to the universe, that there is some basic standard by which men should live? The answer is yes. We have said that the universe has a moral order which man cannot break with impunity. We are now saying that there is a fundamental moral law for all men, a law which is consistent with their nature as creative, rational beings.

The nature of this law must be understood. A moral law is a statement of what *ought* to be, not of what *is* or *must* be. It does not describe specific actions for all men to enact on pain of death. It is a principle or norm which, if intelligently applied to human situations, will allow persons to make the most of their potentialities. A moral law is not a formula analogous to a scientific formula.

For example, the discovery of the scientific formula "force equals mass times acceleration" made it possible for men to design automobiles, steam engines, and every other power engine. Is there a similar formula for ethical living which governs the discovery of human values? Hardly. The physical formula expresses what things actually do. An ethical principle is not a description of *some specific actions* which men perform or ought to perform, but it expresses a principle or norm to guide the specific choices of all men.

This guiding principle has been already mentioned, but we may take another approach. If men like Copernicus, Galileo, and Newton, to restrict ourselves to physical scientists, has not been honest with their data, self-disciplined and persistent in inquiry, courageous in the face of possible failure and social intimidation—indeed, if scientists the world over had not been men of industry, cooperative and unselfish in sharing their discoveries—would the world have enjoyed the results of scientific method? Men for ages have been seeking physical comfort and well-being, social security and order, individual and social freedom, and the general improvement of the race and individual. Would these goals have been approached without the ever-renewed moral discipline of scientists? True, scientists have had their shortcomings as well as their virtues, but the fact stands that their achievement has depended on certain basic attitudes. Too frequently like other specialists, they have shown less concern in their social vision, but even here there are signs of change. For example, in 1941 there came out of the British Association for the Advancement of Science an announcement of "its decision to join with American Scientists in preparing a Democratic Charter of Science to be observed by scientists throughout the world. The first principle to be laid down will be that the fellowship of the commonwealth of science has service to all mankind as its highest aim, and the whole world as its outlook. The Charter will not recognize any barriers of race, creed, or clan."

Are not the scientists here appealing to the guiding principle for all ethical action, a principle which they learned from some source other than science? Is it not true that insofar as men have not willed to be just and merciful, they have been forced to forego much of the good which this world makes possible? Grant that there is much in the world which hampers even man's best efforts: can an objective view of human history contradict the basic truth in the following generalization? If human beings had been willing to respect personality, in themselves and others (as Kant, formalizing the wisdom of the ages, said), if men had refused to use other human beings as mere means to their ends, would not the human spirit have built a society in which the weak and the strong worked together for mutual growth? But rather than sustaining a rich balance of the values of life, men have wasted their substance, and the result has been so much needless pain, despair, and misery. When men prostitute their own abilities and energies, when they abuse and selfishly take advantage of the good available in the lives of others, they accelerate and accumulate evils. But once men develop the willingness to share each other's failures and successes, once they determine to let nothing stand in the way of the development of human relations inspired by tolerance, cooperation, and the search for broader visions of truth and deeper experiences of beauty, they can march together, in cooperation with the cosmic Mind, in the growth of creative and responsible human souls. Is there any reasonable doubt about the central direction in which our value-ventures must go if we are to live in this universe with mutual dignity and security?

Someone will say that to talk thus is to hide behind broad generalizations, when our great need is to break down generalizations into specific commands or imperatives. The reply is that any moral standard which prescribes some one particular form of behavior (such as: Never lie! Never steal!) for every situation is not in fact the kind of guide which will help us in concrete human situations. There is no substitute for intelligent judgment in the application of a moral principle. To be sure: Love one another! is itself likely to become a "sounding brass" or "tinkling cymbal" unless it is translated, for example, into the concrete measures needed in relations between father and mother, parents and children, family and family, teacher and pupil, and pupil and pupil. The concrete expression of love between father and mother, between parent and child, depends upon the nature and specific attitudes of each in concrete situations. Every bit of wisdom at our disposal is needed to work out the concrete meaning of love toward our friends *and* our enemies.

The meaning of God's goodness. Fortunately, we do not need the specific solution to these problems to answer the broader question we are facing: What is the moral law which, if realized in human relations, would indeed produce a human situation that justifies belief in a God of goodness? If our argument is at all sound, we may now say (assuming that the problem of evil can be handled) that the cosmic Agent is not merely an intelligent, creative, Mind. He is a God who not only provides the conditions for the realization of human values, but also decrees that man, in order to achieve the best there is in this world, must practice justice, love, mercy, and walk humbly. Ours is indeed a universe which creates and perpetuates life; in it mathematical and physical order are dominant. But it does more than that. It also prepares men and women for fellowship in the creation of a realm in which men may help each other to realize the best possible in their lives.

It is as if God had said: "Rather than make outright a man and a society in which my will shall automatically be done, as happens among physical things,

I shall make men with physical and intellectual ability, with a wide variety of wants, emotions, and feelings, and with a will which can turn them to realization of the values and ideals their intelligence discerns as they live with each other and in my world. I know that they can hurt each other, that they can act, for they have been given freedom to will and think as if the world and their own minds and bodies belonged only to them for them to use as they please. I know that they can harm the innocent, that they can destroy many possibilities of value and thus forego blessings and undergo hardships far from the moral norms which guide my own thinking and action and which must ultimately guide theirs. But my moral purpose shall be eternal. *They* shall have the joy of cocreation; *they* shall participate in the development of their own characters and personalities; *they* shall know the meaning of self-command in the interest of a worthwhile objective; and *they* shall complete, as it were, the creation. This is the norm for all values everywhere, and this is my task. Mine will it be to establish and preserve the best conditions I can for the realization of the range of values accessible to all kinds of humanity. I shall not swerve from this course because some fatten themselves at the expense of their neighbors; nor shall I be deterred even by war and torture. This is to be a creative world, a drama of life with its rules and its limits, broad but determinative. Some things men can forever depend upon me to do; some effects shall follow dependably from some causes, for I am the source of these regularities. But men will never know the real kingdom of heaven, the creative joys of helping each other and their children to grow, unless *they* seek and find!"[7]

LINK SIX: THE SIGNIFICANCE OF AESTHETIC EXPERIENCE

Aesthetic Experience not a mere addition to human experience. We need constantly to remind ourselves that the mind of man is a varied unity, that his functions are not separated from each other by partitions. The experience of beauty is the experience of a thinking, feeling, willing, and oughting mind. Even if these capacities are not weakened by a neglect of the beautiful, there is no question that the quality of human existence would be impoverished without the aesthetic experiences made possible through nature and the arts. Let human beings be deaf to sounds or insensitive to their expressive possibilities, let them be blind to colors, let them be unresponsive to the sublime or to the tragic—and we begin to realize how the aesthetic experience in all its varied manifestations can contribute to the enrichment of human life.

We must also remember that in his aesthetic experience, whether as artist or appreciator, man is creative. Thus, Beethoven's aesthetic experience in feeling and composing all the meaning in the Fifth Symphony is a re-creation of his life, an extension of its potentialities, and a possible enrichment of quality of life in those who listen. In the arts we have a vast range of conscious human experience which once more distinguishes man from animal. Here the human mind is creating again, this time using the properties of wood, stone, and metals (properties which it did not create initially) for the expression of the meanings man finds aesthetically significant.

If man is to receive satisfaction in his urge to achieve aesthetic value, it must be in a kind of universe which, within limits, conspires with his efforts.

Most of us take for granted the aesthetic quality of our experiences, the fragrance, the delicate colors and structures of flowers, the freshness of laughter, the patterns of music, the proportions of natural and manufactured objects. We seldom ask ourselves whether the experience of beauty and art can ever be supplanted by any other experience without loss to the quality of human existence.

Can we not agree, to begin with, that whatever the ultimate nature of aesthetic experience is, whatever its cognitive value, there is no denying the difference aesthetic experience has made to human existence? Happily, there is no difficulty in finding agreement among different aestheticians on one point: life without aesthetic experience is impoverished in quality and weakened in its ability to grow. Thus an author[8] recently held that "the immediate aim of fine art is to feed intrinsic perception." This means that, in the presence of an aesthetic object, the human being's imagination and feeling are enthralled and expanded, and his associations and desires are so guided that "the backgrounds of memory, knowledge, personality, and character are opened up and allowed . . . freedom."[9] The self is no longer engrossed in the practical concerns of life, nor in gaining knowledge either for practical purposes or for its own sake. "In aesthetic experience, feeling and imagination are freed from the narrowness of a specific practical connection and are more ample and more fertile, as, indeed, all the perceptive powers are."[10] But, what is more important for our purposes, this author goes on: "If we define the spiritual life as a life lived for the spirit of the living, for the intrinsic substance and value of the living itself and the heightening of the self which goes with this, the aesthetic experience, with its concern for intrinsic fullness of objective experience is plainly a part of the spiritual life."[11]

Because the aesthetic experience does develop and sharpen the feelings and imagination, and thereby a person's interests and values, because it sensitizes his vision of what is good in human conduct and in the world about him, it necessarily leaves its stamp upon the moral aspirations and social outlook of a human being. Were not the aesthetic experience such a tonic, were not its effects upon the emotions, feelings, and outlook of human beings so profound, masterminds like Plato would have been less concerned about the problems of censoring the artist. We are not dealing here with a luxury, though the majority of human beings act as if the beautiful is an unnecessary addition. However we ultimately define it and its status, there is no doubt that the depth, the variety, and the very zest of human life is affected by aesthetic experience.

Aesthetic experience as another creative relation between man and the world. We must—if only out of a sense of inadequacy—resist the temptation to become involved in the discussion of whether beauty is real independent of man's experience, or whether it is simply one of the ways a man can feel when he experiences certain perceptual objects; or we may have to accept another position.

Philosophers, it is true, have frequently used the beauties of nature as direct argument for God. Much there is in nature, in its microscopic patterns as well as in the beauty which the naked eye can see, which suggests the reality of a Being who is interested in quality and form as well as content. There is much to suggest the Artist as well as the Mathematician, the Artist whose powers, expressed in myriad forms, seem to give birth in beauty as well as mere order. There are those who would argue that all order is ultimately the order of Beauty.

Suggestive as this line of reasoning may be, we should prefer to say that the world we live in is not so much beautiful as it is the sponsor of the many potentialities for beauty awaiting sensitive appreciation and disciplined skill. Nature's children seem not only to find her own forms worth imitating, or at least suggestive, but they then go on to build (using their own inherited abilities) cathedrals and symphonies, epic poems, sonnets and lyrics, sculptures and paintings. And these abilities, we must remember, bear witness to a life within them nurtured and inspired by the very processes which constitute their being. The beauty men experience is *their* beauty created *with the help and suggestion of nature*. Whatever the structure of the world to which man sensitively responds, this much must be said. Nature, including here all the experiences man can have in the world, does mean more to man and can mean more to him in his capacity as artist than she could mean otherwise. But the artistry in man is evoked, nurtured, and developed in interaction with the universe that brought him into being. If nature is with man in his scientific enterprises, she is with him in his aesthetic experience and creation.

Is nature, then, as might appear in a purely scientific perspective, a skeleton of orderly patterns without beauty? This view is possible only after we have already decided to think of beauty as a garment spun by human imagination in order to clothe the dry bones of what is assumed to be "the real world." Leave out any reference to the enjoyment of the patterns in nature as humanly experienced, see the world through the nonevaluative eye of science or the purely practical concern for prediction, and the beauty as such may indeed seem a meaningless addition to nature. But the fact seems to be that nature does her work in forms and patterns which find a sensitive response and make the difference between light and darkness in man's life, whether he encounters them in flower and field, in physical and animal structure, or in crystal and rainbow. On the other hand, as Tennant says:

> If we do apply this category of design to the whole time process, the beauty of Nature may not only be assigned a cause but also a meaning, or a revelational function . . . If Nature's beauty embody a purpose of God, it would seem to be a purpose for man, and to bespeak that God is "mindful of him." Theistically

regarded, Nature's beauty is of a piece with the world's intelligibility and with its being a theater for moral life; and thus far the case for theism is strengthened by aesthetic considerations.[12]

LINK SEVEN: RELIGIOUS EXPERIENCE AS CONFIRMATORY

The human significance of religious experience. Here I am assuming that the experience of God in itself does not provide adequate *independent* justification for the belief in any specific view of God. Sincere religious persons, we saw, speak in many tongues when it comes to describing in any detail the God they experience. Moreover, when they do interpret their experience, they are forced to speak in words that are coined to express other ranges of experience and tradition and which actually convey no significant meaning to those who do not have the experience or live in the tradition.

This, however, is not to deny the existence of an experience which is a vital, creative, and transforming factor in the life of the experient. Religious experience is not to be dealt with highhandedly and reduced to emotional tonics peculiar to *Homo sapiens*. Yet we felt the need for evidence in other areas to help us choose among the interpretations of God, and even more, to furnish grounds other than that provided by the testimony of the experients themselves, in order to evaluate the evidential value of religious experience.[13]

The common core of all religious experience, among laymen or among mystics, is that there is a Being, independent of the human mind, an objective Presence, or "More," as William James called it, that is not only as real as any other existence, but more significant than any other existent being. Added to this core is the conviction that man never finds his greatest good, his "home," apart from the God thus immediately enjoyed. For in religious experience one stands in the very grip of the Greatest Good, the Ultimately Real, and he knows that (in basic terms) his Redeemer liveth.

The moment we leave this common core to assert that God is a Person, a Redeemer (in a narrower Christian sense), a Father, or an Impersonal One, the Absolute, the Life of Nature, or any other specific view of God, we feel the need of other considerations to guide our belief. Yet we cannot deny that the religious experience points beyond itself to a Being which inspires it. Even though it yields no clear outline of God and his relation to the universe and man, its creative power and suggestiveness would stand as a tremendous fraud in a universe which has no real place for God.

Indeed, as part of a wider teleological argument, the evidential value of religious experience increases, and the experience of God serves to confirm the basic contention in the argument as a whole. If there is ground for believing in a Person whose purpose is the creative growth and development of all values and of human values in particular, then there is every reason to suppose that this

God would make himself felt in the lives of men, indirectly through natural processes, but directly (given certain conditions) in religious experience. The fact of religious experience, then, is consistent with what we would have expected from our hypothesis. The more exact meaning of the experience, on the other hand, may be further developed in the light of the hypothesis explored on other grounds without excluding religious experience itself.

NOTES

1. See Joseph Butler's *Analogy of Religion* (1736), and William Paley's *Natural Theology* (1802). See Frederick Ferré's "Introduction" to selections from the latter (1963).

2. Frederick R. Tennant, *Philosophical Theology* 2 vols. (Cambridge: Cambridge University Press, 1930).

3. See Peter A. Bertocci andd R. M. Millard, *Personality and the Good. Psychological and Ethical Perspectives* (New York: David McKay Co., 1963); Peter A. Bertocci, *The Person God Is* (New York: Humanities Press, 1970).

4. Tennant, *Philosophical Theology*, 2: 102.

5. This fact represents the meaning of *providence* and the *general grace* of God in religious terms.

6. Plato, *Republic*, trans. Francis M. Cornford (New York: Oxford University Press, 1945), Book II, p. 360.

7. See D. Elton Trueblood, *The Logic of Belief* (New York: Harper & Bros., 1942). Trueblood presents similar conclusions but different interpretations of moral, aesthetic, and religious experience. Trueblood is influenced by the scholarly and sensitive treatment of religious and philosophical issues in William Temple, *Nature, Man and God* (New York: Macmillan, 1934).

8. D. W. Gotshalk, *Art and the Social Order* (Chicago: University of Chicago Press, 1947), p. 45.

9. Ibid., p. 23.

10. Ibid., p. 19.

11. Ibid., p. 26.

12. Tennant, *Philosophical Theology*, 2: 93.

13. See H. D. Lewis, *Our Experience of God* (New York: Macmillan, 1960); also John E. Smith, "Religious Experience," in *Encyclopedia Britannica; Experience and God* (New York: Oxford University Press, 1968); idem, *The Analogy of Experience* (New York: Harper & Row, 1973).

PART THREE

Religious Experience and Religious Expression

INTRODUCTION BY JOHN E. SMITH

T HE chief concern of this section is to understand the nature and role of experience in religion and the manner in which experience is articulated in religious language.

In "The Linguistic Key," Frederic Ferré deals with a number of fundamental issues raised by contemporary philosophers concerning the interpretation of theistic claims. He asks whether they can be understood as empirical hypotheses which might be falsified or as unfalsifiable linguistic conventions. He sets forth the verificationist theory of meaning and estimates its impact on the philosophy of religion. In the course of the analysis, noncognitive, quasi-cognitive, evaluational, and heuristic interpretations of religious language are put forward and appraised.

In the next essay, John E. Smith discusses the question of the meaning and possibility of experiencing God and argues that, although mysticism may be thought to be the model of such experience, it does not provide the final answer to the question. The meaning of mystical immediacy depends on the very dialectic the mystic seeks to transcend, and the Western religions have all stressed the need for a *medium* of divine disclosure—person, word, event—as distinct form mystical union. Since modern empiricism has left us with the dichotomy of either "immediately present" or "inferred," a way must be found in experience to transcend these alternatives so that we are not left with the gulf between the God who is *present* in experience and the *must be* God of argument. A consideration of the experiential elements in Saint Anselm leads to the possibility of finding the "is" of God in the "must be" of argument.

In "On Religious Myths," Joseph Kockelmans maintains that most philosophers and scientists who concern themselves with religious myth work with a conception of myth which is both too wide and too narrow. Consequently, he attempts to develop a conception of myth in the light of which the various theories developed by philosophers and scientists can be properly understood and critically evaluated. In addition, he asks the question as to how one is to deal with the myths constituting an integral part of every revealed religion. He rejects demythization and proposes instead a version of demythologization.

Kenneth Schmitz's essay, "Restitution of Meaning in Religious Speech," focuses on the typical characteristics of religious language and the confessed inadequacy of religious speech. Distinguishing between language, usage, and discourse, Schmitz sees in the latter a modification of language in the interest of a critical examination of the cognitive responsibilities of talking about God. He considers three strategies of discourse; the task of accounting for the survival of religious speech in the face of taboo; the problem of restoring meaning to such speech in terms of theoretical discourse; and a threefold recovery, metaphysical, dialectical, and empirical, wherein the very inadequacy of expression indicates the divine reality intended, the sacred presence is sustained by both presence and absence in the religious symbol, and the reliability of religious speech is preserved.

In "The Dialectic of the Mystical Experience," Louis Dupré returns to the problem of the nature of the sacred previously discussed in his essay in Part I. Here he points out that . . . . the term *mystical* should not be restricted to exceptional and strictly subjective experiences. Some degree of passive union is at the core of all religion, including the ordinary and the communal. Different spiritual traditions conceive of this union in different ways. The monistic trend of the Vedanta aims at a total submersion of the finite in the infinite. Negative theology modified this ideal of total union by insisting on the continued reality of the finite while asserting simultaneously the nameless otherness of the transcendent and its full immanence. Christian mysticism, especially since the sixteenth century, has attempted to extend the dwelling presence of the transcendent to the finite *as such* in and through God's creative act.

In the next essay, "The Experience of the Holy and the Idea of God," John E. Smith proposes to reverse the procedure followed by Rudolf Otto in his well-known book, *The Idea of the Holy,* by starting with the distinguishing marks of the experience of the holy and then passing on to the idea of God developed within the tradition of historical religion. Starting with a distinction between ordinary activities and situations in life and those "crucial" occasions—birth, marriage, puberty, choice of vocation, death—upon which we are arrested and forced to focus on the meaning and destiny of life as a whole, the author delineates the awesomeness and seriousness of the holy in relation to all that we think and do. The idea and experience of the holy in and through mundane life provides a basis on which the God of the biblical tradition can be *recognized* when he is disclosed in revelatory events.

Chapter 11

THE LINGUISTIC KEY
Frederick Ferré

THEISTIC LANGUAGE AND FALSIFICATION

One of the logically most interesting discoveries that has emerged from the metareligious controversies of modern times is the sheer fact that despite vast increases in scientific knowledge, theism has survived. It has adjusted to the radical and repeated shocks that it has suffered; it has absorbed them, somehow; and it has continued to command the allegiance of large numbers of modern, well-informed people.

The Empirical Hospitality of Theistic Utterances

In times of tension or conflict, when group interests collide, as in war or civil strife, the claim is often heard that "God is on our side."[1] This very expression, indeed, is found in one of the verses of the well-known civil rights song, "We Shall Overcome." It is no merely abstract example; it is living speech. How, then, shall we understand it?

1. A *falsifiable empirical hypothesis?* One possible interpretation of this utterance would be as a hypothesis used to make predictions about specific expectations of future experience. Then it would have a kind of meaning much like the factual claim: "The sheriff is on our side," which, in context, might very likely mean that at the crucial moment the sheriff will use his powers to aid and not to harass "our" side.

From: Frederick Ferré, *Basic Modern Philosophy of Religion* (New York: Scribner, 1967), pp. 335–70.

It *can* be so used and so interpreted. But the price of such an interpretation is extremely high and in fact seldom paid by modern users of this language. Let us see why this is so.

In the case of a genuine empirical hypothesis, as we have seen, the hypothesis must be held (as the word itself reflects) "hypothetically" or *conditionally*, only as far as is permitted by the actual deliverances of experience. To qualify logically as a hypothesis, that is, a claim must be affirmed with the tacit acknowledgement that it may very well turn out not to be so at all. Thus, if the sheriff regularly breaks our heads and beats our women, we will be prepared to concede that he is "not on our side after all." But the theist is seldom willing to utter his words about God's approval in the same tentative, conditional mood. To do so would require him to be prepared to acknowledge that God, whom he understands to be the supreme source of value and power, might very well *not* be on the side of other values that he holds with great intensity.

This is an expensive concession. It opens the door to radical conflicts between profoundly important valuations. Occasionally, doubtless, this concession is actually made. One good instance is that of the rabbi, Gamaliel, who is reported to have advised the council of Israel against executing Saint Peter and other early Christians on the hypothetical premises that: ". . . if this plan or this undertaking is of men, it will fail; but if it is of God, you will not be able to overthrow them. You might even be found opposing God" (Acts 5:38–39,RSV). On the whole, however, it is with quite a different attitude that theists approach their utterances. Concerning hotly held values it is hard to be as tentative and generous as Gamaliel seems to have been. The hypothetical *attitude* is not a characteristic accompaniment of such passionately important utterances as religious claims are typically found to be.

A second requirement of an empirical hypothesis is that specific experiences be acknowledged as falsifying, or as tending (eventually) actually to falsify, the assertion being made. Even if an apparently open and tentative attitude is claimed by the theist who says that God is on his side, this is not sufficient to establish his claim as an empirical hypothesis as long as every potentially falsifying experience is turned aside or interpreted in an innocuous way. This, however, seems to be exactly what is characteristic of modern advocates of theism. Not only is it obvious that they no longer stake belief—*à la Elijah* (see 1 Kings 18:17–40)—on "signs and wonders," but also that they are highly skilled at evading indefinitely the moment when this particular experience or *that* unwelcome turn of events must be admitted as actually falsifying or tending toward a reasonable rejection of the "hypothesis" they support.

A. GENERAL LOGICAL CONSIDERATIONS

Such a factual claim is an empirical hypothesis and, as every empirical hypothesis must, conveys definite expectations about the future. These expectations, under the appropriate circumstances, will either be satisfied or disappointed. If, when the crucial moment arrives, the sheriff's actions do in fact help "our" side in specifiable ways, then the hypothesis is to that extent "verified"; but if, when the confrontation comes about, the sheriff descends on us in fury, then our earlier hypothesis is shown to be false. It is "falsified."

Clearly, the *disappointment* of our expectations is more definitely revealing about the reliability of our hypothesis than their *satisfaction* would be. The sheriff could be secretly on "their" side plotting a dastardly trick for some later time even while acting in this one crucial situation as though to satisfy the expectations derivable form our hypothesis. Verification, mere compatibility with expectations, is always inconclusive. But no one *really* on our side (we might stipulate) would break our heads and beat our women. ("If this is a friend, I don't need any enemies!") Therefore a single clear case of falsification can count for more, in deciding the truth value of an assertion, than even a large number of inconclusive verifications.[2]

Of course this does not mean that all genuine empirical hypotheses have to be actually falsified. Some empirical hypotheses happen to be consistently re-liable in the expectations they support, and it would be absurd to mistrust them just because they have never been known to let us down. But in all such cases we are able to specify what "letting us down" *would* entail. Perhaps the sheriff *is* squarely on our side; then, as long as he remains so, the hypothesis will not be falsified in the future; but we are in no doubt about what *would* falsify the hypothesis if he should ever change his position.

Sometimes, however, it is hard to tell whether or not a hypothesis has yet been falsified. We have been considering only crucial moments—"moments of truth"—but much of our experience may be more ambiguous. The sheriff acts this way on Monday, another way on Tuesday; he smiles guardedly on Wednesday, but takes some of "our" people into "protective custody" on Thursday. The logical situation is complicated by these considerations, but not radically altered: we still know what sort of definite expectations our hypothesis, "The sheriff is on our side," properly leads us to form, and consequently we still know what kinds of experiences count for and against the hypothesis. The evidence is not conclusive, perhaps, but it can still be generally acknowledged as evidence. Thus, the logical status of our affirmation that the sheriff is on our side is never seriously in question. It is an empirical hypothesis because it encourages certain specifiable experiential expectations and is incompatible with other specifiable experiences that it assures us we need not expect.

B. APPLICATION

Very well, if this is the logic of "The sheriff is on our side," how well does this accord with the modern theistic use of "God is on our side"? We are certainly tempted to anticipate a good deal of similarity: not only are the utterances alike in grammatical form, but, even more, it appears that the theistic expression, like the assertion about the sheriff, has a function in forming expectations about future experience.[3] In context, the intent of this sentence would seem to be: "God is on our side *and therefore our cause will inevitably triumph."* Or in other words, the moral preference of the universe's source of being guarantees that future experience will accord with "our" values and expectations, not with those of the opposition. Such values and expectations can be specified and translated into detailed programs. Contrary experiences can also be specified. It seems, then, that "God is on our side" is a straightforward empirical hypothesis very much of one piece, logically, with "The sheriff is on our side."

"God is on our side," we are told, but our people go on year after year in suffering and degradation; never mind, "Whom God loves, he chastens" (cf. Rev. 3:19), is the answer.

"God is on our side," we are assured, but the other side lives in prosperity and honor; fear not, God "sends rain on the just and on the unjust" (Mt. 5:45, RSV).

"God is on our side," we sing, but we must be prepared for any eventuality, and must certainly not lay down any conditions or time limits or ultimata to God as to what he must do to justify our belief; on the contrary, "We must not put the Lord to the test. . . ." (1 Cor. 10:9, RSV; cf. Mt. 4:7).

We must not put the Lord to the test? But if this warning is heeded, we may not in good logic consider our utterances about the Lord and his ways to be empirical hypotheses. We must not put the Lord to the test? Then literally *any* empirical state of affairs will be compatible with the cry, "God is on our side." And if that is so, then the theist is in principle unable to meet the basic requirement of an empirical hypothesis, that it be incompatible with some specifiable state of affairs.[4] It is hospitable to any and every empirical situation and "verified" by all.

If "God is on our side" and our fortunes prosper, God may be thanked for his blessings. If "God is on our side" and our fortunes sag—even to the point of ignominious death—still God may be praised and trusted. Some believers may fall away in adversity, but this (to unfalsifiable theism) is only "loss of faith," analogous in its religious immaturity to the child who loses faith in God merely because a Christmas present long prayed for fails to arrive; it is not an appropriate response for mature theism, we are told, under any merely empirical circumstances.

Our recent mention of death may suggest a possible opportunity for empirical verification of falsification beyond the grave.[5] But severe logical difficulties weigh heavily against such a proposal. First, there is obviously a radical difference, at best, between what is meant by "empirical" in our ordinary discourse and the alleged postmortem experiences that would be needed on this approach. It is hard to know how to go about specifying, even generally, what the nature of these experiences would have to be like. And we are *ex hypothesi* certainly not in a position to report on the adequacy of these specifications, even if we could work them out, to the living world whose tests they are supposed to be. Second, "verification" beyond this life would be vulnerable to the same open-ended inconclusiveness we have noted already, while the logic of "falsification," too, would seem not to be changed by being merely extended into another life. That is, if appearances in the "next world" seemed contrary to theistic expectations, this "fact" might be taken as one more "test of faith" to be patiently and adoringly endured. Finally, if *no* experience after the termination of physical life should be the case, it is hard to understand how this could conceivably constitute "falsification" of any hypothesis. Falsification *for whom?* The proposal of "eschatological verification" appears therefore to be unable to assimilate theistic utterances into the class of empirical hypotheses.

We seem, then, to be driven to the conclusion that theistic expressions like "God is on our side" or "God made the world" do not typically function among modern theists as empirical hypotheses, despite their superficial resemblances to "The sheriff is on our side" or "The universe began with a big bang." We have not denied the possibility of such a use. There are biblical examples, such as those of Gamaliel, Elijah, Gideon (cf. Jg. 6:11 ff.), or the like, of theistic assertions that appear to follow the logic of clearly falsifiable empirical hypotheses. But the danger of an empirical hypothesis is that it may be disconfirmed by experience. And this is a danger, as we have argued, that most sophisticated theists take pains to avoid, pleading "maturity" of faith against those who would rashly "put the Lord to the test." If the kind of meaning expressed by the language of such sophisticated theists is not that of essentially falsifiable empirical hypotheses, however, what kind of meaning can they claim?

2. *Unfalsifiable linguistic conventions?* Another kind of meaning, and one which permits language to manifest the unlimited sort of compatibility with empirical circumstances that sophisticated theists claim for their utterances, is the meaning possessed by definitions.

A. GENERAL LOGICAL CONSIDERATIONS

Earlier in this essay we had occasion to notice the unfalsifiable character of linguistic rules of usage. Since definitions are useful to us precisely as recording our determinations to employ language in specified ways *whatever* the facts may happen to be, we do not allow any state of affairs to "disconfirm" or "falsify" a definition—though we may evaluate it in other respects with reference to what is empirically discoverable. Is this the kind of unfalsifiability, resting on the security of a linguistic rule of usage, that the utterance "God is on our side" may properly be thought to have?

If so, it might be expected to resemble in logic the similar-sounding expression: "The captain of our team is on our side," when, in context, it is clear that a linguistic determination to link "the captain of our team" with "our side" is being expressed. The problem might arise for someone unfamiliar with the rules of discourse governing the game in question, especially if the captain of our team happens to be a particularly inept player who frequently manages to give the team's advantage to the other side.

"Look!" someone might say, half in exasperation, half in jest, "that captain of ours is the most useful man on *their* team."

"Oh," says the naive visitor, not understanding at all, "but why isn't he wearing their uniform, and why isn't he listed in their roster of players?"

"I was just joking," might come the reply. "He's the captain of our team."

"But you just said . . .," begins the baffled visitor.

"Of course, but you mustn't take my remark in the wrong way. My statement was a joke—if it was—only because it's obviously *impossible*. The captain of *our* team has to be on *our* side."

"Now just a moment," says our visitor, shifting to the offensive, "if the captain's sympathies are really with the opposing team, or if he's entered into some secret deal with the opposing coach, or the like, it's not a bit impossible that he's in fact on their team."

"That kind of fact wouldn't count," says our would-be comedian, "because the captain of our team, if he's really captain of *our* team *must* be on our side. It doesn't matter how he may betray our side *qua* wicked bribetaker or bumbling fool; he's on our side *qua* captain of our team, come what may."

In this exchange we see that our hapless wit has been driven to defend the necessity of his statement, "The captain of our team is on our side," by withdrawing it from relevance to matters of fact. *Come what may* he intends to keep "captain of our team" linked inseparably to "on our side." One of the marks of this sort of stipulative meaning is precisely this: that it is appropriately defended or attacked only on the basis of linguistic proprieties, and that we are free to maintain it apart from any issues of fact that may be raised against it. It is compatible with all possible empirical states because it is dependent on none. Its security is a matter of syntax, dependent on a rule and not an experience.

This being so, we can appreciate why syntactical meaning of this sort cannot possibly be expected to convey any factual meaning. No facts whatever are being claimed by the expression "The captain of our team is on our side" when that expression is functioning to record a linguistic necessity, as in our example. This expression, so used, would hold equally well in a world without captains, without teams, without sides. Only a matter of interconnection between symbols is at stake. This may be very important for the possibility of a developed and stable symbolic structure like a language, but it is clearly incapable of informing us about what is or is not the case.

B. APPLICATION

To what extent, then, is the unfalsifiable theistic expression "God is on our side" logically similar to the also unfalsifiable stipulation "The captain of our team is on our side''? There certainly seems to be one great point in common. Both utterances, we gather, are going to be maintained "come what may." But it is very doubtful that defenders of theism will choose to interpret the meaning of their language exhaustively in this way. To do so would be to surrender the logical possibility of saying anything substantive about what is the case. It would be to purchase empirical unfalsifiability at the cost of factual emptiness.[6]

Theism, however, has traditionally been far more than an exercise in linguistic usage. "God is on our side" has been supposed to reflect triumphal beliefs about what is so, not a linguistic convention. The word *gospel,* central for Christian theism, means "good news." Theists cannot take refuge in the kind of security offered by language used analytically without abandoning what is essential to their interest: some significant *reference* beyond the purely linguistic domain.

The utterances of theism can be neither empirical hypotheses nor linguistic conventions, then; and we are left wondering what may be the consequences of this conclusion.

The Cognitive Difficulties of Theistic Utterances

Our scrutiny of the logic of theistic language has resulted in a negative clarification, at least, by firmly excluding such talk from assimilation into two familiar uses of language with which it might otherwise be confused. But many philosophers in the twentieth century think that these two uses are the only two that may be given any role to play in the quest for understanding. If so, this is obviously a most important consequence for philosophy of religion. This is not a position that is entirely satisfactory, as the later argument of this essay will show, but it has much to recommend it and is certainly crucial to any understanding of contemporary metareligious issues. We must come to grips with it.

1. *The verificational analysis of meaning.* There is no great mystery in the essential reasoning behind the verificational approach to meaning, although the clouds of controversy have swirled endlessly around its details.[7] What, after all, is our language properly doing when it is functioning in contexts connected with "truth," or with the business of understanding? It is either establishing and reflecting linguistic conventions (answer the proponents of the view we shall call "verificational analysis") or it is conveying factual information by means of those conventions. We have said enough in the foregoing about the kind of meaning involved in verbal conventions; what is the nature of factual meaning?

Verificational analysts have a clear reply: the factual meaning of a proposition is essentially exhausted by the observations that would be relevant to the proposition's verification. For example, consider the assertion "There is an apple in this basket." What is the factual content of meaning carried by this utterance, in its functioning context, for those who understand and follow the normal verbal conventions of the English language? The verificational analyst directs us to consider what observations or operations would be relevant to verifying our example. This is quite easy: one such observation would be to look or to feel

in the specified basket. Many more potentially verifying observations and operations—means of verifying the proposition in question—can be thought of.
But this is precisely a sign that we really do understand the proposition in
question. What more, factually, could we mean by it? Its whole factual meaning,
we discover, *is* nothing other than the instructions it gives us for obtaining
various experiences of this kind.

This is a portentous discovery, and may be generalized. "Every synthetic
proposition," says A. J. Ayer, "is a rule for the anticipation of future experience
. . ."8; and if this is so, then specifying any statement's factual meaning will
be the same as listing, in specific cases, the particular experiences that ought to
be obtainable if the relevant rules are followed. The experiences that are promised
by a proposition are, of course, the experiences that will tend to verify it; and
once we know what these are, we have the whole descriptive content of the
proposition.

This is the basic argument that lies behind the so-called verification principle
when it alleges that the factual meaning of an informative proposition is to be
found in the methods of its verification. The verification principle gives us a
way of moving from the realm of words, important as they are, into the domain
of experiences, where factual significance is finally rooted.

But this principle gives us still more than this. What if it is found that certain
kinds of allegedly "factual" utterances purport to be "verified" by anything
whatever? We shall be required, clearly, to conclude that such utterances are
quite useless as rules for the anticipation of our future experience, since literally
anything might equally well be anticipated on their basis. This means, however,
that they carry *no* particular factual content. If the verificational analysis of
meaning is correct, language that is functioning neither to reflect verbal conventions nor to provide particular observational expectations is devoid of any
cognitive significance.

We need not remain merely hypothetical in this matter; the utterances of the
sophisticated theist, as we have seen, are characteristically neither merely true
by definition nor empirically "cashable." Such talk, then, according to verificational analysis, is cognitively meaningless.

2. *The cognitive meaninglessness of theistic discourse?* We have seen already
that apparent assertions about God, such as "God is on our side" or, earlier,
"God made the world," or even "God exists," are typically used in an *unfalsifiable* way by modern theists. Is this exactly the same thing as being *unveri-
fiable?* No, not quite, although the temptation is to pass rather easily from one
to the other. Theistic expressions are so hospitable to experience that *any* observation may be taken to "verify" them. In this sense of "verify," they are
among the most "verifiable" utterances that could possibly be. It is precisely
in this that their unfalsifiability consists.

But if so, they lack just the sort of concrete, specific verifiability that is crucial for verificational analysis. They lack definiteness of content. By "meaning" everything—even mutually incompatible things—these utterances forfeit the right to mean anything in particular; by being too hospitable, by excluding nothing, these utterances lose all their distinctive character. And consequently this kind of language falls short on the verification principle of meaning: it adds nothing in particular to our expectations of future experience, nothing that could not have been equally well expected without it. It might just as well not have been uttered, then, from the point of view of successfully (or even unsuccessfully) adding anything to our knowledge of matters of fact.

Further, empirically unfalsifiable language like this displays another interesting logical trait: the contradictory of every so-called assertion is just as "verifiable" as the assertion itself. If "God is on our side" can manifest a logic that is compatible with any observations, come what may, so also can "It is false that God is on our side." What empirical happening could refute the latter? Prosperity for our cause? No; appearances deceive, and even Satan can give worldly blessings. Adversity and suffering? No; this only "confirms" God's hostility. In fact, exactly the same observations that "verify" a theistic expression will serve equally well to "verify" its negation. But if this is so, there is no factual difference in meaning between what appear as contradictories. What fails to differ in meaning even from its direct denial, however, fails altogether in meaning. It literally *says nothing;* it is empty of all descriptive reference.

If this analysis is correct, *nothing is being conveyed* by such expressions as "God is on our side" or "God exists" that could possibly be believed or even disbelieved under the logical circumstances we have uncovered. These utterances are not verbal conventions and are factually empty. There is no way in which we can judge them "true" or "false," since the basis for such judgments has been withdrawn. Their "assertion" or "denial" makes no difference to what we expect to experience. Therefore they are not the sort of utterances that can be genuinely asserted or denied at all. They are *not real assertions,* according to verificational analysis, but are merely pseudopropositions that have long masqueraded as assertions behind their grammatical or linguistic appearance.

The time, then, is at hand for a linguistic reformation, say the proponents of this analysis. We should drop once and for all the ill-fated attempt of traditional philosophy of religion to discuss the reasonableness of belief in the existence of God. All such enterprises are based on logical confusion about the kind of meaning possessed by the language in question. To search for a reasonable justification for believing or disbelieving that "God exists" is to presuppose that the expression "God exists" is capable of being believed or disbelieved; but if it is not an assertion, if it carries no cognitive content, if it is not an appropriate subject for the adjectives *true* or *false,* then all traditional argumentation is wasted effort.

Still, *some* kind of "meaning" must pertain to language about God, because it is language, as we have seen, to which people get deeply attached. It is at least "meaningful" to them in the sense of seeming *important*. If, assuming for the present the verificational analysis of cognitive meaning, we are no longer able to suppose that the language of sophisticated theists can be used to make claims or affirm beliefs or describe anything, we are still entitled, as comprehensive and critical thinkers about religious phenomena, to explore what other kinds of "meaning" this kind of discourse *may* have. But in this process we soon find evidence of the need to go beyond verificational analysis itself.

"NONCOGNITIVE" THEORIES OF THEISTIC LANGUAGE

The tendency among analytical philosophers today is to acknowledge a more flexible, or more inclusive, approach to meaning than did the logical positivists who first launched what we have termed verificational analysis. Even former logical positivists now tend to temper their early zeal by accepting the later teaching of Ludwig Wittgenstein (himself an early shaper of logical positivism) that there are many varieties of meaning in language, and that the meaning of an expression is best determined by examination of its use or function.[9] But this general preference for what we may call "functional analysis" does not itself necessarily involve a repudiation of the general position on *cognitive* meaning that was advanced by verificational analysis. Functional analysis may awaken us to varieties of meaning not brought to light by verificational analysis, but there is no guarantee that these additional varieties of meaning—however interesting or illuminating—will have any role to play in advancing truth or understanding.

Theories of Emotive Function

Language has to do not only with our intellects but also (perhaps primarily) with our emotions. It is one of our most effective means of expressing and arousing feeling. Here we must be very careful: *expressing* and *arousing* feelings is not the same thing as *discussing* them. Talk *about* feelings, such as we expect from psychologists, must obey the rules of cognitive discourse. But language may be quite otherwise in logical function and still have great potency as a vehicle for dealing directly with feelings.

Were we wordless, we might express these feelings through dance or by whistling; the words are not statements *about* anything but, rather, expressions of the feelings themselves. In this function, they cannot be considered literally "true" or "false" any more than a *grand pas* in a ballet could be so considered. They cannot be "believed" or "disbelieved"; they are simply manifested and observed. But, while the emotive functions of language are completely devoid of cognitive use, they can nevertheless be vital; they constitute a kind of meaning for those who use or respond to such utterances; and what words are used may make a great difference to those involved.

1. *The presence of emotive functions.* This much is generally granted by even the most hostile foes of theistic "beliefs." There is no doubt that consideration of the emotive powers of language can illuminate our philosophic understanding of religious phenomena. "God made the world," for example, may owe a great deal of its meaning to the sense of security it fosters in those who hear or use it. "God is on our side" may function powerfully to buoy up sinking emotions; it may be that its emotive function is so valuable to those involved that this largely accounts for the determination of its users to retain the expression, come what may. If so, we are aided by this analysis to understand one possible source of theism's characteristic unfalsifiability. In addition, it is quite evident that many uses of this language in connection with worship, both public and private, are deeply immersed in emotive significance: theistic language may evoke thrills of anticipation and importance, moods of penitence, feelings of acceptance; theistic language may also express sorrow and determination and awe and the unlimited adoration in which the religious consciousness, understood as one's way of valuing most comprehensively and intensively, consists.

2. *The implications of emotive functions.* While we cannot fail to appreciate the help that a proper analysis of the emotive functions of language can give to philosophy of religion, it is hard to maintain for long that the emotive meaning of this discourse is its *only* meaning. Indeed, even aside from other noncognitive functions, such as we shall soon examine, it is difficult to see how the emotive meanings of theistic language can function apart from the reintroduction of *some* kind of dependence on descriptive meaning. Sheer gibberish does not evoke penitence or express feelings of confidence and adoration. Clearly, theistic utterances are not "utterly empty of content" in every respect. There is "content" enough to direct moods, to influence feelings, to express attitudes. If "God is on our side" is able to arouse or express reassurance, this is finally possible only because the user of the language understands *something* by it.

The emotive powers of language are essentially parasitical upon the provision of some kind of descriptive content. Theistic language *does* have emotive meaning. Therefore, it follows, theistic language cannot be entirely vacuous of descriptive definiteness. Already we must break, then, with verificational analysis. That position leaps too quickly from the discovery that many crucial sentences of theists do not function as falsifiable assertions to the conclusion that these utterances are vacuous. But such a leap is clearly mistaken. The words that are used in theistic utterances are not suddenly rendered empty. We understand them because we know how to use them in nontheistic, empirically falsifiable contexts. The words we employ about God—e.g., *loving, powerful, wise,* etc.—borrow descriptive definiteness from ordinary usage. It is this descriptive definiteness that underlies whatever emotive power religious language possesses.

"God"-talk, then, is given content by vivid imagery that has its roots deep in human experience.[40] Only by appealing to such "ultimate images" can we account for the emotive powers that this language commands. Kant may have been right, then, as we suspected, in his view that we "think" (without "cognizing") God in "phenomenal" terms. With that previously puzzling distinction between "thinking" and "cognizing," he may have been anticipating the distinction we must introduce now between the *descriptive content* of an utterance and its *logical function*. To restate Kant's doctrine in our own way: language about God has definiteness only because of its empirical content, but such language does not properly function to make empirical assertions or to give empirical information.

Provision of phenomenal definiteness for theistic language is not only logically essential; it is religiously essential as well. Here we are obliged to take a stand with Hume's Cleanthes on the inevitability of anthropomorphism. Hume is quite right that all conceptual meanings are in the end human meanings; if we "purify" religious conceptions of all finite limitations, we evacuate them of all content— including even emotive content—for finite human thinkers. Squeamishness about anthropomorphism, at root, is embarrassment about what makes real religion possible. Ludwig Feuerbach was justified in thundering:

> Where man deprives God of all qualities, God is no longer anything more to him than a negative being. To the truly religious man, God is not being without qualities . . . . The denial of determinate, positive predicates concerning the divine nature is nothing else than a denial of religion, with, however, an appearance of religion in its favour, so that it is not recognized as a denial; it is simply a subtle, disguised atheism. The alleged religious horror of limiting God by positive predicates is only the irreligious wish to know nothing more of God, to banish God from the mind . . . . He who earnestly believes in the Divine existence is not shocked at the attributing even of gross sensuous qualities to God. He who dreads an existence that may give offence, who shrinks from the grossness of a positive predicate, may as well renounce existence altogether.[11]

The "gross predicates" will not function, for sophisticated modern theists, in empirical hypotheses: but to discover this gives us no license for claiming theistic language to be "empty." What other functions, besides the emotive, do theism's ultimate images perform?

Theories of Conative Function

We "do things" with words.[12] Our language, that is, can function not only to describe, to establish verbal conventions, and to express or evoke emotion, but also to *change the situation* in direct ways. When someone in the due course of an auction sale, for example, says, "I bid five dollars," and the auctioneer says, "Gone," the situation has been changed; something has been done.

What is it that has happened? Are the buyer and the auctioneer describing some happenings going on behind the scenes, apart from their words? No, the words *are* the happenings. In their context, they function to make a contract, to transfer ownership, and to put the bidder five dollars in debt to the auctioneer. It would be absurd to say to the bidder: "But I didn't notice any bidding on your part, before you spoke"; or to the auctioneer: "Can you verify your assertion that this item has 'Gone' for five dollars?" The absurdity rests in the fact that neither party to the transaction is making assertions about anything, and, consequently, we only display our misunderstanding of the situation when we look for "prior" acts of bidding or for evidence of the "truth" of the auctioneer's closing utterance. The buyer's utterance *is* his making a bid; the auctioneer's utterance *is* his closing the proffered contract. Language here is employed to perform actions that *could* have been accomplished, we know, by waggling a finger or banging a gavel. It is an instance of what is called the "performative" use of language.[13] And this use is no more subject to tests of truth or falsity than are finger-waggles or gavel-bangs. All are instances of doing, not asserting.

Performative uses of language of this sort, of which there turn out to be many, may be characterized as having a "conative" function, from the Latin word for an attempt or an undertaking to *do* something. Whenever, in the appropriate circumstances, language is used to make a promise or to place a bet or to take an oath or to declare a truce, or the like, we find the conative dimension of meaning. And since this use of language—asserting nothing—is freed from the requirements of verification or falsification, it may be that theistic expressions are suited for use in some of these ways.

1. *Committing oneself to a way of life.* The currently most prominent conative analysis of theistic language takes the function of such discourse to constitute the active adoption of a whole way of life.[14] When serious and sincere use is made of the utterances of a religion, this must involve a readiness to place the most intensive and comprehensive values of that religion in the position of highest priority in one's own life. This is a doing, an act of commitment. It does not in itself stand subject to "evidence" or "verification." It has not that kind of meaning. When, for instance, a Christian theist says, "I love God," he is best understood, on this conative interpretation, as committing himself to a life of love for his fellow man. And there is New Testament warrant for this essential linkage: "If anyone says,'I love God' and hates his brother, he is a liar . . . . "(1 Jn 4:20).

Not only is this a "doing," it is by far the most important "doing" that we can engage in. Organizing our basic values, attitudes, and dispositions for behavior has a profound impact on all aspects of life. If this is the meaning of the language of the theist, we can appreciate it as immensely fraught with consequences. Little wonder, then, that religious people insist that their language is vitally "meaningful"; nothing could be more "significant" in that sense. In one's choice of religious language one is in effect choosing what to "do" with one's entire life.

2. *Evaluating conative analyses.* It seems evident that we learn a great deal about the logic of theistic language by paying heed to its conative functions. And, of course, in a fuller account much more could be said. The reader is encouraged to think of other, additional things that we "do" with our religious language.[15]

Once again, however, we can see that this kind of meaning is wholly dependent on the provision of some kind of descriptive content. In the case of our example at the auction sale, we know that there is a considerable difference between the meaning of "I bid five dollars" and "I bid fifty dollars." The language employed, for all its performative *use,* is not without descriptive *content.* And this definite content is essential for the very possibility of "doing things" with our speech.

What, then, of the language of sophisticated theism? If it is possible to use it conatively, to commit oneself by means of it to a life of Christian *agape* rather than of Nazi hostility, then there must be a distinguishable descriptive content that undergirds this possibility. And this content is again supplied by theism's ultimate imagery. Just as the expression "I bid five dollars" is not, in context, functioning to describe anything, but its conative meaning is clear only because "bidding five dollars" can be used descriptively and cognitively, so "God made me" may not, in all contexts, be functioning descriptively. But if it can have distinct conative uses, as it does have, we must grant that "God making . . ." and "God acting . . . and "God loving . . . " expressions must have a descriptive use at least within the imaginative myths of religion. Thanks to their ultimate imagery theists are given a basis, as conative analyses show, for the eliciting and ordering of values. Out of all the mass of possibilities, a few intimately interconnected aspects of human experience are displayed in this imagery as deserving unlimited adoration and as being inescapably relevant to all our existence. These selected aspects are those of human personal experience at its best. God, the object of the most intensive and comprehensive valuation, is pictured as no less than supremely *related* to every actuality, no less than supremely *aware,* and no less than supremely *good* in the exercise of his sovereign, creative freedom. Within particular theistic religions like Judaism or Christianity, of course, God is described as much more than this: e.g., as the righteous lawgiver motivated by steadfast love, for Judaism; and, for Christianity, as the self-giving creator-savior whose triune nature is the paradigm of perfect sociality in the life of the Trinity.

But even at the more general level of theism we find a definite selection of values, from the personal rather than the impersonal, and the theist's own evaluations are strongly elicited from this range. What is "most important" in the ultimate scheme of things? The theistic model points to vividness of consciousness, to creative freedom, to moral excellence. What is "most relevant," ultimately inescapable, in the last analysis? Theism turns to the qualities of richest human life as the basis of its representation of the most comprehensive value. In so doing, it urges a way of life and a set of distinctive attitudes. Values are crucially at stake, not just theories.

Assessing the value judgments involved—i.e., applying the criteria of "practical reason" to religious commitments—is neither an easy nor an impartial task. Fundamental valuations can only be measured by taking comparably fundamental valuations as standards. Given this situation the only responsible recourse is to display one's own basic standards as plainly as possible, so that others will be able to judge them openly for themselves, and (no less important) so that one's own judgments may be conscious and critical. Here the basic standards proposed will be the needs of life for both integrity ("unity" or "wholeness") and fullness ("richness" or "scope"). These are the basic demands that lead to our criteria of practical reason: valuational adequacy, valuational coherence, and valuational effectiveness.

A. VALUATIONAL ADEQUACY

The adequacy of theistic imagery functioning as a value focus for basic attitudes and policies of life is to be measured by the extent to which theists are able to include a rich array of values within its scope; to the extent, in other words, that they are not led, on its basis, to ignore or distort values that are perceived by them as genuine. Failure in coverage is a mark of inadequacy relative to the needs of the person who relies on the imagery.

Specifically in terms of the ultimate imagery of theism, which commends, as we have seen, anthropomorphic values above all others, the question must be raised whether the awesome values, say, of impersonal natural processes or the compelling values of biological rhythms, for two alternative examples, can be included naturally within the life-style of persons who find all of these worthy of inclusion within their range of basic values. A reasonably confident theistic answer to this point can be conjectured: there is nothing necessarily exclusive about the personal focus of theistic value imagery. Personal values do not rule out biological ones but are, in fact, intimately associated with them in our experience. Likewise, the values of mechanical stability are not necessarily in conflict with personal values; frequently the latter are expressed through or made possible by the former. Theistic imagery, therefore (it may be argued), fares well on the criterion of adequacy: personal concepts can without straining include organic or other impersonal ones more easily, in fact, than mechanomorphic or biomorphic imagery can include personal values without distortion or reduction.[16]

And if so, anthropomorphic theistic imagery has a reasonable claim on any who judge the success of ultimate imagery, in part at least, in terms of its capacity to stimulate and sustain valuational fullness in the lives of those who adopt it.

B. VALUATIONAL COHERENCE

Religious imagery cannot be measured simply by its powers of inclusion, however, despite the need for adequacy; it also should *organize* values and give the life lived under its influence a more or less definite form. The priorities implicit in this imagery will provide a basis for orienting the general preferences and policies of people in a unified way. To the degree that people avail themselves of this basis and actually guide their lives by it, their most basic personal policies in behavior should not only avoid interference with each other, internally, but should actually pull together in mutual support. In this way the ultimate images of a religion perform a significant role in orienting or organizing the lives of those who accept them, offering a measure of personal form and unity in place of chaos or disintegration. And as a social phenomenon, the religious community's common allegiance to generally shared imagery can contribute to the cooperation in the pursuit of agreed ends that is the precondition of civilization.

Again a challenge can be put to the ultimate imagery of theism: even acknowledging the relative valuational adequacy of this imagery, can it supply a sufficient degree of *system* to give differentiation and focus to its scope? And once more we may conjecture that the theist can return a reasonably confident answer. The imagery of theistic religions can function to express clear subordination as well as inclusion. Impersonal values, however compelling, are constantly subordinated to personal ones; impersonal structures—though awesome— are depicted in this imagery as made for men, not men for impersonal structures. Here is the valuational significance of the theistic insistence that "God made the world"; and here is the valuational force of the anthropocentric image of the physical universe which, despite its cognitive perils, may not lightly be repudiated or "demythologized" by theists without the most serious consequences. Likewise, biological values, though intimately associated with personal ones and though worthy of high esteem in their right, are kept vividly subordinate to personal values of appropriate kinds. Not merely to live but to live *well*, according to a specified set of personal values, is the supreme life-organizing demand of the imagery of the various theistic religions, all of which are prepared emotively and conatively to support their adherents in sacrificing mere biological survival, if need be, for the sake of comprehensive personal values held with supreme intensiveness.

C. VALUATIONAL EFFECTIVENESS

In this discussion of valuational criteria, however, we must guard against supposing that a person's values are simply given, fully developed, apart from the conceptions by which he lives. Ultimate imagery *elicits* approval, *molds* attitudes. It does not merely summarize or represent independently attained value systems. Once again we find circularity in root matters[17]: religious conceptions deeply influence the very attitudes that, in turn, provide the basis for what will constitute valuational "adequacy" and "coherence." Theism, in particular, cultivates a disposition to venerate personal values as over against mechanistic or purely biological ones. Here seems to be another clue to the difficulty of resolving religious disputes. Theism may strike an individual as "adequate" because it includes his basic values; but these values have largely been elicited by theism itself. Theism may strike the same individual as "coherent" because it organizes his basic values into a viable system; but this system of priorities has itself been at least partly shaped by theistic imagery. Unless some way can be found to break into (or, at minimum, to add a counterinfluence to) this circle, the individual's "tests" of the reliability of his ultimate valuations do not appear to be particularly potent ones.

Basic to all the other criteria, in consequence, must be the question of "effectiveness." The importance of "adequacy," as we have seen it, lies in the desire to make life full; the importance of "coherence," similarly, lies in the concern to keep life whole. Both interests derive ultimately from the underlying criterion of practical reason: long-run viability.

Religious imagery, as we have seen, both molds and reflects values; and as a result of much reciprocal influence the short-run application of criteria like adequacy and coherence is liable to self-justifying circularity. But effectiveness—the actual capacity of the religious imagery to serve the perceived life needs of large numbers of persons over long periods of time—brings the circle down to earth.

A diagram may illustrate what is being suggested here:

The Life-Orienting Function

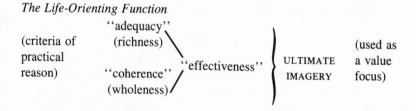

"Long periods of time?" "Perceived life needs?" How do we make such standards precise? There is no way. Nor is this a theoretical matter in which such precision would seem to be called for. But decisions are made and changes gradually do appear as the collective judgments of men and women cumulatively register. In the long historical perspective clear cases of valuational ineffectiveness can be found. Religions are born and die. Theism, too, is altered with shifting assessments of its valuational effectiveness.

For "practical reason," therefore, effectiveness is basic. If you find yourself unable to live by theism's imagery, God is dead for you, no matter how adequately and coherently it may be able to deal with values that are not *your* values. Conversely, if you find yourself grasped by the unconditional value represented in some fundamental imagery, then the motivation to *think* in its terms—however difficult it may be to develop a viable theoretical structure for it—is strongly supplied. We seem, therefore, to be edging back toward the possibility—or necessity—of serious argument, albeit perhaps in a "new key,"[18] about the merits and defects of theism's ultimate imagery for thinking.

"QUASI-COGNITIVE" FUNCTIONS OF THEISTIC LANGUAGE

Theistic religions have historically shown that their ultimate imagery is taken as prior in importance to any other conceptual element on their ideational aspect. This has been shown in the clearest way by simple unwillingness to modify or withdraw this imagery—when forced to make a choice—in favor of any of these other elements

What are these other elements? Analysis of the variety of utterances to be found within the language of theistic religions uncovers some statements having to do with matters of what we shall call "theory." This expression can include theories about the nature and origin of the universe or about abstract properties of God or about the nature of man.[19] Another type of statements might be called "historical," inasmuch as past events are purportedly being described. Still another type of statement occasionally asserts general "empirical hypotheses" about what events may be expected to follow, as a rule, from other events. Still other types of utterances are injunctions rather than statements. They lay down ethical prohibitions and commands, or prescribe proper ritual. But over all this variety of conceptual expressions[20] the ultimate imagery of theism retains its priority.

1. *The priority of imagery over theory.* Theories, we grant at once, are often highly valued, especially if they are held to articulate the imagery of theism in some uniquely suitable way. But despite this fact, it is true that abstract theories, whether about the origin and nature of the cosmos (How was it created? When?) or about man—or even about abstract characteristics of God—have been far more vulnerable to abandonment or alteration than has the basic theistic picture: of a good, all-knowing, actual Person sovereignly engaged with the world and his human creatures.

True, these theories have reciprocal influence on a religion's understanding of its imagery, e.g., by providing standards of interpretation, selection, and the like.[21] But in the long run, abstract theories can be observed to come and go: as when the theoretical scheme of Plato, long in the service of Christian thought, was challenged and largely replaced by Aristotle's rival scheme through the "radical" work of Saint Thomas Aquinas; or when, more recently, Bishop Usher's dating of the universe was replaced by that of modern cosmologists'. There seems to be no immediate prospect of an end to the process.[22]

2. *The priority of imagery over historical assertions.* Some theistic religions are what might be called "historical" religions, heavily committed to the transcendent importance of certain events alleged to have occurred in the past. But reflection shows that historical assertions, however important, do not in themselves command priority over theism's imagery.

One bit of evidence is found in the fact that the advance of historical knowledge, even when it has forced the reluctant modification of a religion's historical claims, has left the imagery basically intact. The events of the past cannot be objectively believed to have occurred, perhaps, just as the religious texts describe. So be it. The trust of faith in "salvation history" need not be shaken.

If this is the typical response of modern theists when the historical assertions associated with their religion are challenged, then it becomes clear that it is not the *historical* element in "sacred history" that counts most for them, but rather the *sacred* element. Historical assertions have been valued, that is, because they are intimately related to the ultimate imagery of the religion: this is what accounts, finally, for their religious significance. What is religiously vital is not, for instance, that a small band of Semite slaves escaped at a certain time from a cruel Egyptian king, but that—according to the imagery of the Old Testament—at one point in history God intervened to save his people and to give them a special mission. Likewise, what is full of import for Christians is not that a young carpenter was executed, like so many others, in Roman Palestine, but that at one time God concretely showed the boundlessness—"even unto death"—of his love. The past is not valued *qua* past, then, even in "historical" religions, but as the temporal setting in which unique acts of divine beings allegedly took place. Thus, historical assertions may be of great importance to theistic religions, but they can never be so important as the imagery of the divine through which alone these assertions gain their ultimate significance.

3. *The priority of imagery over empirical hypotheses.* Among the types of theistic utterance, one sometimes finds assertions of what may be expected in ordinary experience. "God will not permit this nation to be defeated," for example, is a particular empirical statement open to the test of time and observation. General hypotheses, too, concerning the regularities to be found in human life, are occasionally met: e.g., obedience to God and "walking in His ways,"

according to the Deuteronomic tradition, is constantly conjoined to worldly prosperity (e.g., Deuteronomy, chap. 28).

It is obvious that life and history have often forced such statements—particular and general—to be withdrawn or radically modified. The theistic picture, however, is itself basically preserved.

Doubtless this frequently observable primacy of the image over any empirical hypotheses uttered in its name provides the basis for the "unfalsifiability" of basic theistic claims concerning which the verificational analyst complains. To *these* kinds of refutation the imagery has been, over the centuries, securely immunized.

4. *The priority of imagery over ritual or moral injunctions.* Commandments, maxims, and laws all appear also in the variegated discourse of theistic religions; but it is clear that any given set of such commandments is less vital to theism than is its depiction of God as the final source of all good and as the final point of all ritual observance.

Interpretations of the "will of God" regarding ritual or morality may—and do—vary from time to time. But, undisturbed by such changes, the imagery of theism is retained. Thus, the ultimate picture of what is the case takes priority over the significance of injunctions just as it does over the assertions of theory, history, or empirical expectation.

The vision of God is basic. If this is so, then perhaps such a "way of seeing" may have a direct and powerful impact on what one is likely to notice or believe, even though the "vision" itself is not knowledge in any standard sense. This possibility deserves to be explored.

Theories of Heuristic Function

Here, close to the borderline between cognitive and noncognitive functions, we find the interesting possibility that religious language may contribute to cognitive inquiry without itself being subject to the same rules of inquiry. Imagining God as a cosmic designer, for one thing, can give shape and direction to our observations, pointing our attention toward the intimate interconnections between things and spurring us on to search for intelligible principles in every part of nature. Again, picturing God as the one Supreme Being can give a needed sense of unity to our inquiries and place an important demand against all our explanations that they strive toward the "ideal of coherence." As far as Kant was concerned, however, "God"-concepts themselves could never be cognitively justified; utterances about "God" could neither be theoretically true nor false; and the heuristic use of such utterances could not be considered descriptive but, rather, regulative.

Some contemporary analyses of the logic of religious language venture out after Kant on the narrow path between "contributing to knowledge" and "constituting knowledge."

1. "Bliks" *as the unarguable precondition of explanation.* One of these analyses maintains that theistic utterances, although not falsifiable and therefore not assertions, do play a role in thinking: they symbolize our most profound attitudes, "ways of seeing," or (in an invented word now gaining currency) *bliks,*[23] on which hang the very possibility of descriptions or explanations for us. *Bliks,* that is, function as presumed background for any beliefs or disbeliefs whatever. As such, they cannot be falsified empirically, since anything that we would be (attitudinally) prepared to acknowledge as a "fact" must be compatible with the basic attitudes that determine our stance toward experience as a whole. One widespread *blik,* for example, is the profound conviction that the future will be similar to the past in basic ways: e.g., that the principle of causal analogy is trustworthy. Such basic convictions are neither factually empty verbal conventions nor readily surrenderable empirical hypotheses. But though not empirical hypotheses, they are not irrelevant to the facts since "there is no distinction between fact and illusion for a person who does not take up a certain attitude to the world."[24]

Theistic "world models" or "organizing images" would then, on this theory, be among those that most deeply reflect what one would be prepared to take as determinative (heuristically) for one's thinking as well as (conatively) for one's living. Indeed, at the basic level we are discussing there could be no separation of these two aspects of the self. Sane thinking and sound living are assisted by ultimate images, though they are not themselves open to the kinds of arguments that they make possible.

2. *"Ways of seeing" as illuminating "the facts."* Another analysis of the heuristic use of theistic language may be summarized by the statement "What is so isn't merely a matter of 'the facts.' "[25] *Patterns* in the facts cannot be considered merely "more facts," in parallel with the facts that are seen as patterned; and yet patterns, significant arrangements of discretely observable items of experience, are so. What we are likely to notice as significant patterns, however, is very largely dependent upon the conceptual-linguistic screen through which we approach the observable world. To say of a lady's hat, "My dear, it's the Taj Mahal," notes John Wisdom, is not merely to alter the prospective buyer's emotions about the hat. These words, which introduce a fresh frame of reference for this shopper's observations, "alter her apprehension of the hat just as the word *A hare* makes what did look like a clump of earth *look* like an animal, a hare in fact; just as the word *A cobra* may change the look of something in the corner by the bed."[26]

In like manner, then, theistic language, given its definite content by vivid imagery, may function to help our apprehension of what is so; that is, it may aid us to notice patterns in the observable facts around us. These patterns may be too complex and inclusive to be easily proved or disproved ("verified" or "falsified") by any number of closer looks at the discrete facts that make them up; but they may nonetheless be extremely important for our appreciation of, and our living within, the whole observable world around us. If this is the case, then theistic utterances and theistic questions like "Does God exist?" are far from empty. "On the contrary," says Wisdom, "they call for new awareness of what has so long been about us, in case knowing nature so well we never know her."[27]

3. Evaluating heuristic analyses. Heuristic analyses help us to understand the logic of theistic discourse. This remarkably complex language, although not typically used to give us concrete observational expectations, does nevertheless have the capacity, through its imagery, to alter the way in which people who adopt it apprehend things; although not logically equipped to function in scientific explanations, it does have a bearing on what its users take to be at the root of all explanation; and although not properly employed to fashion falsifiable empirical hypotheses, it does seem, at least to those who rely on it, to have an essential and vastly important relevance to what is so.

But if "apprehensions" differ, and if some apprehensions are *better* than others, then perhaps, as John Wisdom says, the old theistic questions "aren't senseless, aren't beyond the scope of thought and reason."[28] What if appropriate criteria of more or less adequate apprehensions of things can be developed? What if *bliks*, as the coiner of the term insists,[29] can be "sane" and "insane" and therefore open to standards and rules of reasonableness in adoption? Then philosophers will be required to withdraw at least one claim: the notion that *bliks* are somehow beyond being argued about. The arguments may not be in the crisply defined terms familiar to the scientist or to those who normally limit their concerns to questions of "the facts"—when "the facts" are taken to be open to clearly delimited observational tests. But if we can find criteria for "better or worse," "more or less sane," "adequate or inadequate," and the like, reasonable men will be able to recommence responsible inquiry.

Responsible *inquiry,* did we say? But inquiry is inseparably part of the cognitive side of human endeavor. We do not need in the least to abandon the discovery of verificational analysis that modern, sophisticated theistic utterances are typically neither tautological linguistic conventions nor falsifiable empirical hypotheses; this is one of the primary findings of contemporary philosophy; yet we must now grant that in some sense this language can function to guide our *thinking* as well as our feelings and our behavior.

COGNITIVE FUNCTIONS: MODELS AND THEORIES

What Are Models?

In the most general sense a "model" can be anything used in any way to represent anything else. Some, as every boy knows, are capable of being built and even being made to work, like certain scale models and mechanical models.

Others—we shall call them "conceptual models"—may merely be drawn on paper, described in words, or entertained in the mind, and range in ideational type from the comparative concreteness of imaginable mental pictures to the formal generality of mathematical analogues.

Models differ, too, in terms of the scope of the subject matter they are taken to represent. Often a model may be used to stand for a single thing (like the *Queen Mary*); equally often models are intended to represent whole classes (like "the hydrogen atom"); and sometimes models are used to refer to even vaster domains of subject mattter (like "the pulsating universe").

This variety in type and scope is due to the variety of purposes that people have in using models. In some contexts (as in art appreciation) a scale model with very particular scope (e.g., Michelangelo's *David*) may assist our aesthetic grasp of the spatial proportions of a huge or distant statue; in other settings (as in microphysics or astronomy) we may call on a conceptual model of wide scope to provide a sense of intuitive familiarity for what is too small or too large or otherwise unavailable for direct observation; in still other enterprises (as in airplane design) we may need a working model to anticipate flaws without the expense and danger of building and testing the real thing. The catalogue of potential uses of models is limited only by the range of our purposes; even within the few enterprises we have already mentioned, we have not exhausted their varied functions. In the case of microphysics, for example, a conceptual model not only offers a sense of intuitive interpretation for the otherwise bare formulas of the physicist's theories, but also can illuminate relations that might otherwise have been missed among theoretical domains, and can suggest fruitful new problems for consideration. These roles of interpretation, integration, and heuristic stimulation, indispensable for purposes of satisfactory understanding, are what make "explanatory models" valuable in cognitive enterprises.

The Function Of Models In Theories

Our present interests, of course, draw our attention especially to those purposes of "knowing" or "understanding" that often lead to the employment of conceptual models for theoretical ends.

1. The benefits of models to theories. A theory "uninterpreted" by any model is liable to be a highly arbitrary set of symbols held together by formal rules to compose what is sometimes called an "abstract calculus."[30] This abstract calculus has a definite formal structure, and when its symbols are connected somehow to specifiable elements of experience, it can have vastly important applications. This is the theoretical matrix; it can, if need be, exist and function without interpretation by a model.

But a conceptual model can add a great deal to the abstract calculus of theories. First, it can bring *ideational definiteness* to what otherwise will remain highly indeterminate. A set of "implicity defined"[31] symbols and formal rules may make some kinds of calculations possible, but the concrete sense of subject matter needs more than this, especially when the subject matter is of a sort that is not, for one reason or another, open to immediate observation: like the inner structure of the atom, or the complex social working of an economic system, or the imperceptibly gradual forces of geological change, or the remote events of the solar system's origin.

Second, in giving ideational definiteness by its concrete representation of a subject matter, a model can help a theory achieve *conceptual unity*. Ideally it can do this in two ways. (*a*) Internal to a single subject area it can suggest additional ways in which the data go together, new areas in which to establish theoretical connections, as, for example, a hydraulic model of an economic system may reveal relations between data that has previously been conceptually isolated. And (*b*) a model may draw together several presumably different subject areas by suggesting hitherto unsuspected similarities of form or structure, as the model of the molecule was able to do in helping to unite the fields of thermodynamics and statistical mechanics.

Third, a fortunate model may have the effect of suggesting potentially fruitful *lines of inquiry* and the making of new discoveries, just as the astronomers' "Big Bang" model of the universe has helped to suggest fascinating applications of radio telescopy to research in quasars and thus has contributed to the revolutionizing of astronomical knowledge.

We have here been considering ideal cases, of course. Sometimes models may actually inject confusion and disconnection: e.g., in the so-called paradoxes of light, wherein some of the physical data are best interpreted by a wave model, other data are most naturally accounted for on a particle model, but the two models are (alas) mutually exclusive. The "paradox," we find, arises from attempts to take the models literally and to push them beyond their appropriate logical limits. Quantum mechanical formulas are capable of dealing consistently, though abstractly, with the data; the conflicts and contradictions arise only in our images. It might be argued, therefore, that sometimes greater understanding is served, after a point, by putting away the models and relying on imageless mathematical theory alone. The aura of intelligibility or "grasp" may indeed by missing from thought shorn of the aid of models; but sometimes, at least when purely theoretical purposes are involved, such an aura must be sacrificed for more basic cognitive interests such as consistency and obedience to the evidence.

We must be cautious, then, in the employment of conceptual models. But assuming a good degree of vigilance, models can be of great value for purposes of cognition. Above all they function to provide conceptual definiteness, to suggest connections in the subject matter, to relate fields to one another, to indicate new lines of investigation, and to afford, when possible, a sense of the familiar and the intuitively intelligible.

2. The "acceptability" of models. Conceptual models, we find, give abstract theories concrete interpretation; theories, in turn, attempt to articulate the formal structure of their subject matter thanks in part, at least, to suggestions derived from the formal structure of their associated models. The relation is mutually supportive, and sometimes powerful models may lead to important modification of theories, just as theoretical requirements may sometimes, as we have noted, result in the limitation or abandonment of models.

Models are accredited as powerful if they give shape and support to theories that perform their conceptual role well. In the sciences one conceptual role of theory, its use as warranting empirical hypotheses, is essentially linked to the task of helping us anticipate specific experiences. Consequently, a scientific model that contributes to the interpretation and improvement of theories that are empirically well confirmed is considered a success. To this extent it is an acceptable vehicle of thought. But the sciences do not exhaust human thinking. We must now consider another conceptual role, another type of theory, another sort of associated conceptual model, and other standards of success.

The Controversial Logic of Metaphysical Models

The various sciences are defined by the conjunction of general empirical methodology with particular subject areas; and, consequently, scientific theories and models are essentially restrained within determinate boundaries. Such boundaries are not externally imposed, they are deliberately—and wisely—chosen.

But the mental urge for conceptual unity seems boundary-indifferent. At least some of the time most of us are open to all-inclusive questions: What are the inescapable, basic features of reality? What is the overall (or underlying) character of the "sum of things entire"? Is there any fundamental pattern to everything that is? Which (if any) features of experience are the realities, and which the temporary (or derivative) appearances? Why should anything at all be, rather than nothing?

Most of us do not take the time or energy to give such questions sustained and critical thought, but a few bold persons attempt to push these questions as far as they can take them, and to supply reasoned answers. In so doing they are thinking metaphysically, at the outer limits of speculative thought.

The defining mark, then, of metaphysical theorizing is its all-inclusiveness. Similarly, the metaphysical use of a model is distinguished from other uses by the proposed *scope* of the model's application. Like other conceptual models, a metaphysical model[32] is intended to provide conceptual definiteness, to suggest connections among apparently diverse things, and to offer the sense of intelligibility that theoretical enterprises aim at. Thus, a metaphysical model is drawn from some particular aspect of experience that is judged to be potentially illuminating for all experience (like Huxley's image of the universe in evolutionary thrust) and is relied upon to give initial conceptual definiteness—a "vision of reality"—to what otherwise is simply formless. It is explored to discover the interconnected patterns in things that such an angle of vision may reveal. And it is valued for its capacity to help make sense out of the otherwise alien complexities of the total environment in which men find themselves living.

Well-chosen metaphysical models must lend themselves to articulation, of course, in metaphysical theories that are themselves capable of self-consistent elaboration, spelling out in depth and in detail the structures of reality as suggested and made concretely vivid by the model. If such a theory performs the conceptual job expected of it—the criteria for which we shall examine in a moment—the model that suggests the theory and gives it concrete interpretation is to this extent accredited or commended for acceptance. That is, we may responsibly use it to give conceptual definiteness to the otherwise empty or abstract phrase "ultimate reality." If, however, the metaphysician's theory develops in directions that require him to modify or abandon his initial model, the model must be expendable. The model, in purely theoretical[33] metaphysical speculation, remains ancillary to the demands of theory.

We shall now argue that in all logical respects (except the last one) anthropomorphic theistic imagery can function on its speculative side as a vivid metaphysical model. It can give conceptual definiteness to the ultimate nature of things by picturing all of reality as constituting either creature or Creator, each with specifiable characteristics; it can suggest patterns and unity in the totality of things in terms of its representation of the various relations between the entities so pictured; and it can give a sense of intelligibility, an aura of meaning and familiarity, by virtue of the appeal to personal purpose, volitional power, and moral principle as the ultimate explanatory categories.

This interpretation of the theist's imagery avoids any confusion of it with either falsifiable empirical propositions or with merely empty linguistic conventions. And at the same time it has the important consequence of providing a foothold for a theoretical assessment of its acceptability, just as any speculative model may be examined for accreditation. That is, insofar as theistic religions are interested in the rational justification of their theocentric vision of reality, it appears now that it must be done, if it can be done, by displaying the success of this model in concretely interpreting some viable metaphysical theory (or theories). If this can be done, then theists will be reasonably entitled to use their imagery as their most inclusive representations of what is so. If this cannot be done, however, theists have no reasonably warranted right to use their God-language to refer to, or stand for, the ultimate nature of things. What, then, will be involved in doing this?

1. The criterion of appropriateness. The first crucial measure of the cognitive power of theism will be the discovery of how all conceptual structures of unlimited range, supposing for the moment that there might exist such stuctures, can be judged to "fit" the primary model. Such structures may either be made to order or, as has usually been the case, adopted from philosophy with some alterations. But whatever their origin, the cognitive justification of a religious model depends upon acceptably appropriate linkage to some theory.

At this point, however, the one major difference in the logical status of theistic imagery from other metaphysical models becomes noteworthy: for the purposes of pure theory, a model must be subordinate to its theory and must be alterable or dispensable according to the dictates of theory; but theistic imagery is not used—even on its speculative side—for theoretical purposes alone. As long as it remains *religious* imagery, the motivation to think in its terms is overridingly practical. This is not necessarily so different, however, from the normal metaphysical situation as it may sound. Seldom, if ever, can metaphysical models, "visions of ultimate reality," be held entirely dispassionately. A metaphysician's view of his world and of himself, as well as his sense of order and intelligibility, is wrapped up in the conceptual models he uses. Theories may be overhauled and rethought to preserve, if possible, a fundamental vision of reality. Theoretical dispassion is always a matter of degree. But granting all this, a difference of degree becomes a difference of kind when religious imagery is at stake, since religious imagery is above all a supremely intensive value phenomenon by which, for the sake of comprehensiveness, men also often try to think.

Theory, then, the abstract articulation and explication of the model, becomes the subordinate partner. Various theories may be seized upon as the conceptual vehicles for the model, as can be clearly observed in the history of Christian doctrine. Plato's abstract metaphysical scheme, for example, may be used at one time to articulate the central model; Aristotle's may challenge and replace it; still others—the conceptual schemes of a Hegel or a Heidegger, a Whitehead or a Wittgenstein—may also be employed to give articulation and application to the value-drenched model at stake.

Each theory has its own abstract formal structure, of course; and this structure may be more or less suited to the natural explication of the key points of the model's own more concrete formal structure. Each theory, conversely, may eventually influence which structural features of the model shall be considered "key." The influence, for instance, of Platonic and Aristotelian theoretical vehicles for Christian imagery has drawn into the foreground those aspects of the Christian model wherein God's changelessness, self-sufficiency, majestic solitude, and the like are portrayed; contrary tendencies to picture God as mutable, developing, or essentially related to the world have been interpreted as "merely figurative" (because not open to explication on those theories) and thus have been deemphasized. The "fit" of model and theory is thereby aided by the reactions of a powerful theory upon the model. But in the end it is the theory that must be appropriate to the model; theistic imagery, in its speculative as well as in its life-orienting use, remains primary.

But how is this "fit" or appropriateness to be judged? That this is a primary requirement is undoubted; that there are any clear standards of "fittingness" seems more dubious. This is a fair question, but one to which no quick—and certainly no quantifiable—answer can be given. In the last resort it would seem to be up to religious believers themselves, collectively and individually, to determine the appropriateness of the "fit" between their model, their primary "vision of reality," and any particular theory. How is this determined?

Perhaps the "fit" of one's imagery to the abstract theory intended to articulate it is finally decided in the same way that one determines the "fit" of the words one chooses to express one's own thought. Each of us engages in the activity of judging the appropriateness of his own choice of words: "Such-and-such a way of putting my thought was not quite right; this other way would be better." But we cannot possibly judge the appropriateness of the manner of our articulation of thought by any precisely articulated standard, as though our thoughts were already articulated somewhere for purposes of comparison before we started articulating them. No, it is the very process of *first* articulation that we are judging; and therefore the judgment must be by means of some prearticulate— essentially unformulable and imprecise—sense of confidence ("That time I said just what I meant") or of discomfort ("No, that wasn't quite the right way to put it") that guides us.[34]

In a similar way, the theist looks to a theory to give articulation to his model; and in a similar way he must in the last resort simply trust his—and his core-ligionists'—"feel" for the appropriateness of the conceptual structure to his prearticulate vision. It is perfectly possible that no theories will be felt as perfectly adequate; but this is a common experience in ordinary uses of language—never to find exactly the right way to articulate something, especially something that means a lot to the speaker. It is certainly no argument against the possibility of finding some ways of articulating thought much more, or less, appropriate than others.

Assuming, then, that this first prerequisite, the criterion of appropriateness, has been sufficiently well met for theists to accept some conceptual scheme as the reasonably "fitting" articulation of their ultimate imagery, the success of the scheme itself in fulfilling its appropriate function must be measured. What is this function? Ideally it is the self-consistent elaboration of an integral, or internally well-connected, way of thinking about the totality of things. In other words, metaphysical theories must, in order to do their job, satisfy the familiar twin criteria (now in their theoretical rather than their practical application) of *adequacy* and *coherence*.

2. *The criterion of adequacy.* Since a metaphysical scheme is designed to deal with questions of unlimited scope, only a fully comprehensive scheme will be

adequate to all the varieties of experience and knowledge that must be integrated. "Adequacy" requires that, at a minimum, no important ranges of human experience and interest be ignored or denied or (as it is sometimes said) "explained away."

Where lies the line, we may wonder, between legitimate *explaining,* by showing a particular object of interest to be an instance of something else already familiar, and *explaining away* by illegitimate reduction? This question cannot be resolved in the abstract. Even in the sciences these issues raise hotly debated judgmental disputes.[35] But the actual practice of inquiry shows that there *is* a difference between the two, though perhaps no a priori "line" can be drawn.

In large part we seem thrown back upon the intuitions of those most affected, whose own cognitive interests and personal experiences are being considered. Do they find the conceptual proposal illuminating? Or do they sense something essential lost by the particular abstractions being employed? If the latter, and if this sense is long sustained, then the verdict of inadequacy seems likely.

What is an "acceptable level" of adequacy? The more of it the better, of course. But perfect inclusiveness, adequacy that satisfies *everyone's* sense that *all* aspects of experience have been considered without distortion, is probably an unattainable ideal. This is especially apt to be so if some elements in the data must be subordinated to other elements, or be put into unfamiliar associations. But problems are compounded by the fact that subordination and unfamiliar association are the inevitable effects of any powerful conceptual ordering: something which is directly sought by our next criterion.

3. *The criterion of coherence.* Ideally, successful thinking about the whole of things calls for conceptual unity, the provision of internal connection that would substitute integrity for fragmentation in thinking. But internal connection, in fact, is never perfect. In fact the more "adequate" a theory attempts to be, the more difficulties are presented for the achievement of "coherence." Scope and system are polar notions. The more tight-knit the system, the more temptation there is to exclude or to explain away parts of the data; but the more that scope is defended, the harder it is to retain system. This is especially true if our knowledge and experience is constantly growing, stretching old coherences to the bursting point.

Still, despite all the difficulties involved, it remains the case that discoverable disconnection is a defect. The more the various elements of a scheme can be shown to entail one another, the more nearly integral, and therefore the more successful, it may be counted as being.

What is the "acceptable level" of incoherence that may be tolerated in a conceptuality intended to represent the whole of things? To ask this question in a vacuum is not likely to be any more fruitful than to ask a scientist, apart from particular cases, how much "complexity" he can tolerate in a theory before he considers his standard of "simplicity" to be hopelessly violated. The answer in both cases will depend on the available alternatives and the consensus of experienced investigators. No one can say in advance how such tests are going to be applied. And yet they remain important for the working inquirer.

The process of human inquiry is not the mechanical affair that is sometimes depicted in simplified logic texts; but neither is it a matter of pure whim nor of arbitrary preference. Adequacy and coherence are not, any more than simplicity or elegance, criteria that lend themselves to programming in computers (though computers might very well help at certain points); still, at the level of comprehensiveness appropriate to the speculative function of theism, they happen to be what inquirers have to work with.

To summarize, the diagram below may be helpful:

Part A of the diagram represents how the life-orienting function of ultimate imagery is to be assessed by the criteria of "practical reason": valuational adequacy, coherence, and (above all) effectiveness. Part B continues the story into the cognitive domain. Though, as it indicates, theoretical reason from a religious point of view is always subordinate to (and derivative from) practical reason, sometimes theistic imagery is given a speculative function. When it is so used it can best be understood to be functioning as a conceptual model of unlimited comprehensiveness. The tests of its success in this role, consequently, are: directly, its perceived appropriateness as an interpretation of some theoretical

THE FUNCTIONS AND CRITERIA OF THEISTIC IMAGERY

A. The Life-Orienting Function

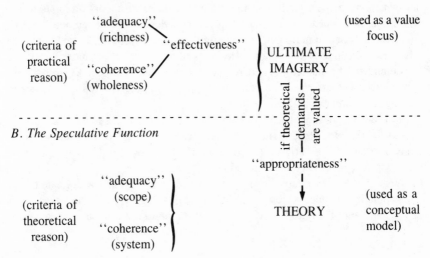

B. The Speculative Function

matrix and, indirectly, the relative adequacy and coherence of the matrix which is taken as articulating it.

Reflecting on the Theoretical Criteria of Theism

This discussion of the criteria appropriate to the language of theism in its speculative function is likely to be acutely unsatisfying to many. These measures are portrayed as so imprecise, so dependent upon a "feel" here, an "intuition" there, a working inquirer's disciplined—but disputable—judgment, that some will be inclined to dismiss them as no measures at all. Worse, we have seen that the two key criteria, such as they are, combine to generate built-in tensions that complicate the situation still further. There is no use evading the fact that speculation at this level of theoretical generality is a problematic enterprise at best.

Some of this dissatisfaction, of course, may be due to a falsely idealized notion of the actual standards and procedures in other domains of inquiry, such as the sciences. "Feel" and "hunch" and trained intuition, even there, play much more of a role than most observers acknowledge.[36] The empirical scientist, however, has a potent appeal to the future and to more particular experiences, which is a great advantage over the metaphysical thinker. The scientist can wait for new specific data to turn up with a significant bearing on his limited hypotheses and theories; but the metaphysician has attempted (so far as he is successful) to account for *all possible* types of experience. He therefore is not in a position to expect clarification or further confirmation of his theories over the passage of time. His criteria, though relevant to all experience, may not appeal simply to more experience for extenuation of their vagueness or for elimination of their element of personal risk.

NOTES

1. This claim is not intended to represent the views of any particular theistic religion, e.g., normative Christianity. Rather, it is taken as typical of a popular theistic outlook widespread in many religions—including Christianity, Judaism, and Islam—whether or not it is a sentiment up to the "highest" expressions of those historical faiths. But its selection as a test example for present purposes seems fair enough, since if a religion is unable to venture the claim that God is in some sense on the side of those who acknowledge the value priorities of the faith centering around him, the question concerning what, if anything, it *can* claim would seem only to be intensified.

2. See Karl Popper, *The Logic of Scientific Discovery* (London: Hutchinson, 1959).

3. Cf. William James, *Essays in Pragmatism,* ed. Alburey Castell. (New York: Hafner, 1948), pp. 13–27.

4. For a now-famous exchange on this point, see the section on Theology and Falsification in *New Essays in Philosophical Theology,* ed. Anthony Flew and Alasdair MacIntyre (London: SCM Press, 1955), pp. 96 ff.

5. See John Hick, *Faith and Knowledge* (Ithaca, N.Y.: Cornell University Press, 1957), for an advocate of this position. Also Ian Crombie's article reprinted in Flew and MacIntyre, *New Essays,* pp. 109–30.

6. This is the basic logical objection to the "Heads I win, tails you lose" type of argument used sometimes by both defenders and opponents of theism.

7. For further, more extended discussion, see Frederick Ferré, *Language, Logic and God* (New York: Harper & Row, 1961).

8. A. J. Ayer, *Language, Truth and Logic* (London: Victor Gollancz, 1956), p. 101. It is interesting to compare this theme to the *savoir pour prévoir* theory of knowledge of classical positivism. Logical positivism, advocated here by Ayer, has fashioned a logical doctrine from the same basic viewpoint.

9. See Ludwig Wittgenstein, *Philosophical Investigations,* trans. G.E.M. Anscombe (Oxford: Blackwell, 1953), e.g., pp. 128, 132.

10. This is a large part of the logical function of the sacred literature of particular theistic religions, to weave together the stories and parables that combine to form what we may call—because the resultant mental picture gives conceptual definiteness to what is taken as ultimately important in that religion— the "ultimate images" of that religion. See Frederick Ferré, "Mapping the Logic of Models in Science and Theology," *The Christian Scholar* 46(1963), especially pp. 24 ff.

11. Ludwig Feuerbach, *The Essence of Christianity,* trans. George Eliot (New York: Harper & Row, 1957), pp. 14–15.

12. See J. L. Austin, *How To Do Things with Words,* ed. J. O. Urmson (Cambridge, Mass.: Harvard University Press, 1962).

13. Ibid., p. 6

14. See, for various instances of this approach, R. B. Braithwaite, "An Empiricist's View of the Nature of Religious Belief," reprinted in *The Existence of God,* ed. John Hick (New York: Macmillan, 1964); Ronald W. Hepburn, *Christianity and Paradox* (London: Watts, 1958), especially chap. 2; and Paul F. Schmidt, *Religious Knowledge* (Glencoe, Ill.: The Free Press, 1961).

15. For further discussion see Kent Bendall and Frederick Ferré, *Exploring the Logic of Faith* (New York: Association Press, 1962), especially chap. 2.

16. See John Macmurray, *The Self as Agent* (New York: Harper & Row, 1957), for such an argument.

17. For the mutual dependence of "truth" and "reality," cf. Frederick Ferré, *Basic Modern Philosophy of Religion* (New York: Scribner, 1967), pp. 25–26, 299.

18. See Susanne K. Langer, *Philosophy in a New Key,* rev. ed. (New York: Mentor, 1958), for a good explication of this musical metaphor.

19. For a closer inspection of the nature of theological theory, cf. Ferré, *Basic Modern Philosophy,* pp. 375–88.

20. This list of basic forms of utterances associated with theistic religions omits expressions without descriptive content, like "Hallelujah!" But all the conceptual expressions that could in principle rival the primacy of ultimate imagery are meant to be covered.

21. See Ferré, *Basic Modern Philosophy,* pp. 380–83, for more details on the nature of this mutual influence.

22. See ibid., pp. 418–35, for a discussion of some current candidates for the role.

23. See R. M. Hare's contribution to "Theology and Falsification" in Flew and MacIntyre, *New Essays,* and his article "Religion and Morals," in *Faith and Logic,* ed. Basil Mitchell (London: Allen & Unwin, 1957).

24. Hare, "Religion and Morals," p. 190.

25. John Wisdom, "Gods," reprinted in *Logic and Language,* 1st series, ed. Anthony Flew (Oxford: Basil Blackwell, 1951), p. 192.

26. John Wisdom, "The Logic of 'God,' " in Hick, *The Existence of God,* p. 278.

27. Ibid., p. 298.

28. Ibid.

29. Hare, in Flew and MacIntyre, *New Essays,* p. 100.

30. See Ernest Nagel, *The Structure of Science* (New York: Harcourt, Brace and World, 1961), pp. 91–93.

31. Ibid., pp. 85, 87, 91, etc.

32. For ease of expression we shall speak of "metaphysical models" instead of continuing the more cumbersome locutions "metaphysical use of a model" or "conceptual model used for metaphysical speculation."

33. If there is any "pure theory" in metaphysical—or any other kind—of thought. All these remarks are much compressed and idealized for the sake of presenting clearly the basic logical structures involved. Some complications and modifications will be introduced later.

34. Cf. Michael Polanyi, *Personal Knowledge* (New York: Harper & Row, Torch, 1964), chap. 5, "Articulation."

35. See Nagel, *The Structure of Science,* chap. 11.

36. There is, for example, no point in principle where a scientist employing a statistical law can decide, without using a "feel for what is reasonable," the exact point at which his law has been "violated" just *too* much. If there is only a 20 percent chance of a certain result, it still *may* (improbably) come up the first time—and (more improbably) the second time, and (much more improbably) the third time in a row, and . . . But the law itself cannot determine when the improbabilities it allows for are simply too improbable in a given case. The scientist, or more accurately the scientific community, must weigh the situation and simply decide whether the evidential weight of such particular cases is more important than keeping the laws unchanged, or whether the law is too useful to

tamper with. Similarly, even apart from statistical laws, "disconfirming" instances can be treated as "freaks" or anomalies" rather than as falsifying instances. Some day, for instance, we shall probably know whether the "feel" of scientists in the mid–twentieth century regarding "unidentified flying objects" and "extrasensory perception" is in the best interests of the advancement of understanding or not.

Chapter 12

IN WHAT SENSE CAN WE SPEAK OF EXPERIENCING GOD?

John E. Smith

THE most obvious fact about our question is that its meaning as a question appears to be infinitely clearer than any of the answers we can give to it—unless, of course, we agree with a popular view and declare that the answer is "in no sense" because there is no reality to experience. If that were my answer, however, I would not discuss the question at all, because such an answer seems to me to follow not so much from an examination of the peculiar circumstances of the case itself as from a theory of experience according to which experience is identified with a tissue of clear-cut and nameable sensible data and nothing more. As we know from the development of modern positivism, on such a view there is and can be no reality answering to the term *God*. And yet the prevalence of a variety of empiricisms in modern philosophy ever since the Enlightenment makes it impossible for us to ignore the vexing question about experience and God. Unless we are to suppose that the approach to God is absolutely discontinuous with our approach to everything else that we seek to know, we cannot arbitrarily decide that experience does not count. There is an important insight in the appeal to experience which most rationalisms have failed to appreciate. This insight, as I shall suggest, is a valid one and must be taken seriously, even if, as I would maintain, no purely immediate approach to God can be self-supporting.

Before proceeding further it is necessary to introduce and then set aside (for good reasons, I believe) the one approach to our problem which many are likely

From: *Journal of Religion* 50:3 (1970): 229–44.

to suppose is *the* approach—the only viable approach—namely, mysticism. For if one understands mysticism in terms of what it has shown itself to be in its many forms, in both East and West, it is clear that mysticism coincides with pure empiricism—even if the association inevitably attached to the latter term runs counter to our most common conception of the mystical temper. The recovery of "what is really there," the capturing of the immediate with "nothing in between" the one who apprehends and what is apprehended, characterize both mysticism and empiricism, at least where empiricism is understood in the classical sense it received at the hands of the great British empiricists of the seventeenth and eighteenth centuries. Mysticism means the persistent attempt—whether by dialectical preparation or moral discipline or, again, by the use of drugs—to transcend, in the sense of "render superfluous," all mediating elements that might be interposed or would interpose themselves between the self and the unity of being that ends the mystic quest. The purpose of the preparation is to remove the layers of ordinary and merely routine experience and habit so as to enable the self to "stand outside itself"—*ekstasis*—and thus be in a position to experience a reality that stands beyond all form. In its religious dimension mysticism means the possession of the divine and the being possessed by the divine in such a mode that rational form and its articulation in language and signs are transcended. That this quest for immediacy, for the possession of what is without the supposed distortion of the interpreting medium, is of the essential nature of mysticism can readily be seen from such diverse sources as the philosophy of Plotinus, where we have the "flight of the alone to the Alone," the Soul's journey to God in Bonaventura, and the realization that Braham is Atman in the Upanishads of classical Hinduism. Moreover, to bring the matter closer to home, running through the forms that constitute William James's "varieties of religious experience" is a large dose of mysticism, so much so, in fact, that many have taken it to be identical with religious experience itself.

Thus there is no question that an answer to our original question about experience and God could be given by citing mysticism; there, it could certainly be claimed, is a sense in which it is possible to speak of experiencing God. And, I might add, there is something of a ground swell on the contemporary scene in favor of a sort of mystical immediacy, even if the enthusiasm is not shared by many philosophers. While, however, I do not want to ignore either the pervasive character of this outlook or the truth that is in it, I do not want to put it forward as a solution. And this for several reasons, not least among which is the paradox that mysticism, in all its forms, derives meaning and sustenance from the very mediation which it seeks to transcend. For example, the sacred silence that cannot be said, emphasized by many mystical writers, is saved from being that bare or empty silence which is not ultimate meaning but actual death, by the fact that its meaning is interpreted through the process by which it is reached. But more important than this paradoxical dependence of mysticism on the finitude it transcends is the fact that neither the dominant religious traditions nor the dominant philosophical traditions of the West have been essentially mystical in character. True, there have been powerful mystical strains in Judaism, Islam, and Christianity; but mysticism is not the heart of any one of these traditions. And, again, there have been philosophers in the Western tradition who have taken mysticism seriously, and we even have the phenomenon of a rationalist like Hegel who proposed to regard mysticism as a kind of ultimate truth if only it were not left in merely implicit form. But in the case neither of religion nor of philosophy has immediacy been the only ultimate criterion with respect to truth and reality. On the contrary, from the religious side, the primacy of mediating factors, the centrality of the interpreting word, and especially the doctrine that God is always to be seen as manifesting himself in and through another, have all militated against the acceptance of mysticism as a final solution. Starting from the philosophical side, we arrive at a similar result. Belief in the necessity of discursive processes of thought and in the interpreting force of both logic and language, and an awareness of the complex structure of experience involving both one who has experience and a world of content experienced, are all factors that run counter to a philosophical position that takes its ultimate stand on the thesis that *to be is to be immediate*.

For these and other reasons it does not seem to me sound to propose the way of mysticism as the answer to our initial question. It was necessary, however, to indicate this negative result at the outset because of the widespread view that the mere mention of experience in relation to God is at once to raise the question of the nature of mysticism. William James is not without responsibility for this view. Quite apart from what has just been said about mysticism not being a dominant and decisive position in either philosophy or religion in the West, there is the philosophically more important fact that experience and the appeals to experience as a criterion in modern thought have not been appeals to mystical immediacy in any sense that would be continuous with classical mysticism. They have been appeals to experience understood as something had or enjoyed by a concrete individual person living in a historical context; there has been little or no emphasis in these empiricisms on the individual's merging with an ultimate reality or on his becoming absorbed in the object of his quest. On the contrary, all modern forms of empiricism have presupposed the validity of the subject-object relationship in experience, even if certain difficulties arising in connection with that relationship have impelled the phenomenologists and existentialists to seek ways of transcending it. We must ask our original question about experience and God in a way that makes logical contact with the concept of experience developed in modern critical philosophy. To rest with mysticism—despite the truth that is in it, and there is much—is, in the end, to accept too easy a solution, for, as has often been said, the mystical citadel is invisible and ultimately beyond the reach of dialectical discussion, even if its proponents have engaged in the most subtle and indirect dialectic to point the way to this conclusion.

Is there another answer that might be given to our question? Happily there is. Let us consider the criticism that has been leveled by the modern appeal to experience, whether from the philosophical side in the form of empiricism, phenomenology, and existentialism, or from the theological side in the form of fideism, theology of encounter, and, again, existentialism, against the entire enterprise of seeking to reach God through the medium of rational dialectic—whether in the ontological form made classic by Augustine and Anselm on the one side, or in the cosmological form of Albert the Great and Thomas Aquinas on the other. I do not want to involve us in an essentially historical discussion; therefore I shall state at once two points at issue, one logical and the other religious, that mark the encounter between the approach through rational dialectic and these forms of the appeal to experience. The principle of empiricism so well expressed by Hegel in his *Encyclopedia* is found in the principle of *copresence;* the self or experiencer is copresent with what is experienced, and that intersection of the two furnishes, for the experiencer, the guarantee of the *reality* of what is thus encountered. Copresence is the warrant for the *is* of what is encountered and in the presence of the *is,* argument aimed at establishing that existence was regarded as either superfluous or impossible. Stated in other terms, the empiricist claim was—and still is—that without copresence, or at least its possibility, no logical argument can function as a surrogate arriving at the *is* through inference of any sort. The difficulty, of course, and it has accounted for all the twistings and turnings of modern empiricism from Locke and Hume to current forms of analysis, is that God is not to be understood as one sensible object among others and therefore forms a special case. This difficulty stemmed from the fact that the empiricism in question was derived entirely from an analysis of our knowledge of sensible objects and their relations to each other, with the result that not only did the knowledge of God become problematic, but the knowledge of human selves or persons did so as well. Confronted with both the demand for copresence and the need to deal with realities such as God and the self where the distinction between ''presence'' and ''absence'' obviously cannot be drawn with the precision possible in the case of a chair or a red patch, this sort of empiricism is bound to be confused. In consequence, from this perspective, God and the self are either ruled out as realities altogether, or some inconsistent exception is made in order to make room for them. It is instructive to note that the founders of classical empiricism in the period of Locke and Hume failed to carry their principle through consistently in the case of God, and all fell back on some form of the older rationalist argument.[1]

So much, for the moment at least, concerning the classical empiricist logical objection to all forms of approach to God through rational dialectic. But there is as well a religious objection to the rationalist tradition, an objection inspired by the empiricist temper and manifesting itself in the diverse forms of fideism, existential theology, and the theology of encounter. This objection, where it is not based on an utter rejection of the appropriateness of all rational argument with respect to God, focuses on what is taken as a fundamental deficiency in the argumentative approach itself, a deficiency which, as will become clear, is felt on both religious and experiential grounds. Unlike philosophical empiricism, which recognized the arguments for God as arguments and attacked them as such, this objection is directed not against the logic of any argument but rather against argument itself, against the sort of relation which is believed to be established by argument between the self and the reality—in this case God— whose existence is being argued for. The objection specifically is this: arguing for the existence of God means the adducing of reasons arranged in accordance with appropriate logical rules that are to compel the reasoner to accept a reality that "must be" or which is necessitated by logical inference. Here the warrant for God is the validity of the argument, and the "must be" is made to serve as the surrogate for the *is* of copresence. Now the objection is that, since we are supposedly arguing from some premises which express what is or is given to another reality which, just because its existence has to be argued for, is *not* present or given, we are in effect arguing to or inferring what is, from the vantage point of experience, absent. Stated in more experiential terms, God has the status of a "must be" in rational demonstration, but he is not met or encountered. It is as if there were grounds for inferring that in all existence, there "must be" at least one person among all the appropriate rational beings that exist who is our friend, except that we never meet or encounter him.

It seems to me that the many rejections of the arguments for God based on logical grounds and the classical conception of experience can be shown to be far from conclusive and to rest ultimately on a dogmatic foundation in the sense that existence must be construed to mean "sensible existence" and nothing else. With regard to the religious objection, however, I am persuaded that there is an important truth in it. Argument which leaves the "must be" of God hanging before the mind, as it were, in a logical space gives rise in the individual to a sense of incompleteness, of something lacking. "Of course," one might say, "a such and such necessarily exists, but I have never encountered it." It is as if the apprehension of necessity (the "must be"), though generally regarded as superior to the knowledge of fact or immediate existence, were now to be regarded as inferior; we would be happy to sacrifice the "must be" of rational dialectic in exchange for the "is" of encounter.

Should anyone propose to dismiss the problem of the gulf between presence and absence, the "is" and the "must be," as either trivial or based on a mere feeling that has no logical import, perhaps he may be persuaded to change his view when he becomes acquainted with the fact that the problem is raised in a vivid way by Anselm himself in the *Proslogion*. I confess that earlier I was inclined to think of the problem as a recent one arising exclusively from the doubts of contemporary existentially—and even mystically—oriented theologians about the validity of argument in the sphere of religion. But this is not so. There is a chapter in the Anselmian program of "faith seeking understanding" which seems to have gone entirely unnoticed by all commentators, and which focuses, in a dramatic way, the experiential issue. To begin with, it would generally be admitted that in the modern sense Anselm was not an empiricist. Although his meditative approach involves the experience of the person to a greater extent than is appreciated by all contemporary commentators, whether fideistic or rationalistic, there is no getting away from the fact that Anselm proposed the most rationalistic argument on record for the existence of God. An appreciation of this fact will enhance the importance of what is to come. The fact is that in two places in the *Proslogion* Anselm raises the same problem of the presence and absence of God to which we have alluded. Let us consider these two crucial passages.

In chapter 13 of the *Proslogion*[2] Anselm is meditating about actually *finding* God. In reiterating the basic ideas of the famous argument set forth in earlier chapters, he describes God as the *summum omnium* and as the reality than which a better cannot be thought. Up to this point in the meditation we have the familiar language and ideas of the ontological argument; suddenly there is a dramatic reversal, and Anselm says: "But if you have found [Him], why is it that you do not experience (*non sentio*) what you have found. Why, O Lord God, does my soul not experience you (*te sentit*) if it has found You?" Two chapters later when Anselm is setting forth the familiar Augustinian figure of the "inaccessible light" in which God dwells and through which everything is seen, he says: "In you I move and in you I have my being and I cannot come near to you. You are within me and around me and I do not have any experience of you (*te sentio*)."[3]

If we consider the context of these statements, that they are part of the meditative and dialectical Anselmian program of "faith seeking understanding" which reached its zenith in the ontological argument, we cannot but be struck by the intrusion of the experiential concern. On the one hand, there is for the Anselmian thinker the utmost rational penetration into the logic of the divine necessity and a comprehension of the reality of God so powerful that it is seen to exclude even the real possibility of the divine nonexistence. That is strong rationalism. On the other hand, there is a clear sense of the failure of even this degree of rational penetration to furnish a concrete realization in experience, an encounter or experience that transcends—in the sense of being richer or more concrete—the force of all argument. This transcendence does not take the form of a something more to know, one more item of "knowledge about" that cannot be known by finite minds; it is rather the demand for an encounter, a meeting ground of the individual and the God he seeks.

No thinker before or since Anselm, with the possible exception of Hegel, has been bolder in pursuing the program of "faith seeking understanding." Understanding for Anselm took the form of a by now familiar argument which has had the peculiar distinction of being refuted more often than any other piece of reasoning on record, and even after nine hundred years a final decision has not been reached. The logic of the argument is well known, even if the meditative framework taken so seriously by Anselm is invariably ignored. According to that logic, the assertion of the nonexistence of the reality denoted by the "that than which nothing greater . . ." formula is a self-contradictory assertion. The thinker moving through the steps of the argument with understanding is to emerge with the further understanding that he cannot both say "God" with understanding and fail to see that God's nonexistence is not, and never was, a possibility. No firmer assertion of the "must be" with respect to God could be found. Even the later defenders of the cosmological arguments, with their own high confidence in reason, thought Anselm rather too bold in arguing for God's existence without even fortifying his premises at the outset with the assumption of some existing things. The point is that, at least in any modern sense, Anselm was no empiricist (and he certainly was not an existentialist!), and yet in the depths of his own meditative rationalism we find him wondering why a reality which so supremely "must be" from a logical standpoint is not made manifest at some focal point or points in experience.[4] The point to be underlined at this juncture is that the problem of meeting or experiencing God is not to be thought of only in terms of existentialist demands that have arisen as a result of dissatisfaction with modern rationalism. There is an essential issue involved, and Anselm's experience helps to focus it. The "must be" of argument seems to provide us at once with too much and too little. The "must be" with respect to God is a rational guarantee of a reality who has been traditionally understood as "omnipresent," but the "omni" does not translate itself into the *hic et nunc* of *presence* to an individual and is therefore too much. We are back again to the analogy of the friend; a "must be" friend can only appear to us in the end as an abstraction if we never in fact meet him, and therefore the "must be" is too little. And from the religious perspective the case is even more urgent with respect to God. An individual related to God through the "must be" of argument taken all by itself is left with a sense of something missing. There is necessity and omnipresence, but no presence.

Now, it may seem strange to have approached our initial question so indirectly, but, as I shall show, there is a method in this madness. Suppose we ask whether we have not been seduced into believing that there must be an irreconcilable opposition between the way of inference and argument on the one hand and experience or encounter on the other. Suppose it were the case that we had been thinking in terms of two erroneous conceptions, an erroneous conception of experience as clear-cut sensible content "given" to the mind and totally disconnected from thought and inference, and an erroneous conception of inference as a disjointed rational move from what is present—the premises—to what is absent, the object in the conclusion. Suppose there were a way of finding the "is" in the "must be," or that there were a way of realizing that "must be" in the concrete unit of experience. Or, again, suppose the classical conception of experience with its roots in certain doctrines set forth by Locke, but more decisively by Hume, were simply inadequate and unable to do justice to all of the many interactions with ourselves and the world to which we can scarcely deny the name of experience. Indeed, it seems to be the case that the tendency of classical empiricism to model experience exclusively on the knowledge of objects in the world for purposes of theoretical science explains why that position found difficulty not only with the experience of God but with the experience of one self by another. These suppositions all point the way to inquiry, and, if they can be justified, we shall have opened up a way of mediating a disastrous split in the modern philosophical and theological consciousness. This split defines the experiential pole as sheer encounter transcending and thus defeating all attempts at analysis, and the rational dimension as an abstract display of terms or signs arranged in accordance with certain rules—formal, austere and unconnected with the experience of anyone, including that of the one who manipulates the terms. In the midst of this polarization it is far easier to see how the gulf can be widened than to see how it can be spanned. As logic becomes more and more formal and machinelike, moving in the thin atmosphere of an implication that is incapable of sustaining the life of an actual reasoner, the demand for immediate encounter is intensified, and, as if to underline the urgency and the importance, encounter is made to appear as something opaque and beyond the reach of analysis. That polarization must be overcome.

Let us begin with experience and then pass on to inference and thought activity. As we shall see, the suggestion that we begin with experience and then pass on to thought is actually misleading if, as I would hold, actual experiencing is shot through and through with thought and inference. There is no objection to starting with the proposition that all we understand and claim to know must find its basis in experience, if it is not supposed at the outset that "experience" has some singular or differential character which determines wholly in advance of actual experiencing what it is that can or cannot be experienced. With regard to a general theory of experience as distinct from actual experiencing, it is necessary to point out that while every interpretation of actual experience presupposes such a theory, it is not by means of it that experience is actually had. I do not want to repeat all that has been said, in the development of American pragmatism and of Continental phenomenologies, about the inadequacies of the classical British conception of experience. The main thrust of the critique can be expressed in three points: first, experience is not an affair that begins with the psychically primitive, well-demarcated, simple data of the senses (with the disjoined enjoying a privileged position over the connected and continuous); second, experience is not a passive reception or duplicative registry of what is encountered exclusive of inference and interpretation; third, experience is not exclusively a matter of knowledge in the sense that the experiencer is not always engaged as a theoretical observer who looks at the world objectively as if his experience were merely material to be known and made no difference to him as a unique individual. By contrast with these features, what I call the reconstructed conception of experience, developed so largely on the American scene, focuses attention on actual experiencing as a complex affair of interaction between what there is, on the one hand, and the language-using animal able to appreciate, on the other. From this vantage point, the simple, primitive data of the classical conception stand out not as ultimate facts but as selective abstractions based on the differential principle that the distinct or separated items of experience are "more real" than the continuous and the transitional. Second, and to this point we must return, experience is not a momentary affair of passive reception but a temporally thick process involving both inference and interpretation so that *as experience* it is shot through with meaning that is realized only in thought. In short, the activity of thought is not a merely subsequent and ancillary activity externally related to the experiential occasion upon which it arises. Third, experience, or, more accurately, experiencing, is a stage in the realization of the person who experiences; it belongs to his life as a complete unity sustaining many stances to the world surrounding—ethical, religious, aesthetic, productive—and is not to be regarded exclusively as a channel for the acquisition of theoretical knowledge where the relation of that experience to the purpose of the individual who has it becomes insignificant.

The first and indispensable step in dealing with the question of the experience of God is taken when we have set aside any conception of experience that precludes at the outset the possibility of experiencing what cannot be uniquely identified with a localizable sense datum. This step is, to be sure, negative and, though necessary, not of itself sufficient for the resolution of the problem. For we are not ever justified in settling the question of the "what" of any experience on the basis merely of a general theory, however rich, that delineates the generic shape of experience. It is necessary to consider specific situations of experience relevant to the subject at hand. From long experience in the Western tradition, at any rate, we have learned that there are two paradigmatic types of situation in and through which the idea of God arises and becomes the subject of dialectical treatment; they are therefore relevant to any discussion about experiencing God. These paradigmatic situations involve the experience of selfhood and reflection on its ground or source on the one hand, and experience of the cosmos in its contingency and its order on the other. As is well known, these two situations formed the starting points, respectively, of the ontological and cosmological traditions in philosophical theology. Because much contemporary discussion focuses exclusively on man and on the self as the only viable way of approach to God, and because this exclusive emphasis tends to submerge the cosmological dimension, there is need to redress the balance. To attempt to do so seems to me especially important at the present time, for if we consider current opinion regarding the three terms in the ancient chain of being—*Nature, Man,* and *God*—the first term in that sequence seems to be taken by most contemporaries more seriously than either *man* or *God.* Let us, therefore, consider a cosmologically oriented paradigm of experience.

Following a line of thought proposed by Charles Peirce,[5] let us each suppose ourselves alone in an open field on a dark but clear night that affords an uninterrupted view of the myriad stars and patterns of stars above. Apart from ourselves, man and culture fade into the background; the experience is all cosmos. Let us further imagine that we have succeeded in attaining that openness of mind and attitude which Peirce called "musement," an attitude of pure play in which we are receptive to what is and are determined by no other purpose than that of enjoying or appreciating the cosmic spectacle. No sooner are we settled in this frame of mind than we find ourselves wondering about the "thereness" or sheer presence of that universe which spreads, as far as we can see, without limit in any direction. Was it always there, and, if so, is it itself an eternal being? Was it, like the pattern of making things in our own finite experience, fashioned in some way to be by a power beyond itself? In short, we find ourselves ineluctably grasping for a ground, wondering how such an arrangement of planetary bodies could have come about. Moreover, we reflect upon ourselves in that setting, aware of our having recollected the previous moment and of a next to come, and we wonder not only about the fact of our own existence, but also about our involvement in this universe and the extent to which we are able to fathom its secrets only because there is some coordination between its structure and our own cognitive apparatus. How has such an order come about? Whence the coordination that makes knowledge possible? Can we in the midst of musing on the world that surrounds us prevent ourselves from thinking, entertaining, the idea of some transcending reality capable of coordinating all the order that we see in the world and in ourselves and in the relations between the two? Some such experience of the universe as standing in need of a coordinator not seen to be identical with any of its proper parts is, in my view, the primordial experiential situation that forms the substance of all cosmological arguments.

But, you may ask, is that what we are to understand as the experiencing of God, some sort of direct perception of God in and through our direct encounter with a world of order that seems not to arrange itself? My answer to the question is *no,* if by experience is meant the direct apprehension of one more reality over and above the discriminable items presented by the starry vault with which our wonder and musement first began. But why may it not be the case that God is actually ingredient both in the portion of the world experienced and in the experience itself in the form of *an actual power of coordinating* the many factors that must be meaningfully arranged if such an experience is to emerge at all?

Here we come to that second topic which I mentioned earlier as accompanying the reconstructed theory of experience, namely, the theory of inference. Must inference, and indeed the several forms of rational activity involved in the interpretation of any experience, necessarily be understood as a logical development *away from* experience, so that it inevitably is made to appear as abstract and as no more than a form of "mere thought" in comparison with the concreteness of the experience from which it sets out? Why may not inference be a real penetration into the depth of experience disclosing what there is reason to believe is ingredient in it but not evident on its surface? Why may not inference disclose what is *present* in a complex of experience and not merely absent in comparison with what is presented on the surface of experience? From this perspective, the gap between experience as something presently had or enjoyed, and inference as a content merely thought, would close. Instead we would think of a distinction between the surface of experience and its depth, the latter being disclosed by thought, to be sure, but still disclosed as the content of experience. To return to our earlier point, the "must be" of argument is the reappearance of the "is" of direct experience in another medium. What is apprehended in and through rational development is no less experienced than what was apprehended on the surface of the direct experience that first gave rise to thought. The problem is, however, can we hope to recover on the current scene this conception of inference as thought moving through a "thick" or experiential medium? I am well aware of the ideas and doctrines that militate against such a recovery.

To begin with, modern logic has suffered from too much practice and too little philosophy. In short, the failure to develop the philosophy of logic more fully has had the unfortunate consequence of obscuring implicit philosophical problems such as the nature of inference or of leading us to suppose that these problems can be resolved entirely by stipulation or convention. The relegation, moreover, of inference to the domain of the "psychological" on the ground that one wants to be concerned with purely "logical" questions has had the effect of removing logic entirely from the continuum of experience. What is truly remarkable in this development is the assumption that the distinction between "logical" and "psychological" is quite clear and that one can always avoid with impunity the problems occurring in thinking as it actually takes place in the psychological domain by a narrow escape into the logical. Thought thus becomes totally formal and is seen as rule-governed relations of implication between some rather peculiar entities called "propositions," which are entirely indifferent to the fact that a thinker somewhere and somewhen actually thinks them. If we add to this the widespread assumption that implication is to be understood as essentially tautological in character, we have a completed picture of thought which cannot function within experience, and, even if it could, there would be no possibility of its bringing forth anything new. In short, with such a conception there could be no rational development of the meaning or depth of experience within experience itself. Thought stands in its universal and formal austerity on one side, and experience, especially where it involves complex meanings in its depth— art, religion, morality—is construed in individual immediate modes so that there seems to be no way in which the full content of experience can be articulated for the individual experiencer.

I see no way of remedying the situation unless we go back to experience in order to gain insight into the mode of functioning which thought exhibits. In an arresting comment written over fifty years ago, Dewey has this to say about experience and inference:

> In the traditional notion experience and thought are antithetical terms. Inference, so far as it is other than a revival of what has been given in the past, goes beyond experience; hence it is either invalid, or else a measure of desperation by which, using experience as a springboard, we jump out to a world of stable things and other selves. But experience, taken free of the restrictions imposed by the older concept, is full of inference. There is, apparently, no conscious experience without inference; reflection is native and constant.[6]

The first step, then, is to return to the experiential matrix in which we have an individual encountering—undergoing, interacting with—some portion of reality. Let us recall our figure of the person engaging in musement confronted with the starry heavens. To begin with, we shall not suppose our individual to be endowed with nothing but a *tabula rasa* for either a mind or a memory. He comes to the situation with past experience, some skill in using language, and a stock of concepts in terms of which he can apprehend what is presented. His grasp of the order in the situation and his reflective wonder at its sheer "thereness" naturally leads him to the idea of a ground or orderer for both the existence itself and the peculiar form it exhibits. The "naturally leads him" means an actual move in thought inside the experiential matrix itself. Perhaps this move is based on analogy with other more familiar experiences involving finite objects; perhaps it is prompted by a more abstract conception of cause and effect; perhaps it is prompted by other beliefs which the person holds. But, whatever prompts the inference, the fact remains that a rational transition is made and, as Peirce so effectively argued, that transition when actually made by an experient in the sort of situation we are considering is not correctly translated into disjointed arguments each with a previously thought premise controlled by a principle of inference which is before the mind of the thinker. The casting of the thought actually had, and the movement from one thought to another into explicit premises and principles of inference, comes as the upshot or end of the process. Explicit formulation is for the purposes of self-criticism and for examining the thought transition to see if it can be substantiated. This, of course, needs to be done, but the translation of the continuous movement of the mind within experience into the explicit argument which is disjointed loses something in the experiential matrix. The important point is that the inference as actually made by the one who muses takes place within the experiential matrix and is thought to disclose ingredients in its depth; the inference appears to be a move into a logical domain wholly distinct from experience only when the natural leading of the mind is replaced by the explicitly formulated argument. When this happens and a cosmological argument with explicit premises is put forth, the experiential matrix with its inference is left behind, and the "must be" God of the conclusion appears not as a reality ingredient or present in the depth of the initial experience but as a reality that is "absent" in comparison with the surface of the experience itself. The proponents of immediacy and encounter who protest the inadequacy of the "merely inferred" God are pointing to precisely this "absent"—by which they usually mean "abstract"—God. What they do not see is that, insofar as they attend to the matter at all, they are making the same mistakes about experience and inference as their opponents. The question is, Is transcendence of the experiential matrix justified? Only if experience is understood as excluding inference. But an examination of what happens in experiences of the sort we are considering shows that inference and even the proposal of rudimentary hypotheses naturally take place. But if inference is not excluded, then it must not only take place within the experience, but must also be seen as the dialectical development of that experience beyond its surface. And there is no reason for excluding the result of that development itself from the sphere of experience. Every experience literally contains and has present in it ingredients that transcend its surface, and these ingredients can only be apprehended in thought. What must be avoided, however, is the supposition that the directly presented represents experience in some preeminent sense while the inferred is all thought construction, abstractions, or mere ideas. To return to our muser and to our original question, there is no reason why we cannot say that he experiences God within his experiential matrix as long as we understand experience as far richer and more complex than its immediate sensible surface, and inference as the development of that experience, a penetration into its ingredients rather than a move away from it. Anselm, then, should have been bolder, if that is not too ironic a suggestion. In accordance with his own dialectic and especially with his own understanding of God, he should have seen the "must be" of his argument, developed out of his matrix of reflective thought, as the "is" or presence of God ingredient in that reflection—the presence of the Uncreated Light. There was, on the view I have been developing, no need for him to ask, after he had worked through his ingenious reasoning, *Why do I not experience you?* The *is* is present in the *must be*.

In conclusion, I have not, to be sure, considered the question of the validity of particular rational arguments for God, or what I have called the "must be." That was not my purpose. Instead I wanted to acknowledge and take seriously the element of truth in the criticism that traditional arguments have not done justice to the experiential pole. I believe it is true that a merely "must be" God is inadequate for religious purposes, however sufficient it may be for philosophers, if such there be, who retain God without religion. On the other hand, unless we adopt a totally mystical position as a way of preserving the experiential element, the present climate of philosophical opinion so much determined by the classical conception of experience does not make it easy to speak of experiencing God in a way that would be intelligible to a critical empiricism. Hence I was led to question the adequacy of the classical conception of experience, and also the adequacy of the wholly formal conception of logic as an instrument for disclosing the depth of actual experience. In the end it is imperative, not only for the philosophical and religious concerns, but for the whole of modern culture, to overcome the disastrous split in modern consciousness between experience as something wholly immediate, opaque, anxious, and undisciplined, and thought as no more than an empty logic. Perhaps if the split can be overcome in relation to the problem of God, we shall have gone a long way in making good the claim of Whitehead that God should be the supreme exemplification of our categories and not a reality invoked to prevent their collapse.

NOTES

1. See my *Religion and Empiricism*, Aquinas Lecture Series (Milwaukee: Marquette, 1967).

2. M. J. Charlesworth, *St. Anselm's Proslogion* (Oxford: Oxford University Press, 1965), p. 135.

3. Ibid., p. 137.

4. Anselm's expression *"te sentio"* need not be rendered by an English term that means "sensing" through the so-called five senses. *Sentio* embraces a range of meanings revolving about "perceiving," "experiencing," and "being aware of." The point is that Anselm's contrast is not between the apprehension of God's existence through *reason* and his being *sensed;* it is rather a contrast between the deliverance of an argument and some more intimate form of encounter. In this connection, I believe Charlesworth is correct in translating *sentio* as *experience* in chaps. 14 and 16 of the *Proslogion*.

5. "A Neglected Argument for the Reality of God," in *Collected Papers of Charles Sanders Peirce,* ed. Charles Hartshorne and Paul Weiss, 6 vols. (Cambridge: Harvard University Press, Belknap Press, 1931), 6:452–93. I mention this paper not because I want in any way to invoke the authority of Peirce but to acknowledge what I believe is an important and, ironically, a neglected paper.

6. "The Need for a Recovery of Philosophy," in *Creative Intelligence: Essays in the Pragmatic Attitude,* ed. John Dewey et al. (New York: Holt and Co., 1917), p. 7.

Chapter 13

ON RELIGIOUS MYTHS
Joseph J. Kockelmans

IN this essay I wish to explain what I take to be constitutive of religious myths. In so doing I shall try first to locate our contemporary concern with myths within our Western tradition in which the phenomenon of myth has been examined from various perspectives for many centuries. Then I shall attempt to focus on the most important aspects of *religious* myths by commenting on certain ideas proposed by some contemporary philosophers in whose works reflections on religous myths play an important part. Finally, I wish to conclude this essay with some critical thoughts on the question of what attitude we should adopt today in regard to religious myths. Here I shall be concerned primarily with the Judeo-Christian conception of religion.[1]

MYTH AND THE STUDY OF MYTH IN OUR WESTERN TRADITION: SOME INTRODUCTORY REMARKS

In the literature on myth and mythology several authors have pointed to the fact that in attempting to answer the question of what myth really is, it is relatively unfruitful to undertake an etymological study of the word *myth* (from the Greek *muthos:* word, speech, saying; tale, story, fable). Obviously such a study is not meaningless, but it would shed little light on the contemporary problem of the meaning and function of myths. Even an appeal to ordinary language usages of the term is not very illuminating in that in the various sciences concerned with myth, the term has received a kind of "oper-

This is a revised version of part of "On Myth and Its Relation to Hermeneutics," *Cultural Hermeneutics* 1 (1973): 47–86. Copyright © 1973 by D. Reidel Publishing Co., Dordrecht, Holland.

ational'' meaning which in many instances goes far beyond, or in other case is much more limited and refined than, that used by people in their everyday language.[2] For this reason a critical approach to the questions seems to be more adequate. But before turning to such a critical analysis of *religious* myth, a brief introduction to the problem of myth as such seems to be of some importance as a way of placing the modern views in their historical perspective.

The question of what myth precisely is, cannot easily be answered in a few statements. One of the greatest difficulties one encounters when approaching this phenomenon is the fact that the greater part of our knowledge concerning myths has come to us via written documents which in many cases refer to a much older oral tradition. Most of these documents have been preserved and are studied mainly because of their historical or literary value. The consequence of this practice has been that for many centuries people have quite commonly believed that myths are either a kind of literary art, or documents in the form of stories which somehow have to do with the origin of history, of a nation, a religion, etc. Many contemporary authors, on the other hand, believe that basically myth is not a story of some kind but a certain way of understanding or even a way of living which underlies all story-myths and to which these story-myths refer. At any rate, in contemporary literature the term *myth* is very often used in a sense in which it refers to a very special mode of understanding and/or living.[3]

A second difficulty is connected with the fact that the phenomenon of myth has been studied by a great number of modern scholars with quite different scientific interests: history of religion, philosophy of religion, psychology of religion, philology, history of philosophy, classics, sociology, cultural anthropology, psychoanalysis, history, to mention some of the major areas. It is understandable that sociologists with an interest in understanding the origin and life of a society will stress quite different elements in the phenomenon of myth from those who are interested in philosophy of religion, or in literary phenomena. This has led to views about the very essence of myth which at first sight are contradictory or at least somehow exclusive in regard to one another. The confusion has become so complete that today it is even difficult to specify the genus to which the phenomenon ''myth'' belongs: is myth a kind of story? a work of art? a way of thinking? a way of living? a peculiar form of interpretation? etc.

Myths and theories about them are almost as old as our Western civilization, at least insofar as we have any historical knowledge of it.[4] The oldest conception of myth is the *allegorical,* first defended by the Alexandrian rhetoricians on the basis of a suggestion by Theagenes of Rhegium (fl. ca. 525 B.C.) and then systematically developed by the Stoics. The gods and heroes of the ancient myths must be reduced to cosmic forces and events, or to physical and ethical principles.

According to Euhemerus the gods of the ancient myths are deified heroes or kings. Myths represent the confused memory and an imaginative transfiguration of the deeds and vicissitudes of the primitive kings.

Thus, although the need for an interpretation of myths was already experienced in the ancient world, there was not yet at that time a real "hermeneutics" of myths. This was due to the fact that all people originally conceived of myths exclusively in terms of stories of some kind and limited themselves to two basic interpretations: gods and heroes are either to be reduced to abstract concepts (allegoric interpretation) or they are to be reduced to fictive historical personalities (euhemerism). The goal of these interpretations was not to explain what myth is and how myths function in the life of a society, but mainly to maintain and preserve from these myths what seemed to be pedagogically important. Until 1795 all authors stressed the *utility* of the interpretation for the individual or for society.

A new, *hermeneutic*, approach to myths was prepared by Vico and Herder and subsequently formulated for the first time by Moritz.[5] According to Moritz, myths must be considered as a work of man's imagination in the creation of a mythical world. This world is a world of its own separated from the world of real things but somehow related to it. Myths try to communicate something about the world view as it has been developed in prehistoric times. In trying to understand a myth, one must interpret it within the context of the civilization to which it belongs and about which it tries to communicate something. In so doing one must take the myth as such, in the way it itself is, without any reference to anything else it could mean either allegorically or euhemeristically, and which thus could still be in some sense important for us. However, myths should not be interpreted as historical data, either. Moritz's conception of myth has become part of many contemporary views of myth, mainly through the works of Schleiermacher, Schelling, and the so-called young Hegelians.[6]

Whereas originally interest in the problem of myth came mainly from the side of classics, classical philosophy, philology, and theology, in the nineteenth century, studies by cultural anthropologists, historians, psychologists, and sociologists started to gradually appear. In these very different approaches to the problem of myth most scientists have been quite onesided in that they stressed mainly those elements in myth which from their own scientific point of view appeared to be obvious and relevant. The consequence of this development has been that today we find ourselves with a great number of different theories about myths. Some people believe that it is still possible to adopt a general point of view from which then contributions by the various scientists who have written on the subject can be evaluated and then incorporated into an overall theory.[7] Others have defended the view that one should come to a single general theory of myth with the intention of ousting all other theories as unscientific.[8] Finally, some authors are of the opinion that it is impossible to develop an overall theory of myth, in that myth appears to be a "many splendored thing."[9]

Although the arguments which Kirk has set forth for his view are not without merit, I nonetheless feel that in the final analysis his position is logically untenable. For, if Kirk were completely correct, it would be impossible for us to distinguish between a myth on the one hand, and a novel, a scientific theory, a religious creed, etc., on the other. However, Kirk's arguments have definitively refuted Malinowski's view and any other view which tries to single out and define one particular conception of myth which establishes in a univocal manner the "true" nature of myth and on the basis of which then all other conceptions of myth can be rejected as unscientific. That is why as a working-hypothesis Cohen's suggestion seems to be more promising. With this hypothesis in mind I now wish to turn to a critical analysis of some contemporary conceptions of *religious* myths. In so doing I shall focus first on some aspects of one of the best-known contemporary conceptions of myth, namely, that proposed by Mircea Eliade.

RELIGIOUS MYTHS NARRATE A SACRED STORY: ELIADE

According to Eliade[10] it is difficult to define myth in a way which is acceptable to all scholars and at the same time intelligible to a larger audience. Myth is an extremely complex phenomenon which can be approached and interpreted from various, complementary points of view.

As a general definition Eliade suggests the following: Myth narrates a sacred story. Myth is a story which relates an event that took place in primordial time. In other words, myth tells us how through the deeds of supernatural beings a reality came into existence, be it the whole of reality (the cosmos) or only a fragment of reality (an island, a river, a species of plant or animal, a particular form of human behavior, an institution). Myth, then, is always an account of a creation; it narrates how something began to be.

Myth tells only of that which *really* happened. The actors in a myth are supernatural beings. They are known by what they did. Hence myth discloses the creative activity of these beings and the sacredness of their works. Myths describe the diverse and sometimes dramatic breakthroughs of the sacred into the world. Since the myth is regarded as a sacred story, it is a true story; it is a true history which is verified by the facts. The cosmogonic myth is true because the existence of the world is there to prove it. The myth of the origin of death is true because man's mortality proves it.

Most primitive people make a clear distinction between true and sacred stories (myth) and false stories (fables and tales). Whereas myths have a religious and educational meaning, other stories have a recreational meaning.

Myths narrate not only the origin of the world, of plants, animals, and men, but also the primordial events in consequence of which man became what he is today: mortal, sexed, organized in society; myths finally "explain" the most important social institutions. What happened *in illo tempore* can be repeated through rituals. For a member of a primitive society it is essential to know the myths, and by reenacting them ritually he is able to repeat what the "gods" did *ab origine.* Myths are to be *lived,* and in so doing one emerges from profane, chronological time and enters a sacred time at once primordial and indefinitely recoverable. Thus, living a myth implies a genuinely religious experience in that it differs from the everyday experience, witnesses and reenacts the creative works of supernatural beings, and makes modern man become a contemporary of the gods.

Eliade distinguishes two major types of myth which then are subdivided. There are first the myths of the beginning and the end of the world, to which cosmogonic, apocalyptic, and millennialist myths belong. Then there is the group of myths concerning gods, the creation of man, myths about the subsequent modification of the world and of the human condition, myths associated with celestial bodies, and, finally, heromyths.

From the above brief summary of some of Eliade's views it is quite clear that Eliade's conception incorporates elements of a number of other theories of myth: myth is inherently a linguistic phenomenon, it is a story of some kind; the content of the story is at once historical, sacred, religious, and of great social value; myths are taken to be true and not as mere fables; myths are closely related to rites and rituals. Now, although one perhaps can accept that all of this is to some degree true for myths which are inherently *religious* in character, he will still wonder whether Eliade really comes to an encompassing theory of myth. Yet he often suggests that his conception of myth captures the essence of all myths and that only religious myths are *genuine* myths. But even if one limits his reflections to Eliade's conception of myths insofar as they are religious in nature, there are still at least three large areas in which our account of his theory is inadequate. First of all, the relationship between myth and symbol is not yet stressed. Secondly, we have not yet explicitly explained the typical form of experience from which the myth-stories originate, nor why the mythical stories for some people at some point in time "work mythically," whereas for other people or for the same people at different times, they do not (or no longer) work as myths. In other words, we have not yet explicitly answered the questions of what is typical for a mythical experience of world, why this experience is to be expressed in stories, and, as far as the myth-stories are concerned, precisely what makes these stories inherently different from other kinds of stories. Finally, we have not yet explained what attitude one must adopt in regard to religious myths as members of a society that has become predominantly oriented toward science and technology.

I plan to examine these questions in the order in which they have just been formulated. In so doing I shall no longer take my point of departure in a reflection on ideas suggested by Eliade, even though he did address some of these questions, but rather in ideas suggested by Ricoeur, Cassirer, and Bultmann, respectively.

MYTH AND SYMBOL: RICOEUR

Ricoeur[11] begins by stating that he is interested in religious myths only. Although he leaves room for myths which are not inherently religious in character, most of the time, however, he, too, seems to suggest that only religious myths are *genuine* myths.

In his view myth is not a false explanation by means of images and fables, but a traditional narration which relates to events that happened at the beginning of time, and one which has the purpose of providing grounds for the ritual actions of men today and, in a general manner, of establishing all forms of action and thought by which man understands himself and his world.

Myths once also had the character of explanations. For us moderns a myth is merely a myth, and all etiological character and intention is now to be excluded. By thus excluding the explanatory character of myths, we wish to make free their symbolic function so that they may reveal their exploratory significance and their contribution to understanding. The symbolic function of a myth consists in its power of discovering and revealing the bond between man and what he considers sacred. Once it is "purified" through contact with scientific history, and once it is elevated to the dignity of a genuine symbol, myth is still a dimension of modern thought.

Myth can be recognized as a myth only by modern man, because he alone has reached the point where history and myth have become separated. We are tempted today to eliminate all myths from our modern world view. However, there is another alternative; it is precisely because myth and history are separated for us that it is possible for us to understand myth *as myth*. This we do in a process of interpretation in which we purify the myth from its pseudoknowledge or false *logos* such as it is found, for instance, in the etiological interpretation of myths.

Ricoeur takes his point of departure in the following working hypotheses:

1. The first function of the religious myths is to embrace mankind as a whole in one ideal history.
2. The universality of man manifested through religious myths receives its concrete character from the movement which is introduced into human experience by narration: in recounting the Beginning and the End, the myths confer upon this experience an orientation and tension: from Genesis to Apocalypse.
3. Still more fundamentally the myths try to get at the enigma of human existence, namely, the discordance between its fundamental reality (state of innocence) and the actual modality of man (sin). The myths account for this transition by means of a narration precisely because there is no logical nexus between the fundamental reality and man's present existence.

From this it follows that a myth must not be taken as an allegoric story. A myth cannot be translated into a clear language. What the myth shows, while hiding it, cannot be said in a direct discourse that replaces the myth. By its triple function of concrete universality, temporal orientation, and ontological exploration, myth has a way of revealing things which is not reducible to any translation from a language in cipher to a clear language.

Thus, myth is neither history nor explanation. Although one must choose between *gnosis* and science, one is not forced into a choice between myth and genuine knowledge. Myth taken positively is a second-degree function of primary symbols. A myth is a narration which means symbolically, not etiologically. In elaborating this idea Ricoeur borrows from Van der Leeuw, Leenhardt, and Eliade. But instead of moving from the narrative to the pre-narrative root of the myth as they have suggested, Ricoeur wants to follow the opposite course from the pre-narrative consciousness to the mythical narration because the whole enigma of the symbolic function of myths is precisely centered in this latter transition. In so doing two basic characteristics of myths are to be explained carefully: 1) myth is an expression in language; 2) in myth the symbol takes the form of narration.

For the phenomenologists of religion just mentioned, the myth-narration is the verbal envelope of a form of life felt and lived before being verbally formulated. This form of life expresses itself first in an inclusive mode of behavior relative to the whole of things; this behavior is expressed more completely in rite than in narration. Furthermore, both ritual action and mythical language taken together point beyond themselves to a model which they repeat: imitation in gestures and verbal repetition are the broken expressions of a living participation in an original act. By participation is meant here the special relation of man to the sacred.

Thus there is a mythical structure that is the matrix of all the images and all the particular narrations underlying all concrete myths. The ultimate significance of this mythical structure is to be found in the fact that it indicates the intimate accord of the man of cult and myth with the whole of being, the cosmos. It aims at an indivisible plenitude in which the supernatural and the natural, the real and the psychological are not yet separated. It is only in intention that the myth restores some wholeness; it is because man himself has lost that wholeness that he reenacts and imitates it in myth and rite. Since primitive man is already a man of division, the myth can only be an *intentional* restoration or reinstatement of this wholeness; in that sense it is essentially symbolical.

Ricoeur then points briefly to the view on myth suggested by Gusdorf,[12] who stressed the distance between experience and intention by attributing to myth a biological role of protection against anxiety. Myth is an antidote to distress because the man of myths is already an unhappy consciousness; unity, conciliation are things he has to speak about and to reenact precisely because he does not experience them as given.

Claude Lévi-Strauss has also pointed to the discrepancy between the experienced limitation and the signified totality. This totality, signified in the myths but so little experienced, becomes available only when it is condensed in sacred beings and objects which become the privileged signs of the significant whole. The sacred takes on contingent forms precisely because it is "floating"; it cannot be divined except through the indefinite diversity of mythologies and rituals. If the plenitude were experienced, it would be everywhere in space and time; but because it is only aimed at by means of symbols, it first requires special signs and then a discourse on the signs. Hence the narrative myth has the function of guarding the finite contours of the signs, which in their turn refer to the plenitude that man aims at but does not experience. That is why primitive civilizations have in common almost the same mythical structure, although this structure exists nowhere without a diversity of myths. Ricoeur thus explains the narrative character of the myth by pointing to the fact that, that in which myth and rite lead us to participate, has the character of a drama. The reason why the narration-myth must refer symbolically to a drama is that mythical consciousness not only does not experience the plenitude of meaning, but does not even indicate it except at the beginning or the end of a fundamental history in which the plenitude is established, lost, and recovered. The myth receives from this primordial drama the mode of discourse peculiar to narration.

Ricoeur concludes his reflections by again stipulating that two characteristics of myth are essential in his view: 1) the surplus of signification, the "floating" significance constituted by the sacred which is *intended* versus the limitation of what is *experienced;* 2) the reference to a cosmic drama which *once upon a time* marked the foundation of the world.

On several occasions Ricoeur stresses the point that myth is a second-degree function of certain primary symbols and that these symbols open up and disclose a dimension of experience that without them would remain closed and hidden.[13] In his own works Ricoeur has tried to justify this view by a critical analysis of symbols of good and evil. In the section to follow I wish to try to come to a better understanding of the typical kind of experience from which all religious myths originate without making the assumption that primary symbols necessarily are symbols of good and evil. In so doing I shall start with a brief reflection on certain ideas first developed by Cassirer.

MYTH AND EXPERIENCE: CASSIRER

For Cassirer[14] myth appears at first sight as mere chaos, a shapeless mass of incoherent ideas without rhyme or reason. Thus, it seems to be meaningless to seek the reasons for these ideas. Almost every natural and human phenomenon is capable of a mythical interpretation and calls for such an interpretation. That is why any attempt to unify mythological ideas, or to reduce all of them to a certain uniform type is bound to end up in failure. And yet the myth-making function in man does not lack real homogeneity. Although the religious symbols, for instance, may change incessantly, the underlying symbolic activity remains the same; and the same may be said for social and other symbols often found in myths.

A theory of myth is inherently laden with difficulties in that myth is non-theoretical in its very essence and meaning. Philosophy and contemporary science have never been willing to accept this essentially nontheoretical character of the myth. People have tried to explain myths by interpreting them allegorically or by subjecting them to scientific analysis in order to classify the mythical objects or the motives guiding the myth-making function. Cassirer is convinced that it is impossible to make us understand the mythical world by a process of intellectual reduction.

In Cassirer's view myths combine a theoretical element with an element of artistic creation. As such, myth has a close relationship to poetry. However, there is also an essential difference between myth and poetry. Poetry is indifferent to the existence or nonexistence of its object, whereas myth implies an act of faith in the reality of its object. Myth and science (as well as philosophy) have in common that both are in quest of reality, but in so doing both follow a different type of "logic" and pursue different aims.

Myth has, as it were, a double face: it shows a conceptual and a perceptual structure. A myth is not a mass of disorganized and confused ideas, and thus it depends upon a definite mode of perception. Contrary to scientific thought, which is interested in constant features and the invariable structures or laws governing them, and which thus presupposes an analytic and empirical form of perception, myth is perceptively not interested in objective qualities, but in physiognomic characters. For science nature is the totality of real things insofar as it is determined by general laws; for myth nature is a dramatic world, a world of actions, forces, and conflicting powers. That is why mythical perception is always impregnated with emotional qualities which call for an atmosphere of joy, grief, anguish, excitement, etc. This explains why a scientific approach to nature tends to eliminate the mythical approach to the world. However, by foregoing these physiognomic characters science does not and cannot annihilate myth; in addition to their objective and cosmological values, things also possess their anthropoligical value and meaning. And in the genetic order the latter seem to precede the former, as is clear from investigations into the ways small children perceive.

Thus, if one wishes to account for the world of mythical perception and mythical imagination, he must not begin wih a critique of both from the viewpoint of science and philosophy. In other words, what is needed is not a scientific explanation of thoughts and beliefs, but an interpretation of our mythical life. Myth is not a system of beliefs or dogmatic creeds, but consists much more in actions and rituals. Thus, even if we should succeed in analyzing myth into ultimate conceptual elements, we would still not yet grasp its vital principle, which is a dynamic one. Primitive man expresses his feelings and emotions not having no other means available for opening up such a world. Although appealing in mere abstract symbols, but in a concrete and immediate way in actions. One must study this whole of man's expression in order to understand the structure of myth.

Cassirer is very sympathetic in regard to the ideas developed by the French sociological school since Durkheim and Lucien Lévy-Bruhl, namely that fundamentally myths have a social character. But following Malinowski he disagrees with the French school and claims that myth is alogical or prelogical. Myth and science are different and even essentially so, and that is why any attempt to intellectualize myth must fail. The real substratum of myth is not a substratum of thought, but of *feeling*. The coherence of a myth does not rest upon any logical rules or laws but much more upon a unity of feeling. Myth does not work with fixed concepts; its basic characteristic is not a static, conceptual framework, but the law of metamorphosis. The primitive man does not approach the world logically, but sympathetically. Primitive man by no means lacks the ability to grasp the empirical differences of things. But in his conception of nature and life all these differences are obliterated by a stronger feeling: the deep conviction of a fundamental and indelible solidarity of life that bridges over the multiplicity and variety of its single form.

Language and myth are very closely related to one another. At the early stages of culture it is almost impossible to separate one from the other. The faculty of speech and the myth-making function are both fundamental and characteristic traits of man, but they cannot be reduced to one another, as Max Müller, for instance, tried to do. But although both these functions are basically different, in primitive man they worked together closely and this was connected with the fact that for primitive man nature and society constituted one unity, the great society of life. The belief in the magic power of the word was built upon this solidarity of life. At a later stage of his development man realized that the magic function of the word is to be replaced by its semantic function and thus that *logos* and *mythos* are to be separated. When at a still later stage the sciences develop, then each science has to go through a mythical stage in order gradually to achieve an increasing simplicity in the understanding of the relevant phenomena by setting up and carefully following logical and methodical laws and rules.

In an attempt to critically evaluate Cassirer's contribution to the problem of myth I wish first to point to the fact that Cassirer throughout uses Kantian insights. Cassirer broadens these insights and develops a critique of man's theoretical knowledge of nature into a critique of culture, although it is doubtful whether this can be done without destroying the Kantian perspective. It seems that a new and more primordial approach to the problem is needed here.[15]

Furthermore, Cassirer does not explain *why* there are two modes of thought, namely a scientific and a mythopoeic one, nor why sometimes the one dominates and sometimes the other. He seems to suggest that when scientific thought emerges, mythopoeic thought declines. But this positivist view, influenced by

Durkheim, is in conflict with what we observe in our contemporary societies.[16] Finally, Cassirer's conception of myth and the myth-making-function is in need of an ontological foundation, which it does not receive in his own work. Cassirer should have tried to found his interpretation of man's mythical life on a central characteristic of man's comprehension of the world. And in order to do so Cassirer should have explained man's *basic* mode of being in regard to the world, his transcendence. For the question precisely is, What aspect of man's basic mode of being brings him to mythical thinking? In the basic mode of being of man precisely what is it that leads him to turn toward mythical thought? It seems that a man turns to myth when he realizes that he *finds himself* in a world which is not of his own making and over which he does not have "full control." Realizing that he has been "thrown" into a world that is already constituted, a man can feel overpowered by this world and thus may turn to myths where the overpowering world manifests itself in the very special temporal mode of that which has been.

Cassirer has somehow intuitively felt the problem. He thought he had found an answer to the question by stating that man's mythical form of being manifests itself in its own mode in the form of *desire*. But why should this be so? And what kind of desire is meant here? How is this type of desire related to man's basic mode of being? If desire constitutes a form of involvement between the world and me, then one must realize that this kind of involvement is merely *one mode* according to which man's transcendence toward his world is *revealed,* but not necessarily *the mode* in which this transcendence becomes *constituted.* In myth man's transcendence takes on a very special modality, which Cassirer did not explain adequately.[17] We shall return to this issue later in this essay.

TOWARD THE ESSENCE OF MYTH[18]

As I see it, myth refers primarily to an inherently *human* form of understanding or conceiving. What is typical for this mode of understanding is that it is oriented toward a certain totality of meaning or world and *not immediately* toward concrete events, states of affairs, or entities of some kind. This form of understanding or conceiving has the character of a *firm belief* in the totality of meaning or world which it discloses and which is its immediate subject matter. On the basis of this firm belief, actions of some kind become possible and meaningful. The kind of action which is made possible by this firm belief ranges over a very broad domain and extends in principle to all forms of man's experience: theoretical understanding, religious conceptions and ritual action, social praxis, political action, economic behavior, etc.

A man appeals to this typical mode of understanding or conceiving any time he is in need of a totality of meaning or world in order to be able to act theoretically, practically, or otherwise, *and* he finds himself in the position of to this typical mode of conceiving is a genuinely human possibility for each individual man, in most cases a man will share this belief with other human beings and particularly with all the members of the society to which he belongs.

It is important to note here that as soon as a realm of meaning or world has been disclosed by a myth, man's interest usually turns immediately to the possibilities which the myth has opened for him. One could say that the firm belief which constitutes the myth remains on the level of the "unconscious" and can in many cases be made explicit only by means of reflexive analysis. In other words, although individual as well as social myths are at work in almost all realms of man's experience, man is sometimes reflexively aware of the presence of these myths, but in many cases he is not.

Finally, the firm belief which forms the mythical mode of conceiving can in many, if not in all, cases be articulated, and since all articulation is, or at least ultimately leads to, language, there is a very close relationship between myth and language.

From the foregoing it becomes clear why an adequate understanding of the phenomenon of myth is so difficult. For first of all, myth is a mode of conceiving which is *presupposed* in many forms of our articulated understanding as well as in many modes of action, whereas this articulated understanding and this action is immediately oriented not toward the totality of meaning disclosed by the myth, but precisely toward that which this world made understandable and meaningful. Secondly, in all realms of man's experience myth can be at work without his reflexive awareness of it, at least so long as his main interest keeps focusing on the possibilities which the myth precisely made accessible to him. Finally, what we know about myths is to a very great extent made available to us through the stories in which former generations have articulated and expressed their mythical understanding concerning a certain set of human phenomena. Today it is very difficult for us to clearly distinguish between the original myths and the linguistic articulation and expression of the firm belief in which they consist, as well as between the characteristics of the myth as myth and the characteristics of the myth as story.

In the literature which is available on the subject of myth many authors have pointed to the fact that myth is somehow related to man's *emotional* life, that man appeals to myths when he *feels overpowered* by his world, that myth is closely related to desire, that myth anchors the *present* in the *past,* that there is a very close relationship between myth and *language,* and so on. It seems to me that although all of this is true, no one has as yet been able to incorporate all of these insights into a harmonious conception of myth. As I see it, this is due to the fact that until now no one has tried to systematically analyze how man's mythical mode of being is related to man's *basic* mode of being. It seems to me that if one were to take his point of departure in the realization that each human being finds himself "thrown" into a world which always is already there and which, because he has no complete control over it, seems to overpower him, all of these isolated, true statements immediately begin to fall into place.[19]

The meaning of this last remark is not to suggest that this conception of man's being is the only ontological conception of man which allows us to come to a genuine understanding of myth. I only claim that we shall never come to a real understanding of the phenomenon of myth if we do not integrate all the insights we have about this complex phenomenon into an all-encompassing conception of man and explain how man's mythical mode of being is precisely related to his primordial mode of being.

At any rate, as I see it, a myth is a basic mode of understanding or conceiving, very closely related to man's primordial attunement to the world in which he finds himself being thrown. This mode of conceiving opens up a field of meaning, or world, within which reasonable action of some kind becomes possible. If this world is a *religious* world, we need symbols if and only if we try to articulate this form of understanding. Such an articulation is necessary if the myth is to have a social function and to be handed down to future generations. Symbols may appear in the articulations of myths other than religious myths, but this is by no means universally the case.

From this it follows that myth taken *as such* is not an interpretation, nor does it *as such* ask for an interpretation. A myth is precisely meant to make an interpretation of some kind possible. If something is to be interpreted, it is to be *taken as* something or other. In order to be able to take x as y. I need a horizon of meaning in which x may appear as y. A myth can provide such a horizon, although it is obviously not the only form of understanding which can provide us with such a world.

And yet a myth can also be interpreted. But this can be done only after the myth has already been *articulated* and if, in addition, there is a more encompassing horizon of meaning available within which the myth may then appear *as* either this or that. It is important to note that such a new horizon in some instances presupposes an appeal to a new type of myth. Furthermore, every *linguistic* articulation of the firm belief which constitutes the myth is itself already an interpretation of that belief, which, in turn, as linguistic structure, is open to a second-order interpretation.

Concluding this part of my essay I wish to make a few additional remarks in order to avoid misunderstanding. It has not been my intention to suggest that the understanding or conceiving characteristic of myth is the only means available to man to open up a horizon of meaning or world. However, it does seem to me that myth is a privileged mode of understanding in that it can make action meaningful even though man is unable to (completely) rationally account for his behavior.

Since all myths imply elements which are beyond our rationally justifiable insights, myth is essentially different from science and philosophy. Myth and philosophy have in common the fact that in contrast to science both are oriented toward worlds rather than to intramundane things, events, or states of affairs. But whereas philosophy tries to explain the acceptance of a world rationally, myth limits itself to accepting such a world on the basis of belief. In other words, contrary to myth, philosophy attempts to methodically examine the basic acceptance of the world which underlies all of our ways of living and thinking by purifying them of any uncritical beliefs and by interpretatively explaining and justifying them. But although myth as such is essentially different from science and philosophy, my view does not necessarily exclude the possibility of myth's constituting an essential part of some philosophical and scientific conceptions. It seems to me that in view of the fact that science presupposes a totality of meaning within which the rational and scientific dialogue can take place, it follows that all sciences explicitly or implicitly presuppose either myth, philosophy, or both.

Since the practical possibilities for rational justification vary from society to society and within one society from epoch to epoch, it is understandable that phenomena or realms of phenomena formerly "explained" on the basis of myth can now be explained by science or philosophy. However, this thesis does not entail that myth one day will be completely superfluous. It seems to me that the finitude and historicity of man's understanding make the use of mythical thought in many instances unavoidable in that there are realms of experience in which man sometimes is unable to act except on the basis of a firm belief, taken individually or socially. If in projecting a realm of meaning or world necessary for theory or action a man appeals to myths, then he does so either because there is no other means available to him for discovering such a world, or because (if there is another access to such a world, for instance through tradition) there is at least no way of rationally accounting for that world.

Finally, it seems to me that the difference between myth and religious faith and belief is found mainly in the fact that whereas religious belief presupposes a reference to a supernatural source and thus rests upon revelation, myth does not necessarily refer to a source which lies beyond the human order, although it certainly refers to a totality of meaning for which man at a particular moment in time is unable to give a completely rational account.

In the remainder of this essay I wish to focus on the last issue mentioned earlier in this paper: What attitude is the modern believer to adopt in regard to religious myths in light of recent developments in the sciences? In so doing I shall first describe certain ideas developed by Bultmann; then I shall try to analyze these ideas, critically employing certain suggestions made by Ricoeur. A brief summary of the ideas gained in this process will finally conclude this essay. As was mentioned before, in all of this I shall limit my reflections to the Judeo-Christian conception of religion.

DEMYTHIZATION OR DEMYTHOLOGIZATION?

According to Rudolf Bultmann the interpretation of biblical texts is not subject to conditions different from those applying to other kinds of literature. However, there is a special task here for the theory of interpretation. In many cases the religious message is formulated in the form of myths which are unacceptable for a Western man of the twentieth century in that they are in plain conflict with his self-understanding and the understanding of the world in which he lives. That is why a good interpretation of biblical texts involves a process of demythologization.[20]

In elaborating upon this program of demythologization Bultmann states that the cosmology of the New Testament is essentially mythical in character.[21] The world is viewed as a three-storied structure with the earth in the center. In addition to cosmological myths there are Jewish apocalyptic and Gnostic redemption myths. The latter both assume a basic dualism of two powers: good and evil. Standing between these two powers man is attacked by the one power and must be helped by the other. The religious meaning of these myths lies not in their imagery, but in the understanding of human existence which they try to express and of the world in which man must live. That is why these myths must be interpreted existentially.

The mythological view of the Old and New Testaments is incredible to modern man, for he is convinced that this mythical view is obsolete: science, technology, the modern self-conception of man, his conception of history, etc., have brought modern man to this view. This attitude in regard to myths affects not only the dogmas concerning God, world, and Christ, but equally the doctrine of the sacraments.

The process of demythologization does not consist in a reinterpretation which leaves out some or all mythological elements (Barth). Nor is it possible with the nineteenth-century liberals to throw away mythology and kerygma (demythization). Whereas the older liberals used criticism to eliminate the mythology of the New Testament, our task today is to use criticism in order to *interpret* the mythology. In interpreting mythologies the issue is not to come to an allegoric interpretation which sprititualizes the mythical events so that they become symbols of processes going on in the soul; nor is the issue about reducing the kerygma to a rationalized religion (Harnack); nor finally is demythologization an attempt to go back to pietism as found in the history-of-religion school. "It seems to me that the revelation of that which Christian faith means, thus the revelation of the all-decisive question, is the only but also the decisive task which theology has to achieve. . . . "[22]

Bultmann explains his real concern as far as demythologization is concerned as follows. The real purpose of the myth is not to present an objective picture of the world as it is, but to express man's understanding of himself and the world in which he lives. Myth should be interpreted not cosmologically, but anthropologically, or, better still, existentially. Mythology uses imagery to express the otherworldly in terms of this world, and the divine in terms of human life. For instance, divine transcendence is expressed as spatial distance. Its genuine message, however, is to communicate man's conviction that the origin and purpose of this world in which man lives are to be sought not within it, but beyond it, beyond the realm of the known and tangible reality. Myth is also an expression of man's awareness that he is not the Lord of his own being. Finally, myth expresses man's belief that in this state of dependence he can be delivered from the evil forces within the visible world. What is to be criticized in the myth is its imagery with its apparent claim to objective validity; what is to be maintained in and through the criticism is the genuine purpose of the myth, namely, the fact that there is a transcendent power which controls the world as well as man. The importance of the Bible's mythology lies not in its imagery but in the understanding of man's existence which it enshrines. The real question is whether *this* understanding is true. Faith claims that it is, and this faith is all the more acceptable to modern man as it is not tied down to the imagery of the Bible's mythology.

Bultmann touches here on a great number of important and highly complex issues. Although in principle I agree with Bultmann's approach to the problems underlying these issues, nonetheless I feel that in two aspects he has underestimated his task. It seems to me that a more thorough study of the problem of myth would have led immediately to the view that not all myths found in the Bible are of the same kind. If this is so, then the process of demythologization is a very complex one which cannot possibly suggest the same answers for all myths. It is obvious to me that cosmological myths are *not necessarily* religious, whereas apocalyptic as well as redemption myths are inherently religious. When Bultmann states that the mythological view of the Bible is incredible to modern man, this may be true in an absolute sense insofar as the mythical views which conceive of the world as a three-storied structure with the earth in the center are concerned. But this is certainly not true in an absolute sense as far as inherently religious myths go. Unacceptable cosmological views can be eliminated altogether without damage to the religious message (demythization); inherently religious myths cannot be eliminated altogether; perhaps they are to be changed, perhaps they are to be replaced, perhaps, and this seems most likely to be the case, they are to be *interpreted* in such a way that the symbolism which is essential to religious myths points again to the religious message which the original myth more conceals than shows (demythologization). One must realize that one cannot speak of the transcendent except in terms of symbols and that these religious symbols cannot be adequately translated into a nonsymbolic language.

Furthermore, when Bultmann states that biblical mythology is to be interpreted anthropologically and existentially, he touches again upon something which in my view is very important. But he should have made it clear that that to which this type of hermeneutics is to be applied is not the myth, but man, the world in which he lives and to whom the myth is addressed, and his interpretation (*logos*) of the myth. When a man comes to genuine self-understanding in authenticity, he is ready to listen to the "real" message addressed to him by the religious myth in a symbolic language.

As far as my first remark is concerned, it seems to me that this has been the main issue in Jasper's criticism of Bultmann,[23] a criticism that, as I understand it, was later taken up by Ricoeur and developed into a more harmonious view on the relationship between myth and interpretation. That is why I wish now to say a few words about Ricoeur's view.[24]

We have seen that for Ricoeur myth necessarily implies the use of symbolic language. If this is true, then it is obvious that myths are to be interpreted. For nowhere do we find a symbolic language without an interpretation. Wherever a man dreams or raves, another man arises to give an interpretation. The question now is one of whether such an interpretation could be *philosophical* in character. For there seems to be a basic conflict between the immediacy of the symbol and the mediation of philosophic thought. Ricoeur believes that the enterprise would indeed be hopeless if symbols were *radically* alien to philosophical discourse. But this is not so for at least two reasons. First of all, symbols are already in the element of speech. And secondly, there exists nowhere a symbolic language without some kind of philosophic interpretation. Contemporary philosophical thought wishes to give an interpretation, also; but in so doing it wishes to remain within the line of critical thought. It tries to dissolve the myth as explanation in order to restore the myth as symbol. One could say also that modern philosophical thought shows myth as myth and then demythologizes it so that it no longer appears as pseudoexplanation, but precisely as symbol.

Modern man cannot be critical without separating the scientific and historical from the inherently mythical. We never can return to the primitive naiveté which led to the original myths. That immediacy of belief is lost forever. But by interpreting the myths critically we can learn to *hear* again. No longer can we *just* believe: we must understand in order to believe, but we must also believe in order to understand. We must believe in order to understand: on the part of the interpreter there must be a preunderstanding of the things about which he interrogates the texts. As Bultmann says: the presupposition of all understanding is the vital relation between the interpreter and the thing about which the text speaks directly or indirectly. But I must also understand in order to believe. This requires that we exorcise the *logos* of the *mythos,* that is, the pseudoscientific and pseudohistorical from the symbolic. By demythologization contemporary philosophical thought can penetrate the dimension of the symbol as a primordial sign of the sacred.

However, it is not sufficient merely to try to understand symbols through symbols as Eliade tried to do. The philosopher will have to go beyond this in a venture that attempts to acquire a better understanding of man and of the bond between his own being and the whole of meaning, by following the indication or the pointing of symbolic thought in a kind of transcendental deduction of symbols. Ricoeur believes he has done so successfully in his book *Finitude and Guilt* (trans. Charles Kelbley [Chicago: Regnery, 1965]).

In his book on Freud, Ricoeur explicitly admits that he decided purposely to link the problem of symbolism and myth to the problem of interpretation.[25] He feels that the issue of myth and symbol and of interpretation is a very complex and complicated one and that the extreme confusion of vocabulary in these matters calls for a decision which implies a whole philosophy. "I have decided to define, i.e., limit, the notions of symbol and interpretation through one another." For him a symbol is a double-meaning linguistic expression that requires interpretation, whereas an interpretation is a work of understanding that aims at deciphering symbols. In deciphering symbols one should not try to conceive of interpretation as an unmasking, demystification, or reduction of illusions, but rather as recollection and restoration of meaning. But one should also be willing to suspect all idols.

Furthermore, in regard to the question of how an interpretation of symbols is to be coherently interrelated with philosphic reflection Ricoeur admits that his position as found in *The Symbolism of Evil* remained somehow enigmatic in that he limited himself to a kind of contradictory solution: on the one hand he argued that we have to *listen* to the rich words of symbols and myths which precede reflection, instruct and nourish it; on the other he defended the thesis that our philosophical exegesis of symbols and myths must continue the tradition of rational and critical philosophy. Symbols give rise to thought. In suggesting this as a solution for the problem, Ricoeur explicitly admits that he does not believe in a radical and presuppositionless philosophy: philosophy begins nothing since the fullness of language precedes it, and yet it begins from itself in that it formulates the questions of meaning and of the foundation of meaning. But what then is the precise relationship between myth, interpretation, and philosophical reflection?

As long as we pay attention merely to the semantic structure of symbols, their excess of meaning due to their overdetermination, we see that they ask for interpretation. However, the moment we realize that they are embodied in ritual, emotions, and, above all, in myths, we see that they contain something of universal validity as regards our human experience, temporality, and the ultimate ontological import of our own self-understanding. At that level symbols have not only an expressive, but also a heuristic value. But this means that symbols ask for philosophic reflection. Another reason why symbols and myths ask for philosophic reflection is the fact that each one of them belongs to a meaningful totality which demands expression at the level of reflection itself. The question still is how such an expression can be materialized.

This perplexing question has traditionally been put in the following terms: what is the place of myth in philosophy? If myth calls for philosophical reflection, does philosophy in turn call for myth? At first sight this question is to be answered in the negative. Since the time of Aristotle and certainly since the time of German idealism there has been an unbridgeable gap between *muthos* and *episteme*, between myth and *Wissenschaft*. Furthermore, symbolism and myth remain caught within the diversity of languages and cultures, whereas philosophy strives for universally acceptable knowledge. Finally, there are always many interpretations of symbols and myths possible, but how could philosophy ever allow for the possibility of a multiplicity of interpretations?

One can deal with these questions provisionally by pointing out that an absolute and presuppositionless philosophy is impossible. The problem of equivocity can be solved in principle by admitting a transcendental logic in addition to a purely formal one. And finally, the multiplicity of interpretations is not a basic problem as long as the philosopher is aware of the multiplicity, is able to comprehend the multiplicity by justifying the multiple views and embodying them in his own work. Yet these reflections obviously do not go to the heart of the matter in that the realm and scope of philosophy is much broader than that of morality and religion, and, on the other hand, symbolism and myth reach much farther than man's religious and moral experiences.

As for the question concerning demythization and demythologization, it seems that an absolute and complete *demythization* is impossible in view of the fact that there are realms of experience in which man is unable to live without myths, realms in which he thus must believe in order to be able to understand and to act reasonably. And religion is one of these realms. However, there are many other realms of experience in which former generations have appealed to myths, where we today perhaps have other means available to open up a world necessary for theoretical or practical actions. In these cases demythization is necessary.

Demythologization, on the other hand, is a process that is meaningful only in those realms of man's experience in which myths are unavoidable and essential. As far as *religious* myths are concerned one should note once more that that which is to be demythologized is not the religious myth as such, but its interpretation, and in some cases its archaic articulation in language, its *logos*. As for the latter, demythologization is necessary only where the archaic articulation made use of nonreligious myths which have become meaningless for modern man, or where the archaic articulation in language employed ideas which implicitly or explicitly are connected with insights which are no longer acceptable today in light of modern science and philosophy.

NOTES

1. The reflections to follow are taken from my article "On Myth and Its Relation to Hermeneutics" which appeared in *Cultural Hermeneutics* 1(1973): 47–86. © 1973 by D. Reidel Publishing Company, Dordrecht–Holland. Reprinted in part with minor changes by courtesy of Reidel Publishing Company.

2. Karl Kerényi, "Was ist Mythologie?" *Europäische Revue* 15(1939): 3–18; G. S. Kirk, *Myth: Its Meaning and Functions in Ancient and Other Cultures* (Berkeley: University of California Press, 1970), p. 8.

3. Ernst Cassirer, *The Philosophy of Symbolic Forms*, 3 vols. (New Haven: Yale University Press, 1966), 2: 27–231; Gerardus van der Leeuw, *Religion in Essence and Manifestation: A study in Phenomenology*, trans. J. E. Turner (London: Allen & Unwin, 1938); Karl Kerényi, *Wesen und Gegenwartigkeit des Mythos* (Munich: Knaur, 1965), pp. 128–44; Walter F. Otto, *Mythos und Welt* (Stuttgart: Ernst Klett Verlag, 1962), pp. 258–66.

4. Cf. Jan de Vries, *Forschungsgeschichte der Mythologie* (Freiburg: Karl Alber, 1961), pp. 360–68; Karl Kerényi, *Die Eröffnung des Zugangs zum Mythos* (Darmstadt: Wissenschaftliche Buchgemeinschaft, 1967), introduction, p. ixff.

5. Karl Philipp Moritz, "Gesichtspunkt für die mythologischen Dichtungen," in *Götterlehre oder mythologische Dichtungen der Alten* (1795), (Lahr: Schauenburg, 1948), pp. 1–6.

6. Kerényi, *Die Eröffnung*, pp. ixff.

7. Perry C. Cohen, "Theories of Myth," *Man*, 4(1969): 337–53.

8. B. Malinowski, "Myth in Primitive Psychology," in *Magic, Science, and Religion and Other Essays* (Boston: Beacon Press, 1948).

9. Kirk, *Myth*, pp. 1–40 and 252ff.

10. Mircea Eliade, *Myth, Dreams and Mysteries*, trans. Philip Mairet (London: Hawill Press, no d.); idem, *Patterns in Comparative Religion* (New York: Meridian, 1958); idem, *Yoga: Immortality and Freedom* (New York: Pantheon, 1958); idem, *From Primitives to Zen* (New York: Harper & Row, 1967). cf. *Encyclopædia Britannica*, 15th ed., s.v. "Myth."

11. Paul Ricoeur, *The Symbolism of Evil*, trans. E. Buchanan (New York: Harper & Row, 1967), pp. 3–9, 161–71.

12. G. Gusdorf, *Myth et Métaphysique* (Paris: Alcan, 1953).

13. Ricoeur, *Symbolism of Evil*, pp. 7, 165.

14. Cassirer, *Philosophy of Symbolic Forms*, vol. 2; idem, *An Essay on Man* (New Haven: Yale University Press, 1965), pp. 72–108, 109–11, 208–9, and passim.

15. Martin Heidegger, *Being and Time,* trans. John Macquarrie and Edward Robinson (London: SCM Press, 1962), p. 490, note xi.

16. Cohen, "Theories of Myth," pp. 339–40; Kirk, *Myth,* pp. 263–68.

17. Cf. Martin Heidegger's review of the second volume of Cassirer's *The Philosophy of Symbolic Forms,* in *Deutsche Literaturzeitung* 21(1928) Col. 1000–1012.

18. Cf. F. W. Schelling, "Einleitung in die Philosophie der Mythologie," in *Sämmtliche Werke* (Stuttgart: J. Mertzler Verlag, 1856), vol. 2. See also the publications of Kerényi, Otto, Cohen, and Ricoeur quoted above.

19. Heidegger, *Being and Time,* secs. 29, 31, 41, 65, 68, and passim.

20. Rudolf Bultmann, "The Problem of Hermeneutics," in *Essays: Philosophical and Theological* (London: SCM Press, 1955), 234–61, pp. 234–35, 252–61.

21. Idem, "New Testament and Mythology," in *Kerygma and Myth: A Theological Debate,* ed. H. W. Bartsch, trans. F. Fuller (London: S.P.C.K., 1953), pp. 1–44 (especially pp. 1–3, 11–12, 15–16); idem, "Zum Problem der Entmythologisierung," in *Kerygma und Mythos,* 3 vols., ed. H. W. Bartsch (Hamburg: Herbert Reich, 1960, 1952, 1957), 2: 179–211.

22. Idem, "Zur Frage der Entmythologisierung," in *Kerygma und Mythos,* 3: 51.

23. Karl Jaspers, "Wahrheit und Unheil der Bultmannschen Entmythologisierung," in *Kerygma und Mythos,* 3: 1–46; Bultmann, "Zur Frage," pp. 47–60.

24. Ricoeur, *Symbolism of Evil,* pp. 347–57.

25. Idem, *Freud and Philosophy: An Essay On Interpretation,* trans. Denis Savage (New Haven: Yale University Press, 1970), pp. 20–56.

Chapter 14

RESTITUTION OF MEANING IN RELIGIOUS SPEECH
Kenneth L. Schmitz

RELIGIOUS speech displays a variety of terms and imagery which cannot be reduced to any easy consistency. It is notoriously difficult to arrive at valid statements about the nature of religious speech as a whole. Even if we were to set aside the plurality of languages, cultures, and religions in which the sacred is expressed, and were to concentrate upon only one religion and one language, we would still face a variety of intentions and modes of expression. I will try to maintain some control of the matter by considering only one religious theme. It is an important and even central theme which is often voiced in the biblical religions of Judaism, Christianity, and Islam. It is the theme of *magnifying the Lord*. I will consider it chiefly as it is voiced in the Christian speech community. Nevertheless, I hope that much of what is said will hold also for the other biblical religions, and that it may even prove illuminating for at least some other religious speech as well.

The philosopher of religion must take seriously any phenomenon which he sets out to understand, and so he must let religious speech lay itself out before him as it arises out of religious life. Now, the totality of religious speech sustains itself by the interplay of three exigencies: Religious speech *about* the sacred is ultimately not separable from speech *to* the sacred, nor is either separable from speech *by* the sacred. And so the speech of objectivity (theology) and the speech of subjectivity (prayer and worship) pay homage to the sacred presence attested

From: *International Journal for Philosophy of Religion* 5(1974), pp. 131–51. This paper was read at the Thirty-Sixth Annual Meeting of the Society for Philosophy of Religion on March 8, 1974 in New Orleans.

in theophany, oral tradition, and scripture (revelation). A particular religious expression bears the impress of these three religious exigencies, which are to be found in the mélange of expressions with which our reflection begins:

> The Lord walks in the cool of the garden. He is a rock, a mighty waters, like the very ocean and the mountains. He is a great tower, a pillar of fire who leads the way, a mighty fortress to his Israel. God is like a refiner's fire; he will sift the house of Israel. God is judge and law-giver, he is patient and filled with mercy. God is creator, he gave thee birth. He is a nurse to his children. The Lord is a vine, an oak whose branches shade his faithful. He is a lion, fleet and graceful as a deer. God is father and potter. He is an avenging sword, lord of armies. He is the only true king. He is a husband in love who will not abandon his cuckolding wife. The Lord is the friend who leads us beside still waters, even through danger and death. The Lord speaks, and things are made, deeds done.
>
> The Lord is the Word, he is the light, truth, life and way. He is the Word made flesh, crucified, died, buried, risen. He is Messiah, Son of Man, Son of God. The Lord is my deliverer, our redeemer, ransom, sacrificial offering, Paschal Lamb. God is love. God is the Comforter. God is Father, Son, and Holy Spirit.
>
> The Lord God is a trinity of persons. The Lord endures, he is eternity. The Lord is, and he is perfect being, infinite wisdom, the fullness of substance. The Lord is commanding presence, all-powerful, all-knowing, all-loving, all-desirable. The Lord is providential. God is not man. He is transcendent, yet immanent. God is pure actuality of existence. God is *Nihil*.

The rich, extravagant imagery is undoubtedly awakened by a numinous awe. An exhilaration and exuberance pushes religious speech towards a peculiar form of intimacy and familiarity in the face of a presiding taboo. For the taboo marks the sense of inadequacy that is built into such religious speech. Much of any language is self-referential, it is language about language. But the very *raison d'être* of speech points to real and imaginary situations beyond itself. Indeed, religious speech witnesses to a source where human words and images cannot go. It points ultimately, therefore, to mystery and to silence. "Were you with the Lord when he laid the foundations of the universe? How incomprehensible his ways! How ineffable his glory!" In this moment of awe, religious speech reaches an awareness of its limits and becomes conscious of its inherent self-denial. A curious mixture of asceticism and profligacy weaves throughout religious speech. It multiplies names and images as it hurries on from the insufficiency of one to another, like a man crossing a stream by pushing away one rock after another from under his slipping feet. To stop is to sink. Or, to use another simile, religious speech is like a maze. It takes the worshiper into a broad corridor (a holy name, a key term), and then invites exploration of the region thereabouts by taking side branches (that is, by deriving subsidiary and cognate terms which cluster about the major one). Some of these branches are useful and lead to further branches and even to new main corridors. But others only cause him to lose his way, bringing him to a dead end, or leading him away from his intended goal. Thus, names such as *lion* and *fortress* or *judge* or *being* may illuminate to a point and suggest further speech, but some of their associations and connotations may turn speech into lies and its images into idols. Religious speech, then, is not random profusion, but is rather selective multiplicity. It is subject to a certain discipline. Not every name is appropriate, and some are less appropriate than others. Still others are irrelevant, misleading, or even blasphemous. In sum, typical expressions of a religious theme, such as magnifying the Lord, are varied and not easily rendered coherent, given to a certain extravagance and profusion of terms, yet exhibiting selectivity and discipline, and ultimately a sense of the radical limitations of speech uttered in the service of the sacred.

Exegetes, linguists, and historians of religion have made us aware of the variety of settings, intentions, and forms in religious speech. Within this variety a philosopher of religion may be expected to ask about traits of an epistemological and logical character. He might even ask whether religious speech is, after all, so extraordinary, profuse, and negative that it defies all attempts to make coherent sense of it? Religious speakers may protest that it makes good sense to them, and that they are not interested in theoretical reconstructions of religious speech. Their instincts are good, but not good enough. If we remained with instincts we should have no philosophy. That prospect may not send out tremors, except to those who in addition to using religious speech or studying it may also want to understand what it is that they are doing. Their number is greater than the relatively few philosophers of religion. For religious speech has become puzzling to many, even to some believers who, believing, seek to understand. They have come to adopt a self-conscious and critical attitude towards their own use of language, and especially to its religious use. It is out of such a critical interest that the philosophical question is here posed: How can it be meaningful to magnify the Lord?

[Religious speech attempts to satisfy all the expressive needs of a faith community. Discourse, on the other hand, is a tighter, more systematic organization of language. It is preoccupied with the cognitive possibilities of language, and has a more or less explicit theory of truth, criteria of evidence, and canons of argumentation. Earlier strategies of discourse have included Saint Thomas Aquinas's doctrine of analogy, Moses Maimonides' predication by negation, Saint Anselm's transcendental affirmation and the negative way leading to silence.]

These four earlier strategies may be held as the background for profiles of three more recent attempts to recover the meaning of religious speech. As in the earlier strategies, here too theoretical discourse copes with the peculiar ignorance that invests our speech about God. Discourse brings the radical negative into disciplined association with our structures of cognition and speech. In the first attempt, theoretical discourse proposes a *metaphysical distinction* based upon the transcendental relation between being and its modalities. In the second, discourse follows out a *dialectical symbolism* based upon the dynamic of being and nonbeing. In the third, discourse qualifies contemporary model theory in order to construct a *model empiricism*. We have, then, metaphysical, dialectical, and empirical strategies for the discursive restitution of meaning in religious speech.

Already present in Saint Thomas Aquinas, the metaphysical recovery has received reemphasis in recent Thomism.[1] If we accept the conception of wisdom as somehow appropriately said of God, we might begin with the simple affirmation that God is *wise*. In order to make explicit the infinite and unrestricted range and depth of his wisdom, however, it is better to say that God is *all-wise* and *always wise*. Still, the adjectival form of the predicate and the attributive type of predication do not sufficiently distinguish the nature of divine wisdom from human wisdom. It seems to assign to God what is, after all, only human wisdom writ large. Now, divine and human wisdom do not differ merely in scope and duration. Religious speech, therefore, must intend to mark out the difference in essence, nature, and substance between God and man. Man is sometimes imperfectly wise, and even when he is fitfully wise, his being wise is only one aspect of his manifold being. God, on the other hand, is richly but wholly simple. He does not *have* the characteristic of being wise as a property which is only an aspect of his being. He *is* wholly, fully, absolutely what he is. He is substantial Wisdom. The copula, then, must not merely express a qualified and relative identification of a property with a substance. It must express the absolute and unrestricted identity of the predicate-as-substance with the subject-as-substance. God is not wise; he is Wisdom. But we have not yet said enough to realize the intention of religious speech. For God is also his Power, Freedom, Goodness, Being, and Love. In its reflection upon religious speech, metaphysical discourse has come upon its own version of the impasse felt by religious speech (*scandalum*). It is faced with the scandal of the plurality of divine names said of the divine simplicity. On the one side stands the unutterable simplicity of the divine, and on the other the undeniable complexity of human speech. The worshiper intends to speak of and to God, but human speech introduces a complexity alien to God's rich simplicity. Moreover, the difficulty is not manufactured solely by theoretical discourse in search of the cognitive values of religious speech. It merely sharpens the dilemma already well known to the worshiper who is conscious of the impotent clutter of human speech in its attempt to magnify the Lord. He cries out. "Lord, unless you quicken my tongue, what shall I say?" Indeed, revelation is primordial for religious speech because the word of God alone can break open the possibility of such speech. It is the taboo again, an integral part of the evidence available to theoretical discourse as it reflects upon the theme of magnifying the Lord.

The metaphysical restoration which we are presently considering tries to make this impasse intelligible by introducing a radical distinction between two factors of religious speech. It distinguishes the intention of religious speech from its mode of expression, the *res significata* from the *modus significandi*.[2] In order to intend what he says, the worshiper must deny the manner in which he says it. A linguistic sign, such as a predicate, can function only within a plurality of other linguistic signs. Signs are determinate interrelated units which in referring to something other than language have a side reference to each other, a sort of concomitant reference (parasemiotic). This side reference is inseparable from their manner of signification. In speaking of God, religious speech intends something richly simple, but its manner of speaking is not simple. So far the present metaphysical reflection has distinguished between various parts and modes of speech. It began by denying that every term is an appropriate predicate for magnifying the Lord. It then distinguished between modes of predication, rejecting the adjectival and selecting the substantive. The present distinction, however, insinuates itself between the inseparable factors which attend all speech. It distinguishes between the reality meant, viz., the divine simplicity, and the manner in which it is signified, viz., the complexity of the sign system. Religious speech means more than it can say.

The present theoretical discourse, however, must pose this question: Is religious speech entitled to cling to an ineffable reality that has no proportion with the human modes of expression? Does not the very distinction render all speech about God false, and even meaningless? The answer cannot be a simple yes or no. We might begin modestly by pointing out that to the worshiper some speech about God is more false than other speech. The intention has operated in order to influence the selection of terms, the preference among predicational forms, and, finally, for the rejection of all modes of expression. Discourse can recognize here a certain direction which meaning must take if it is to be in harmony with the intention of the worshiper. No sign is the thing signified. Even in mathematics numerals are distinguished from numbers. So, too, the signs on the road to Paris are not Paris. Nevertheless, reliable signs are true indicators of the way to Paris. Now, the sacred reality intended is taken as the measure which establishes an order among the signs and modes of signification. The distinction undermines the truth of any religious assertion taken in its entirety. Moreover, it denies the efficacy of all signs used in religious expression. Nevertheless, it is important to notice that the denial does not bear indifferently upon the whole expression. We have already seen that it presupposes a discrimination among the signs, ranking them according to their lesser or greater inefficacy. It is just this discrimination which is the ground for the metaphysical distinction between manner and intention. For the prior discrimination determines the character of the distinction, just as the principle of the discrimination is the reality intended. The distinction is not meant simply to erase religious speech. It is meant, rather, to isolate the nature of the deficiency. The deficiency lies not in what the worshiper intends to say but in the manner of saying it. Now, to isolate the deficiency is to introduce a distinction between what in the expression is deficient and what is not. It is the mode which is deficient, but the meaning is not comprised simply of the mode. Indeed, the expression itself is not wholly deficient or discourse could not draw the present distinction which presupposes a deficiency of meaning that is not total. For the meaning of religious speech includes the very measure of the deficiency. The thing intended by religious speech (*res significata*) is not just an empty meaning-intention waiting to be filled by other ordinary cognitive acts. On the contrary, it is a fullness of meaning in relation to which the actual filled modes of signification are all but empty perspectives. If they are taken in themselves, they become idols before which the worshiper must not bow his knee. The distinction, then, does not *separate* out the mode from the reality in such a way that the worshiper can throw away the empty shell of the mode and directly confront the kernel meant. The distinction does not divide speech, but rather surrounds the whole expression and brings into relief a certain intended reality which overflows the confining modes of speech. Can meaning which lies beyond the structures of speech be expressed? The answer must be both yes and no. The meaning is ineffable in that no form of speech can incorporate it and express it adequately. Yet the meaning of religious speech is constituted not only by its mode, but also by the presence of the reality meant. In distinguishing the mode of speech from what is meant, the distinction discloses the meaning that lies beyond the form, without separating it out and reabsorbing it into additional forms of speech. The meant is apprehended indirectly because it can never be separated from the denial of the adequacy of the mode which expresses it. It is reached expressively only through the mode and the denial based upon it. But conversely, the denial of the mode is reached only through the effective presence of the intended reality as it presides over the intention to speak properly of the sacred reality.

A corollary returns this theoretical discourse to the exigencies of religious speech. The distinction drawn in metaphysical discourse is not alien to the needs of religious speech. Our mode of speech is itself an expression of our way of being. The denial of the adequacy of our human mode of expression, then, places our human being within the restricted area and discloses a sacred reality which escapes the speaker on all sides. In noticing the deficiency without being able to discard it, metaphysical discourse illustrates the ultimate religious condition, not simply for human speech, but also for being human. In making its distinction, discourse seeks to expose the relation between worshiper and sacred reality and to reconstruct the conditions under which religious speech can magnify the Lord.

A second strategy for recovering the possibilities of religious speech by means of discourse proposes a theory of *diaelectical symbolism*.[3] The corollary of the previous metaphysical distinction involved the religious speaker in the very speech which he utters. Religious symbols illustrate even more dynamically the intimate and mutual relationship between the worshiper and the sacred reality. Religious faith takes a religious symbol to be a sign of that reality. Such a religious sign differs from a natural sign such as smoke, however, because its referent is unseen. It differs also from a conventional sign, such as the function of the square root, because *pi* designates an operation we can perform, whereas the religious symbol—even when we perform it—intends a presence which escapes us and is never simply under our control. Then, too, faith apprehends more in a religious symbol than a means of inference to something as yet unknown. It apprehends in the symbol a promise which transforms it into a means of transference into the sacred presence. Faith apprehends in a symbolic sign a symbolism which is the process initiated by the resident power of the sacred in the symbol. For the religious symbol does not only signify. It signifies in such a way that it embodies, discloses, and transforms. It embodies the numinous, making it present in a distinctive but authentic manner. It discloses the identity of the numinous presence in some definite way. It transforms the faithful through the power inherent in the symbol.

It would be a mistake, however, to take the religious symbol as a straight-forward affirmation of the presence of God. Faith apprehends the reality in and through the symbol as a reality that remains ineluctably mysterious. The symbol hides more than it reveals. There is within its movement an interplay of presence and absence. A moment of negativity and mystery is inseparable from the symbol. For the worshiper, the reality is present in the symbol, but not without quali-fication. Faith apprehends a reality which energizes the symbol and empowers it to transform and transpose the plane of existence of the recipient. Being, nonbeing, and becoming, presence, mystery, and power constitute the inner tension of the symbol. As faith penetrates the meaning of a symbol, it no more discovers a straightforward absence that it does a straightforward presence. If there is a certain darkness at the heart of the symbol, it is a manner of hiding that announces that it hides more than it reveals. For it discloses the sacred presence as that which stands essentially free from the symbol. It is present in it, but not enclosed by it. The inner process of symbolism, therefore, leads out onto a transcendent reality which turns back, so to speak, upon the sign elements and discloses a numinous presence which outstrips them absolutely. The sacred moves away to a great distance. How great is dependent upon the tension between seen and unseen in the religion. Within the symbol the reality draws the worshiper on by an evanescent attraction, so that the deeper he penetrates into the signif-icance of the symbol, the more does the sacred reality manifest itself as with-drawing. It withdraws from the conditions of the sign, however, in order to draw nearer to the worshiper. In fleeing it reveals itself. It is a manifestation of that absence which is required both for human meaning and human freedom in the face of the reality of the sacred. Yet that distancing is overcome by a more genuine presence than simple positive adjacence. What would be a defect in an ordinary sign has become an essential condition for the symbolic significance of the sacred. The interrelation of sign, presence, and absence in the symbol arises through the tension of sign and signified within it. It is the taboo again, a form of the *tremor fascinans et repellens*. The transformative meaning expressed in and by the symbol lives in and among these comings and goings. While it never gives a direct apprehension of the religious reality which it signifies, its indirectness is not the simple absence within which a road sign indicates a direction and a promise. It is an effective sign, a prayer, a meal, a dance embodying sacramental presence. Nevertheless, like the road sign, a religious symbol need not resemble the sacred reality which it inadequately embodies. There is usually some, at least remote, equivocal likeness between an aspect of the sacred reality and the sign elements. Thus, bread nourishes those hungry for life. But the thrust and power of the religious symbol lies in another direction than resemblance. It lies in its transformative power to achieve the copresence of man and God in a sacred communication. What is decisive in the religious symbol is that it is an initiative taken by God. Great religious symbols are taken to be instituted and sanctioned by God rather than invented by men. Religious symbolism is the history of God in search of men. When the worshiper takes up the great symbols in speech, gesture, and action, he participates in this traffic between God and man.

The remote source of the first strategy is Saint Thomas, and of the second, Hegel. John Locke is the remote source of the third strategy, the *model empiricism* developed by the late Ian Ramsey.[4] According to Ramsey, theoretical recovery of religious meaning must begin by recognizing the sort of empirical situation which lies at the base of religious speech. It is a situation in which objects are given in and through language for our consideration. But along with empirically observable objects, such as the empty tomb or the bread and wine, something "more" is given, something inobservable, unseen, transempirical. The faith which "sees" is more concrete than the cognition of objects, because its "noninferential awareness" apprehends the personal presence of God in his activity. For this reason, the religious situation needs first-person language, and can never be described in scientific objective language. Consider how a situation is "thickened" and "quickened" when a judge about to try an accused suddenly finds that he is an old friend. Ramsey also noticed the odd logical behavior of nicknames. They are not simply proper names, but are rather invitations to intimacy which transform the general tenor of a situation into which they are introduced. Speakers who accept such a situation find themselves committed to the other person. A situation becomes religious when it yields a disclosure of God in his personal creative or redemptive activity.

Ramsey thought that the philosophy of religion should show how there can be reliable speech about such a situation and such a disclosure. Adapting the work of Max Black,[5] he focused upon the explanatory power of models. He was not interested in simple isomorphic scale models, for they can explain only that which can be pictured by a point-for-point correspondence. They can shed no light upon what transcends observation. The analogue models used in the natural and social sciences, on the other hand, do not correspond point for point with the phenomena they illuminate. They offer "hints rather than identities." These hints enable the scientist to interpret hitherto uninterpreted aspects of a phenomenon, to see congruences among its various elements, and to suggest further lines of inquiry. In this indirect and oblique way an analogue model engenders, confirms, and promotes disciplined methodical discourse about the phenomenon. Thus, the analogue model of light as a "linear propagation" does not claim to be a copy of the true essence of light. Nevertheless, when it is brought into association with certain selected traits of a phenomenon, it generates an insight that permits the scientist to make reliable correlations which he could not otherwise make.

Ramsey modified the notion of the analogue model into what he called the disclosure model, so that it could accommodate what he called the "logically odd" behavior of religious speech. A central affirmation of Christian speech is that "God did something through Jesus." As this expression came to be understood more deeply, old terms exploded and speech was transformed until it evoked a unique series of disclosures about Christ and the Trinity.[6] Around this series of disclosures there grew up a network of terms which became brothers in a new linguistic fraternity, Christian religious usage. Consider, for example, the attempt to express the sonship of Jesus. In saying that he is the "son" of the "Father," it is added that he is "eternally begotten." The model of sonship is familiar enough, but it points towards the subordination and separation of Jesus from the Father, and to the contingency of their relationship. The model threatens the disclosure of the full divinity of this son. In order to prevent the ordinary meaning of sonship from wiping away the unique disclosure of God in Jesus, therefore, religious speech gives the model one or more *qualifiers*. The qualifier, *eternal,* is an oddity, a logical and linguistic safeguard of this son's divinity. It removes the contingency of the normal relationship between father and son, and insists upon a logically necessary connection between Jesus and the Father. In this way it brings *this* Father and *this* Son closer together until . . . And here, according to Ramsey, there bursts upon us another illuminating impropriety: the Son is "of one substance" with the Father. Their unique and necessary relationship has been secured in religious speech by another qualifier. So, too, beginning with a familiar model, religious speech transforms the meaning of the word *Father* by adding "Who art in heaven." The limitations of the model of sonship taken in its ordinary sense have been overcome, and yet the model remains present within the religious expression as its empirical undertone.

Heresy, according to Ramsey, is language caught in the limitations of the model. Such a disclosure model cannot be taken as a literal, point-for-point description of the relation between God and Jesus anymore than the linear model of light depicts that phenomenon. There is no point-for-point identity between divine and human paternity. No model can exhaust the mysterious relationship between Jesus and the Father. That is why each model was qualified by such words as *eternal, necessary, only,* infinite, and *hypostatic.* In this way a disclosure model permits the believer to speak reliably of God and Jesus. Familiar models are taken up into religious speech, qualifiers there transform them so that they point beyond the empirical and allow the believer to be articulate about what is modeled. The disclosure is not straightforward and face to face. The light it casts is shadowed, indirect, and oblique. Nevertheless, it is as though the model "echoes and chimes in with" the reality at which it hints.

Just as a model must be qualified in order to serve as a disclosure, so must several models be interlaced with one another to form a network of hints and suggestions. Ramsey modified Max Black's interaction theory of metaphor in order to show how two models brought together in an unusual locution might spark a disclosure of meaning. According to Black,[7] when someone laments that "man is a wolf," two systems of commonplace meanings are brought together in such a way that they filter each other out to produce a single meaning. The subject, *man*, comes to have some of the properties commonly associated with wolves. Of course, it is not intended that he have them all, four feet and a hairy body, but rather that he is fierce and cruel to the weak and that he overruns his environment. The two systems of commonplaces interact with each other, filtering out discordant and irrelevant meanings. The resultant clash generates a new meaning under pressure. We thereby come to organize and apprehend a whole line of human behavior in an oblique but distinctive way. The metaphor is tired. But consider a fresher one, cited by Max Black in a discussion with Paul Ricoeur. Wallace Stevens has said that "a poem is a pheasant." Now, if we bring together certain accepted commonplaces about poetry and about pheasants, we will at first strike a blank wall which turns us back to Stevens in order to see what a poem is for him and why he should call it a pheasant. The two systems of commonplaces have not been enough for this creative metaphor and we have to reshape them. Once reshaped, we can bring them together again, so that in using the metaphor to control our speech we can attain a new disclosure about poetry. Ramsey found this suggestive for explaining what often happens in creative religious speech. Pre-existing speech patterns are systems of commonplace meanings which must be refashioned, just as commonplaces about love had to be refashioned by Christian speech. The systems of commonplaces function as familiar models which are driven together under the pressure of trying to say what God has done in Jesus. In their clash, what is meant is disclosed in the very words which do not quite say it. To call God king and shepherd, potter and physician, nurse and warrior, avenger and cuckold is to heap up models and metaphors towards a disclosure of meaning that is reliable because the models are authoritative, but that is still inadequate because the models, even when qualified, give hints rather than identities. So, too, to call Jesus both "Son of Man" and "Word made flesh" is to move towards generating a disclosure of Jesus as the extraordinary God-man. The qualifier, *made flesh,* sponsors an ontological commitment to the reality disclosed by the meeting of the phrases, "Son of Man" and "Word made flesh." The words are given a sense which points to a reality which stands mysteriously beyond the familiar and ordinary. Under the initiative of revelation, authoritative models and metaphors help the believer to speak reliably of that which descriptive speech cannot express. The domain of significant religious speech opens up when attention is shifted from the observable to the reliable as the measure of the significance of religious speech. An adaptation of theories of models and metaphors has been used in the discursive recovery of meaning in religious speech.

To summarize. We began by noticing the exuberance, hesitancy, familiarity, and confessed inadequacy of religious speech. We took this to be evidence of the taboo operative in that speech. It is the threat to meaning which the worshiper somehow experiences even as he continues to talk to and about God. We then distinguished between language, usage, and discourse. The latter is the modification of language in the interests of a critical, reflective, methodical examination of the cognitive responsibilities of religious speech. We then brought together three current strategies of discourse and placed them within this common problem: the task of accounting for the survival of religious speech in the face of the taboo, the problem of the restitution of meaning in religious speech in terms of theoretical discourse. In the metaphysical recovery the intended reality is indicated by the direction of the progressive inadequacy of all modes of expression. In the dialectical recovery the sacred presence sustains itself in a sublated way through the dynamic interplay of its presence and absence within the religious symbol. In the empirical recovery religious speech sustains its reliability by the qualification and clash of familiar and authoritative models.

Each strategy makes explicit the situation of the worshiper and treats language as a distinctive totality within that situation. The first invokes the energy of *being* (existence, *esse*). The worshiper, his speech, and the sacred reality are translated into the vocabulary of being and its modes. The sacred reality arises as the fullness of *actuality*. The second calls upon the energy of *life*. The worshiper, his speech, and the sacred reality are translated into the process of revelation itself, in which the sacred reality arises as a *manifestation* which includes hiddenness as its counterpoint. The third counts on the energy of *speech* itself, and translates the worshiper, his speech, and the sacred reality into the clash of meanings which generates a cosmic disclosure. The sacred reality discloses itself in the making of authoritative models which sustain reliable speech about the sacred as creative and redemptive *person*.

Each tries to take the measure of the negative element in religious speech and the measure of the worshiper's ignorance. Each uses negation to purge the complacency of ordinary speech. Each qualifies negation in different ways in order to bring it into a disciplined and constructive relationship with affirmation. This answers to the words of religious speech itself: that we see darkly as in a mirror. Religious speech is veiled and indirect. The first strategy looks beyond the sign towards the reality intended. Not surprisingly, it looks to inference and demonstration as a primary task for theoretical discourse, and maintains a philosophical theology distinct from a philosophy of religion. The second strategy hands the worshiper over to life situations and draws him into a search as a participant. The third strategy delivers the worshiper over to a disclosure which generates further speech and further disclosure. We have in these three strategies an emphasis upon creature in the first, cult in the second, and witness in the third. Undoubtedly, each highlights an aspect of religious speech and its cognitive responsibilities. Each employs a different epistemological device: sign, symbol, and model. Each rests upon a different ontological foundation: being, life, and person. An epistemology and ontology that undercut these differences might provide a more unified theory for recovering the meaning of religious speech, and with it the cognitive responsibilities of that speech.

NOTES

1. See the excellent and too-little-known work of Gerard Smith, S.J., *Natural Theology* (New York: Macmillan, 1951), p. 174ff. Cf. idem, *The Philosophy of Being* (New York: Macmillan, 1961), p. 329ff.

2. Cf. St. Thomas Aquinas, *Summa Theologiae,* I, 13, 3c.

3. What follows is my own version of a contemporary position which finds at least analogous expression in the work of Paul Tillich and others. It arises out of the confluence of a recovered sense of religious symbol and of the dialectic operative in religion. It traces its dialectical ancestry back to Hegel and its understanding of religious symbol to the Middle Ages.

4. See especially Ian T. Ramsey's Inaugural Lecture at Oxford (1951), "Miracles: An Exercise in Logical Mapwork," in *The Miracles and the Resurrection* (London: SPCK, 1964). Also, idem, *Religious Language: An Empirical Placing of Theological Phrases* (New York: Macmillan, [1957] 1963); idem, *Christian Discourse: Some Logical Explorations* (London, New York: Oxford University Press, 1965); and idem, "On the Possibility and Purpose of a Metaphysical Theology," in *Prospect for Metaphysics*, ed. I. T. Ramsey (London: Allen & Unwin, 1961), pp. 153–77. For his relation to Locke, see his edition of Locke's *The Reasonableness of Christianity*.

5. *Models and Metaphors: Studies in Language and Philosophy* (Ithaca: Cornell University Press, 1962), especially chaps. 3 and 13.

6. *Religious Language*, chap. 4: "The Language of Christian Doctrine." Cf. *Christian Discourse*.

7. *Models and Metaphors*, pp. 39ff.

Chapter 15

THE DIALECTIC OF THE MYSTICAL EXPERIENCE
Louis Dupré

Today the term *mystical* is usually restricted to exceptional and strictly private states of ecstasy. But a mystical element permeates the entire religous experience; indeed, it is that experience itself in its purest form. To be sure, the mass of religious people never reach the passive states of contemplation. But all of them have occasionally experienced the unique joys and sorrows of their faith. The communal feeling which fills the participants at the end of a Passover meal, the inexplicable joy of Christmas night or Easter morning, the silent peace of a private visit to a church—all these experiences are fully continuous with the passive forms of contemplation. The drive toward mystical union is the vital principle of all religious life. Without it religion withers away in sterile ritualism or arid moralism. This mystical power is at work in all true prayer. Whoever prays is on his way toward total union. Few ever reach the end of the journey, but that is no reason to sever the beginning from the end. Nor is this experience essentially private. As far as I can ascertain, never during the entire patristic period in which the term *mystical* gained acceptance among Christians did it refer to a private, exceptional experience.

Nor was the subjective connotation which we so easily attach to the term *mystical* present in the beginning. For the Greeks the *mystikos* was someone initiated in the mystery cults. Early Christians gave the word a different, but not a more subjective, meaning. For Clement of Alexandria, a "mystical" interpretation of the Scriptures was one in which the text of the Old Testament yielded

"The Dialectic of the Mystical Experience" is a shorter version of the concluding chapter of *The Other Dimension* (New York: The Seabury Press, 1979).

a new, hitherto hidden meaning when read in the light of Christian redemption.[1] Hence *mystical* came to denote all that was sacred to the Christian, particularly the sacramental reality. As Christ is hidden in the Scripture, so is he hidden in the Eucharistic bread and wine.[2] Origen gave the Biblical meaning a slight but decisive twist by applying it to the direct, experiential way of knowing God through the Scripture. The scriptural connection will disappear later but is still present in Pseudo-Dionysius, the author mainly responsible for the modern usage of the word. Even today the Eastern Orthodox tend to look upon the mystical state as a normal feature in the life of the spiritual community.

MONIST MYSTICISM

Rudolf Otto has distinguished the outward mysticism of unifying vision from the inward mysticism of introspection.[3] Both ways appear in the East as well as in the West. Although clearly distinct, they must not be separated too strictly. For the unifying vision requires an attitude of recollection, while the method of introspection leads to a unifying self. Let us first consider the second way—the intuition of the self. The mind has an ordinary cognition of itself through reflection upon its acts. Yet, as Jacques Maritain points out, the self knows its existence only indirectly and its essence not at all. It is aware only of its operations and its psychic states, not of subjectivity as such.

> Doubtless, the more my attention comes to bear upon the existential experience of my soul, the more shall I tend to neglect the diversity of objects and of operations the reflexive grasp of which is nevertheless the very condition for such an experience. Yet it remains true that as long as we go in the direction of nature, the experiential folding back of which I speak, however powerful it may be in certain "interior" souls, leaves the soul prisoner of mobility and multiplicity, of the fugitive luxuriance of phenomena and of operations which emerge in us from the darkness of the unconscious.[4]

By an ascetic self-concentration the mind can stop reflecting upon its operations, purify itself from all images, and come directly face to face with its own selfhood.

The awareness of the self's own being may be religious, although it need not be so. What makes it specifically religious? In both cases the mind reaches the innermost self and the absolute in one and the same act. Yet in religious introspection the attainment of the absolute through the self is accompanied by a negation that simultaneously opposes the absolute to the self. This movement is of a most complex nature. For the opposition occurs *within* the self—not outside it. The religious absolute, then, is still discovered as a self, not as a nonself; and the opposition is one between an absolute Self and an ordinary self. The inadequacy of ordinary language to cope with those distinctions has led to a great deal of confusion. For the mystic describes his experience exclusively in terms of a self which others are likely to understand as referring to the finite self. Semantic problems make it almost impossible for a Westerner to evaluate properly Eastern descriptions of introspective mystical experiences. The absence of a reference to a transcendent, personal God makes him suspect an absence of religion. Rather than for traditional "religious" terms we should search for signs of an internal opposition within the experience. It is in the withdrawing movement from the finite self to the absolute that the experience becomes religious.

The same rule applies to outwardly unifying mysticism. Natural mysticism does not maintain or constitute oppositions—as religious states of contemplation invariably do—it merely dissolves the existing ones. On the other side, even the monist mysticism of the Upanishads retains a basic opposition between the finite, ordinary self and the deeper self. They may negate the reality of the finite, but that is not the same as to declare everything divine. For they continue to assert the finite as the appearance or illusion opposed to the infinite. Even if the infinite, then, is declared to be the only true reality, it remains transcendent. The concept of the absolutely One may not be adequate, but one cannot dismiss it as non-religious. For as long as a dialectical negation takes place, mysticism retains a transcendent terminus. The process of religious negation is a very complex one, and such Christian mystics as Eckhart and Angelus Silesius also struggle with the problem. Even John of the Cross uses language that could be interpreted in a monist sense. Much depends upon speculative clarifications of the concept of God which are the outcome of a long and gradual process. But perfection in expressing the divine is always a matter of degree, since no concept is entirely adequate. We should rather judge the mystics by the living experience which reveals itself through their inadequate concepts. By these standards most monist mysticism must be regarded as clearly religious. For it describes the movement of the mind toward a terminus that continues to transcend the finite.

NEGATIVE THEOLOGY OR HENOLOGICAL MYSTICISM

Monist mysticism originated in the East. Yet the West also knows a type of introspective mysticism that, though less negative in its overall attitudes toward the finite world, nevertheless shares some essential features with the Eastern variety. Its followers belong to no single school. Nor has the tradition remembered them under a single common name. It usually refers to them by the more comprehensive (i.e., including also nonmystical theologies) title of negative theology. Like the monist mystic, the negative theologian negates any common bond between God and the finite. Yet instead of denying the *reality* of the finite, he denies of God all predicates that can be attributed to finite beings. No positive name can be given to the ultimate, undivided principle. Henological mysticism goes back to Plotinus.[5] Like the Oriental mystics by whom he may have been influenced, Plotinus situates the Absolute beyond the multiplicity of all ideas. The knowledge of it is by nature ecstatic and can be attained only in the unity which the mind possesses in itself before moving outward into its determinations. The soul's endeavor is to become exclusively aware of that point where it proceeds from the ultimate One and is one itself.

> Awareness of the One comes to us neither by knowing nor by the pure thought which discovers the other intelligible things, but by a presence transcending knowledge. When the soul knows something, it loses its unity; it cannot remain simply one because knowledge implies multiplicity. . . . Having freed itself from all externals, the soul must turn totally inward; not allowing itself to be wrested back towards the outer, it must forget everything, the subjective first and, finally, the objective. It must not even know that it is itself that is applying itself to contemplation of the One.[6]

Unity must not be understood as a positive attribute of God. It expresses no objective determination, but is a sign of the Absolute or, more correctly, a sign of the mind's relation to the Absolute. The term *one* in no way reveals what God is.[7] In itself unity is a determination of quantity, and thus still belongs to the intelligible order. But this order is immediately negated, for the absolute "One" admits no other points of comparison and thereby ceases to be quantitative. Still, the affirmation of the One is more than a thought-destroying process, for it posits the Absolute as ultimate end of all affirmation and expresses the mind's need to move beyond the multiplicity of the intelligible order. Negative theology has its roots in a heightened awareness of divine transcendence. It is not merely negative, for it strongly asserts that God is so totally and exclusively himself that his reality can be understood only by himself.

Still, negative theology would have little appeal to the mystic if it did not express the presence of God. Philosophers commonly assume that a heavy emphasis upon transcendence eo ipso excludes immanence. But it is precisely the strong awareness of the immanence of the divine light that drives the mystic beyond all categories of intelligibility into the dark of total incomprehension. The more God is experienced, the more the soul moves beyond itself. The intensity of the awareness leads to the ultimacy of negation.

According to Eckhart, the best-known Christian representative of henological mysticism, God differs so radically from his creature that one cannot speak meaningfully about him in positive concepts. Nor is it sufficient to expurgate these concepts from their finite determinations and then predicate them *per eminentiam,* for concepts themselves are inherently creaturelike.[8] The dissimilarity is due not to a lack of creaturelike reality on God's part but to the absence of any true reality on the part of the creature. "To see God is to know that all creatures are as nothing.''[9] This does not mean that the creature is an illusion, as the monist would claim, but rather that there is a basic equivocity between God and the specific being of the creature, that is, its existence. "Where the creature ends, there God begins to be."

At the same time, the creature is identical with God, for its true Being is God. Eckhart never attempts to harmonize the two opposite aspects. He envisions the relation at once as more intimate and more remote. In its essence the creature is identical with God, for in its *esse primum* the creature is a living idea of God. This essential Being is God himself insofar as he is immanent in the expression of himself in the Word. The Father begets the Son in an eternal *now*. That *now* is preserved in the essence of all creatures. The *now* of creation and the now of God's self-expression are identical, for the creature is in the Son and the Son in the creature.

When the soul is totally possessed by God, God no longer exists for it, but the soul itself becomes a divine presence. Nor does God live "in" the soul, since the soul is being "lived by" God. The final state of union, then, is one of total Godlessness, for the soul has lost the power to objectivate what it has become.

What is reached, then, at the end of the decreation process is an absolute which is at the same time the essence of the self. Self-renunciation is more than a means to an end: it is the negative side of the Absolute. To come face to face with the uncreated self is to shed one's creaturehood. Only when the self coincides with the Absolute is the true nature of the soul revealed. The soul discovers its essence in the act in which God knows himself.

POSITIVE MYSTICISM

Most Christian mystics have not followed the extreme negative tradition. Though they do not hesitate to declare God to be beyond all predication and the soul in need of total abnegation, they differ on the significance of the finite. Reasserting the independence of the creature, they allow it a value in its own right, and they do so by means of a second, more radical negation, allowing them to overcome the human viewpoint itself and to adopt a divine attitude toward the creation—which is entirely positive. According to John of the Cross, the most articulate interpreter of this type of mysticism, first all finite determinations are declared incommensurate to the divine reality. But then, the mystic abandons the right to judge the finite on his own terms. Rather than denying that the finite truly exists as finite, he asserts that it depends, even in its finitude, upon the infinite. After denying his own determinations in God, he adopts God's own viewpoint with respect to the finite. To George Morel, a French commentator of John of the Cross, the radical negation of the finite is an attempt to grasp the divine as it is itself; it therefore culminates in a divine reaffirmation of the finite. "Only in this perspective does the apophasis receive its full meaning. Until then the notion of infinity, for instance, appears under the mode of negation and relativity: God is not this or that as the contingent realities are. As long as man attempts to define God from the spatial and the temporal, the very concept of difference still posits a relation."[10] This second negation has excluded the relational viewpoint itself. God and the creature must not even be compared. "Although it is true that all creatures have, as theologians say, a certain relation to God, and bear a divine impress . . . yet there is no essential resemblance or connection between them and God."[11] The creature then may be reaffirmed in its distinctness. In himself, beyond the relation of the creature to him, God is not opposed to the creature.

The sacred now entirely takes over the profane and retains its opposition to it only as a conquered moment within itself. Thus, divine transcendence ceases to mean negation of the creature, and instead becomes its elevation. Transcendence is no longer found above creation but in creation. The creature is in God and God is in the creature. In its very finitude, and not only in its uncreated essence, the creature manifests God as the ultimate dimension of finite reality, the inaccessible in the accessible. Unlike negative theology, positive mysticism refuses to consider God's transcendence to the creature as final. For all its radical denial of creaturely determinations, negative theology never overcomes the creaturely standpoint. As a result, its religious reassertion of the finite is also weaker. For in spiritual life certainly the rule holds that one possesses as much as one is willing to lose. Only the mystic who has lost the whole world will gain it in return. Francis's universal love, Ignatius's practical sense, Teresa of Avila's warm humanity were made possible only through their renouncement of creaturely desire and even of creaturely knowledge. It is precisely this complex and demanding character which makes creature mysticism the most human form of mysticism, accessible only to men of heroic religious virtue. To have produced it so abundantly is one of the glories of the Christian faith.

How can the creature first be totally renounced and then continue to survive in God? Rather then answering this question speculatively, mystical writers describe the actual purification of the soul which leads to total negation, and the subsequent reintegration which overcomes it. Yet they are clearly aware of the complexity of the movement. At the end of the first book of the *Ascent of Mount Carmel*, in which he deals with the abnegation of the creatures, Saint John of the Cross already anticipates their readmission:

> *In order to arrive at possessing everything,*
> *Desire to possess nothing.*
> *In order to arrive at being everything,*
> *Desire to be nothing*
> *In order to arrive at knowing everything,*
> *Desire to know nothing.*[12]

The soul must purify itself, then, of the *desire* of the creature, but the motive, spiritual writers insist, must be the union in love.[13] Not pleasure, then, but desire, that is, the self-centered aspect of pleasure, must be renounced. Even the renunciation of desire must not be self-centered, as, for instance, the drive to attain a higher state of perfection would be. Nor must the purification aim at the attainment of a future good. Its sole purpose is to express its *present* love of God. Remarkably enough, this drive to convert suffering and contempt into positive values is found primarily in Christian mysticism. In spite of the emphasis on abnegation of desire, the Hindu and Buddhist attitudes toward suffering reflect resignation rather than preference. Apparently because of his active recognition of and deep involvement with the created world, the Christian needs this counter balance to maintain his upward attitude.

Nevertheless, the active purification, however intensive, remains essentially insufficient for mystical progress. A *passive* night is required in which God purges the senses of the many impurities which no mortification can ever eliminate. One such impurity is attachment to the pleasure of divine love, which diverts the soul from the Beloved himself.[14]

In the rhythm of spiritual life the purgation of the senses is followed by the perception of a new, transcendent reality. Some consider the overwhelming awareness of divine presence which characterizes this mystical stage as *the* fundamental mystical phenomenon. Spiritual illumination may occur on several levels: sense perception, imagination, understanding. On the first two levels we find the more sensational phenomena of the mystical life, hallucinations, revolutions, which the outsider is all too often inclined to identify with mystical illumination as such. The masters of spiritual life caution against this emergence of the unconscious at the moment when the mind is about to reach another level of consciousness. Visions to them are imperfect stages of mystical illumination, the main function of which is to prepare the soul for the passive illumination. The latter takes place in a state of negative simplicity and spiritual emptiness which Saint John of the Cross calls "dark contemplation." Here the highest illumination consists of the so-called intellectual visions, states of awareness that "can be felt in the substance of the soul." They no longer relate to particular matters, but directly reflect the union between God and the soul.

The term *intellectual* is not entirely appropriate for a unifed experience which is no more "knowing" than "loving," and which, as the fourteenth-century English mystic Walter Hilton wrote, consists in "the enlightening of the understanding joined to the joys of his love."[15] Clearly, the "intellectual vision" is the purest form of the religious experience as such, in which the mind concentrates entirely on the single awareness of its own unity. To speak of infused knowledge is misleading, for there is no evidence that mystics in this state know *more* than before. They use the word *knowledge* often enough, and some have even maintained that they learned more in one moment of illumination than in an entire lifetime. Yet those words refer not to an increase in the ability of comprehension but to a new *dimension* of consciousness in which what they knew previously takes on a different meaning. From the constant usage of such terms as *indeterminate knowledge* and *night,* we may safely conclude that no new ideas are being infused. Rather does the total transformation of consciousness have unique repercussions upon the cognitive power of the mind. With Maritain we might name this "practical knowledge," that is, a connaturality of the mind with that which is directly present to it.[16]

Still the term *intellectual* is not altogether gratuitous. For aside from its non-sensuous character the highest mystical illumination possesses a permanence comparable to that of an intellectual insight, which is absent from the transitory visions of the imagination. This must not be understood as if the flow of divine light were always even. But the intermittent intensive illuminations do not entirely disappear in the subsequent period, as imaginary visions do. They are retained in some sort of habitual state of enlightenment, compared by Saint Teresa to the awareness of a person's presence which continues after the shutters of a bright room have been closed.

NOTES

1. *Stromata* 5–6. Migne, P.G. 9, 64A.

2. Louis Bouyer summarizes the early Christian development as follows: "For the Greek Fathers the word *mystical* was used to describe first of all the divine reality which Christ brought to us, which the Gospel has revealed, and which gives its profound and definitive meaning to all the Scriptures. Moreover, *mystical* is applied to all knowledge of divine things to which we accede through Christ, and then, by derivation, to those things themselves. Finally, the word, evolving always in the same direction, comes to describe the spiritual reality of worship 'in spirit and truth,' as opposed to the vanity of an exterior religion which has not been quickened to new life by the coming of the savior" ("Mysticism" in *Mystery and Mysticism* [New York: Philosophical Library, 1956], pp. 127–128).

3. *Mysticism East and West,* trans. Bertha Bracey and Richenda Payne (New York: Macmillan, 1970), pp. 57–72.

4. Jacques Maritain, "The Natural Mystical Experience," in *Redeeming the Time,* trans. Harry L. Binsse (London: Geoffrey Bles, The Centenary Press, 1946), p. 239. Maritain's interpretation is based upon Ambroise Gardeil, *La structure de l'âme et l'expérience mystique* (Paris: J. Gabalda, 1927).

5. Etymologically the term *henological* does not basically differ from *monist,* but its actual usage is restricted to a Neoplatonic, negative theology. Since we are speaking of a type of mysticism rather than a particular current of thought, the term *henological* seems preferable to *Neoplatonic.*

6. *Enneads,* VI, 9 (4, 7), trans. Elmer O'Brien in *The Essential Plotinus* (New York: New American Library, 1964).

7. Ibid., V, 3, 14.

8. Sermon *"Scitote quia prope est,"* in the translation of Raymond Bernard Blakney, *Meister Eckhart* (New York: Harper & Row, 1957), p. 131. Compare also *"Omne datum optimum,"* Blakney, p. 185, and *"Elisabeth impletum est tempus,"* Blakney, p. 153.

9. *"In hoc apparuit caritas,"* Blakney, p. 127. Rudolf Otto gives the exact distinction: "They (the creatures) must exist somehow in order that this judgment of their nonexistence may be cast in their faces. They 'are' not does not mean that they have no empirical existence, no physical reality. They cannot be nonexistent in this empirical sense, for they could not then be 'pure nothing' " *(Mysticism,* p. 111).

10. *Le sens de l'existence d'après S. Jean de la Croix* (Paris: Aubier, 1960), 2:1 167.

11. John of the Cross Saint, *The Ascent of Mount Carmel,* trans. E. Allison Peers (Garden City, N.Y.: Doubleday, 1958), II, 8, 3.

12 Ibid., I, 13, 11.

13. As John of the Cross expresses it: "Every pleasure if it be not purely for the honor and love of God, must be renounced and completely rejected for the love of Jesus Christ" (ibid., I, 13, 4).

14. John of the Cross, Saint, *Dark Night* in *Complete Works,* 3 vols., trans. and ed. E. Allison Peers (Westminster, Md.: Newman Press, 1946), vol. I, Book I, 1, 3.

15. *The Ladder of Perfection, Scala Perfectionis,* trans. Leo Sherley-Price (London: Penguin 1957), Book I, chap. 9, p. 8 John of the Cross also writes that the highest vision can neither be seen nor understood but only "felt in the substance of the soul, with the sweetest touches and unions, all of which belong to spiritual feelings" *(Ascent,* II, 24, 4).

16. Jacques Maritain, *The Degrees of Knowledge,* trans. Gerald Phelan (New York: Scribner 1959), p. 449: cf. also 338–39.

Chapter 16

THE EXPERIENCE OF THE HOLY AND THE IDEA OF GOD
John E. Smith

THE phenomenological approach to any philosophical problem means an approach through the analysis of primary experience and the reflective grasp of what we actually encounter. This view, though positive, implies the negation of certain other views. First, it means that experience is not to be understood either as a way of transforming reality into mere phenomena devoid of power and otherness, or of reducing reality to the data of sense; second, it means that experience is not to be identified with an exclusively private or "mental" content confined to an individual mind; third, it means that ingredient in experience is a real world of things, events, and selves transcending the encounter had by any one individual or any finite collection of individuals. The general assumption behind these negations is that experience is neither a substitute for reality nor a veil that falls between us and what there is, but rather a *reliable medium of disclosure* through which the real world is made manifest and comes to be apprehended by us.

Our task here is to seek an understanding of the experience of the holy, to mark out distinctive features of the situations in which the presence of the holy is felt, and then to express the relation of these features to the idea of God as the supremely worshipful being of religion. Rudolf Otto, in his well-known study *The Idea of the Holy*, began with the record of certain experiences or encounters with God which played a special role in the foundation of the Hebraic-Christian religion. The question might be raised, however, whether instead of beginning

From: James M. Edie, ed. *Phenomenology in America* (Chicago: Quadrangle Books, 1967), pp. 295–306.

with the special experiences that are recorded and interpreted in the biblical, especially the Old Testament, literature, it would be more in accord with a phenomenological approach to start from a broader base and consider certain recurrent situations that are to be found universally in experience. In this way we can face more directly the difficult problem of passing from the experience of the holy to a historically specific idea of God.

Let us approach the holy by the method of contrast. A distinction to be found in some form in every culture known to us is the distinction between those persons, objects, events, and places that are said to be "holy" and those that are called "profane." The most distinctive and yet most abstract characteristic of the holy is that it is *set apart* from what is ordinary in human life, because of the sense that the holy is powerful, awe-inspiring, dangerous, important, precious, and to be approached only with fitting seriousness and gravity. The holy stands over against the profane, which is, by contrast, open, manifest, obvious, ordinary, and devoid of any special power to evoke awe and reverence. The profane belongs to the ordinary or customary course of events and harbors no mysterious depth within itself. Whereas the holy can be approached only with due preparation, profane existence is readily available and is taken for granted without evoking much thought or concern.

The initial contrast that enables us to make the fundamental identification of the holy is a distinction—not a separation or total disconnection. The holy is "other than" the profane but not "wholly other." In order to avoid separating the two spheres so that they are severed of all intelligible connections, it is important to notice the dual nature of their relations. On the one hand, the holy is set apart from the profane, but on the other hand, its disconnection from the profane is not the final fact about its being. Otto tended to emphasize their separation and the "wholly other" character of the holy because he was trying to present it as an ultimate and irreducible feature of reality, and also to avoid the reduction of the holy as a religious reality to the sphere of morality. But the holy must impinge upon and become ingredient in life, including the activities of profane or ordinary existence; it cannot be merely set apart. The holy is not to break through life or destroy it as if life were of no account, but rather to consecrate and sustain human existence. In addition, therefore, to the awe and reverence expressing our sense that there is a *gulf* between the holy and our ordinary life, there is also the concern on our part to have communion with the holy, to partake of its power and thereby elevate profane existence to a new level of importance.

In the course of experience we discover that the situations we encounter divide themselves into two basically different sorts. On the one hand, there are situations such as traveling to work, purchasing a book or an umbrella, meeting friends for luncheon, calling for information about train schedules, and so forth, which reduce to routine, which do not challenge or arrest us in any way, and which we do more or less habitually, regarding them as "normal" or "regular" parts of the business of living. On the other hand, there is another type of situation running through experience, and it calls for a different description. This type of situation has an insistence that arrests us and leads us to reflect on the seriousness and import of life as a whole. Such arresting situations are encountered in their most insistent form at the two boundaries of natural life—birth and death—but they are also to be encountered during the course of life in the form of certain "crucial" times that mark what may be called the "turning points" or times of decision, judgment, and risk in the life both of individuals and nations. In addition to birth and death, there is the time of marriage, the time of attaining adulthood, the time of serious illness and recovery, the time of war and of the concluding peace, the time of choosing a vocation and of launching a career, the time of setting out upon a long journey. Each of these times is marked off from the "ordinary" course of events, and in every case we frequently describe it as a time of "life and death," by which we mean to express our sense both of the power manifested and of its special bearing or import for our life as a whole. We are vaguely aware in such situations of something that is powerful and important, and our most universal response is that of "celebration." Such times, we feel, must not be allowed to sink to the level of ordinary routine; in some way they must be kept apart from all that is usual or taken for granted. On one side, these times set themselves apart from the ordinary because of their own arresting character; on the other side, there is our response or sense that these times must not be allowed to pass away unnoticed or to be reduced to the sphere of the ordinary. Celebration or ceremony is the attempt to preserve and intensify the importance of the crucial junctures of life.

The various forms of celebration which take place on these occasions are evidence both of their arresting character in themselves and of our human capacity to be arrested by them and to acknowledge their power. Everyone, even the most completely rationalistic person who regards himself as committed only to the pursuit of truth and objectivity without ceremony, experiences the seriousness and arresting character of weddings and funerals and the anxiety attaching inevitably to the birth of a new being. The philosophical task posed by such situations is to discover what there is about these events that evokes our response so that we come to identify them as times when the holy is present. Assuming, as we may, that the cycle of human life contains such special and arresting times as we have indicated, we must attempt to discover wherein their special power resides and ultimately how they are related to the idea of God.

The most basic fact about the special events is their temporal position in life; most of them occur once and do not recur. Birth and death have an obvious "once-for-allness" about them, as do the attainment of manhood and the time of marriage. The latter, at the very least, is *meant* to be the establishment of a permanent relationship. What happens but once in life cannot be placed on the same level of importance with the endlessly repeated and repeatable events of the daily round. The unique temporal position of these events harbors in itself a special capacity, a capacity for calling attention to the being of the self and to life as a *whole*. This feature is, of course, most evident in the two boundary events of life. In birth and death we have to do with absolute beginnings and endings, with the coming into being or the passing away of an individual being who is unique. In both cases it is the total being who comes before us, the person as an indissoluble unit. The focus of attention on the person as such helps to direct attention to the *being* of the person and away from the parts and details of life.

In the case of the crucial events falling between the boundaries of life and death, attention is also directed to the *course* of life viewed in its total quality or worth. Life as such and the purpose of living come into view at points where decision affects the direction and destiny of life in its entire cycle and not just in one aspect or part. We experience awe in the face of the crucial events because we see in them, at one extreme, the possibility of death and the destruction of our hopes or, in less serious situations, the possibility of a failure so basic that the purpose of living may seem to be destroyed. Conversely, the crucial events may prove to be occasions of creative self-realization and the laying of foundations for lasting achievement. A crucial event is said to be a time of "crisis" because it means a judgment upon life in the sense that a time of decision reveals the quality of a life and opens the possibility for success or failure with respect to that life as a whole.

The use of the term *crisis* to describe the crucial event expresses the dual sense of *choice* and of *judgment* appropriate to such situations. From the standpoint of the agent who contemplates marriage, for example, there is the responsibility of choice, commitment, and the attendant risk that comes with realizing freedom at a specific point in life; an unwise or ill-considered choice at this point affects the course and quality of life as a whole and not only in some part or limited aspect. Choice in a crisis situation is "momentous" just because of the holistic nature of the consequences. In a trivial situation concerning a part of life, one can "experiment" and, through a process of trial and error, gradually arrive at the best method for achieving success without at the same time involving one's entire being in the process. But trivial situations are very different from the times of crisis; the latter involve our entire being, and the idea of "experimenting" with a marriage, for example, as if one could enter that relationship casually and sporadically, is inappropriate and severely damages the personal relations that must exist if the union is to be a success. The notion of experiment and trial is inappropriate at those points where the being of the person as a whole is in question.

On the other hand, a crisis situation brings with it more than the demand for decision on the part of the agent; a crisis brings us to a juncture where the direction and quality of life are judged or tested by the nature of the situation itself. The attempt to lead the quiet or sheltered life is generally the attempt to avoid becoming involved in situations that call for, i.e., demand or exact from us, a response that at once reveals the nature of our persons, our most intimate desires and values, our ultimate beliefs and commitments. The situation by itself, of course, exercises no "judgment," but its nature forces us to reveal ourselves, even if we try to avoid meeting the demands it makes upon us. In this sense the special events in life are literally the "times that try men's souls." The time of "crisis," as the Greek term from which the word is derived means, is a time of "judgment."

The crucial times, moreover, reveal the precariousness of our existence and underline the truth that in existence no realization is absolutely guaranteed in advance. Precariousness is seen as affecting not only the details of life, but life in its entire being. The crucial times make clear that we confront not only problems *in* life, but a fundamental problem *of* life, namely, the problem of finding the power upon which we depend for our being and our purpose. The arresting character of the special times consists largely in their shocking us and thus forcing us out of the routine established within the framework of ordinary clock time into an awareness of our being and its purpose in a total scheme of things. Concern for details and the partial interests that make up so large a part of ordinary existence gradually deadens our sensitivity not only to our problematic being as selves in a precarious world, but also to the ultimate questions about the world itself. Where all is "ordinary," open, manifest, and devoid of either depth or mystery, awe and reverence disappear and are replaced by boredom and indifference. But life has a structure of its own that works against the reduction of everything to the level of the profane. Life has its critical junctures, and these exert power over us, so that however completely the affairs described as the "ordinary business of living" prevent us from attending to what Socrates called the "care of the soul," the crucial times serve to bring us back to this concern and to a grasp of the problematic nature of our individual existence.

Thus far, the experience of the holy through the crucial junctures of life has been understood entirely in terms of the *temporal* pattern of life, and we have referred exclusively to crucial *times* and *events*. But the whole of life is not exhausted in its temporal features; we are creatures of space as well as of time, and the question naturally arises, Are there special or crucial *spaces* that have an arresting function, driving us out of the uniformity and the habitual routine of ordinary life and leading us to respond in awe to the holy, to become aware of our own being and of the need to find a pattern and a purpose in life as a whole? Since space has its quality in itself and contemporaneously—a holy space does not possess its holy character in virtue of any *summing* of its parts, but immediately and at once—it will not intrude itself upon us as the temporal event does, but rather we shall have first to seek such a space and place ourselves in it in order to experience its power. When we are actually *in* such a space, it will have its own insistence and arresting force, but its effect can take place only when we have opened ourselves by going to the appropriate place. Here space differs from time and crucial events in that the latter descend upon us whether we will or not, whereas we must go to a special space or structure one for ourselves in order to realize its holiness.

The best-known form of holy space is the sanctuary or physical enclosure clearly marked off from profane space and consecrated as a special place where the holy is present in the form of the divine to be sought and worshiped. Once again, it is well to consider whether, instead of beginning with a readily acknowledged holy space, we can find features belonging to the spatial environment of life that would help to explain how it can be the mediator of the holy in and through its own character. We may begin with the distinction evident in experience between the open, public, and neutral space in which the activities of ordinary life take place and shape, and those spaces where it is possible to break through routine and habitual responses in order to find ourselves confronted with the fact of existence and with the question of the purpose of our life as a whole. For example, a stadium filled with people waiting to see a football game is a singularly inappropriate space for discussing a matter of theological concern or for expressing thoughts most intimately expressive of our being and purpose. The space is too completely open and public; it has no arresting power to drive us back to a consideration of what is highest in importance or ultimate in being. On the contrary, such space is entirely extroverted and calls for self-forgetful expressions of enjoyment; the space of the stadium harbors no mystery within itself. Moreover, in such a space we are not elevated in either reverence or awe, and indeed it seems to prevent our withdrawal from the scene and makes it impossible for us to contemplate our being or the ultimate nature of things. For the consideration of what involves our lives as a whole and concerns us most intimately, we need a different kind of space.

We must have a space that is not public in the sense that it is a scene where ordinary business is generally conducted, or where anyone may enter without warning or preparation. We must have a space different from one we normally pass through in the course of going to another place. A space that is able to express the sense of the holy has three characteristics: first, it is set apart from ordinary or routine experience and thus cannot be universally accessible; second, it must have historic associations which remind us of the experiences of the holy had by others in the past, as in the biblical example of Moses turning aside to see the burning bush, where a previously open and profane space became a holy space in virtue of the arresting experience associated with it; third, the holy space must be so structured as to direct our thoughts to ourselves and our own being and at the same time away from ourselves to an awareness of the holy power upon which all existence depends.

The crucial times and the holy spaces may arrest us and bring us to a realization of the problematic character of our existence, of our dependence upon a power not ourselves, and of the need to find an object of supreme devotion. But by themselves these events and spaces do not solve our problem. The most they can do is arrest us and impel us to consider the question and the possibility of a form of holy life upon which our existence depends. There is no necessary, logical transition from an experience of the holy, in encountering the crucial events and places, to the reality of God as understood in a specific, historical tradition such as the Judeo-Christian understanding of God represents. On the other hand, the experience of the holy belongs to the structure of life and the world; it is not dependent on the assumption of certain traditional religious ideas, as if there were no experiential content in the crucial events themselves but only a "religious interpretation" in the form of a tissue of ideas. There is therefore a clear distinction to be drawn between the idea of God, specifically and historically understood, and the experience of the holy. On the other hand, the two need not remain unrelated to each other. There is an ultimate connection between the experience of the holy as a pervasive fact of human life and some idea of God or other, but there is no necessary transition from the experience to a historically specific conception of God. There is a missing link that remains to be supplied. The idea of God as the holy power in existence arises in our consciousness on occasions when we are arrested, taken out of our daily routine, and led to contemplate our being only if we have the belief that the power we sense is one upon which our ultimate destiny depends and is a reality that demands our worship and the devotion of our entire being. The sense of the holy, with the awe we feel on the occasions when the holy becomes manifest to us, is connected with the idea of God *only* if we identify that holy with the controller of destiny and the supremely worshipful being.

It is, however, an error to identify the experience of the holy, as it is open to any human being, with the apprehension of a definite Being as such, as if the approach to God through the holy was a form of empirical confirmation of the divine existence so understood. Here there are too many possibilities for interpretation. We may hold that the structure of human life remains universal in character despite the undeniable differences that exist in the staggering variety of cultural forms and practices in religion, art, and morality. But just because there is such a plurality of religious traditions and cultural forms, we are not justified in identifying the experience of the holy, taken as a phenomenon of universal scope, with the intuition of God as understood from the standpoint of any one religious tradition.

On the other hand, it is an error to suppose, as contemporary nonphilosophical theologians do, that because there is no necessary logical transition from the experience of the holy as a pervasive ingredient in experience to the God who is called "the God of Abraham, Isaac, and Jacob," there is no logical relation at all obtaining between the two. Unless we are prepared to show that, for example, the sort of experience in which Abraham participated is absolutely discontinuous with human experience as known to us, there is no ground for denying an intelligible connection between our contemporary experience of the holy and the God of the Judeo-Christian tradition. The way is left open for *interpreting* the power present in the crucial events and places encountered in living experience in terms of the doctrine of God to be found in that tradition. Insofar as the power encountered in the experience of the holy is regarded as that upon which our being, the purpose of our life as a whole, and our destiny depend, it is legitimate to introduce the idea of the biblical God at this point. That there is no logical necessity in the transition from the holy to the God described in the Bible, such as might be based on an intuition of the individual Being of the Judeo-Christian tradition, does not preclude our interpreting the holy in that sense.

The transition from the holy to God, while not logically necessary, is nevertheless not without some ground; it is rooted in a mediating concept which we may call the general *concept* of God derived from reflective analysis of recurrent experience and presupposed as part of the meaning of every specific religious doctrine of God. The topic calls for more extended treatment, but one essential point can be elucidated. The term *God* need not be restricted to use as a name (although there are contexts in which it so functions) but stands as well for a concept that finds its basis in philosophical reflection on the world and ourselves. This concept embraces the idea of a supremely worshipful reality which gives being to and controls the final destiny of all finite realities. If the term *God* were merely a name, significant exclusively within the confines of a special religious tradition, there could be no intelligible connection between the experience of the holy and God. But because there is a concept of God available for our use, it is possible to connect the concept of God with the experience of the holy in which we become aware of the dependence of our being on a power that is at once the supremely worshipful being, and that upon which we depend for our final purpose and destiny.

The general concept of God as the object of supreme devotion, derived from reflective analysis of experience, including encounter with the environment and ourselves, mediates between the pervasive experience of the holy and the specific idea of God existing within a historical religious community. The latter idea is itself dependent on experiences of the holy, but those experiences are selected, historically specific encounters which have served as the foundation for an identifiable religious community. Thus, the Hebraic community finds its unifying and identifying reference point in the historic encounters of the patriarchs, Moses, and the prophetic figures with the holy; likewise, the New Testament communities were rooted in the historic encounters of Jesus, Paul, and the disciples with the holy, this time mediated through a historic personage. The historic encounters with the holy, however, demanded in each instance an interpreter whose task was to set forth the specifically religious meaning of these encounters. At that point the generic concept of God comes into play. The experiences of the holy come to be understood as encounters with God through the identification of these experiences as religion, i.e., as encounters with that reality which alone is worthy of absolute devotion. Once the transition from the holy to God has been made via the generic concept of the supremely worshipful reality, the specific character of the historic encounters supplies the concrete content. For the Judeo-Christian tradition, for example, God is understood as Will and Righteousness, as Love and Mercy, because of the nature of the encounters had by Moses, the prophets, and Jesus with the holy.

PART FOUR

Religion and the Human Predicament

INTRODUCTION BY JOSEPH J. KOCKELMANS

IN the preceding parts of this book the contributing authors have expressed their ideas on the religious dimension as a whole, the question of how far it is possible for man in the natural condition to know God and to "prove" His existence, and, finally, on issues that are directly related to man's religious experience and to religious language. We must now focus on the implication of these ideas for the human predicament. From the numerous topics we could have selected for discussion we have chosen those that seem to be most relevant to modern people today.

After stressing the historical character of revelation, we turn to the question concerning the meaning and function of religion in societies that are deeply influenced by modern science and technology. These reflections are followed by investigations about how today to explain evil and what we are to think about immortality. Finally, the book concludes with a brief note on the sense of mystery in our modern world.

In "History as Revelation" Louis Dupré tries to answer the question of how a religious message can be historical without being for that reason subject to all changes that inherently affect human history. According to the author, the concept of history as divine revelation remains entirely a matter of theological interpretation. Only the interpretation can isolate certain events as revealing a special divine intervention. But since the events are also claimed to be truly historical, the question arises of how they can continue to be decisive for the relation to the transcendent for later generations. The answer must lie in a constant reinterpretation of the past through the present.

"Explanation in Science and Theology" constitutes a reflection on what we are trying to do when interdisciplinarily we seek to understand our world as scientists, philosophers, and theologians. Frederick Ferré analyzes what explanation is and how explanations can be given in science, philosophy, and theology.

Next Joseph Kockelmans presents some historicocritical reflections on the relationship between science and religion. According to Whitehead, there has always been a conflict between religion and science, and both religion and science have always been in a state of continual development. It is the combination of these two "facts" which can explain why, since the sixteenth century, many Christian scientists have concerned themselves with natural religion. The author makes an attempt to explain the historical origin of natural religion as well as the reasons why natural religion began to play an important part in the concern of many scientists wih Christianity. Special attention is given to the ideas proposed by Boyle, Locke, and Newton.

In "Alien Universe" Frederick Ferré defends the view that science was the most influential agency that formed the consciousness of modern man and shaped his world. In his view it cannot be denied that, all positive elements and aspects notwithstanding, there are fatal flaws in our modern world. The author traces these flaws to flaws in our modern consciousness itself and argues that the latter were caused by misinterpretations of the meaning and function of science in society.

In the next essay Peter Bertocci has characterized the Person-Creator by attributes that can be rooted in the interaction of persons and their supreme values with Nature. The attributes of God must not be settled by appeal to the Mystery of Being. Too often when this is done conclusions are drawn that conform to the assumed validity of the classical view of Perfection. This tendency results in opposing any change or growth in God, and any limitation of his knowledge and power that is not self-imposed. Thus, most theists hold that God's "infinite" goodness and "infinite" power insure the ultimate victory of the good in the best of compossible worlds. This view of God, his goodness and his power, does not cohere with the evils in natural and in human processes that are beyond human control and can hardly be conceived as disciplinary values. Thus, given such nondisciplinary evil, why not think of God as a continuing Creator-Person "persuading" a coeternal Impediment within His own nature to fit into His purposes? Bertocci defends this view from the objection that it dichotomizes God's unity; and he also argues that we cannot reasonably continue to conceive of God's experience as immune from creative insecurity. This especially is so if we are to conceive of the divine purpose as involving unrelenting, moral creativity in achieving and orchestrating the good—a human divine, responsive-responsible community. Is any perfection worthy of worship, indeed is it perfection, if it does not accept the "cost" of such creativity?

The book concludes with some reflections on the importance of preserving the sense of mystery in a postmodern world. Frederick Ferré argues in favor of a polymythic organicism which reflects a religious stance that affirms as legitimate and exciting the possibility of pluralism in mythic imagery within a context of undergirding fundamental values. The author particularly stresses the need for preserving and even revitalizing a sense of mystery in our belief systems, in the sciences, in our concern for the environment, in our caring for one another, in a word, in all our human experiences.

Chapter 17

HISTORY AS REVELATION
Louis Dupré

So much interpretation goes into the presentation of "religious" events that we must raise the question whether revelation as history may still be called history. A first part of the answer is easy enough. History always interprets events. Facts remain meaningless until they are compared with previous occurrences and are linked to subsequent events.[1] A theological interpretation of events, then, does not a priori rule out their historical character, particularly if this interpretation was given by the men (Jesus, Moses, Muhammad) who initiated the events. But the difficulty reaches much deeper. Sacred history cannot be resolved into the sort of phenomenal continuity which seems to be essential to the scientific concept of history. Granted, the historian uses models, perhaps even myths, in his interpretation of events, but empirical evidence must be the ultimate criterion for their adoption or rejection. The types and interpretations of the sacred historian, on the contrary, can never be borne out by the facts, for they belong in the final analysis to a nonempirical realm. His way of telling a story is ultimately nonhistorical, not because it is interpretive (all history is), but because his interpretation cannot become more or less acceptable by additional evidence.[2] Most of the time there is no evidence or insufficient historical evidence to favor a religious interpretation above a nonreligious one. Professor Austin Farrer underscored this point in a lecture given toward the end of his life: "Theological history [i.e., history as revelation] does not and cannot resolve its mythical diagrams into the succession or interplay of human acts; they must stand for a reality which is the continuous operation of the divine will. . . . [Believers] unquestionably hold that God is an historical

From: Louis Dupré, *The Other Dimension: A Search for the Meaning of Religious Attitudes* (Garden City, N.Y.: Doubleday, 1972), pp. 299–313.

agent not pinned to a point of time, but able as out of another dimension to exert his power at every moment; and if sacred history does not show the hand of God it neither is nor mediates divine revelation.''[3] If history consists of a coherent interpretation on an *empirical basis* of observable events, revelatory history cannot be called history at all. Its interpretative models differ entirely from the ones which scientific history uses. Nor can sacred history claim a separate set of facts as its own, for facts alone are not sacred. The same historical science deals with all facts, the ones which theology declares "revelatory" as well as others; and it deals with all in the same way. The notion of revelation history belongs in theology and nowhere else.

This does not mean that history as such is of no concern to the believer. It obviously is, since the believer must interpret his faith *within* the events of the past, not *à propos* of them. Historical verification of some sort, then, becomes an essential ingredient in any faith which claims to rest upon historical revelation. Such historical research becomes abusive only when it takes itself as ultimate criterion for the interpretation of faith.[4] In what sense can history be said to be revealing for religious man? Not by attributing a hierophantic meaning to time, for, as Mircea Eliade has shown, all religions recognize a sacred time.[5] Nor by giving history a place in the religious attitude, for it does so inevitably once man starts attributing any meaning at all to history. At that moment every experience, including the religious one, attains a historical dimension.[6] But that is obviously not what the Hebrews meant in saying that God reveals himself through history. In a historical faith, such as that of Israel, history occupies a *privileged* revelatory position: it is more revealing than anything else.[7] But how? Once again, the revelatory quality of an event does not reside in the event alone but in the *interpreted* event. As a rule this interpretation itself is not immediately settled. It is an ongoing process in which the past is constantly reinterpreted. The first chapters of Genesis articulate Israel's vision of the beginning at a particular stage (or stages) of its history. Later reports in Ben Sirach 42:15–43, 35; Baruch 3:24–35; Job 37–40; Psalms 8 and 104 cover the same ground and reinterpret it according to new needs and insights. But at each stage of the process events are presented in such a way that they cannot be explained as the deeds of men only. Sacred historiography endows its facts with a mysterious quality which requires further investigation. The suggestion of something that cannot be explained by ordinary laws of history, it has been said, is what distinguishes the narratives of Genesis from those of Homer.[8]

But here a difficult problem arises: How can a message be historical without being subject to all the changes of history? A historical revelation is necessarily restricted by the symbolic idiom of a particular civilization. Its images and ideas are part of the same cultural totality as those literary creations which the believer does not regard as revealed. The writings of the New Testament share a number of conceptions and prejudices with the late Hellenistic culture in which they originated. Ideas about magic, slavery, and nationalism are not divided along the lines of scriptural inspiration. Moreoever, the events of revelation are with all other events woven into a single historical fabric. A revelation *through* history is necessarily subject to the laws of history. Believers in a historical faith are anxious enough to claim the first half of this statement but reluctant to admit the second. Yet, whatever stands in history becomes part of a changing process. The past takes on new meanings as it moves into the future. If we are fortunate enough to retrieve the original meaning of a historical message (no mean task, indeed), we must still integrate it within our own, different universe of discourse. Language develops as culture expands, and in developing it articulates the on-going revision of values in man's axiological creativity. The revealed message does not escape this common fate of all historical expression. Most often the evolution happens so gradually that the believer is hardly aware how he is adapting old texts to new contexts. Yet at certain times the words of revelation seem to come from a strange past which has vanished forever. How can the religious consciousness survive this ordeal?

A positive revelation inevitably takes place at a particular moment of a cultural process which continues to develop afterward. Since man constantly recreates himself and his world, no concrete statement concerning his situation in the world can be definitive. To the extent that a historical revelation contains such judgments—as it invariably does—it must be subject to change. Christians are usually startled when confronted with these inexorable consequences. If Christ was truly human in more than a biological sense, as his followers so strongly proclaim, he was bound by the cultural limitations of his time.[9] His message contained elements which would be developed long after him and other elements which later believers could no longer accept in their own world view. The price to pay for a historical revelation is some sort of contingency.

At the same time a revelation must possess a lasting quality which allows its central message to resist the flux of historical change. By itself the purely historical cannot convey a permanent message. If revelation became mere process, it would cease to be revelatory. H. Richard Niebuhr, after having conceded the relative nature of all that is historical, rightly concluded: "Revelation, if it be revelation of God, must offer men something more immovable than the pole star and something more precise than our measurements of the winds and currents of history can afford."[10] Some theologians hope to escape the dilemma of stability and historicity by settling for a continuous message rather than a permanent one. But this compromise does not solve anything until it appears that continuity can exist without permanence.

How could events and words of a historical past ever be permanently decisive in establishing a relation to the transcendent? The full moment of the question was first perceived by Lessing. How, he wondered, could the acceptance of Jesus' resurrection as a historical fact ever lead one to conform his entire existence today to the claim that he is God? "What is the connection between my inability to raise any significant objection to the evidence of the former and my obligation to believe something against which my reason rebels?"[11] We may discard as an odd reminder of Lessing's own historical relativity the rationalist belief that every person would indeed be willing to stake everything on a revelation of the necessary truths of reason.[12] Yet the main question stands: How can the purely historical ever attain a transhistorical status? Or, how can the past remain permanently present? In spite of the strong historical awareness of our own age, I find little desire among current theologians to tackle this problem. Most of them are perfectly satisfied with "historical" or "scriptural" theology, optimistically hoping that a better understanding of the past will somehow make the original revelation reverberate into the present. The position implies the remarkable contention that revelation will reach us as it reached the early community if only we study history, while it is precisely its past character which seems to make the message irrelevant or even unacceptable.[13] The underlying argument, I believe, is the easy analogy that, since the events and words of revelation at one time sparked off a new relation to the transcendent, there is no reason why they could not do so again if properly placed in their original context. But there is a reason! For the better we understand the past, the more we realize that it is not the present. Others, steeped in hermeneutics, promise less and deliver nothing. They are too busy showing the uniqueness of the events and the inevitable change of every subsequent reading of it to explain how throughout all these changes it can still remain identical.

What we need is a proof that a historical event can convey a lasting message to each subsequent generation. To provide such a proof is beyond the scope of this essay, since it would imply a full clarification of all the ways in which the past can be present.[14] Yet restricting ourselves to religious symbols, we find that they always surpass the immediate present, insofar as they always point beyond their actual appearance. Unlike some other symbols, symbols of the transcendent are not tied to their historical form and expression. The awareness of the intrinsic inadequacy of expression, which is inherent to the religious symbol, gives it a unique flexibility. Thus, the symbols of a historical revelation are able to adopt new meanings while maintaining a full continuity with their past.[15] Their religious intentionality enables them to transcend their historical context and to overcome the cultural restrictions of their origin.

Surely, to point out the tension between the noema of the religious symbol and its forms of expression is not to solve the entire historical problem. For one might think, with some theologians of the recent past, that the culturally antiquated form of the revelation can be detached from its lasting content. Such an endeavor, as a moment's reflection might have suggested, is wholly unsatisfactory. For one thing, it presupposes that man can lift himself sufficiently out of his historical condition to commit a perennial content to a historical form and subsequently translate it out of this form into a "universal" language. If this were the case, one wonders why the content was not formulated directly in its universal form. The historical embodiment, then, appears to be a mere detour. But if the original expression is historically determined, so is the later interpretation. A complete "demythologization"—which eliminates all historical determinations—is therefore intrinsically impossible.

A reflection on the nature of the symbol exposes even more the methodological error in all attempts to separate form from content. A symbol never consists of a disposable form wrapped around a permanent content. More than any other characteristic, the indissoluble unity of form and content is essential to the symbolization process. A change in form affects the content of the symbol. No one would question this for the work of art, but the reason is just as cogent for the religious symbol, for its function is precisely to open a *perspective* upon the transcendent reality, and for this purpose the form cannot be an indifferent matter. The Churches have, therefore, upheld in the face of major difficulties that also the revealed form must be preserved and that divine inspiration extends to the wording itself. Fundamentalists corrupt this profound insight by attributing to the original expression a magical and superhuman quality which conflicts with the nature of the symbol. The confusion results from the mistaken assumption that if the wording is revealed it cannot be human and must thus escape all historical relativity. Relevation, in this view, retains its divine quality only by freezing its symbols into immutable past facts. The role of the sacred writer is confined to that of an amanuensis, a secretary who contributes nothing but a pair of ears to perceive the inspired whisper and a hand to write it down.

Our purpose in defending the indissolubility of expression and meaning content of revealed symbols is the exact opposite. Instead of eliminating all possibility of development, as the fundamentalist does, we extend the development to the entire symbol—form and content. The original expression must be preserved, but that is only half the work. It is not sufficient to let the façade stand and erect a new building behind it, as communities pressed for change and unable to justify it tend to do. (One recalls the farfetched "interpretations" of Catholic theologians during the antimodernist repression of the Holy Office.) The meaning must be preserved with the expression, yet in such a way that it fully incorporates the entire evolution from the moment of revelation to the present. To discover this meaning is the true task of hermeneutics. Beyond an up-to-date exegesis of the past as past, it must attempt to understand the past in the light of the present. The present introduces a new element which ought to be fully accepted if the past is to be understood as a living reality. Attempts to bypass the distance between past and present inevitably reduce the message to a dead letter and a purely historical event.[16]

Still, reading the past in the light of the present is not without risk, for we bring to it a number of presuppositions. Which ones are legitimate? Which ones are biases of our time? Time alone will determine which principles of today will turn out to be prejudices tomorrow. But one rule would seem to provide at least a basic principle of discernment to prevent destructive innovations. The interpretation of the past through the present must fully acknowledge the tradition in between the two historical points.[12] Man never thinks alone: he always stands in a tradition, and his only possibility of attaining truth lies in fully recognizing this tradition. This is particularly true in the case of a historical revelation where the believer's faith attains the original events only through the various stages of interpretation. We have assumed the legitimacy of historical development. But is this assumption justified, particularly in view of the erratic and often irrational character which marks the process of religious traditions? Is a revelation able to transmit its transcendent message through subsequent interpretations which cannot reasonably be claimed to have been present, even "implicitly," in the original message? If historical faith originates in a clearly defined message, all later additions would seem to jeopardize the purity of the origin. The existence of a tradition, which has caused so much legitimate concern in theology, can be justified only by establishing the traditional character of the original revelation itself. If the events and writings of revelation had been delivered directly, without the intermediacy of interpretation, all later interpretations would be spurious, since they would always deviate from the original, uninterpreted message. Yet if the revealed events and words were interpreted from the very beginning, then revelation may be considered as traditional in its very nature. In the past, the Christian Churches usually posed the problem in the narrow terms of a dilemma between "Scripture" and "tradition." Catholics would uphold tradition, Protestants Scripture. But revelation is neither Scripture alone nor Scripture interpreted by a *subsequent* tradition. Underneath their violent polemics, the antagonists harmoniously agreed in misstating the problem. To its lasting credit, *Formgeschichte* has placed tradition *before* Scripture, thereby changing the terms of the problem to a point where pertinent discussion becomes possible. Scripture does not come first. Jews have always known that Israel existed as a religious society long before prophets and priests, sages and historians, interpreted its unique experience; and Christians were aware that the community of their earliest predecessors flourished long before Paul and Mark started writing. Yet *Formgeschichte* had made it unambiguously clear that the Scriptures were intended as *interpretations* for the instruction of the communities. Thus, tradition and interpretation are established in the very heart of scriptural revelation. Even Jewish theologians, with their profound respect for the Word of God, do not hesitate to refer to the Bible as a *midrash* of revelation, that is, a commentary upon the original mystery.[18] The new insight is not limited to Scripture; it goes back to the original events and words. For events become religious and, a fortiori, revelatory only in and through interpretation. By themselves they all belong to the one skein of history, the raw material of historical science, which is neither religious nor profane. The religious consciousness alone makes an event stand

out as religious and even as revealing. This may be done during its very occurrence. One and the same intentionality made the acts of Jesus' adult life both
into historical facts and religious events. He himself *intended* (that is, interpreted)
his acts religiously and thereby constituted them into revelations. Henry Duméry
defined the original event of Christian revelation with great precision: "The fact
Jesus is nothing if not constituted by the subject Jesus, not only on the psycho-
empirical level but also on the level of its profound spiritual meaning (where
faith perceives the person of the Word). Once constituted, it carries a meaning.
This meaning may be recaptured, literally reconstituted by other subjects."[19]

Yet there is more than reconstitution, for the religious event does not end at
the moment of its occurence. The great deeds of the liberation of Israel were not
completed after Moses had finally looked down upon the promised land, or even
after David had conquered and pacified the new country. Centuries of prophetic
proclamation and sapiential reflection were to complete the *process of meaning*
initiated by the exodus. They also belong to the revelation. Similarly, Jesus'
message was not delivered after his final words were spoken on the mountain
in Galilee. The Christian revelation consisted as much in interpretations after
the events—by the synoptics, by Paul, who never witnessed any of them, by the
theologian who authored the Fourth Gospel, and, before all, by the primitive
Christian community. Even Jesus' words were not final, for they also required
that unique process of meditation which lately we have come to call "proclamation." The religious intepretation of the revelation is for a major part *reinterpretation*. It was so from the beginning. Scripture is a privileged part of the
tradition,[20] decisive in that it gives tradition a definitive turn, but not, as the
term *inspiration* has all too often suggested, in that it starts the revelatory process
or closes the tradition.

NOTES

1. Wolfhart Pannenberg rightly remarks: "The events of history speak their
own language, the language of facts; however, this language is understandable
only in the context of the traditions and expectations in which the given events
occur" ("Dogmatic Theses on the Doctrine of Revelation," in *Revelation as
History*, trans. David Granskou [New York: Macmillan, 1968], p. 153).

2. There are exceptions to this rule. The resurrection of Christ must be considered an essential fact. Theoretically it is conceivable that new historical evidence would confirm or weaken the establishment of this fact. This would have
a direct impact upon sacred history as such. We might add that all miraculous
facts are of this nature. They carry their own interpretation to the extent that if
the mere *fact* is proven false, the entire religious interpretation of it collapses;
if it is proven to be true, the presumption is strongly in favor of the religious
interpretation.

3. Austin Farrer, *Faith and Speculation* (New York: New York University Press, 1967), p. 93.

4. This point is well developed in Louis Monden, S.J., *Faith: Can Man Still Believe* (New York: Sheed & Ward, 1970).

5. *Images and Symbols*, trans. Ph. Mairet (New York: Sheed & Ward, 1961), p. 170.

6. History-conscious man, whatever the nature of his revelation may be, cannot but agree with the words of Eliade: "There is no such thing as a pure 'religious' datum, outside of history. For there is no such thing as a human datum that is not at the same time a historical datum. Every religious experience is expressed and transmitted in a particular historical context" ("History of Religions and a New Humanism," in *History of Religions,* Summer 1961, p. 6). As soon as man becomes aware of history the sacred takes on a historical dimension.

7. To say this is not to say that believers in a historical revelation invented the historical science, as is often maintained. None of the Hebrew historians compares with Thucydides or Polybius. See James Barr, "Revelation Through History in the Old Testament and in Modern Theology," in *New Theology,* ed. Martin Marty and Dan G. Peerman (New York: Macmillan, 1964), vol. 1.

8. Erich Auerbach, *Mimesis* (Princeton: Princeton University Press, 1953), p. 15.

9. This would seem to be clearly implied by the definitions of the Council of Chalcedon (*Enchiridion Symbolorum* No. 148). It is obviously not sufficient to take refuge from these consequences in his divine nature, for the whole problem is how the two must be synthesized. One does not have to be Arian or Monophysite to understand that a person can have only one consciousness. Nor does the hypostatic union imply that the God-man could grasp the fullness of divine nature. For an intelligent discussion of this problem see Gabriel Moran, *Theology of Revelation* (New York: Herder & Herder, 1966), pp. 68–71; also Avery Dulles, "The Theology of Revelation," *Theological Studies* 25(1964): 47.

10. *The Meaning of Revelation* (New York: Harper & Row, 1962), p. 54.

11. Gothold Ephraim Lessing, *Werke,* ed. Karl Lachmann et al. (Leipzig-Stuttgart: G. J. Göschen, 1886–1924), 6: 224. "On the Proof of the Spirit and the Power," in *Lessing's Theological Writings,* trans. Henry Chadwick (Stanford: Stanford University Press, 1967), p. 54.

12. Kierkegaard would say that every risk requires an act of faith: a commitment to a historical event is in that respect on a par with an irrefutable, "necessary truth."

13. See Moran, *Theology of Revelation,* p. 53.

14. Karl Rahner went to the roots of the problem: "Only when it can be demonstrated in a metaphysical anthropology that the foundation of man's spiritual existence in historical events (and hence the question about historical hap-

penings) belong *a priori* to the nature of man and form part of his inescapable duties, do we find that a basis for the assumption of the proof of a specific historical fact and the difficulty of a rationalist and enlightened philosophy such as Lessing's can be basically resolved" (*Hörer des Wortes* (Munich: Kösel, 1963), p. 36. *Hearers of the Word* (New York: Herder & Herder, 1969), p. 21.

15. Karl Jaspers is wrong in regarding the symbols of revelation as univocal and unambiguous, and therefore ultimately unsatisfactory as symbols of the transcendent. (*Philosophical Faith and Revelation*, trans. E. B. Ashton [New York: Harper & Row, 1967], pp. 104–114.) Revealed symbols are no more self-contained than other religious symbols. If they did not point beyond themselves, they would cease to be religious altogether. That a symbol is revealed does not mean that the transcendent reality is "contained" in it, but that religious man considers it a privileged, less inadequate way of speaking of the transcendent.

16. The hermeneutic task of understanding the past through the present does not consist exclusively, or even primarily, in an interpretation of words. Words are the illuminating side of events. Far from being the whole problem, they provide most of the assistance for the solution. Gerhard Ebeling has aptly drawn attention to this extension from word to event. "The primary phenomenon in the realm of understanding is not understanding of language, but understanding *through* language. The word is not really the object of understanding—and thus the thing that poses the problem of understanding—the solution of which requires exposition and therefore also hermeneutics as the theory of understanding. Rather, the word is what opens up and mediates understanding, i.e., brings something to understanding. The word itself has a hermeneutic function" (*Word and Faith*, trans. James W. Leitch [Philadelphia: Fortress Press, 1963], p. 318).

17. In an enlightening study on the hermeneutical problem in theology Edward Schillebeeckx illustrates this principle: "Thanks to the distance in time between, for example, the Council of Trent and our present, we can understand the Council of Trent in the light of the present. Thanks to this distance which is filled by the continuity of tradition, we can make a distinction in our understanding between legitimate and illegitimate prejudgments" (*God the Future of Man*, trans. n. d. Smith [New York: Sheed & Ward, 1968], p. 27).

18. Abraham Heschel, *God in Search of Man* (New York: Harper & Row, 1966), p. 185.

19. Henry Duméry, *La foi n'est pas un cri,* 2nd ed. (Paris: Éditions du Seuil, 1959), p. 253.

20. Privileged more by the content and circumstances in which it took place than by the mode of expression.

Chapter 18

EXPLANATION IN SCIENCE AND THEOLOGY
Frederick Ferré

IS the idea of a theology of nature intelligible in an age of science? Is the formulation of an ecological theology a legitimate undertaking that can be defended on methodological grounds? Might theology have something significant to say about nature—or is nature the exclusive domain of science? We must try to answer these basic questions about the justification of the theological enterprise itself before we can attempt to formulate specific details of a theology of nature.

My aim in this essay is to consider what we are trying to do when we seek to understand our world as scientists, philosophers, theologians—and, more importantly, as whole men concerned about the whole earth. Ecological awareness has taught us, among other things, that there are too many compartments in our society and in our thought. We must think, and think wisely, if we are to find an adequate philosophy for living together on this small planet.

This essay will aim, therefore, at clarifying what I believe to be the proper relationship between the kinds of thinking done by scientists, philosophers, and theologians. It will do this by analyzing various kinds of "explanation." The essay will also challenge the common assumption that explanation and evaluation must always be kept in compartments sealed from each other. An epistemology suited for an ecologically conscious age must learn how to relate not merely different facts, not merely different modes of explanation, but different essential aspects of our own human consciousness itself. Only when we come to terms

From : Ian G. Barbour, ed., *Earth Might Be Fair: Reflections on Ethics, Religion, and Ecology* (Englewood Cliffs, N.J.: Prentice-Hall, 1972), pp. 14–32.

with the attitudinal component always effective in our fundamental modes of thinking about the universe will we be able to recognize and utilize the very human logic of ultimate explanations.

To the reader unfamiliar with the discussion among philosophers of science in recent years, the first part of this argument may seem uncomfortably dry. I ask such readers, however, to bear with the next few pages. Scientific explanations are the key to our culture's understanding of explanation itself; thus, without seeing how the interests of science themselves create a deeper thirst than some philosophers have been willing to recognize, we would miss seeing the essential human continuities between proximate or limited explanations and the larger explanatory forms toward which we are fumbling—with such urgent need—today.

One of the more nerve-shattering challenges to theology from science—or what has been widely supposed to be from science—has been the raising of grave doubts about the logical possibility, or the intellectual propriety, of dealing in what I shall call "ultimate explanations." This challenge arises from a view of scientific method rather than from any substantive discoveries made by the sciences. It is therefore better thought of as a challenge coming from scientists and philosophers reflecting on scientific procedures, rather than from science directly; but this challenge is nonetheless a serious inhibition to one of the traditional roles of religious thinking, particularly in regard to a theology of nature, as long as it is able plausibly to claim the authority and prestige of first-order scientific practice to support it.

EXPLANATION AS DEDUCTION FROM SCIENTIFIC LAWS

The attack consists of two claims, both of which I intend to dispute. The first claim is that an explanation *within science* is always analyzable into a deductive pattern in which the statement of what is to be explained is derivable as a conclusion from a set of premises, premises usually containing particular statements of initial conditions and always containing the statement of at least one general law. According to this view, "subsumption under a law" is crucial for every scientific explanation. In agreement with widespread usage, therefore, I shall call this first claim the "covering-law" view of scientific explanation: a scientific explanation is provided if and only if the event or law to be explained is brought under, or "covered" by, a law expressing a general regularity of nature. For example; the bursting of one's frozen water pipes might be explained in this manner by reference to the universal proposition that *all* water expands upon freezing.

The second claim is that scientific explanations, as conceived by the covering-law view, are *the only genuine explanations*. Anything else is, at best, only an "incomplete explanation" in which whatever is put forward as explanatory—

whether it be similarities with already familiar domains, "understood" personal motivations, or the like—will have "explanatory value only if it involves at least tacit reference to general laws."[1] Mere familiarity, for instance, may give us a comfortable feeling or a sense of being at home with the subject matter, but according to the covering-law view, this is both potentially misleading[2] and logically irrelevant ("the extent to which an idea will be considered as familiar varies from person to person and from time to time, and a psychological factor of this kind certainly cannot serve as a standard in assessing the worth of a proposed explanation"[3]). Likewise, a sense of understanding motives may give emphatic vividness to an explanation of personal behavior, but this is cognitively unreliable and really nothing more than a special case of the appeal to familiarity, familiarity that comes from our own experience of purposive behavior.[4]

It is claimed, in short, that *every* sound explanation must subsume the event to be explained under general laws.[5] Since theological thinking is not engaged in the enterprise of formulating general laws of nature, it must be supposed that any explanation offered by theology will be methodologically unsound.

Now it is not my heroic—but absurd—intention to deny that many theological explanations of the total scheme of things have been unsound, since I suspect that a great many such candidates for ultimate explanation have been egregiously faulty, for a variety of reasons. But I believe that the wholesale disposal of them is at least equally unsound, and that the dismissal of all efforts at constructing ultimate explanations (culminating, as I shall argue, in religious forms of ultimate explanation) does injustice to the flexibility and power of human thought on several fronts, the scientific as well as the metaphysical and theological.

Let us start by looking at the sciences themselves. The covering-law view has serious defects as a "reconstructed logic of scientific method,"[6] and these have been the subject of an extensive literature in the past decade. I shall not attempt even to summarize recent debate, but for our purposes three areas of weakness are particularly pertinent. First, it is doubtful whether one can long maintain that *only* when a covering law is known can we claim to possess a genuine explanation. We may, I think, agree that *often* the deductive scheme portrayed by the covering-law view is present in scientific explanation, particularly in such fields as physics or astronomy. We may even admire the precision and rigor of such deductive explanations and begin to wish that all explanations could be similarly patterned. But it becomes costly to insist that unless our explanations in science conform to these few fortunate ones, they are not really scientific explanations at all. In light of the actual situation within recognized and responsible scientific enterprises, it becomes increasingly evident that such tenacious holding to the covering-law view slips quietly into techniques of persuasive definition for "explanation."

What is the actual situation? The simple but unavoidable answer is that a great many of our explanations in science cannot provide laws of the sort deemed necessary by the covering-law view. The explanatory power, for example, of the concept of evolution—including even the so-called law of natural selection—does not function in the way we would expect if only subsumption under a specific natural regularity qualified for scientific explanation. These principles do not permit deductive prediction of the specific course of the history of biological forms, though they do greatly aid our understanding of it. Even more obviously, social and phychological sciences must function without recourse to such covering laws from which (taken together with statements of initial conditions) the phenomena could be uniquely deduced. Laws permitting us to deduce the outbreak of civil war in society, or the falling in love of a particular couple, are not even a realistic hope on the horizon. Even an author who has defended the covering-law view acknowledges that in the sciences of human behavior we simply lack covering laws that will fulfill the supposed requirement, and (he adds significantly) "it is worthy of note that we do not deny ourselves the claim that we have explained . . . because of this."[7]

It appears, then, that there is a wider but still legitimate and needed use of the concept "explanation," even within science, that is not included in the covering-law view. Subsumption under a law may indeed form an important kind of scientific explanation, but it turns out not to be a necessary condition for all such explanation. The weakness of the covering-law view is hidden, for a time, behind the vague assertion that the general laws need only be implicit. But where it becomes evident that there simply are no known laws of the sort called for in the appeal to "at least tacit reference to general laws,"[8] the case either fails or it driven to the high but barren ground of a priori assertion and persuasive definition.

Second, even the presence of general regularities of nature may not, by itself, be sufficient to provide a complete scientific explanation. That an event can be shown deductively to be an instance of a more general pattern of events observed in nature very often will not satisfy a scientist that it has been explained. Why is *that* pattern found and not some other? What is it that *accounts* for this general regularity? Sometimes, perhaps, the answers will be sought, as the covering-law view holds, in subsuming the law in question under some still more general law, deducing the regularity from other wider regularities, just as one might attempt the "derivation of the general regularities governing the motion of double stars from the laws of celestial mechanics. . . ."[9] But sometimes even this will not be enough to answer the scientist's quest for explanation. He wants to have some idea of the structures, the underlying mechanisms, by reference to which the regularities he observes may become intelligible rather than merely arbitrary. All the laws in his possession, together with a full grasp of their deductive relationships, may not add up to a single explanation in this fuller sense of the word. On the contrary, the natural regularities themselves, even the widest he can observe, may become the problematic phenomena crying out for explanation rather than supplying it. The covering-law view thus fails in its account of the scientific enterprise, since it may be possible to have laws in abundance but still not to have an explanation.

THE EXPLANATORY POWER OF THEORIES

This consideration brings us, then, to the third and most revealing defect in the covering-law claim I am criticizing. This defect is the failure to make adequate provision for scientific *theory* in the "reconstructed logic" of science. It would be dangerously misleading, as much current discussion has shown, to make the distinction too sharp between the laws and the theories of a science. What we observe is deeply influenced by what theoretical language we employ, just as our theories are scientifically useful to the extent that they remain in fruitful touch with observation. But be this as it may, there is in the covering-law view a strange neglect of the differences between what constitutes the statement of an observed regularity of nature and what constitutes the statement of an inferred "regularity" of a theoretical entity or structure. This neglect is illustrated in the following passage:

> To an observer in a rowboat, that part of an oar which is under water appears to be bent upwards. The phenomenon is explained by means of general laws—namely, the law of refraction and the law that water is an optically denser medium than air—and by reference to certain antecedent conditions—especially the fact that part of the oar is in the water, part in the air, and that the oar is practically a straight piece of wood. . . . But the question "Why?" may be raised also in regard to general laws. Thus . . . the question might be asked: Why does the propagation of light conform to the law of refraction? Classical physics answers in terms of the undulatory theory of light, i.e., by stating that the propagation of light is a wave phenomenon of a certain general type, and that all wave phenomena of that type satisfy the law of refraction. Thus, the explanation of a general regularity consists in subsuming it under another, more comprehensive regularity, under a more general law.[10]

What is evident here is the running together of two quite different types of laws. The first is a law that we may say, roughly, is a law of gross observation. We see oars as bent regularly under certain circumstances. We see refraction effects of other sorts, inside and outside the laboratory. But neither in nor out of our laboratories do we *see* light waves being propagated like water waves in a pond. We can, indeed, observe regularities of various sorts—interference patterns and the like—that are highly encouraging to our theories that light can sometimes be represented as being in certain ways like "wave phenomena of a certain type." The point is, however, that in moving from explanation by subsumption under *observable* natural regularities (what Comte called positive general facts[11]) to explanation by reference to *supposed* regularities of structure (which make sense out of the given observable regularities of nature), the step has been taken to a logically very different type of explanation. The crucial importance of this step is obscured by the covering-law view.

There is a practical consequence, too, embedded in this logical distinction. There is a difference between, on the one hand, treating nature as a black box whose behavior we note, generalize upon, and predict with considerable effectiveness, and, on the other hand, approaching the world with additional interests in understanding what may be behind the visible structures and behaviors. If we ignore this distinction, we may be lured uncritically into the false belief that the discovery of uniform correlations between events is the most important part of our cognitive endeavors. And this may, as a practical consequence, lead us to focus attention too fixedly on the quest for uniformities and still more uniformities in nature—to the neglect of the search for theories and models through which alone these uniformities can be made intelligible to us.

The methodological point here at issue is the difference between what Margenau calls the *correlational* and the *theoretic* procedures within science,[12] or what Toulmin more vividly, and with perhaps more glee, contrasts as "natural history" (or "mere bug-hunting"[13]) versus "physics."[14] The former is interested in finding "regularities of given forms," whereas the latter is in quest of "the form of given regularities."[15] This distinction—of the greatest importance however it may be phrased—is ignored and indeed denied by any proposal that "to explain an event is simply to bring it under a law; and to explain a law is to bring it under another law."[16] Such an account would send us hunting on the surface of our experience for more empirical regularities, whereas actually what may be most needed (even for eventual practical control) are what Margenau terms the "subsurface connections," always most highly acclaimed by working scientists.[17]

Illustrations of the enormous difference of explanatory power exhibited by these "subsurface connections" as contrasted with "uniformities" are not difficult to find. For example, practical knowledge of the relationships holding between the lengths of the sides of the three-four-five right triangle long antedated the Pythagorean theorem; this regularity of form was used for surveying land before the time of Pythagoras as well as after. "Yet we pay homage to Pythagoras' mathematical demonstration. . . . Why should it be so important to devise a proof which adds nothing to the empirical knowledge already available? What distinguishes the Greek philosopher from the careful observers in Egypt? The answer is: Through his act a *theory* was born; the surface of mere correlation was broken, subsurface explanation had begun."[18]

The usefulness of theory, on the basis of which we may give *reasons* for a particular event happening or for a particular correlation, is further illustrated by the explanatory advance represented by Bohr's theory-*cum*-model of the hydrogen atom, an advance that gave *reasons* for the success of Balmer's formula in stating the "uniformity of nature" discovered in the absorption lines of the hydrogen spectrum. "Again, in the proof, a theory of the atom was born. An internal luminosity suddenly shone through the empirical formula."[19]

What is it about a theory-*cum*-model that provides our higher-level explanations with this "internal luminosity" that is denied to less powerful explanations limited to statements of empirical uniformities? The answer, were it to be fully developed, would center around the *connections in thought* provided by theories, the finding of shared patterns in widely diverse concepts about quite varied phenomena, the fittingness of our ideas together according to the canons of logic, and the discovery of analogues where previously none had been evident—in sum, in the replacement of sheer multiplicity with coherence, the substitution of imaginative acquaintance for opaque strangeness, the elimination or diminution of the sense of the sheerly disconnected and arbitrary.

Perhaps we may have discovered at this point the correct logical place of "familiarity" in explanation. The covering-law view was no doubt quite correct in rejecting, as we saw, the oversimple appeal to the familiar; such an appeal would, if allowed, short-circuit the entire theoretical enterprise by demanding that explanations be forbidden to venture beyond the already known. But granting the dangers implicit in premature concern for the familiar, we may also recognize the large role which familiarity—of pattern, of operation, of conceptual relation, and the like—plays in the logic of explanation. True, familiarity is a relative notion, but explanations, likewise, must explain to *someone* if they are to function as explanations at all. To this extent, explanation is also a relative notion; but in this sense—in which all language is relative to some user/interpreter—the relativity of both notions becomes decidedly innocuous.

EXPLANATORY PARADIGMS IN SCIENCE

The battle for understanding is none other than the war against "unfamiliarity," in its widest sense of incoherence and arbitrariness; science is the human spirit's most carefully constructed and consciously invented instrument for the waging of this war. Thus, the internal demands of all the sciences press toward wider and still wider models and theories. The special sciences themselves, as we shall see, cannot remain true to their own particular role in man's cognitive quest and at the same time respond to the drive toward theories and models of *unlimited* comprehensiveness; but the push toward such all-encompassing theories is implicit within the sciences, and therefore the rationally disciplined attempt at forming such schemes of unlimited scope is continuous, though not identical, with the goal of the sciences.

That the special sciences are in search of explanations that would be *basic relative to their own fields of application* has long been recognized by philosophers of science. "*Basic*" here does not need to involve "finality" in the sense of "never-to-be-superseded"; basic explanations are not usefully defined as "incorrigible" ones. Instead, they should be recognized as "final" in the sense that although accepted they themselves do not call for, or admit of, further explanation. That such explanations have in fact been part of the logic of the special sciences, and that these explanatory paradigms have not proved incorrigible, has been reemphasized, among others, by Stephen Toulmin and Thomas Kuhn.[20]

Toulmin points out that underlying the lesser explanations of the sciences have always been what he calls "ideals of natural order."[21] It is on the basis of some such ideal that the scientist is content to rest his case. Ideals may vary with the era, but the reliance on them is undeniable; the ideal of natural order represents what the scientist considers to be beyond the need of explanation. For Copernicus, Toulmin shows, this self-explanatory principle was uniform circular motion. "He felt no need to look for interplanetary forces in order to explain why the planets follow closed orbits: in his opinion, a uniform circular motion needed no further explanation, and would—in the nature of things—continue to maintain itself indefinitely."[22] Scientific explanations may seldom in practice be pushed back to these bedrock concepts, but "about any explanatory theory . . . we can always ask what it implies about the Natural Order. There must always be some point in a scientist's explanation where he comes to a stop: beyond this point, if he is pressed to explain further the fundamental basis of his explanation, he can say only that he has reached rock bottom."[23]

Still, the ideal of natural order that serves the scientist as a basic explanation within his field (e.g., "The natural state of motion is circular") will never—so long as it remains a scientific conception—be a totally inclusive one (e.g., "All events happen as God wills"). The reason for this is the fact that the scientist *qua* scientist has contracted for the task of discovering "why this happened *rather than that,* and the theological explanation will not enable him to make this discrimination. . . ."[24] To protect the very *specificity* of the *special* sciences, it is essential that even their most wide-ranging "ideals of natural order" renounce every pretense at providing a basis for the coherent understanding of *all* things. In a sense, perhaps, this reminder may be no more than a tautology: that the special sciences have specialized jobs to do. But if it is a tautology, it is an important one to keep in mind. And it has practical consequences: e.g., that the physicist *qua* physicist may properly remain aloof from certain phenomena that the biologist *qua* biologist finds extremely important, and, in like manner, that a thinker is no longer acting simply *qua* special scientist when he considers the connections between all that lies within the purview of each of the sciences. Every special science contributes toward our understanding; but no one should too quickly suppose (nor is it any part of the special scientist's job to claim) that all things can be understood in terms of the explanations, even the basic explanatory paradigms, of any such science. It may have made sense to Copernicus, for example, that the only "natural and self-explanatory" notion would be circular; but this had to do with motions and not with "the sum of things entire." For Newton and for ourselves, his descendants, the one form of motion not requiring further explanation (straight-line motion in a vacuum) is of a quite different character. The consequences for physics of the change in these explanatory paradigms are of the highest importance; yet the difference between the Copernican and the Newtonian notion of "rock bottom" for the explanatory regression remains a difference *within physics,* with clear physical implications and clear conceptual boundaries.

We may here note in passing that although such concepts as these remain part of the explanatory logic of the special sciences, the means of testing them is considerably more elaborate and indirect than is often acknowledged by many popular analyses of scientific procedure. Hospers, for example, insists that every concept used as an explanatory premise in a science must be open to empirical falsification. "Without this condition it would not be considered an explanation in any science."[25] True, but the meaning of falsification—once one admits the role of theories as well as experimental laws, and explanatory paradigms of natural order as well as theories—must be enriched beyond the simplistic look-and-see concept of the "crucial experiment" that has hobbled the philosophy of science—though not the sciences themselves—for far too long.

The means of verification or falsification of these most far-reaching concepts or models of the natural order depend upon the scope, the coherence, the consistency, and the practical effectiveness of the entire theoretical structure of the science founded upon them. "Such models and ideals, principles of regularity and explanatory paradigms, are not always recognized for what they are; differences of opinion about them give rise to some of the profoundest scientific disputes, and changes in them to some of the most important changes in scientific theory. . . ."[26] The substitution of Newton's view of straight-line motion as needing "no explanation" in place of Copernicus's satisfaction with the "self-explanatory" character of "natural" circular motion had more to do with the entire schemes of thought of which these models were a basic part than any simple empirical observation. And the adoption of Galileo's fundamental concept of impetus in place of Aristotle's was (despite the "Leaning Tower" myth) more the result of harder cerebration than the result of closer observation.[27]

METAPHYSICAL EXPLANATION AND THE SEARCH FOR COHERENCE

But, at last, when the most wide-ranging concepts of any science—those to which other explanations keep returning—are "verified" by the cognitive and practical effectiveness of the articulated science, there yet remains an element of the arbitrary and the disconnected. The logical element of disconnection must haunt the basic concepts of every special science, as we have seen, *just as long as these sciences defend their specificity;* and the sense of the arbitrary must cling to every notion that is accepted as rock bottom, to which one can only shrug and say, "That's just the way it is." Something in all of us dislikes this shrug. That something is what initiated the cognitive quest and initially set the sciences their task: to bring us understanding. Must the quest end here?

Hospers believes that it must, and although he cautions us against prematurely supposing that we have *found* a basic law or a rock bottom explanation, he points out that if we did actually have a basic law, it would not only be a waste of time but would also be logically self-contradictory to request an explanation of it, since such a move would be "a request for explanation in a situation whereby one's own admission no more explaining can be done."[28] The demands of theory, that "basic" must mean what it says, would seem to lead inevitably to the frustration of our unquenchable thirst for understanding! Hospers adds:

> Like so many others, this point may seem logically compelling but psychologically unsatisfying. Having heard the above argument, one may still feel inclined to ask, "Why are the basic uniformities of the universe the way they are, and not some other way? Why should we have just *these* laws rather than other ones? I want an *explanation* of why they are as they are." I must confess here, as an autobiographical remark, that I cannot help sharing this feeling: I want to ask why the laws of nature, being contingent, are as they are, even though I cannot conceive of what an explanation of this would be like, and even though by my own argument above the request for such an explanation is self-contradictory.[29]

To account for this psychological dissatisfaction, Hospers blames habit—the mere habit of asking "Why?" even when it makes no sense to do so.

But perhaps the source lies deeper. Our previous analysis of the concept of explanation in terms of the drive to theoretical coherence and completeness may dissuade us, first, from accepting Hospers's identification of the source of our unrest as *merely* psychological. Perhaps there is a built-in drive within the logic of explanation that refuses to be quieted until satisfied; perhaps the human mind properly declines, therefore, to accept the boundaries often proposed for its cognitive aspirations. Perhaps it *must* so decline, for good reasons, despite acknowledgment (with Kant) that the terms of its explanatory paradigms can never be known to be meaningfully applicable in precisely the same ways as are those of its less ambitious theories.

But, second, granting that there are "psychological" sources to our reluctance to abandon the quest for ultimate explanatory satisfaction, the existentialists direct our attention—possibly with some perceptiveness—to a less trivial human basis than "habit." They point to man's anxiety for himself and for his world in the face of (what used to be called) its "contingency," and to his fear of the abyss of meaninglessness that yawns behind the starkly arbitrary. But it is here, poised over this abyss, that the special sciences are entitled—and obliged—to leave us. Whether all men actually feel, or are capable of feeling, or latently feel (deep down), such "ontological anxiety" is not a question that needs to be answered in this essay. It is enough to note that at least some men find their cognitive aspirations reinforced by profound anxieties about what we have learned to call man's "existential situation." And they discover that even the broadest explanations of the special sciences are unable to answer fully either the cognitive or the personal demand.

Still, the creative energies behind the human struggle against arbitrariness and disconnection have not been exhausted in giving birth to their offspring, the sciences. Prior to the development of the sort of rational inquiry that gave rise to the sciences, of course, conceptual syntheses were frequently attempted—and with sometimes impressive results. But we shall find that adequate ultimate explanations for our own time cannot be divorced from the principles and findings of the scientific method, undoubtedly the most significant intellectual fact of our modern world. How, then, can we proceed responsibly beyond the special sciences in quest of cognitive satisfaction?

First, to overcome "disconnection" by coherence and to provide familiarity of pattern in the place of sheer diversity, theories and models drawn from the special sciences as well as from other sources are quite often used outside the methodological restrictions of scope imposed by their strictly scientific uses. Julian Huxley's or Pierre Teilhard de Chardin's concepts of "evolution," for example, or Alfred North Whitehead's thoughts on "organism"—one could multiply examples—these are in their new contexts given conceptual functions as all-embracing interpretive principles for thought, feeling, and behavior that far transcend the boundaries of their original employment. As a result, these new uses are as vulnerable as fish in a barrel to the accurate fire of those[30] who proceed to demonstrate that these new uses, in attempting to bring coherence to reality as a whole, no longer have the right (in this new employment) to claim the authority and precision of the special sciences from which they were borrowed.

These critics are right—of course. This much is built into the very nature of the case. What is not so clear is whether or not such a line of criticism meets the relevant issues: *Must* all explanations have no more than specialized scientific uses? May not concepts be put to work in disciplined ways to bring coherence to our account of reality as a whole as well as to reality as delimited by our departments of science? The demands for conceptual coherence are surely not *prima facie* irrelevant to the *whole,* though relevant to the *parts,* of our account of reality.

Some more profound point must lie behind these recent criticisms than the mere platitude that attempting to explain the whole is not the same thing as attempting to explain the part! It may be that underneath such criticisms there still persists the view—residuum of more exciting "principles" from positivist days of not so long ago—that "explanations of the whole" *cannot* be put to work in a "disciplined" manner, since "discipline" implies "testing," and "testing" (here lurks the ghost) implies "looking and seeing." But this assumption is false. It must be questioned and questioned again, until the spook is exorcised. Disciplined inquiry does demand tests, but there are conditions under which the tests, on their theoretical side, must be extremely general and, on their experimental side, must be extremely indirect. We have already seen examples of this indirectness and generality of verification in connection with basic explanatory paradigms in the special sciences. We should be prepared for a like situation—intensified—when we turn from models and theories that are taken as "basic relative to a given field" to evaluate models and theories that are offered as ultimate for all knowledge.[31]

Supposing, then, what is at least possible, that our account of things has (to some extent) been unified and given coherence through the disciplined employment of a conceptual synthesis of some kind. We will have overcome (to that extent) the enemy of "disconnection." What, though, of the threat to cognition posed by "arbitrariness"? There are those who maintain that the latter is inescapable and that we shall do well to settle peacefully for the greatest degree of coherence we can find. Alfred North Whitehead puts it: "In a sense, all explanation must end in ultimate arbitrariness. My demand is that the ultimate arbitrariness of matter of fact from which our formulation starts should disclose the same general principles of reality which we dimly discern as stretching away into regions beyond our explicit powers of discernment."[32]

ULTIMATE EXPLANATION AS VALUATIONAL

Shall we rest content with this verdict? From the viewpoint of pure theory, it is probably the most that can be said, especially if we may also hope, as Whitehead does, that "the sheer statement of what things are may contain elements explanatory of why things are."[33] But man's cognitive quest, although carried on in the terms and by the canons of theory, is not for the sake of theory alone. The sense of values and the need for action are as much a part of the demand for explanation as the thirst for theory. It may even be the case, indeed, that all theory is for the sake of the life-oriented domain.[34] And if so, then the very concept of cognitive satisfaction at its ultimate levels may require analysis in terms that include the *whole* man's quest for understanding, i.e., not only the defeat of disconnection through logical coherence among our concepts, but the victory over arbitrariness as well.

Is this, though, to embark upon a journey without hope of arrival—or worse, as Hospers tells us—to begin a search for the answer to a senseless question?

What "answer" could *possibly,* in principle, satisfy the insatiable demand? Would we recognize the answer if we found it? On the plane of pure theory, let it be repeated, there can be no such answer, no such "arrival," no such satisfaction. In theory it is possible to go on asking the question "Why?" as Hospers says, forever.

The notion of the arbitrary needs further inspection, however, for its poignancy extends beyond the theoretical domain. We tend to be bothered by the arbitrary when confronted with that which seems either void of meaning or downright *wrong* (note the overtones of the phrase "brute fact"). Whatever is *right* or valuable, on the other hand, needs no further justification for its being. Our ultimate cognitive resting place as men—whole men who are valuers and agents as well as thinkers—would seem to lie nowhere short of that elusive point where ultimate *fact* is seen also as perfect *good,* where our most reliable account of "the way things are" shows also the ultimate *rightness* of things. Such rightness, of course, is properly predicable only of the *whole* state of arrairs referred to in our ultimate explanations. It would be not only methodologically self-defeating, but also logically a category mistake to characterize partial or proximate explanations as though they were ultimate ones. We can allow no shortcut to the termination of the cognitive process through premature appeals to value considerations; but, equally, we shall find no cognitively satisfying termination of this process at all, apart from a vision of the whole of whatever *is* as also that which *ought* to be.

But wait a moment! If we adopt this view, are we not in danger of begging the question about the character of reality as a whole? To say that explanations of unlimited generality *must* show the "rightness of things" in order to avoid the irrationality of arbitrariness may, at first glance, seem to be a blatant *petitio* concerning what may be the case. Such a supposition, however, would be mistaken. There is no claim made here that any logically coherent and experientially grounded explanation of unlimited generality *will* in fact exhibit the unity of *is* with *ought.* It may even be that constructing a conceptual synthesis, relevant to the formidable (and growing) mass of contemporary knowledge, undigested, incoherent, and unstable as it is—a conceptual synthesis, in other words, that succeeds merely in overcoming the single enemy of disconnection— may alone prove (though perfectly legitimate in principle) practically impossible at the present moment in history. And even if, by dint of generous efforts from geniuses as yet unknown, a fortunate model should prove fruitful in the development of such an omnirelevant account of things as we have in mind, it would still *remain to be seen* whether this account answered man's nontheoretic (practical and valuational) thirst for explanatory satisfaction. It may be that the arbitrary, at the furthest reaches of our conceptions, will never be eliminated from the human situation. But if so, this is a discovery to be made, not an axiom to be assumed. And inasmuch as the arbitrary *is* ever genuinely overcome in cognition (as is the present writer's contention), the palm will go to the ultimate explanation that combines the unsparing standards of theoretical success with the fruitful satisfaction of human aspiration.

It is here that we discover again the profound insight into the human cognitive situation displayed by such giants of conceptual synthesis as Plato, Aristotle, or Spinoza. In each of their attempts at offering ultimate explanations the Real is inseparable from the Right; the *is* and the *ought* are seen *sub specie aeternitatis,* one and the same. The arbitrary is overcome; brute fact is seen not to be just "brutal" but to display a necessity that is also acceptable; the demand for understanding comes, for a time at least, to fulfillment.

Plato, Aristotle, and Spinoza will not, of course, satisfy our conceptual needs today. The concepts that they were attempting to bring into coherent relation are not our own; human knowledge, thanks very largely to the spectacular successes of the special sciences, has vastly increased. It is our own knowledge, not the concepts of an earlier day, that we demand to see "steadily and whole." But these thinkers, though chosen only as examples, are properly of more than antiquarian interest. Their diagnosis of the cognitive demand was basically correct, although their specific prescriptions for its treatment no longer satisfy. In thus stressing the *continuing* nature of the quest for ultimate explanations—frankly recognizing these to be corrigible, like their distinguished forerunners—we embark upon this philosophic enterprise perhaps more adequately forewarned concerning the logical character of our task. Just as long as human knowledge continues to grow and human judgment to develop, so long will the search for fresh and fuller syntheses be required. The cognitive demand for ultimate explanations is not a threat, therefore, to the wholesome excitement of the hunt. The satisfactions of the search are no less genuine than the pleasures of possession. Ultimate explanation in our interpretation is no enemy, then, to free minds; instead, the common enemies of responsible thought at all levels are dogmatism, prejudice, and that unadventuresome temper so bound by orthodoxies, and by what Hume called modes, as to shun the risks always present in creative "venturing far out." Every ultimate explanation, religious or secular, is an invitation to take a change.

THEOLOGICAL EXPLANATION IN TERMS OF PURPOSE

Finally, we may at last explicitly consider the status of theological explanation in the light of what has been maintained. In a sense, those are right who scornfully curl a logical lip at explanations of the nature of things *via* appeals to "God's purpose." It is true, as far as we can tell from anthropology and studies of infant logic, that animism and the attempt to account for all things in terms of purpose are, as Hospers tells us, the most primitive conceptions of explanation.[35] But the case may not be left on this level. If ultimate explanation, to be cognitively satisfying, demands in principle a union of fact and value, the explanatory model of a perfectly good personal purpose joined to creative sovereignty over all being may—if, *but only if*, it is rigorously articulated, coherently and illuminatingly related to all knowledge and experience, and successfully defended against prima facie incoherences—deserve our philosophical attention and respect. The fact that explanations in terms of purposes are ubiquitous would then prove to be significant for positive as well as for negative reasons. The most primitive concept of explanation is, perhaps, best qualified to be our ultimate basis for explanation as well! Just as familiarity may be seen after all to reflect the victory over disconnection, so also purpose in the last analysis may turn out to represent our most effective weapon against arbitrariness.

If this is so, however, it will not be so because of the appeal of *purpose* alone or even primarily, but because purpose, taken as an explanatory model, proves capable both of undergirding a successfully coherent conceptual synthesis and of being recognized as *good*. In a footnote of his discussion of the blank contingency of ultimate explanations, Hospers writes: "Explanation in terms of divine purposes again will not help: if we are told that the laws of nature are as they are because God willed it so, we can ask why He should have willed it so; and if here again an answer is given, we can once again ask a why-question of this answer."[36] Who is to tell Hospers that he is wrong here? Of course one can do as he describes, asking over and over again the theoretical "Why?" or rejecting every stopping place as theoretically arbitrary. But to shift the emphasis so that theological explanation is seen not so much in terms of "divine *purpose*" as "purpose that is *divine*"—and to understand the "divine" as that which is worthy of our worship—this (or something of this *kind*) may conceivably offer a way through which men can responsibly cope with the cognitive bottomlessness of the arbitrary.

Those who take the procedures and practical aims of the special sciences as determinative for all respectable cognitive endeavor will in all likelihood be shocked by this injection of value consideration into the notion of explanation and hence into cognition. There is little recognized room in the methodology of the special sciences for consideration of value—at least when it comes to choosing between proffered explanatory schemes. The franchise of the scientist is vast but not carte blanche. It is to give us understanding for the sake of coping with nature, and for this pursuit our role as valuers remains normally and methodologically subordinate (though not entirely inactive, as witnessed by the importance of such aesthetic values as "elegance" and such practical values as "simplicity," in our decisions between scientific theories).

The franchise of the philosopher is also to provide us with "understanding," but not alone for the sake of coping with nature. The postanalytical, ecologically aware philosopher who determines to move carefully, self-consciously, and rigorously toward synthesis will attempt to construct—not only with the aid of the specialized scientist but also with the aid of the artist, the moralist, the theologian, the man of affairs, and the poet—a coherent and effective conceptual context within which he and other men may cope with *all* of their environment and the *totality* of their experience, including felt demands of value and of action. To deny philosophers the right to engage in this synthesizing explanatory activity is to deny ourselves, and others, the possibility of substituting a rational and responsible for an irrational and irresponsible means of coping with life as a whole and the earth as a whole.

Finally, the theologian deserves to be drawn back once again into his rightful place in the thoughtful community. If my account is correct, it is only the theologian disciplined by science and philosophy—or the philosopher prepared to venture into the theological domain of ultimate value commitments—who will bring the cognitive quest to whatever approximate completion may be hoped for by any generation. It may be that the current situation is ill suited to our generation's hopes of cognitive satisfaction; it may be that synthesis is less needed (or possible) in turbulent times than is a constant alertness to the ever-changing data—data of value as well as of empirical belief. But if the human spirit continues, as seems likely, to demand ultimate explanations, we shall at least be in a position to ask certain crucial questions of any candidate for our acceptance. First, is this proposed explanation in keeping with the best findings of the special sciences, whose explanatory models and theories lie at the beginning of the quest for understanding and may not be ignored without cognitive peril? Second, has the candidate for explanation overcome the disconnection of separate explanatory paradigms in the various special sciences by some coherent principle of theoretical unification that is also adequately inclusive? And, finally, has the value dimension of human life been seriously considered and tested against humanity's most profound intuitions of ultimate worth? It is by these criteria, I submit, that a theology of nature must be evaluated. The functions of scientist, philosopher, and theologian in explanation are not identical; they are, I believe, continuous. Therefore, if we continue to hope for understanding as whole men, we shall wish success to each.

NOTES

1. Carl G. Hempel and Paul Oppenheim, "Studies in the Logic of Explanation," reprinted in Edward H. Madden, ed., *The Structure of Scientific Thought* (Boston: Houghton Mifflin, 1960), p. 22.

2. Ibid., p. 28.

3. Ibid., p. 29

4. Ibid., p. 29.

5. Ibid., p. 29, italics added.

6. See Abraham Kaplan, *The Conduct of Inquiry* (San Francisco: Chandler, 1964), especially chap. 1.

7. John Hospers, "What Is Explanation?" in Anthony Flew, ed., *Essays in Conceptual Analysis* (New York: Macmillan, 1956), p. 105.

8. Hempel and Oppenheim, "Logic of Explanation," p. 22.

9. Ibid., p. 21.

10. Ibid., p. 20.

11. See August Comte, *Introduction to Positive Philosophy*, ed. Frederick Ferré (Indianapolis: Bobbs-Merrill, 1969).

12. Henry Margenau, *The Nature of Physical Reality* (New York: McGraw-Hill, 1950), pp. 25–30.

13. Stephen Toulmin, *The Philosophy of Science* (New York: Harper & Row, 1960), p. 54.

14. Ibid., p. 53.

15. Ibid.

16. Hospers, "What Is Explanation?" p. 98.

17. Margenau, *Nature of Physical Reality*, p. 29.

18. Ibid., p. 28.

19. Ibid., p. 29.

20. Stephen Toulmin, *Foresight and Understanding* (Bloomington: Indiana University Press, 1961), p. 28; Thomas S. Kuhn, *The Structure of Scientific Revolutions* (Chicago: University of Chicago Press, 1962).

21. Toulmin, *Foresight and Understanding*, p. 41ff.

22. Ibid., p. 42.

23. Ibid.

24. Hospers, "What Is Explanation?" p. 107.

25. Ibid., p. 108.

26. Toulmin, *Foresight and Understanding*, pp. 42–43.

27. Cf. Herbert Butterfield, *The Origins of Modern Science: 1300–1800* (New York: Free Press, 1968) for an account that does not overlook the experimental elements contributing to Aristotle's overthrow but that at the same time makes vivid the *conceptual* revolution underlying the birth of modern science. For further examples, see Toulmin's *Foresight and Understanding*, especially chaps. 3 and 4.

28. Hospers, "What Is Explanation?" p. 116

29. Ibid.

30. See Stephen Toulmin, "Scientific Theories and Scientific Myths," in *Metaphysical Beliefs*, ed. A. MacIntyre (London: SCM Press, 1957).

31. For a more detailed discussion of the appropriate tests that may be applied to models and theories of this latter kind, see the present author's chapters in

Exploring the Logic of Faith, by Kent Bendall and Frederick Ferré (New York: Association Press, 1962).

32. *Science and the Modern World* (New York: Macmillan, 1925); Mentor Books edition, p. 88.

33. Ibid.

34. Cf. Bendall and Ferré, *Exploring the Logic of Faith.*

35. Hospers, "What Is Explanation?" p. 95.

36. Ibid., p. 117.

Chapter 19

REFLECTIONS ON THE INTERACTION BETWEEN SCIENCE AND RELIGION
Joseph J. Kockelmans

INTRODUCTION

In this essay I wish to present some ideas on the question of how in the Western world man's experience with the sciences has affected his experience with the Christian religion. The fact that his experience with Christianity was deeply influenced by his experience with modern science cannot be questioned. Numerous publications have addressed this issue and they contain convincing arguments which place the *quaestio facti* beyond any reasonable doubt. However, in the same literature there is no agreement on the question of how deeply this influence has reached into our conception of the Christian religion and of how this influence is to be understood precisely. Some authors have described this interaction in a positive manner, whereas others have evaluated the interaction predominantly negatively.

In *Der Garten des Menschlichen*[1] von Weizsäcker states that, in his view, contemporary physicists generally adopt an agnostic, but positive, attitude toward religion. An antireligious attitude today is seldom found among physicists; such an attitude is adopted more readily by biologists and is very often found among social scientists. According to von Weizsäcker, the reason for this seems to be that the confrontation between physics and the churches today goes much further back in history than the conflict of biology and the social sciences with the churches. Von Weizsäcker suggests that the conflict between the churches and certain scientists or groups of scientists is at the root of the negative attitude that

"Reflections on the Interaction between Science and Religion" is published for the first time in this volume.

many scientists adopt in regard to the Christian religion. The persecution of Galileo is often quoted in this connection.

Indeed, it cannot be denied that confrontation of the churches with certain leading scientists is an important element of our heritage in this regard. Yet I doubt whether this conflict is not more a sign of a much deeper conflict than it is at the very root of the attitude many scientists adopt today. I can imagine that an individual scientist whose scientific ideas were criticized by representatives of a church became gradually alienated from that church. But this does not explain why he, as has often been the case, became an atheist, or why others not related to that church became unbelievers. I would rather tend to agree with Whitehead's statement that, "in a generation which saw the Thirty Years' War and remembered Alva in the Netherlands, the worst that happened to men of science was that Galileo suffered an honorable detention and a mild reproof, before dying peacefully in his bed."[2] This is not to say that the negative and critical attitude of the churches in regard to the ideas of some scientists has not been a factor in the manner in which we now conceive of the relationship between religion and science. Yet it seems to me that we shall never get to the root of the tension between science and the Christian religion by merely pointing to this factor taken in isolation.

To understand the relationship between science and the Christian religion it is important to distance oneself from the actual situation and examine the issue in a broad historical perspective. The interaction between science and religion took place over a period of almost four hundred years. Many ideas developed in this long process of interaction have now become sedimented into our modern conception of the world in such a manner that they are now no longer consciously present in our awareness. If we study the interaction between science and religion in a broad historical perspective, we shall see that both science and religion have always been in a state of continuous development, that there always has been a tension between the two, and that it is incorrect to assume that the interaction between science and religion was confined to contradiction and antagonism.[3]

From the time of Copernicus and Galileo the relationship between science and the Christian religion has been *problematic*. The basis issue that makes it so manifested itself first in modern physics; only in the nineteenth century did it manifest itself in biology, the behavioral, and social sciences. From the beginning some scientists *assumed* that science obviously contradicts religion and, thus, that science makes traditional religion superfluous. This view was gradually adopted by more scientists and became the dominant view in the later part of the eighteenth century. It has found its clearest and most convincing expression in the works of the *philosophes* of the Enlightenment, and later in the works of Comte, Nietzsche, Marx, and Freud. By going back in history to the origin of modern science, I will show precisely why there is a tension between science and the Christian religion, how the discussion of this very issue led some to natural religion first, to deism later, and finally to atheism.[4] After this historical introduction, I wish to reflect on the meaning and function of science in an attempt to discover precisely what it is in science that prompted this development. This reflection will show that a conflict between science and religion, although historically understandable, is by no means necessary. I wish to conclude this essay with some reflections on the question of how the tension between science and religion can be given a positive meaning.

FROM SUPERNATURAL TO NATURAL RELIGION

Since the beginning of Christianity there has always been a tension between scientific knowledge and the Christian religion, between reason and faith. Between the second and the sixteenth centuries attempts have been made to relate reason and faith in a meaningful manner. For many centuries Saint Augustine's view, according to which the safest way to the truth is that road which starts in revelation and faith and leads from there to reason (*credo ut intelligam*), was quite universally accepted. In the thirteenth century Albert the Great and Aquinas proposed another way to relate reason and faith which then was quite generally accepted until the sixteenth century. This view can perhaps be briefly summarized as follows: 1) reason and faith are both genuine sources of knowledge; 2) reason does not presuppose faith; 3) faith does not depend upon reason but on revelation; 4) reason can discover certain truths which are also the subject matter of faith; 5) the truths about God's existence and his attributes that can be known by natural reason "are not articles of faith, but are preambles to the articles."[5] Between the eighth and sixteenth centuries there have been a number of authors who, contrary to the commonly accepted views proposed by Saint Augustine on the one hand and Aquinas on the other, propagated a view which was influenced by negative natural theology. According to these authors, natural theology does not exclude the possibility of reason to prepare man for the existence of an absolute and transcendent Being; yet all natural knowledge of this absolute Being is knowledge of what He is not, and all positive knowledge of God and his attributes presupposes revelation.[6]

In the seventeenth century most Christian scientists explicitly or implicitly subscribed to some form of Neoplatonism and, thus, accepted that God had created the world according to a perfect mathematical order. In their opinion, the function of the new science was to rediscover this order and to formulate the natural laws according to which the universe runs in harmony with God's will. They realized that this conception of natural order was somehow in conflict with the Christian conception of Providence. And they also knew that the basic assumptions underlying the new science were materialistic and mechanistic and that both these assumptions were often linked to Lucretius's atheism. However, the authors felt that natural philosophy (= modern science) could easily be used as an aid to the Christian religion and that its "irrefutable" arguments for the existence of God could be employed to destroy the menace of atheism once and for all. What they did not realize fully is that their well-meant efforts to defend the Christian religion against atheism would ultimately become the most powerful force to promote natural religion and deism, which in turn would finally lead many to atheism. For even though these scientists originally conceived of the new science as a preparation for and an aid to the Christian religion, their works focused, in fact, almost exclusively on those truths which natural reason can ascertain and gave little more than a superficial treatment to the supernatural elements of Christianity.[7]

I wish to illustrate these general theses with concrete ideas developed by Locke and Newton. However, before turning to their ideas on the matter, I shall make a few observations which will help us to better understand their position on the relationship between science and the Christian religion.

For most English authors of that time faith was a strictly *personal* matter; no church authority could establish what is true; this can be done only through reason seeking faith (*intellectus quaerens fidem*). The Bible is the only source of supernatural truths and each human being must interpret the Bible personally according to the guidelines of reason. This is one of the reasons why, for many of these authors, Christianity became gradually reduced to natural religion, and the examination of reason's scope in religion was for them no more than an examination of the human capacity for truth. It is thus fair to state that natural religion finally came to be the result of the efforts on the part of many seventeenth-century philosophers and scientists to find a harmonious balance between reason and faith.

Furthermore, the Reformation and the religious wars that followed upon it had convinced many people that not dogma, but the good Christian life constitutes the essence of Christianity. Several authors defended the view that the various denominations within Christianity as a whole should refrain from sectarian, emotional excesses, and that the very spirit of Christianity demands tolerance, not persecution and war. This drive toward religious "rationalism" led first to a reduction of the essence of Christianity to those truths which are universally shared by all denominations, and later to the reduction of Christianity to natural religion. I shall return to this issue shortly. Here it suffices to stress the point that the concern with natural religion gradually began to take the form of a severe criticism of sectarianism, superstition, liturgical pomp, and other emotional extravagances. It should be noted also in this connection that in the seventeenth century very few, if any, scientists were driven toward natural religion because of skepticism or agnosticism. At first no one made the explicit claim that natural religion was really a substitute for Christianity; it was thought to be no more than an aid toward "genuine" Christianity; it was supposed to merely secure its foundations and purge it of superstition and excesses. Later, however, many authors tended to forget this, as well as the fact that the Christian faith inherently transcends reason and natural proof. What then ultimately was left of Christianity was no more than a "reasonable" religion for rational men. In the final analysis this development would lead to a complete reduction of Christianity to a rational moral theory (Rousseau).[8]

To avoid misunderstanding it is necessary to point out here that the idea of natural religion itself did not originate in the works of these authors and that this idea was not promoted on the basis of arguments explicitly connected with the conception of the new science. As a matter of fact, several reasons can be cited why many authors in the sixteenth and seventeenth centuries were deeply concerned with natural religion. One should realize first that after the fifteenth century several new continents were discovered and that particularly in the sixteenth and seventeenth centuries a close contact between these continents and western Europe developed. One of the consequences of this development was that one began to realize that many peoples lived according to very high moral standards, even though these standards were not derived from or supported by the Christian religion. This realization led some authors to believe that there must be some kind of natural religion shared by all peoples and of which the various concrete forms of religion one actually had discovered, revealed and not revealed, are no more than further articulations. Most reflections in this direction were at first not inspired by any criticism of Christianity and certainly not intended to reduce Christianity to natural religion.[9]

One of the first authors who wrote about natural religion was Thomas More, who in so doing was clearly inspired by his desire for religious tolerance. In his *Utopia* (1516), More makes an explicit distinction between natural religion and Christianity. In his view there are several sorts of religions. Most of them worship and adore one eternal, invisible, infinite, and incomprehensible Deity whom they call the Father of all. Even though these religions differ concerning other things, all agree that there is one supreme Being that made and governs the world and that whoever is the supreme Being, He is also that great Essence to whose glory and majesty all honors are to be ascribed by the consent of all nations.[10]

Similar ideas were developed at that time by the Italian academics with the explicit intention of promoting religious tolerance among Christians. These efforts led there first to a reduction of the essence of Christianity to those truths explicitly formulated in the Apostles' Creed and later to the six basic beliefs formulated first by Ascontius, namely: "that 1) there is one God, his son Jesus Christ, whom He sent, and the Holy Spirit; 2) there is a resurrection to eternal happiness or damnation; 3) Jesus Christ, whom God sent, was made man, died for our sins, and rose from the dead; 4) we shall obtain life if we believe in the son of God; 5) there is no salvation save in the name of Jesus, and no righteousness in the law, or in the institutions of man; and 6) there is one baptism in the name of the Father, the Son, and the Holy Spirit."[11]

The author most often quoted as the "father" of natural religion is Edward Lord Herbert of Cherbury, who laid the foundation for his view on natural religion in his treatise on truth, *De Veritate* (1624), and then gave a systematic account of it in *De Religione Laici* (1645). For Herbert, in order to be valid faith, it must be such that it can be justified by natural reason. Reason cannot comprehend all truths, for in that case there would be no room for faith; yet neither can there be truths of faith which are in conflict with reason.[12] On the basis of these principles Herbert comes to the conclusion that natural religion can be reduced to the following five articles: "1. That there is some supreme divinity. 2. That this divinity ought to be worshiped. 3. That virtue joined with piety is the best method of divine worship. 4. That we should return to our right selves from sin. 5. That reward or punishment is bestowed after this life is finished."[13] It is important to note here again that Herbert, who was not an original thinker and merely reflects a view to which many had come during the period of the religious wars, was not led to develop these ideas because of a concern flowing from philosophy or the new science, but because of the deep desire to make a positive contribution to the struggle for religious tolerance.[14]

These ideas, to which the protagonists of the idea of "natural religion" during the first half of the seventeenth century had gradually come on grounds not related to the origin of modern science, were then readily employed by philosophers and scientists who during the later part of the seventeenth century were concerned primarily with an attempt to establish a meaningful relationship between the new science and the Christian religion.[15] With respect to reason's competence in regard to religious matters, among these authors there was a more moderate and a more extremist group. According to the moderates, to whom Boyle and Ray belonged, there are truths which reason cannot comprehend, even though we can understand them to some degree after they have been revealed to us. However, there may be things revealed also which *seem* to contradict reason; these, too, may be accepted by faith, provided one can prove with certainty that they were so revealed. The seeming contradictions are due to the limitations of finite understanding; only God's word can reveal these truths to man. The extremists, to whom Locke and Newton belonged, made a distinction between truths according to reason, truths above reason, and truths contradictory to reason. God can reveal to man truths which are beyond reason, but there cannot be any religious truths which contradict reason.

In the works of Locke, natural religion is at first still expressed in the traditional terminology of Christianity. In the *Essay Concerning Human Understanding* (1690) he delivers proofs for the existence of God, the immortality of the soul, and for the thesis that natural law implies a strict moral obligation.[16] In *The Reasonableness of Christianity* (1695) Locke gives reasons in support of the fundamental Christian doctrines. He does not try to defend Christianity against atheism, but attempts to purify it and prune it of every doctrine not susceptible to human reason. In fact, he reduces Christianity to natural religion, while waging his battle against what he thought to be superstition and absurdity in the convictions of sectarians and enthusiasts. His final view on these matters is a clear form of rationalist natural religion, which in part seems to have been developed to disprove the claim made by certain deists that Christianity contains doctrines that are beyond human comprehension.[17]

It is reasonable to assume that Locke did not believe in the Trinity and, thus, equally rejected the divinity of Christ. Yet Locke did not deny that Jesus was the promised Messiah. In his view, Christ was sent to confirm the existence of the one and omnipotent God, to establish the (natural) moral law more firmly, to reform the mode of worship, which was filled with excessive pomp, to encourage virtue and piety and stress their reward, and to give the promise of assistance to the virtuous life.

Generally speaking, Locke was concerned more with morality than with the Christian faith. The Christian religion "is not a notional science to furnish speculation to the brain or discourse to the tongue, but a rule of righteousness to influence our lives."[18] In his view the moral law can be discovered by natural reason. Given the idea of God, his power, goodness, and wisdom, and given the idea of man as a rational creature, morality should be subject to accurate demonstration. Christ helped people rediscover the natural law, but the Christian law is really identical with the natural law.

As far as content is concerned, Locke's natural religion is practically identical with what later would become known as an anti-Christian form of deism, and as a matter of fact prepared the ground for it. Yet Locke himself was convinced he was a good Christian, and his personal life certainly testifies to this. Nevertheless, he had systematically eliminated all supernatural elements from Christianity and, thus, reduced it to a form of natural religion.[19]

Like Locke, Newton tried to mediate the tension between science and religion by reducing Christianity to natural religion. For Newton natural science can reveal the ultimate cause of the universe, and, thus, natural philosophy and religion are really concerned with the same basic truths. The more one knows about the first Cause through natural philosophy, the greater his awe for God will be and the less superstition will affect his faith. The physical universe is a beautifully ordered cosmos which reveals in every detail the infinite Intelligence, God. As for God, Newton maintained only those characteristics which he thought natural philosophy could account for: God is infinite, omnipresent, omnipotent, transcendent, and the Creator of the universe. Divine Providence is for Newton identical with God's absolute dominion over the cosmos which maintains the natural laws. Newton did not believe in miracles.

Yet for Newton, God is not to be identified with the God many philosophers of his time spoke about; He is not just an uninterested first Cause, or the utterly indifferent and world-absent God of Descartes. He is the God of the Bible.

This Being governs all things, not as the soul of the world, but as the Lord over all; and on account of his dominion He is wont to be called Lord God, *pantokrator* or Universal Ruler. . . . The Supreme God is a Being eternal, infinite, absolutely perfect; but a being, however, perfect, without dominion, cannot be said to be the Lord God; for we say, my God, your God, the God of Israel, the God of Gods, the Lord of Lords; but we do not say, my Eternal, your Eternal, the Eternal of Israel, the Eternal of Gods. . . . these are titles which have no respect to servants. The word *God* usually signifies Lord; but every Lord is not a God. It is the dominion of a spiritual being which constitutes a God. . . .[20]

In Newton's view, then, two things are essential to Christianity as the true form of natural religion: knowledge of, awe for, and worship of, God, and a morality of *caritas* as propagated by the New Testament. The knowledge of God is revealed to man through natural philosophy as well as through the Scriptures. As far as the moral order is concerned, it is sufficient to assume that Christ came to stress a new morality of love. Newton did not believe in the Trinity, nor in the Divinity of Christ. His reduction of Christianity to natural religion implied the elimination of supernatural faith, redemption, and grace, even though Newton himself believed that in so doing he had merely purified Christianity from superstition. In "Irenicum" Newton argued strongly in favor of an ecumenical movement among Christians; this movement should rest on nothing but natural religion and on a commitment to the moral order of love.[21]

These ideas would find their most systematic expression one century later in the works of Kant. For Kant all religion is to be reduced to morality; religion for him is the representation of the essential, rational, moral laws and the commandments revealed by God, and of virtue as a correspondence between a finite will with the Will of the holy and good Creator of the world. Thus, religion is founded upon morality and the science of religion is moral theology.[22] For Kant a religion is a revealed religion if one must first accept something as a divine commandment before he can take it as his personal obligation. In natural religion, on the other hand, one must acknowledge something to be his basic obligation before he can acknowledge it as a divine commandment. Everyone can convince himself of the truths of natural religion with the help of natural reason, and one can convince others of its truths through scientific reflection and argumentation.[23]

In the final analysis, what Kant calls "religion" can no longer be identified with Christianity; religion is for him essentially rationalistic and moralistic in character. Everything which, apart from a moral way of life, man believes himself capable of doing to please God is mere religious delusion and spurious worship.[24] This view implies that a unique revelation of religious truths and the belief in the Church as the "official" custodian and accredited interpreter of revelation are to be rejected.

Kant describes here in his own way and in harmony with the basic principles of his critical philosophy the fundamental ideas of Rousseau, who in his *Emile* wrote that natural religion consists in the belief of the existence and goodness of God, in the spirituality and immortality of the human soul, and in the obligatory character of genuine moral actions to the degree that all of this is "revealed" to consciousness by means of an "inner light" that illuminates all human beings.[25]

THE SCIENTIFIC REVOLUTION IN THE SEVENTEENTH CENTURY: THE ESSENCE OF MODERN SCIENCE

If we look from a distance at the development briefly described in the preceding section, it is quite clear that natural religion is something artificial and unnatural, a late extract from the Christian religion (Blondel). Natural religion, far from being the essence of all religions, is merely a special by-product of modern Western thought. As a matter of fact, natural religion is no more than the Renaissance conception of monotheism reduced to a pale and abstract moral system (Lévy-Bruhl).[26] For an unbiased observer it is quite obvious that it is impossible to reduce Christianity to a rationalist system of thought or to an individual's system of basic beliefs and feelings without destroying it. But if this is so, why then did the leading scientists and philosophers of the seventeenth century turn toward natural religion? The reasons which we have given thus far are, even taken together, incapable of accounting for this development. The real reasons why, for these authors, the move from the Christian religion to natural religion seemed to be a very plausible one, is intimately connected with the manner in which the same authors conceived of the essence of modern science. A few introductory remarks may be helpful to explain and justify this thesis.

In the sixteenth and seventeenth centuries the history of scientific and philosophical thought were closely interrelated; separated from one another they are not understandable. Science and philosophy then constituted a unity, as they were both legitimately concerned with nature, patterns of action, and, above all, with the nature and structure of human thought. Thus, it is science and philosophy, represented as often as not by the same men (Kepler, Descartes, Boyle, Newton, Leibniz), that join and take part in the great debate that starts with Giordano Bruno and provisionally comes to a conclusion with Leibniz.

It is generally agreed that the sixteenth and seventeenth centuries underwent and accomplished a very radical revolution of which both modern science and modern philosophy were, at the same time, the root and the fruit. This revolution changed the very framework and patterns of our way of thinking. This "crisis of European consciousness" has been described and explained in different ways. Some historians have seen its most characteristic feature in the secularization of consciousness, its turning from transcendental goals to immanent aims, thus, in the replacement of the concern for the life to come by a preoccupation with this life. Others have seen in it the discovery of the essential subjectivity of man's consciousness and, thus, in the substitution of the subjectivism of the moderns for the objectivism characteristic of the thought of ancients and medievals. Others have seen it in the change of the relationship between theory and practice, between the *vita contemplativa* and the *vita activa;* whereas ancient and medieval man aimed at the contemplation of nature, modern man wanted domination and mastery. Others have stressed the replacement of the teleological and organismic patterns of thought and explanation to the mechanization of the modern world view. Still others have simply described the despair and confusion brought about by the new "philosophy" into a world from which all coherence was gone and in which the heavens no longer announced the glory of God.

All of these authors admit that the development of the new cosmology which replaced a geocentric world of classical astronomy by the heliocentric universe of modern astronomy played a paramount role in this process. This is why Alexandre Koyré conceives of the crisis as flowing from two fundamental and closely connected actions, the destruction of the closed and ordered cosmos and the geometrization of space. By the first factor is meant the substitution for the conception of the universe as a finite and well-ordered whole, in which the spatial structure embodied a hierarchy of perfection and value, by that of an indefinite or infinite universe no longer united by a natural order, but unified only by the identity of its ultimate and basic components and laws. By the geometrization of space is meant the replacement of the Aristotelian conception of space as a differentiated set of innerworldly places by that of Euclidean geometry, an essentially infinite and homogeneous extension. In this complex process man lost his place in the world, or perhaps he even lost the very world in which he had been living, because the process implied the discarding by scientific thought of all considerations based upon the concept of value (perfection, order, harmony, meaning, and aim), and, in a word, the divorce of the world of value from the world of facts.

When this revolution started God was still the Creator of the world and the Father of all men; when the revolution came to a close He was as a *Dieu fainéant* declared a superfluous hypothesis. At the beginning of the process man was still God's child and the crown of His creation; at the end he was no more than a part of nature possessed by an unbridled desire for power and domination.[27]

These characteristics of the revolution are by no means false, and all of them point to some rather important aspect of it. It is true that the modern era is to be characterized by the secularization of consciousness, the origin of subjectivism, the separation of theory and practice, the replacement of teleological and organismic patterns of thought by mechanistic principles, the switch from a closed geocentric universe to an open heliocentric universe, the separation of fact and value, and so on. Yet one will still have to address the question of precisely why this complex development could ever take place and why it did take place in the seventeenth century. Most authors feel that the development of the "new science" after Galileo and Newton is at the root of it, but as far as I know none of them has fully succeeded in explaining why and in what sense this is so. In order to be able to discover the basic characteristic of the modern era, from which all the other characteristics seem to flow, one must first turn to the question of precisely what constitutes the essence of modern science.[28]

One usually characterizes modern science, in contradistinction to ancient and medieval science, by stating that modern science starts from facts, whereas ancient and medieval science started from general, speculative assumptions. There is some truth to this view; yet it is undeniable that ancient and medieval science observed facts and that modern science works with universal assumptions. The contrast between the ancient and the modern attitude in science can thus be explained only by paying attention to *the manner in which* in both cases the facts are conceived and the question of *how* the basic assumptions are established in both instances. Many positivists will object to this approach to the issue. Yet one should note once more that all great scientists of the sixteenth and seventeenth centuries were all philosophers (Galileo, Descartes, Newton, Leibniz). They all clearly understood that there cannot be any bare facts; a fact is only what it is in light of the fundamental conception with which man approaches nature and natural events.

Secondly, the difference between the old and the new science is often determined by saying that the latter uses experiments and proves its insights empirically. But both experiment and test to get information about the behavior of things were already used in ancient Greece and in the Middle Ages. One should not forget that this kind of experience is implicit in all technological contact with things in the arts and crafts as well as in the use of tools. Here, too, it is not the experiment and test as such, but *the manner in which* experiments and tests are set up and the *intention* with which they are undertaken, that are different in both cases. In both instances the manner of experimentation is intimately connected with the kind of conceptual determination of the facts.

Thirdly, it is often said that it is characteristic of modern science that it uses calculation and measurement. But these were also used in the preceding centuries and in ancient times in Greece. It is again *the manner in which* both are being employed that is characteristic for modern science.

These three ways of characterizing modern science, thus, remain inadequate as long as we do not find the *basic* characteristic of modern science which rules and determines the basic movement of science itself. This characteristic consists in the typical metaphysical projection of the mode of being of the objects of modern science. Let us try to explain why this is the case.

Modern science did not appear all at once. Its origin lies partly in Greek science, partly in the conception of science formulated in the Renaissance of the twelfth century.[29] This conception was developed further in the later Scholasticism of the fourteenth and fifteenth centuries. In the sixteenth century sudden advances and setbacks occurred. Only during the seventeenth century, after a definitive clarification of the foundations of modern science was accomplished, did modern science begin to flourish. The entire development found its first systematic expression in Newton's *Principia* (1686–7). This work was not only the culmination of the preceding efforts in the same direction, but at the same time the foundation for the subsequent development in the natural sciences. It has both promoted and limited this development.[30]

The basic difference between ancient and modern science already shows itself clearly in Newton's first law, with which the first Book of the work begins. The first law reads: "Every body continues in its state of rest, or uniform motion in a straight line, unless it is compelled to change that state by forces impressed upon it."[31] This law was immediately accepted by all natural scientists, as Roger Cotes remarks in the preface of the second edition of the work (1713). Most scientists at that time as well as most scientists today consider this law to be self-evident. Yet one hundred years before Newton put the law in this form, it was completely unknown. During the preceding two thousand years it was not only unknown, but it would have been completely meaningless. Its discovery by Galileo, Baliani, and Newton and its establishment as the fundamental law of physics by Newton belongs to the greatest in human thought; it provides the real ground for the turning from Ptolemy to Copernicus, as we shall see shortly.

The idea of the universe which reigned in the West until the seventeenth century was largely determined by the works of Plato and Aristotle. Both Aristotle and Newton agree that physics wishes to deal with what shows itself of what is (phenomena), and the issue in physics is the unimpeachable evidence of perception as to each fact.[32] In Rule IV of Book III Newton expresses this idea as follows: "In experimental philosophy we are to look upon propositions inferred by general induction from phenomena as accurate or very nearly true, notwithstanding contrary hypotheses that may be imagined, till such times as other phenomena occur, by which they may either be made more accurate or liable to exceptions."[33] And yet the basic position of Newton is substantially different from that defended by Aristotle, because both view the phenomena from a totally different a priori perspective.

Both Aristotle and Newton agree that natural things are the subject matter of natural philosophy; these things are either in motion or at rest; this fact is given in direct experience. How bodies and their motions are to be conceived and what relations they have to each other is *not directly* given in experience; nor is this directly evident. Aristotle conceived of locomotion as *one* particular kind of motion, whereas for Newton it is *the* motion of all natural things. For Aristotle things move from themselves; the body itself is the first *arche* and *aition* of its own motion. Each body moves naturally to that place which is natural for it: earthy bodies move downward, fiery bodies move upward, because the natural place of earthy bodies is below, whereas that of fiery bodies is above. If a body is not in its proper place it must have been brought there by an impressed force. Its not being in its proper place is to be explained by an appeal to forces. All natural motions of sublunar things are motions in a straight line; celestial bodies, being perfect bodies, move in perfect, circular orbits. Celestial movements are eternal, terrestrial movements always come to an end, namely, when the thing has reached its proper place. Celestial movements need not be explained by means of an appeal to forces as long as the bodies stay in their natural orbits. Forces are necessary only where bodies do not move "naturally" (*phusei*). It should be stressed here that the most important claims that Aristotle made correspond distinctly to the common conception based on direct experience: celestial bodies continue to move in circular orbits, whereas a motion imparted to a sublunar body continues for some time and then ceases, passing over into a state of rest.

Contrary to this view, Newton formulates as the first law of motion that every moving body left to itself moves uniformly according to a straight line. Newton eliminates the distinction between terrestrial and celestial bodies; *all* natural bodies are essentially of the same kind. The circular motion has no priority over motion in a straight line; on the contrary, motion in a straight line is taken to be fundamental; it is the one that needs no explanation. There are no privileged places for different kinds of natural bodies. Place is merely a position in space in regard to other positions. The motions themselves are no longer determined according to different natures of things, but the essence of force is determined by the law of motion. A moving body, left to itself, moves uniformly in a straight line for all eternity; a force is that whose impact results in a declination from the rectilinear, uniform motion. It should be stressed again that this law is by no means suggested by our immediate experience. For Aristotle the moon moves in a circular orbit because it belongs to the nature of a celestial body to do so; no forces are necessary to explain this motion. For Newton the moon ought to have moved in a straight line uniformly; the reason why it moves in a circular orbit is due to the fact that a gravitational force is exerted by the earth. Since the concept of place has basically changed, motion is now only seen as a change of position in regard to certain bodies. Motion is defined by means of distances which can be measured. Thus, motion is now defined as the amount of motion; Newton does not define what motion itself is, he merely defines its quantity. The same is true for mass and weight. There is no difference between natural and forced motions, and nature no longer is the inner principle out of which the natural motions of a body necessarily follow. Finally, space and time become domains for the positional determinations of order among the natural bodies. Thus, *the manner of questioning* nature changes completely, and to some degree the two modes of questioning become opposites.

We must now try to understand in what sense the new manner of questioning becomes decisive in the explanation of Newton's first law. The law speaks of a body's motion which is not caused by impressed forces. But where does one find such a body? There obviously is no such thing. There also is no experiment which could ever bring such a body to direct perception. Modern science thus presupposes a fundamental presentation of things which "contradicts" our ordinary experience, even though it claims to be based solely on experience.

Thus, it is quite clear that modern science ultimately rests on a peculiar claim, namely, the claim that a determination of the things' mode of being is to be applied which is not derived from our immediate experience of the things and yet lies at the base of every further determination of these things, making it possible for them to appear in a certain way. Such a fundamental conception "a priori" of the things' mode of being is neither arbitrary nor self-evident. This is the reason why it required a long discussion and controversy to bring it to acceptance, why it required a change in the manner of approach to natural things, why it required the development of a new mode of thought for both modern physics and modern metaphysics.

When Galileo performed his famous experiment at the Leaning Tower of Pisa, the bodies of different weights, which according to his new theory should fall with equal velocity, did not arrive at *exactly* the same time.[34] Galileo nonetheless maintained his theory, whereas opponents interpreted the outcome in favor of Aristotle's theory of motion. Both parties saw the same facts, but they interpreted them differently; they made the same events visible to themselves in different ways. Both contemplated something that in their opinion was connected with the essence of bodies and the nature of their motions. Even before the experiment, Galileo was convinced that the motion of every body is uniform and rectilinear, if every obstacle has been excluded; and that every body's motion changes uniformly when an equal force affects it, regardless of its weight or shape. There is here a prior grasping of motion as well as of what should be uniformly determinative of all bodies: all bodies, all places, and all moments are alike as far as motion is concerned; motion is nothing but change in place; forces become determinable only by the change of motion which they cause; natural processes are nothing but the space-time determinations of the motions of point masses.

We are now in a position to describe more clearly the basic model of questioning that is characteristic of modern science: It is a taking cognizance of something in which man's knowledge gives to itself and from itself what it itself in advance takes a thing to be. We can specify this by saying that the scientific activity, as an act of man's thinking, is a projection of the mode of being of the things under investigation. This projection opens a domain in which things of a certain kind show themselves. In the projection there is *posited in advance* an outline of the mode of being according to which things are to be perceived and how they are to be evaluated. The cognition which is posited in the projection is of such a nature that it sets things on their proper foundation. Insofar as the projection is expressed in propositions, the anticipating determinations which are implicit in the projection take the form of fundamental propositions or axioms. The projection is the anticipated conception of the things to be examined, which sketches in advance the ground plan of the basic structure of every relevant thing and of its relation to every other thing.

Finally, we must try to understand the essence of modern science in its deeper meaning and in its relationship to modern metaphysics. In the Christian era before the sixteenth century, the truth proposed by faith and the Church was taken to be authoritative in an absolute sense. Whatever other experience and knowledge had been won was subordinated to this fundamental truth. Basically, there was no real worldly knowledge. Knowledge that was not based on revelation did not yet have an intelligibility and ground of its own. The essence of modern science, on the other hand, implies a specific will to a new formation and a new self-grounding of *natural* knowledge. Thus, revelation is not the first source of *all* truth concerning *all* things, nor is tradition *in all cases* the authoritative means of knowledge. Man, who projects the objects of his science, posits himself as the projector of the things' mode of being, including his own mode of being. In this process there is equally implied a new experience of freedom. From now on man wants to bind himself freely to obligations which are self-imposed (Kant).

Thus, in modern science and modern philosophy since Descartes, man no longer conceives of himself as the one who receives the truth about all things, but rather as the one who posits the conditions under which things may appear in truth. In every positing act the "I" (or the "We") as the positor is always coposited and preposited as that which is already present as what is. The mode of being of what is, of both the positor and that which is posited, is determined by the positing act. In the essence of positing as such lies the proposition: *I* posit. This latter proposition does not depend upon something given beforehand; it only gives to itself what lies within it. This proposition has the peculiarity of *first* positing that about which it makes an assertion. What is so posited first is the "I" as the positor. The "I" is the *subjectum (hupokeimenon)* of the very first principle, the *subjectum* of the positing as such. Thus, this *subjectum* must be called *the* subject.

Before the time of Descartes every thing could be called a subject; from Descartes onward the positor is *the* subject as such. The things from now on are called objects, because they always lie over against this primary subject of the basic positing act. The word *object* then received a meaning which it had never had before. From then on all certainty and truth will be based on the "I posit." Reason becomes now posited explicitly and according to its own demands as the first ground of all knowledge and the basic guideline for the determination of the mode of being of all things, including the mode of being of man himself.

From this general perspective it finally becomes understandable why modern man gradually came to the view that even in regard to religious matters, man must first determine in advance what kind of religious truths he can legitimately accept. In other words, by stipulating the relevant conditions of all knowledge *scientifically,* he was quite naturally led from a revealed religion to natural religion.

SCIENCE AND RELIGION IN THE MODERN ERA

It will now be clear why in the modern era the relationship between faith and reason had to become problematic in a sense in which this had never been the case before. Reason posits itself as the highest court of appeal for the determination of the mode of being of all beings, and thus as the ultimate judge about truth. On the other hand, faith must submit itself to the word of God and accept on his authority truths that cannot be discovered or justified by reason. By taking one possible way of knowing *certain* things as the privileged and primary way of knowing *all* things, modern man was forced to eliminate from religion all those truths which are beyond reason. Thus, Christianity was gradually reduced to natural religion and natural religion to a postulate of practical reason.

Yet it is obviously impossible, and most certainly not necessary, to conceive of modern science as the ultimate judge of truth in all matters. If this were to be the case, then in addition to religion, the entire moral, sociopolitical, and aesthetic domains in a man's life would equally have to be reduced to the scientific knowledge of the relevant phenomena. But such an attempt would make our lives empty and inhuman, because it would mean the reduction of all culture to natural processes.

Both science and religion form an essential part of our Western world. As part of the same world they did and should continue to influence one another as they have over the past four centuries. Today this interaction often has the character of a painful conflict. This conflict need not lead to skepticism or agnosticism, but can be used as a positive opportunity which may help us see again the genuine Christianness of Christianity. In such an effort the following reflections seem to have some importance.

1. Both science and the Christian religion are constantly in development. As far as science is concerned, the history of science has shown us the details of this development for both the formal and the empirical sciences. As for the Christian religion, it is true that Christianity is really concerned with eternal and invariable truths; yet these truths must be handed on, time and again, to concrete living human beings who find themselves in a constantly changing world which continuously places new demands on them. Thus, the invariable truths of religion

must repeatedly be adapted to the concrete situations in which people actually find themselves.

Thus, it is not correct to assume that either in science or in the Christian religion will man ever be able to formulate truths in a manner which will be once and for all definitive. Every truth that is formulated by man presupposes a perspective of related conceptions which is to be modified periodically. If there seems to be a conflict between science and the Christian religion, one should not hastily abandon doctrines for which there is solid evidence on either side. The clash is often merely a sign that there are wider truths and more encompassing and finer perspectives within which science and Christianity can be reconciled.[35]

2. However, this does not mean that the genuine and all-encompassing truth would consist in a kind of synthesis of science and religion. On the contrary, both science and religion refer to irreducible domains of man's experience. This is precisely the reason why modern man in regard to science and religion finds himself in a paradoxical situation. On the one hand, both science and religion are constitutive parts of our Western culture, of our world. Taken as such they cannot be kept separated from one another. Yet on the other hand, they cannot directly influence one another either. If modern science and metaphysics flow from a positing objectivation, then obviously neither can say anything meaningful about that to which the religious attitude is oriented: God can neither be posited by finite understanding, nor can he be objectified. In science man posits himself as the positor of all (scientific) truths; in his religious attitude man submits himself to the Word in which God revealed to him what is indispensable for his salvation. In reflecting on this paradox, one should keep in mind that it is not typical of the relationship between science and religion alone; this paradox also manifests itself when one tries to relate science to the arts or to our interpersonal relationships.

Yet it is true that the paradox between science and religion is experienced today as much more acute than ever before, due to the fact that contemporary man finds himself in a world which is so dominated by modern science and technology that the holy seems to have lost its meaning and all attempts to express our relationship to God appear as being empty shells.

3. In the process of the gradual adaptation of Christianity to the scientific conception of world, the churches have played an important part. It cannot be denied that in many instances the churches have failed to give guidance and to seize valuable opportunities. Particularly in regard to the sciences, the attitude of the churches has often been an unduly negative one, one of suspicion, fear, criticism, or apathy.

4. Because of the radical difference between science and religion it is incorrect to try to use scientific theories either to defend or to criticize strictly religious beliefs. Russell was correct in pointing out that it makes no sense to appeal to quantum mechanics or modern biology to "prove" the immortality of the soul

or man's freedom, or to modern cosmological theories to "prove" the existence of God.[36] On the other hand, Whitehead was correct when he explained that it makes no sense to use scientific theories to criticize the Christianness of Christianity.[37]

It is equally incorrect for the same reason to try to employ scientific ideas in a natural, philosophical theology. It has been only since the time of Descartes that philosophers have really believed that man is able to "prove without a doubt" the existence of God and to describe accurately some of his basic attributes. In former centuries there was never more than a faith searching for understanding (*fides quaerens intellectum*). At any rate, it is unquestionable that the meaning and function of philosophical theology in modern philosophy since Descartes are completely different from the meaning and function of the philosophical reflections about God in preceding centuries.

To summarize, religion, as the reaction of man to his search for the holy, implies a vision which from the viewpoint of science and modern metaphysics stands beyond the passing flux of immediate things. Religion implies a vision of something that is real and yet waiting to be realized, a remote possibility and yet the greatest of present facts, something that gives meaning to all that passes and yet eludes apprehension, something whose possession is the final good and yet is beyond all reach, something that is the ultimate ideal and yet the hopeless quest. The immediate reaction of man to religion and its vision is worship, and worship is the surrender to the claim for assimilation urged on by the motive of love. That religion is strong which in its modes of thought and ritual evokes an apprehension of this commanding vision and for which worship is not a rule of safety, but an adventure of the spirit.[38]

NOTES

1. C. F. von Weizsäcker, "Notizen zum Gespräch über Physik und Religion," in *Der Garten des Menschlichen* (Munich: Carl Henser, 1977), pp. 441–43.

2. Alfred North Whitehead, *Science and the Modern World* (New York: Free Press, 1967), p. 2.

3. Ibid., pp. 181–83.

4. The terms *natural religion* and *deism* are often used interchangeably. The expression *natural religion* was introduced in the sixteenth century by authors who believed that there is a natural religion shared by all peoples and of which the diverse forms of religion that were actually discovered are no more than further articulations. These authors did not intend to criticize Christianity, nor was it their intention to reduce Christianity to natural religion. In the seventeenth century many scientists explicitly reduced Christianity to some form of natural religion and in the eighteenth century protagonists of natural religion often adopted a critical and negative attitude in regard to Christianity. Their position

has often been referred to by the term *deism*. It is in this sense that the term is used here. For many people the term *deism* refers to the view according to which God exists and created the world but thereafter assumed no control over it. One should realize, though, that very few philosophers and scientists, if any, have defended such a view.

5. Thomas Aquinas, *Summa Theologiae*, I, q. 2, a. 2, ad 1.

6. Cf. Etienne Gilson, *Reason and Revelation in the Middle Ages* (New York: Humanities, 1939).

7. Cf. W. C. Dampier, *A History of Science and Its Relations with Philosophy and Religion* (Cambridge: University Press, 1971); E. A. Burtt, *The Metaphysical Foundations of Modern Science* (Garden City: Doubleday, n.d.); A. Koyré, *From the Closed World to the Infinite Universe* (Baltimore: Johns Hopkins University Press, 1976); Richard S. Westfall, *Science and Religion in Seventeenth Century England* (Ann Arbor: University of Michigan Press, 1973); R. Hooykaas, *Religion and the Rise of Modern Science* (Grand Rapids: William B. Eerdmans Publishing Co., 1974); R. Popkin, *The History of Scepticism from Erasmus to Descartes* (Assen: Van Gorcum, 1964); E. J. Dijksterhuis, *The Mechanization of the World Picture*, trans. C. Dikshoorn (Oxford: Clarendon Press, 1961); P. Rossi, *Philosophy, Technology, and the Arts in the Early Modern Era*, trans. S. Attanasio (New York: Harper & Row, 1970); Arthur Koestler, *The Watershed: A Biography of Johannes Kepler* (Garden City: Doubleday, 1960); B. Willey, *The Seventeenth Century Background* (New York: Columbia University Press, 1967); R. K. Merton, "Science, Technology and Society in Seventeenth Century England," *Osiris* 4(1938): 360–632; Paul H. Kocher, *Science and Religion in Elisabethan England* (San Marino, Calif.: Huntington Library, 1953). Several authors who wrote in the seventeenth century claimed that natural religion, in view of the fact that it is supported by "natural philosophy," is the strongest weapon against atheism. This reason for promoting natural religion is somewhat puzzling, for at that time there were virtually no known atheists. What is now called atheism is a product of the eighteenth century, and it is most certainly not true that in the seventeenth century people were very concerned about the dangers of atheism. It is true that Hobbes may have been considered to have been an atheist. But even for Hobbes the label *atheist* is to be used with caution and restrictions. It seems that the authors mentioned turned to an attack on atheism for basically two related reasons: 1) they knew very well that the new science made presuppositions which were taken from a materialist philosophy (Democritus); 2) they also knew that they themselves could have been legitimately accused of promoting atheism. When these authors join Charleton when he wrote: "England has of late produced, and does at this unhappy day foster, more swarms of atheistic monsters . . . than any nation has been infested withal," they usually have certain materialistic Epicurians and Hobbes in mind (cf. Westfall, *Science and Religion*, pp. 106–116; Charleton's quote

from *The Darkness of Atheism Dispelled by the Light of Nature* is cited on pp. 107–8). Cf. Fritz Mauthner, *Der Atheismus und seine Geschichte im Abendlande,* 3 vols. (Hildesheim: Georg Olms Verlagsbuchhandlung, 1963), vol. 2; Cornelio Fabro, *God in Exile. Modern Atheism: A Study of the Internal Dynamic of Modern Atheism from Its Roots in the Cartesian Cogito to the Present Day,* trans. A. Gibson (New York: Newman Press, 1968).

8. Cf. Westfall, *Science and Religion,* pp. 107–45.

9. Leslie Stephen, *History of English Thought in the Eighteenth Century,* 2 vols. (London: J. Murray, 1927), vol. 1, chaps. 2–4.

10. L. Gallagher, *More's Utopia and Its Critics* (Chicago: Scott Foresman, 1964), p. 57; cf. pp. 57–59.

11. *Lord Herbert of Cherbury's De Religione Laici,* ed. and trans. Harold R. Hutcheson (New Haven: Yale University press, 1944), p. 65.

12. Ibid., pp. 87, 89f., 103, 119, 131.

13. Ibid., p. 129.

14. Ibid., p. *vii.*

15. In addition to the philosophers B. Pascal (1623–62), J. Locke (1631–1704), and G. W. Leibniz (1646–1716), the following English scientists must be mentioned in this context: R. Boyle (1627–91), W. Charleton (1619–1707), N. Grew (1641–1712), R. Lower (1631–91), J. Mapletoff (1631–1712), W. Petty (1623–87), T. Sydenham (1624–89), I. Barrow (1630–80), J. Flamsteed (1646–1719), J. Ray (1627–1705), E. Halley (1656–1742), and I. Newton (1642–1727). These scientists were representatives of mathematics, physics, chemistry, astronomy, biology, and medicine. Similar ideas were proposed by scholars primarily concerned with literature and education; in this connection T. Browne (1605–82), J. Wilkins (1614–72), and J. Glanvill (1636–80) can be mentioned.

16. John Locke, *Essay Concerning Human Understanding,* ed. P. H. Niccitch (Oxford: Clarendon Press, 1975), Book. IV, chap. 10.

17. John Locke, *The Reasonableness of Christianity,* ed. I. T. Ramsey (Stanford Calif.: Stanford University Press, 1967).

18. "Creed for the Society of Pacific Christians," composed by Locke, in H. R. Fox Bourne, *The Life of John Locke,* 2 vols. (New York: Harper, 1876), 2:185–86.

19. Cf. S. G. Hefelbower, *The Relation of John Locke to English Deism* (Chicago: University of Chicago Press, 1918).

20. Isaac Newton, *Mathematical Principles of Natural Philosophy,* trans. A. Motte (1729), ed. F. Cajori (Berkeley: University of California Press, 1962), *General Scholion,* pp. 554f.; idem, *Opticks,* ed. I. B. Cohen (New York: Dover, 1952), pp. 400–406.

21. Koyré, *From the Closed World,* pp. 206–72; Westfall, *Science and Religion,* pp. 193–220. Some of the drafts of *Irenicum* which Newton never pub-

lished are printed in: *Theological Manuscripts,* ed. H. McLachlan (Liverpool, University Press, 1950).

22. Immanuel Kant, *Critique of Practical Reason and Other Writings in Moral Philosophy,* trans. and ed. by L. W. Beck (Chicago: University of Chicago Press, 1949), pp. 227–34; idem, *Critique of Judgment,* trans. J. Bernard (New York: Hafner, 1966), pp. 292–98, 327–29; idem, *Religion within the Limits of Reason Alone,* trans. T. M. Greene and H. H. Hudson (New York: Harper & Brothers, 1960), pp. 87–138.

23. Idem, *Religion Within the Limits,* pp. 139–55.

24. Ibid., p. 158.

25. J. Rousseau, *Émile,* Book IV, in *Œuvres complètes,* ed. V. D. Musset-Pathay, 26 vols. (Paris: P. Dupont, 1823–25), vol. 4.

26. Cf. André Lalande, *Vocabulaire Technique et Critique de la Philosophie* (Paris: Presses Universitaires de France, 1962), pp. 915–18.

27. Koyré, *From the Closed World,* pp. vii–ix, 1–3, 273–76.

28. For what follows here, cf. Martin Heidegger, *What Is a Thing?* trans. W. B. Barton, Jr. and Vera Deutsch (Chicago: Henry Regnery, 1967), pp. 65–119 (passim).

29. Cf. C. H. Haskins, *The Renaissance of the Twelfth Century* (Cleveland: World Publishing, 1957); A. C. Crombie, *Medieval and Early Modern Science* (Cambridge: Harvard University Press, 1963).

30. Cf. Dampier, *A History of Science,* pp. 97–177.

31. Newton, *Mathematical Principles,* p. 13.

32. Aristotle, *De Caelo,* 7, 306a6, 16–17.

33. Newton, *Mathematical Principles,* pp. 398ff.

34. The fact that the experiment may not have been performed from the Leaning Tower of Pisa is irrelevant for the point being made. Cf. Dampier, *History of Science,* p. 130 and the sources quoted there.

35. Whitehead, *Science and the Modern World,* pp. 181–83.

36. Bertrand Russell, *The Scientific Outlook* (New York: Norton, 1962), pp. 101–33.

37. Whitehead, *Science and the Modern World,* pp. 181–83, 186–88.

38. Ibid., p. 192.

Chapter 20

ALIEN UNIVERSE
Frederick Ferré

MY position, briefly, is as follows: that science was the most potent agency that formed the consciousness of the modern world; that there are fatal flaws in the modern world which make its ending certain; that these flaws are directly traceable to flaws in modern consciousness; and, therefore, that science when functioning beyond its secular limits as mythic matrix of our obsolescent culture is itself significantly flawed.

ONE

First, is it clear that scientific practice is capable of being extended to generate a spiritual vision? I shall argue that this is indeed the case, and that the scientistic vision is at the root of much that is characteristic of modern culture.

Any fundamental religious phenomenon is organized by deeply felt values issuing in characteristic behavior that is considered linked to the "sacred" or ultimately worthy. Sometimes it is difficult or impossible to distinguish whether the linkage is a ritual or an ethical one. Abstaining from meat on Fridays, when this was required of Roman Catholics, seems a pretty clear case of a ritual linkage, while abstaining from adultery, for example, seems a pretty obvious case of ethical linkage. But the categories have a way of merging under some circumstances. Many strict Catholics felt moral compunctions about meatless Fridays—and is it not an ethical failing to violate one's duty of obedience to legitimate ecclesiastical discipline? One old monk, I am told, felt so deeply about

From: Frederick Ferré, *Shaping the Future: Resources for the Post-Modern World*, New York: Harper & Row, 1976), pp. 19–39.

the prohibition that the first Friday it was lifted (by legitimate ecclesiastical authority), he refused to eat the celebration steaks served by the monastery cooks: "The Holy Father can go to hell if he wishes," he moaned, "but I'll not eat meat on Friday." Such "scrupulosity," as Catholic moral theologians call it, even where no ethical point seems at issue, is a good sign that we have entered a religious context, where valuing is intense and zealotry is always only a step away from zeal.

Likewise indicative of religious dynamics at work are those cases where what looks like ethical injunctions function like ritual ones. Refraining from adultery, normally, is an ethical policy with much ethical point. But under some circumstances, where the ethical point is lost, the prohibition, if regarded, serves instead as a ritual. To take an extreme example from a science fiction story I read long ago, the plot entailed that the entire population of the world had somehow been wiped out except for two adult human beings, a man and a woman. The human race would perish unless they had children who could begin to replenish the world. But, alas, the couple were not married and there were no clergymen left alive to tie the sanctifying knot. The man was willing to risk it, but the woman took the Seventh Commandment absolutely. The world ended, as I recall, with a whimper.

It is not easy to draw a line, then, when sacred values are at stake, between behavior relevant to such values linked by ethical or by ritual sanctions. Let us, however, as a very rough rule of thumb say that ritual action is action relevant to sacred values which is performed for its own sake or as a symbol of the ultimately worthy. Let us say that religiously sanctioned ethical action is action relevant to sacred values which is performed for the furtherance of some religiously valued end or good. Then I believe we can see that scientific practice involves both sacred ritual and religiously sanctioned ethics.

A *ritual* of science would involve a way of doing things whose propriety is deeply felt to touch on the ultimately worthy, which is valued for its own sake, regardless of whether good is gained or lost thereby. One such sacred ritual, present since Descartes' famous founding of modern thought in methodological doubt, is deliberate suspense of judgment in the absence of sufficient evidence. Scientific thinkers must not believe anything to any degree more strongly than the objective evidence warrants, even if it means failing to believe something that is in fact true, and missing, to that extent, the good end of maximizing the stock of true beliefs. The bad-in-itself, avoided by this sacred ritual, is credulity, the state of consciousness most disvalued by the scientific community. The good-in-itself, symbolized by and implicit in this central ritual, is critical objectivity.

The most famous defense of such ritual scrupulosity, despite the possible loss of truth, was made by W.K. Clifford in the nineteenth century when he wrote: "If I let myself believe anything on insufficient evidence, there may be no great harm done by the mere belief; it may be true after all, or I may never have occasion to exhibit it in outward acts. But I cannot help doing this great wrong towards Man, that I make myself credulous."[1]

Most of us now, I am sure, share Clifford's disapproval of credulity. We admire critical objectivity as an intrinsically valuable state of consciousness. We are, after all, dwellers in the latter days of the modern world sharing most of the values that science-generated objective consciousness has victoriously instilled throughout our culture. But we should at least notice that Clifford's argument, though we may instinctively nod when we hear it, supports a mode of behavior that other types of consciousness might not find self-evidently valuable at all. Belief without objective evidence—belief, that is, by subjective hunch, by poetic suggestion, by authority of shaman, by sheer delight in what is believed, by fear of disbelief, by social solidarity, by moral duty, by love or loyalty or the like—such believing is an ever-present human possibility which under different value priorities might be affirmed as far better than critically objective suspense of judgment. What, it might be asked, is so absolute about objective consciousness *as such* that it merits losing the potential values of believing beyond or without evidence? What is so sacred about ritual avoidance of credulity that it makes modern scientistic consciousness prefer to lose friendship, or beauty, or even truth itself, perhaps, rather than to profane objectivity?

These, if uttered, would be basic rival religious challenges to basic science-generated religious values. We should not expect a ready answer, since the highest value can never—in principle—be justified. As highest, it is the ground of all justification. To attempt to justify it by some other value would be to make the other value higher; it can only be justified by itself, therefore, which means that it is beyond the context of justification. Thus, we must view scientific ritual avoidance of credulity as touching upon a functioning religious ultimate, symbolizing and incarnating the intensely valued objective-critical consciousness itself.

I have started at the top, as it were, of the ritual hierarchy in scientific practice. But even minor practices reflect the centrality of sanctified objective consciousness. There is, for example, a ritual way of writing up experimental reports that strikes me as portentous, for all its familiarity. The ritual is to write everything in the passive voice, with all references to the experimenter eliminated, if possible, but if not, at least transformed into the third person. All first-person remarks or actions are systematically eliminated. Instead of: "Then I put the test tube into the Bunsen burner while glancing at the clock," we are taught to write: "Next, the test tube was introduced into the flame and the time noted." Men and women don't see or hear or smell things; in this ritual "observations are made." People don't put things on scales or place rulers against things: "measurements are performed." The ritual of scientific writing style systematically impersonalizes. Why? Is there any practical or ethical point to such a formal practice? I suspect that neither clarity nor precision would need to be sacrificed in a laboratory report that used first-person active language;[2] but the mood, the tone, the subliminal feel would be very different. And so would the symbolism, which now works to cultivate a consciousness in which the peculiarities of individual subjectivities count not at all. The persons who do or see or measure don't matter; what matters, as symbolized and reinforced by the ritual language, are the objective events, the recorded observations, the performed measurements. It is negligible that some particular person did this or that; it is important only that this or that happened under carefully defined circumstances. The ritual writing style of science, though a minor symbol, no doubt, points to the sacred value matrix of objective consciousness and participates in it as well.

TWO

I hope by now that I have succeeded in my first aim, namely, in replacing what Scheffler calls the "myth" of the "cold, aloof scientist"[3] with some sense—however sketchy—of the vibrant valuational power implicit in scientific enterprises. What seems cold to others is passionate self-discipline in the service of sacred and rigorous clarity; what seems aloof is dedication to impersonal standards by which objectivity is maintained. Objective truth is the end; objective reason is the means. End and means cohere and reinforce one another, vision and practice, ritual and morality—into a unity that makes objective consciousness the motivating center of a major functioning religious phenomenon.

By asserting that it is a functioning religious phenomenon, of course, I do not mean to suggest that the modern world actually lives fully by or through the ideals of objectivity. No more did medieval people live fully by or through the ideals of Christianity. But as Christianity—fully exemplified only in a few saints, supported by priests and ecclesiastical institutions, and generally accepted at the instinctive level as authorative by the bulk of medieval society—put what White-head call its "impress" on the thought, feelings, perceptions, and characteristic institutions of Christendom, so objective consciousness—fully exemplified only in a few scientific heroes, supported by working researchers and their institutions, and generally accepted at the instinctive level as authoritative by the bulk of modern people—has put its "impress" on the thought, feelings, perceptions and characteristic institutions of modernity whenever and wherever in its progressive expansion the modern world has reached.

It is appropriate, then, to trace the impact of scientism on our cultural history— that is, how this phenomenon has manifested its most basic traits in the institutions, the policies, and the character of the modern world—just as historians trace the impact of Christianity on medieval Christendom. In this project I shall select three basic traits of scientific practice for attention: connecting each to the value-laden images of reality that extend scientific practice into a mythic vision; illustrating each from the work of Galileo, as "saint" and "martyr"; and tracing each to consequences in the modern world around us that show the valuational limits of scientism's objective consciousness—and that spell practical ruin as well.

First, an essential trait of objective consciousness, as we have seen, is its requirement that *belief be strictly tied to objective evidence*. No merely private whim, hunch, or feeling is to be allowed standing in the court of objective reason. Without such a requirement it is impossible to conceive of modern science as we have known it.

Galileo grasped this point unerringly. What counts as objective evidence is what can be tested by public methods of weighing, timing, measuring. These characteristics of things can be quantified, checked, and rechecked by anyone, regardless of mood or other private, subjective considerations. More generally, any merely subjective aspects of experience must be irrelevant to the steady progress toward objective truth. What is merely personal or private is unconfirmable, unmeasurable, and secondary for scientific purposes. What will be primary for purposes of providing objective evidence will be aspects of reality that can be checked on by others (that is, "public" aspects of things) and that allow precise, quantitative measurement.

Galileo consequently introduced (and Descartes greatly elaborated) a vital distinction required by objective consciousness between the *primary* qualities of things and their *secondary* qualities. The primary qualities of, say, a billiard ball will be its weight, or massiveness, its shape or figure, its motion (including both quantity of time and quantity of distance covered); the secondary qualities will consist, among others, in the shade of color we perceive, or the quality of the sound we hear when one ball strikes another, or the texture as we feel it on our palm. These latter are all qualitative, not quantitative. They are not public and confirmable. What quality of color you see is private to your subjective awareness. Perhaps you are color-blind. Perhaps the quality you privately experience and call "green" is in fact the quality I privately experience and call "red." How could we ever know? What difference would it make?

Moreover, all such qualities seem to be produced by my subjective interaction with the objective world. If a tree falls in the forest and no one is there to hear, so the most famous philosophical puzzle of the modern world runs, is there any sound? The obvious answer, given Galileo's distinction, is that in the sense of "sound" in which *primary* features are understood—the interactions of material bodies with shape and weight, the setting into measurable motion of particles dancing as sound waves pass—there *is* sound; but in the sense of "sound" in which the *quality* of the crackling branches is meant, there obviously is only silence. For the totally deaf (and for the world itself) there are no sounds, only vibrations. The vibrations, as primary qualities, are consequently the objectively real features of the universe; qualities of tone are merely subjective.

The real world, the objectively true world, consequently, is made up of what can be apart from the private irrelevancies of human subjectivity. Just as there is no *pain* in the objective fire, but only in my awareness if I let my body get too close, so by the same token there is no *warmth,* in the sense that I feel its comforting glow. What there really is, in what we subjectively call heat, is more or less rapid movement (measurable) of tiny molecules (with mass and length and shape). Color, as we of the modern world all believe, is "really" only electromagnetic vibrations, and different hues are "really" only different frequencies on a spectrum of energetic wave phenomena that extends well above and well below the narrow range called visible light, where human subjectivity alone supplies the many-hued rainbow.

This is a compelling image, and one that rises directly and essentially from objective methods. It is familiar. It enters into our authoritative vision of the universe. What is real and basic is the measurable, the material. What is suspect and relative is the qualitative, the private, the merely mental. Thus, at last, if the sound of the tree in the forest and the colors of the rainbow must be credited to the human mind, not to the objective world, so much more must the values we experience along with them—the thrilling dissonance of the crash or the subtle beauty of the rainbow. If the tree-in-the-forest problem is the modern world's most famous and characteristic metaphysical saw, the most characteristic aesthetic cliché comes out of the same consciousness: "Beauty is in the eye of the beholder." And so, of course, must all values be in a world devoid of quality. Whitehead sadly sums it up: "Nature is a dull affair, soundless, scentless, colourless; merely the hurrying of material, endlessly, meaninglessly."[4]

Protests against this vision of the world, including Whitehead's protest, have been heard. Various lines of criticism have been taken. Whitehead, for instance, argues that it is simply unbelievable. He marshals evidence from poetic insight to show that the basic, concrete data of human experience are overwhelmingly in opposition. Then he concludes that between concrete data of experience and mere theory, one must side with the data and conclude that the theory is wrong. I agree with Whitehead in principle: theoretical abstraction must give way to concrete experience. But I wonder whether Whitehead takes seriously enough the fact I have been stressing here: that for the modern consciousness this is no mere theory to be used or discarded at will, but, instead, this has become a value-laden vision of reality—a way of feeling and relating to the universe. We shall require not merely a different theory—though new theory will be needed— but a change of consciousness itself in order to experience the world another way.

Another recent critic is Lewis Mumford, whose attack has been from the standpoint of morality. The "crime of Galileo" was to alienate humanity from the fullness of our own experience as well as from our universe. It was not so much merely to break with the authority of the Church but, worse, to break down respect for personality. As Mumford writes:

> By his exclusive preoccupation with quantity Galileo had, in affect, *disqualified* the real world of experience; and he had thus driven man out of living nature into a cosmic desert, even more peremptorily than Jehovah had driven Adam and Eve out of the Garden of Eden. But in Galileo's case the punishment for eating the apple of the tree of knowledge lay in the nature of knowledge itself, for that tasteless, dessicated fruit was incapable of sustaining or reproducing life. . . .
>
> From the seventeenth century on, the technological world, which prided itself on reducing or extruding the human personality, progressively replaced both nature and human culture and claimed indeed a higher status for itself, as the concrete working model of scientific truth. "In 1893," Loren Eiseley reminds us, "Robert Monro in an opening address before the British Association for the Advancement of Science remarked sententiously . . . 'imagination, conceptions, idealizations, the moral faculties . . . may be compared to parasites that live at the expense of their neighbors.' " To have pointed the way to this devaluation of the personality, and its eventual exile, was the real crime of Galileo.[5]

To Whitehead's epistemological warning and Mumford's passionate moral protest, I would like to add a word on the practical social consequences of this aspect of scientistic mythos. It has, through its world picture with its implicit values, reinforced the supreme importance of the "hardheaded" in modern institutions and policies. What really counts is the countable—the measurable, the tangible, the material. The objective consciousness of the modern world can count money, size, output, speed. "More," "bigger," "faster" become transcendent and unexaminable values drawn from fundamental functioning religious imagery and supportive of tendencies toward greed, conflict, and war. Likewise, modern consciousness puts its faith in its hardware—to preserve it from military destruction and ecological collapse. To challenge this instinctive faith in the "technological fix" is to challenge something very deep in our souls. Most of us cannot even imagine another way. In the same way we find it hard to take values other than measurable material values with any great degree of seriousness. The pervasive *ugliness* of the modern world wherever it has spread—from Jersey City to Japan—is one of its most obvious features. It is slightly unfair to compare a medieval cathedral with a modern oil refinery, but not entirely so. These are typical institutions of their respective civilizations and well represent where the basic values have been invested. Aesthetic considerations in our modern world are arbitrarily split off from the rest of life and are supposed to be left for the women (and effete poets, environmentalists, or other such weaklings), while the real world pursues real interests: that is, economic ones. Wherever material, quantifiable, "real" values (jobs, production, income) are threatened by merely subjective, qualitative concerns, the people tend to recoil and their politicians with them.

Conflict, obsessive material consumption, adulation of growth, and pervasive ugliness are not the only social consequences of the modern mythos. In addition, the objective world without intrinsic values becomes mere resource pit and dumping ground. There are no values in the objective world to slow us down. Pollution is in the eye of the beholder. And so it is, painfully! And so it will be, increasingly, until it becomes—as we must hope it is not already—too late to turn back from ecological collapse. One consequence of objective consciousness, then, is *alienation from quality in the universe* with all that this portends for human life.

The supreme value of objectivity requires public evidence, as we have seen, but second, it demands *rigorous clarity* as well. The muddling of things together that can be seen dispassionately apart is the enemy of scientific reason. Scientific practice leads to *analysis* of its subject matter, therefore, and best of all to mathematical analysis with its power and precision.

Galileo, again, led the way: "Philosophy is written in this grand book, the universe, which stands continually open to our gaze. But the book cannot be understood unless one first learns to comprehend the language and read the letters in which it is composed. It is written in the language of mathematics, and its characters are triangles, circles, and other geometric figures, without which it is humanly impossible to understand a single word of it; without them, one wanders about in a dark labyrinth."[2] To understand the whole, divide the problem, Descartes urged modern thinkers, and analyze it in terms of the mathematics of its smallest components. The objective truth will become clear when these elements are distinctly known, together with the quantifiable laws of their combination.

The stress of early modern scientific practice on clarity through analysis gives us more than a method to follow, it also gives us a vivid image of how things are, fundamentally: things are aggregates of tiny parts which have laws of their own, by virtue of which the larger wholes are constructed. The more basic reality is the tiny part, obviously, and the derivative reality is the compound everyday object, the resultant of many parts working according to their laws.

The cell is more basic than the whole living body, on this world view; the molecule is more basic than the living cell; the atoms of the molecule are more basic than the molecule; and the subatomic particles—electrons, protons, and all the other swarm—are more basic than the atom. They are the "ultimately real." But of course they are not living. Thus, nonlife is more ultimate than life, and physics is the fundamental science in every sense: it deals with the fundamental particles of which everything is derived, and it is in principle fundamental to all the sciences which, one by one, reduce to physics. Sociology, that is, reduces to individual psychology; psychology reduces to brain physiology and general biology; biology reduces to molecular chemistry; and chemistry in its turn reduces to the subject matter of physics.

This familiar imagery of reductionism coheres well with the objective world picture of quantifiable material in motion and refines it still further. The most important of the material realities are the smallest particles. All else is derivative and secondary. And therefore the kinds of properties that fundamental particles have are basic to the universe. That rules out life as having any basic status, of course, and further locks mind, the ephemeral third-order by-product of the physical universe, firmly into its subjective limbo. Perhaps subjectivity isn't even there at all, muse some extreme reductionists.

Reductive analysis, however, though implicit in objective consciousness, contains seeds of its own destruction. I do not refer, merely, to the obvious awkwardness of a living being devoting intense efforts of thought in attempting to show that he or she is neither living nor thinking. That would be a tactic successful only against those few who hold that derivative realities are not real at all, but are mere illusions. Most reductive analysts do not take this extreme position, though admittedly they then have the difficult task of explaining where phenomena like life and subjectivity—apparently ungrounded in the basic realities of the universe—can possibly come from. I will not press the fact, either, that reduction is not an accomplished scientific achievement but only a program believed to be possible in the assumed progressive future of objective consciousness. There have been remarkable reductionist successes. The science of thermodynamics has been reduced to that of statistical mechanics; and molecular biology is currently showing new relationships between genetic stability and molecular chemistry. Such relationships should, after all, be expected in a unified world.

What is fatal about reductionist analysis is its claim to be exhaustive and complete in its vision. But this is impossible in principle, as Michael Polanyi stresses.[7] Before we begin to analyze an interesting whole, he points out, we must first be able to recognize the whole as interesting. Any consciousness operating by analysis alone could never recognize the difference between the atoms of the frog and of the fly and of the air and water surrounding them. We must—logically must—move *from* holistic awareness of significant unities, *then* to the detailed parts that find their meaning and importance in the wholes within which they function, if we are to understand the universe as it is. Unless we get the gestalt of things first, the process of analysis would never give us unities again.

To this logical point I would like to add another practical dimension which arises when analysis claims exclusive adequacy for consciousness. The ecosphere within which we dwell is a delicately woven web of life. To be understood—

more urgently, to be saved from collapse—this vulnerable and immensely complex network must be approached holistically, contrary to the habits of modern analytical consciousness. The consequences of our failures to think and perceive our world in multivalent rather than analytically monovalent ways are already painfully apparent. Barry Commoner repeatedly points these out in *The Closing Circle* and names the proper culprit. Regarding the complex holistic chemistry of air pollution, for example, he writes: "In order to describe the course of a particular chemical reaction, it is necessary to study it in isolation, separate from other processes that might change the reaction under study. However, if, for the sake of such an analysis, a few ingredients are isolated from the mixture of polluted air, this artificial change destroys precisely the complex of chemical reaction that needs to be understood. This is the ultimate theoretical limitation."[8]

An ultimate theoretical limitation? Yes, at least as long as scientistic consciousness remains intent on analysis as the only possible sort of responsible thought. Genuine science may be leaving the typically modern scientistic mythos behind, of course, since exclusive emphasis on analysis and reduction is being replaced by holistic systems approaches in certain frontier sciences, notably in ecology itself. I shall have more to say about the possibility of postmodern forms of science later in this essay; but here it is important to recognize the continuing pervasiveness of reductive analysis and professional overspecialization as dangerous legacies from the modern mythos. The danger, as Commoner shows, is in continuing to relate to our environment through technologies (and policies) that themselves arise from reductive-analytical modes of consciousness.

> In sum, we can trace the origin of the environmental crisis through the following sequence. Environmental degradation largely results from the introduction of new industrial and agricultural technologies. These technologies are ecologically faulty because they are designed to solve singular, separate problems and fail to take account of the inevitable "side effects" that arise because, in nature, no part is isolated from the whole ecological fabric. In turn, the fragmented design of technology reflects its scientific foundation, for science is divided into disciplines that are largely governed by the notion that complex systems can be understood only if they are first broken into their separate component parts. This reductionist bias has also tended to shield basic science from a concern for real-life problems, such as environmental degradation.[9]

The modern world, then, has alienated itself dangerously from the natural environment, on which all, ultimately, depend for life. This has been done enthusiastically through the very successes of modern technology, the practical offspring of modern science. We are alienated not merely because we deny intrinsic value to the real world, not merely because we are obsessed with material growth and heedless of the ugliness we spread. We are alienated—and in imminent danger of terrible retribution for our self-alienation—because we have not thought or felt or perceived holistically but rather have torn into the delicate web of life with tubular vision, reductionist assumptions, and exclusively analytical logic. Our tools of objective consciousness have been powerful, but their very effectiveness, ironically, is leading remorselessly to the undoing of the modern world.

Finally, we should note a third scientific practice extended dangerously into religious vision. Objectivity is no respecter of persons, as we have seen. On one level this stands for fearless independence in the face of intimidating authority; 50 another level, we discover, this stands for deep-seated disregard for personality and its subjective traits. In the latter sense the methodological decisions of modern science may be seen as fueling a consistent attack *against anthropocentric and anthropomorphic visions of the universe.*

Galileo battled anthropocentrism when he argued for the Copernican displacement of the earth from the center of the astronomical picture; he also battled anthropormorphism when he fought Aristotelian dynamics with its baggage of "final causes." The stone does not fall to the earth because it is "seeking" its own proper place, Galileo argued; and it does not accelerate as it falls "in order" to hurry home to Mother. The stone moves as it does according to fixed mathematical laws. There are no purposes in nature in the modern imagery of things. There are forces and particles and regularities of happening; but never purposes. As Jacques Monod, the noted French molecular biologist, put it: "The cornerstone of the scientific method is the postulate that nature is objective. In other words, *systematic* denial that 'true' knowledge can be got at by interpreting phenomena in terms of final causes—that is to say, of 'purpose.' "[10]

Galileo was right about the stone, was he not? Can there be serious objection to the systematic elimination of purpose or subjective interiority from the objective universe by modern consciousness? Indeed there can. One of the most vivid such objections was voiced by Theodore Roszak in *The Making of a Counter Culture*. In essence he contends that the deliberate elimination of purpose from the natural world has destroyed human sensitivity to nature and has thereby undermined human sensitivity to the intrinsic independence of the world's being. By rigorously eliminating anthropomorphism from the objective world, the modern vision is left with an absolute gulf between human subjectivity (the In-Here) and everything else (the Out-There). Even other human beings start losing their inwardness before such a consciousness. Roszak writes:

> Now, in fact, anyone, even the most objective scientist, would fall into a state of total paralysis if he *really* believed that Out-There (beginning with his own organism and unconscious processes) was totally stupid. Nevertheless, In-Here is committed to studying Out-There as *if* it were completely stupid, meaning without intention or wisdom or purposeful pattern. In-Here cannot, if it is to be strictly objective, strive to sympathize in any way with Out-There. It must not attribute

to Out-There what cannot be observed, measured, and—ideally—formulated into articulate, demonstrable propositions for experimental verification. In-Here must maintain its alienative dichotomy at all times. And like the racist who cannot under Jim Crow conditions come to see the segregated black man as anything but a doltish and primitive nigger, so In-Here, as the unmoved spectator, cannot feel that Out-There has any ingenuity or dignity. Under this kind of scrutiny, even the other human beings who inhabit Out-There can be made stupid, for they were not made to function within laboratory conditions or according to the exacting needs of questionnaires and surveys. Under the eye of an alien observer they also begin to lose their human purposefulness.[11]

Assuming Galileo to be correct about the stone's fall, is the animal and vegetable world also barren of inwardness or intentions? If we are "objective" in Monod's sense, the question cannot even be taken seriously. Scientistic assumptions rule out the possibility in advance. But from within such a set of assumptions, cultured into a common sense, a consciousness, and a way of life, terrible consequences may follow. One consequence is callous abuse of the natural environment, dismissing any thought of the intrinsic dignity of nonhuman nature and (anthropocentrically!) reducing all thought of purposes in the universe to human purpose. Another is similarly callous abuse of men and women, as well, once they are effectively depersonalized by the habits and values of the objectivistic mythos. Torture and mass death, especially when further distanced by impersonal technology, are acts which we recognize, all too painfully, as marks of the modern world.

The high spiritual vision grown out of modern science has led to this, then. The spiritual flaws in objective consciousness have given rise to materialism, overconsumption, obsessive growth, ugliness, ecological crisis, anthropocentric insensitivity to nature, and contempt of human dignity. We stand before an alien universe created, ironically, by the best and most characteristic of our own modern heritage. Let us reflect, then, on the words of Jacques Monod, apostle of the objective consciousness but sensitive to the spiritual costs, the debit side, of modernity. "But there is this too:" he writes, "just as an initial 'choice' in the biological evolution of a species can be binding upon its entire future, so the choice of scientific *practice*, an unconscious choice in the beginning, has launched the evolution of culture on a one-way path; onto a track which nineteenth-century scientism saw leading infallibly upward to an empyrean noon hour for mankind, whereas what we see opening before us today is an abyss of darkness."[12]

NOTES

1. Cited in Jacob Bronowski, *Science and Human Values* (New York: Harper & Row, 1965), p. 66.

2. Since writing this I have been assured by Professor Priscilla Laws that good scientific work has indeed been done in this personal style, including the work of Rutherford at the turn of this century.

3. Israel Scheffler, *Science and Subjectivity* (Indianapolis: Bobbs 1967), p. 2.

4. Alfred North Whitehead, *Science and the Modern World* (New York: Free Press, 1967), p. 54.

5. Lewis Mumford, "The Pentagon of Power," *Horizon* 12 (1970): 10.

6. Cited in E. J. Dijksterhuis, *The Mechanization of the World Picture* (London: Oxford University Press, 1961), p. 362.

7. Michael Polanyi, *Personal Knowledge* (New York: Harper & Row, 1962), pp. 347–58.

8. Barry Commoner, *The Closing Circle: Nature, Man and Technology* (New York: Bantam, 1972), p. 73.

9. Ibid., p. 191.

10. Jacques Monod, *Chance and Necessity: An Essay on the Natural Philosophy of Modern Biology* (New York: Vintage, 1972), p. 21.

11. Theodore Roszak, *The Making of a Counter Culture* (New York: Doubleday, 1969), pp. 221, 222.

12. Monod, *Chance and Necessity*, p. 170.

Chapter 21

A THEISTIC EXPLANATION OF EVIL
Peter A. Bertocci

$\mathbf{I}$T is now time for us to face the problem of evil. Evil is a part of the universe we are trying to understand here, and no interpretation of the universe is adequate if it does not provide the most coherent hypothesis about the nature and purpose of evil. This is not the place to hedge; nor is it the place to be overcome by emotional resentment against evil. Our stand, if we are to be objective and reasonable, must be determined by the hypothesis most consistent with the known facts.

WHAT IS HAPPINESS?

At the very outset we encounter what in some respects is the most difficult question: What is to be considered evil? And immediately we find ourselves reaching for an answer to the question, What is the good? Now *the good* must not be wholly identified with *moral goodness*. To be morally good is to will consistently what one believes to be the best. But a person might consistently will the best he knows and be a Judas. A conception of the good life is needed to guide us in our willing. What is the ideal goal of life? Any word we use for it will have some drawback. The word *happiness*, which we shall use as a synonym for the good, suggests to many a kind of pleasure-seeking which we would immediately repudiate.

Fortunately, we can begin by referring back to the underlying theme in the conception of a perfect being (God). A perfect being, in contrast to ourselves,

From: Peter A. Bertocci, *Introduction to the Philosophy of Religion* (Englewood Cliffs, N.J.: Prentice-Hall, 1951), pp. 389–441.

lives in constant fruition or realization of all his capacities. In him there are no conflicting purposes and emotions, no inconsistency between aims and actions. All other beings depend upon him, and there is nothing in his nature or beyond it which can keep him from realizing his purposes. There emerges, then, a definite suggestion as to the nature of happiness, namely, the fulfillment of capacity in harmonious activity with all related beings.

But, the reader will say, you are talking about God and not man. Surely such happiness is impossible in the human situation with all of its limitations. And this must, of course, be granted. But need we give up the essential insight here, namely, that the good or happy life is the life which harmoniously realizes its own potentialities to the utmost? Let us see what this would mean concretely in the human situation.

An individual's happiness (his *whole*-some satisfaction rather than pleasure) would be found in his ability to develop his native endowment to *his own* limit. This undertaking calls for maximum physical health so that he may be free to meet physical hardship and enjoy the spring and vigor possible in a human body at work or play. It means mental development which will allow him not only to solve the problems of physical survival but also to satisfy and expand his intellectual interests in the many environments which encompass his life—in conversation and reading, in mathematical computation, in vivid and appreciative sense perceptions, in the enjoyment of memory and imagination, in the reflective consciousness which takes him beyond things immediate and lays open before him the many possibilities of existence. The good life involves the development of emotional sensitivity, the cultivation of the feelings so that one's emotional activity may take one from the bogs of fear, anger, self-pity, greed, and lust, to the higher land of sympathy, reverence, tenderness, wonder, joy in mastery, and forgiving love. The good life is vivified, refreshed, and expanded in the experience of beauty, and it is recreated in the experience of God.

This, of course, calls first for conscientiousness (moral goodness), the willingness to live by the best one knows, if only to discover what one can do and be. But it also calls for the wise selection from day to day of those experiences which will not only be satisfying in themselves but also will protect, as far as possible, the values in other phases of life. This means pruning the vines of one's life, encouraging growth here, limiting it there, but always with a view to the greatest possible yield. The happy life for each of us at every stage of life is always the achievement of a "concert"; each basic theme—the physical, mental, emotional, aesthetic, and religious—is woven into the pattern of the others, and each enriches the whole. Discords are there as a menace, but they bring strength and variety when surmounted. It is *creative conflict, creative control,* this matter of happiness; and success means a symphony of values, a song of gratitude to man's powers and a memorial to his success in gracefully interweaving his endowment with opportunities in the world.

This is what is meant when one says that the deepest human happiness comes only through the development of character (moral goodness). *Character is the willingness to persist in doing what one thinks is right to the best of one's ability.* However different human beings may be in their satisfactions owing to variation in their endowments, every human being capable of willing has a chance at the satisfaction which comes with the effort to achieve character. The blind man cannot enjoy the satisfactions of color experience and of vision generally, but he can have the satisfaction which character brings, however else he may compensate for his lack of sight. Whatever his abilities, whatever his circumstances, a man cannot be denied his ever-present opportunity to know that he has done his best in the pursuit of his ideals. When he is well-endowed, when the circumstances of his existence have been fortunate, and when he has done his best to make the most of his surroundings with his endowment, he does indeed enjoy more quality and the higher ranges of satisfaction in his life. But no person, regardless of endowment or circumstances, knows the height of human satisfaction if he does not know the meaning of character in his own life. To work and play with others, to trust and be trusted by others, to become a creative member of a group, to love and be loved, to enter into the never-ending joys and concerns of family life, to participate in the work of the world and feel that one "belongs" to the human venture in community living—here is human living full of conflict in values, but here is opportunity to grow as one can never grow if he walls himself out of the lives of others! Every human joy is increased if one can feel that others too participate in that enjoyment; every human joy is decreased by the thought that others are needlessly shut out of one's own joys.

To sum up: the good human being must be perfect in his kind, with his limitations. This means that, so far as possible, he will keep even his limitations from afflicting others so as not to detract from their effectiveness. His own goodness must find its proper relation to the creative control others also can achieve. Where there is "symphonic" growth, there is happiness; it is against this background that evil must be described and, in the end, evaluated.

THE NATURE OF EVIL

Hardship is not necessarily evil. Let it be clear, then, that in terms of the conception of human happiness here advocated, hardship is in itself no evil. Human beings are not lifted to their highest resourcefulness without the many inner and outer conflicts which beset them. Normal conflict is not evil, and frustration is in itself no tragedy. As a person responds to "good" or to "evil," he can develop attitudes, habits, and traits which make him a monument to human dignity and power—or he can develop attitudes, habits, and traits which smother his ability to meet other conflicts and rob him of self-confidence and independence. Human happiness, as we enjoy it from day to day and as we know it in the great souls of the race, is impossible without great risks, even without the willingness to live *with* uncertainty.

When we talk about hardship, we are likely to think of it as being caused by an absence of something normally needed for physical or mental security. But the actual fact is that many people feel insecurity or face hardship even though they are blessed with enough and more of this world's goods. Would that it were only the poor and dispossessed who miss happiness! That handsome fellow and that glamorous young lady who have been using charm and not good brains to get what they wanted may someday find themselves in situations requiring not "charm" but the capacity to perform disliked work. Their very wealth of personal attractiveness may become a menace to them. Every human being needs to use his assets effectively and responsibly. Weaknesses in personality structure do not stem necessarily from forced limitations in one's life; they may issue from abuse of rich endowment.

Hardship and evil as disciplinary. Ultimately then, good and evil in human life, however conditioned by forces inside and outside of us, are largely a matter of the spirit. "Good" conditions do not necessarily create happiness, and "bad" conditions do not necessarily help or hinder happiness. A human being must find his happiness *through* his conditions but not *in* his conditions; bitterness of spirit, defeatism, insecurity, and suspicion can be developed in both good and bad "external" conditions. Until a man has overcome evil in his own spirit, until he has kept it from maiming his zest for cooperative living, he is not cured. Evil is never overcome and goodness is never achieved unless the inner victory is won and the value in every event is appreciated. We come back to our first suggestion. Evil is not simply hardship, but it is any condition which keeps the individual, and the commonwealth of individuals, from the self-fulfillment of which each is capable.

We have been saying that even if we lived in circumstances which everywhere encouraged goodness, this in itself would not necessarily make human beings happier. The decision to use the world for better or for worse would still remain with them. We have also said that no matter how bad a situation might be, there is always an attitude that can be taken to it which will help quarantine the evil and force it to contribute to some good. There is, therefore, real point in Ferré's remarks: "Those who suffer, incurably ill, often embody the fullest answer. What matters most in life is not how we explain but how we accept suffering. Having accepted it, we find a new light breaking through. . . . To accept suffering as a gift from God *to be used for others* is hard, but suffering so accepted opens the door to a new world and to the real God."[1] Indeed, it may well be said that there is no situation in life from which some good and evil cannot conceivably be realized. No matter what else we say about good and evil in what follows, let it be clear that we would not deny that moral good and moral evil must be a part of any universe in which creativity is to be a fundamental factor in human happiness.

But now we must emphasize the other part of the picture: the limitations and suffering for which man is not responsible. Men do sin; they do transgress their own ideals. The suffering which they initiate by so doing is a necessary part of any "vale of soul making." But men do not suffer simply because they have disobeyed the moral law. Indeed, if all the suffering were punishment for the abuse of free will, the question might still be raised whether the suffering actually inflicted fitted the crime. The undeniable fact is that there is much more suffering in the world than neatly fits any moral purpose. Granted that much suffering can be used as a means to goodness, the stubborn fact remains that there is a great deal of human and animal suffering which falls beyond any disciplinary purpose. If suffering is the shadow which helps human beings to appreciate the light, there is altogether too much shadow in multitudes of lives; there is much more, certainly, than is necessary to throw goodness into relief.

Nondisciplinary evil. We must, then, not allow our interest in looking on the sunny side of suffering to leave us insensitive to the reality of pain, mental and physical, which not only makes moral effort difficult but actually destroys goods otherwise available. However suffering may be used for goodness, suffering in itself can never be good, for its very nature is to destroy some good. Were this not so, why resist it? Why plead that it be turned to goodness? "The real problem of suffering comes not because it denies us what we actually and sometimes cheaply want, but because it cuts across our critically judged wants and blocks the reasonable good."[2] In other words, it is all too easy to talk about the necessity of suffering in a moral universe. It is all too easy to forget that in a given life, suffering, especially to the degree often experienced, is neither merited nor necessary to deepen appreciation. Which of us does not know the parent who has been able to turn the incessant illness in his family into strength of character? But would the contour of his life have become more rounded had better health prevailed?

A particular man can be challenged to grow in character by some evil, but let it be poured into his life in a continuous stream, and that particular life simply may not stand the strain. If the spirit and body do not break, the mind often does, and a life which could otherwise have enjoyed beauty, human service, fellowship, work, and play is now reduced to dependence and to a mere shadow of existence. War has in some cases helped to create the "happy warrior" with all those manly virtues the militarist extols. But for how many men, forced to unloose upon each other the forces of nature, physical and psychological, has it reduced the quality of life, the very belief in life as more than an urge to survive? Man does need a certain amount of physical, mental, and emotional stability if he is to fulfill his own potentialities even reasonably well. It is only the hero of melodrama who can successfully withstand all odds. The upheavals of nature, the floods, cyclones, earthquakes, the cancers, the excruciating pain and mental torture—these and their effects man does not create; he simply has to accept and make the most of them. Even if he overcomes the ordeals, he does not come through unscathed. There is such a thing as too much strain, and in that excess of strain the very power to grow becomes gnarled and stunted.

It becomes necessary, then, to distinguish the evil which is the result of man's abuse of free will (*moral* evil) from the evil which comes to him against his will (*nonmoral* evil). As we have seen, both moral evil and nonmoral evil can, to some degree at least, be transmuted into goodness. The fact nevertheless remains that both moral and nonmoral evil are frequently greater than human effort and intelligence can cope with. There is more evil than can serve any disciplinary purpose. We must, therefore, discriminate *nondisciplinary* evil—that is, all evil, whether it be man's fault or not, whose destructive effect, so far as we know, is greater than any good which may come from it. One may take the best attitude one can toward his limitations, his blindness— "They also serve who only stand and wait." But it is probably even better for Milton, and for his society, if he is less impeded in action and word. If a Miltonic spirit needs to be curbed, isn't blindness a rather drastic discipline? In such instances, there is simply too wide a residue of disvalue, granted the partial good which may be realized through it.

Such effects of evil raise again persistent questions. In the light of the disciplinary and nondisciplinary evils which lie about us on every hand, does it make sense to believe in God? In particular, how can we claim that God is a Person, omniscient, omnipotent, and all-loving. Certainly, if God is all-powerful and all-knowing, he could have framed a universe in which the unnecessary afflictions of evil were absent. If God is omnipotent, and therefore the creator of so much evil, how can he be good? Or if he is good, and did not intend evil, can he be omnipotent in the sense defined? Must there not be something beyond the control of his good will which is the source of evil in the world?

The traditional answer to the question, affirming that God is omnipotent and all-good, has much in it to merit our consideration. But there are weaknesses, too, and these will have to be indicated.

WEAKNESSES IN THE TRADITIONAL EXPLANATION OF EVIL

Weakness of procedure in argument. It has been a central thesis of this essay that any conception of God or of the universe should be justified by its ability to explain the facts of human experience as a whole more completely than can any other hypothesis. Now, the traditional explanation of evil does not seem to be adequately grounded in human experience. The traditionalist claims that all evil performs a moral function. But in order to defend this claim he argues not from what he knows about the world, but from a conception of what might be. Nondisciplinary evil, he thinks, can be seen in a light which transforms it into a *necessary* part of the *best* (compossible) world. If we knew enough about the world, he insists, we would realize that it is one symphonic system of goodness. So much of what we know is good that we are justified in assuming that a broader vision would prove that the whole is a perfect system for moral development.

The reply is: Much of what we experience is not morally beneficial; in the world as we know it there is no doubting the fact that more evil exists than is needed to provide a sparring partner who will extend us for our own good in the moral fight. To raise the warning: "If we knew enough . . ." works both ways. If we knew enough . . . we might know how wrong the traditionalist hypothesis is. If empirical coherence is to be our test of truth, such *ifs* don't count. Our hypothesis must be built on what we do know, on what we have experienced, and not what we might experience—for what we might experience may well invalidate both hypotheses.

Let us underscore this matter of procedure in argument. We have every right to build imaginative conceptions of the world and God, such as the traditionalist's, and to consider whether the facts do fit in with that conception. But we have no right to allow any *conception* of the world and God to bias our interpretation of present and past facts of experience, especially if it outruns those facts. The conception might help us to look for facts we do not have, or it may help us to see what the facts may be like; but it should not find acceptance unless it does explain the known facts better than any other conception does. The *absolutistic* conception of God, as we shall now call the traditional view, gives a possible explanation of evil, but in dealing with nondisciplinary evil it seems to force the facts instead of being consistent with them. What we need to remember is that conception of an absolute, omnipotent, all-good God is not based on any more facts than those we actually have, and in the last analysis it must stand or fall by them. It has no theoretical precedence, as such, over any other conception.

A second fallacious assumption presses on the first. The absolutist presupposes that a universe in which God is all-good *and* omnipotent is closer to the mind's desire than any other conception of God. But this view of perfection is itself debatable. There are those who hold that only the traditional conception of perfection is consistent with religious experience. But religious experience is certainly subject to more than one interpretation. In sum, absolutists frequently assume that their conception of God is necessarily superior to any other, when, as a matter of fact, this needs to be argued. If it were true that an omnipotent, all-good God is preferable to an all-good God who is growing in power in *some* respects, it would still be necessary to show that such a superior conception of God did fit the facts of good and evil more coherently. As we shall see, there seem to be good reasons not only for denying that it does, but also for affirming that another conception of God is more coherent and at least equally inspiring. *This world is not an ideal training ground for persons.* Granted that moral freedom does involve the possibility of evil as well as the possibility of good, we must realize that even the advantages of moral freedom, precious as they are, seem to exact superfluous loss of value. As Brightman says:

> Nevertheless, human freedom leaves many aspects of evil, even of moral evil, unexplained. Why are there in the nature of things, independent of human choice, so many temptations and allurements to evil choices? And why are the consequences of some evil choices so utterly debasing and disastrous? It is very hard to reconcile some religious utterances on temptation with the facts. Saint Paul says: "God is faithful, who will not suffer you to be tempted above that ye are able" (1 Cor. 10:13). Yet the pressure, physiological, psychological, and social, to which some men, women, and children are subjected seems to most observers to be unendurable. Is it just to ascribe all of the sins and vices of poverty-stricken refugees or un-employed families to their own freedom, or even to all human freedom put together?[3]

This comment and others take on greater force if we try to frame for ourselves a conception of an ideal training ground for the development of moral personality, an ideal "vale of soul-making." Granted freedom to choose between alternatives, we have insisted that man's freedom would have to be limited, and that man would have to live in a world so constituted that he could dependably predict the consequences of his actions. But another requirement is called for if we are to be challenged without being discouraged—if, indeed, we are to be so challenged that we can, on our own initiative, continue to make progress despite setbacks. This requirement is that we should not face odds, either as consequences of our own free action or as environmental conditions, which are too heavy for our abilities to bear, and thus cause unfruitful frustration and despair as well as the loss of other values.

To suggest an analogy: every teacher who is concerned about the growth of his students is faced with the problem of assigning the amount and quality of work which will call for effort on the part of each student and yet be within his range of abilities and educational preparation. A perfect classroom situation would be one in which there could be the assignment of work which would keep each student on his toes and yet not allow his mistakes, moral or nonmoral, to cost him so dearly that whole ranges of value are lost to him and others. Similarly, a perfect "vale of soul-making" involves not only a dependable world in which freedom and effort are basic, but one also in which the consequences of moral and nonmoral evil do not exceed human ability to transform them into good.

Is excess evil due to a recalcitrant aspect of God's own nature? Professor Edgar S. Brightman shares Montague's insight that the explanation of excess evil must be found within the being of God himself. But his view of God's relation to the world of nature enables Brightman to avoid the difficulty with which Montague is faced. For reasons which will appear as we proceed, Brightman's hypothesis seems more adequate than these others we have considered. Although Brightman's view of nature is not absolutely essential to his conviction that the cause of nondisciplinary evil is within God's nature, we shall understand his reasoning all the more if we glance briefly at his conception of the world.

Brightman is a personal idealist. This means that for him what we call the physical universe is not some nonmental stuff or electrical energy which God created, as many dualistic theists have held. For Brightman what we call the physical or spatial world is a part of God's nature, and as such it is mental in structure. A chair, crowbar, or mountain *is* the energizing of God's will. This is not to identify God with the physical world. The spatial world is an expression of God's nature, but God is more than the physical universe, as some pantheistic or monistic thinkers would hold. Indeed, God creates free persons, and these persons are no part of God, though they are ever sustained by him. *Personal idealism,* then, refers to the view that everything in the "physical" world is the energizing of the cosmic Person; and all other distinct mental beings are the creation of God and not part of him. Brightman, then, escapes the difficulty we noted in all views which hold that there is something not God which is coeternal with him. For the world is in reality one with God, a part of his eternal nature.

How, then, does Brightman explain nondisciplinary evil? He cannot resort to some being outside of God which God must "persuade" to conform to his will. But he does postulate that there is an aspect of God's mind, which he calls The Given, that God must take account of in all his creative activity. God is finite because he cannot completely control The Given.

In order to understand Brightman's view of the relation of The Given to God's mind, we must become aware of the basic structure of the human mind which is analogous to God's mind up to a point.

Every finite mind is a unity of three factors—not separate parts, but distinguishable phases. The first is agency, or activity, or what we commonly refer to as will. But activity would be meaningless unless it took some form. We cannot think, for example, without manifesting logical principles, or trying to satisfy the idea of coherence. Moreover, when we choose between actions, we do so in the light of some moral principle. Formless human activity is a nonexistent fact, though, of course, we do not always completely con-form to the ideals of reason or goodness which we have in mind.

But what keeps us from such conforming? Specifically, what in our lives do we have to think about and act upon? Not our desires alone, but sensations—of color, touch, smell, sound, and so forth. We construct the world we perceive by selectively thinking about these "brute" sensations which are continuous with our sconsciousness. As we shift our gazes from this book, we find ourselves flooded by more sensations that we can count. All we can do about them is to select among them and to organize them in certain ways. For example, we organize the sensations composing "window" and distinguish them from those continuous with them composing "wall." Our desires and interests, it is true, influence where we look and help us to select what we pay attention to; but there is no escaping the stream of sensations forced upon us.

Our perceptual experience, however, is only part of the story about the content of our conscious experience. We find ourselves experiencing pleasantness and unpleasantness in many forms; we cannot do much about the fact that they are there, although we can control our attitude toward them. A toothache is both sensory pain and unpleasant, but it is unpleasant in a different way from a pinprick. We can will to interpret these feelings and sensations in one way rather than another, even if we cannot do anything about their being what they are. *These* sensory experiences, *these* pleasant and unpleasant feelings are the content which our thinking must organize and our will-agency do something about; but our thinking and willing can never do without these "brute parts" or others; our wills can neither create nor destroy these feelings and sensations, although we may direct and control them.

We must add one more factor on the content side of experience. We all have desires, wants, and emotions which, once more, we do not create, but which we simply find. It is our task to control them in accordance with some ideal of reason and goodness. These brute facts, of sense, of feeling, of desire, are stimuli and challenges to activity. "In fact, all experience is a constant activity, which seeks to impose the forms of reason on the content of brute fact."[4]

We can phrase this description of human experience in another way. We can say that to the human will both an unreasoned, "raw" content and rational norms are *given*. After all, our wills cannot alter the content of sensations, and our wills cannot change the validity or invalidity of a syllogism; these are *given* to our wills. Obviously, the word *given* has a special meaning here. It means that no human being ever creates either the laws of reason or the sensations, feelings, and desires which he finds in his experience. To summarize, there is a *given* in any human experience: rational form and ideals, on the one hand, and unreasoned desires, feelings, and sensations which may be brought into conformity with the rational principles on the other.

To the extent that we, in willing, consistently strive to organize our sensory and emotional experiences, and to the extent that we realize and enjoy the utmost value possible in our lives, we are *controlling* our unreasoned (nonrational) *given* in accordance with the rational *given*—namely, the norms of reason and the values which we approve. To the extent that the will is overcome by the nonrational *given*, we can be said to be controlled by it. Our problem in life is to will to control the nonrational *given* in the light of the rational ideals we recognize. Evil comes into our life in two forms: (a) as moral evil, when we do not will the best that we know; and (b) as nonmoral pain, frustration, and destruction of value owing to factors beyond the control of our will.

In basic structure, God's experience does not differ from ours. There is form and content in God's mind, and there is challenge, enjoyment, and struggle in his life. Thus, arguing from analogy, Brightman holds: "Our experience of activity would be evidence for the cosmic will of God; 'our experience of form' would be evidence for his uncreated eternal reason; and our experience of brute fact would be evidence for his uncreated nonrational content."[5] What this means specifically is that God's will creates neither his rational norms nor the brute fact in his experience.

One may ask why Brightman holds that rational norms (and ethical, for that matter) are uncreated? Why does he hold that the structure of logic is coeternal with God, the being who is unbegun and unending? The answer is that if reason were not coeternal with God's will, we would have to say that his will could create the laws of logic. In other words, before that creation, God's will and nature would be completely nonlogical! This hypothesis is not only psychologically inconceivable; it is inconsistent with what we know about the world and human experience. A nonlogical God would have no reason for anything. How could nonlogical, unreasoning being create a logical structure never exemplified anywhere? Or, if it existed outside of his mind, how could he appreciate it, being logically ignorant? No, if we are to explain whatever logical structure the world exemplifies and minds enjoy, it must be because the unbegun and unending Mind of God finds rational norms in its very nature. It is the very nature of logic to be eternally valid.

We are now ready for Brightman's own statement of the nature of his finite-infinite God.

> God is personal consciousness of eternal duration; his consciousness is an eternally active will, which eternally finds and controls The Given within every moment of his eternal experience. The Given consists of the eternal, uncreated laws of reason and also of equally eternal and uncreated processes of nonrational consciousness which exhibit all the ultimate qualities of sense objects (*qualia*), disorderly impulses and desires, such experiences as pain and suffering, the forms of space and time, and whatever in God is the source of surd evil. The common characteristics of all that is "given" (in the technical sense) is, first, that it is eternal within the experience of God and hence had no other origin than God's eternal being; and, secondly, that it is not a product of will or created activity. For The Given to be in consciousness at all means that it must be process; but unwilled, nonvoluntary consciousness is distinguishable from voluntary consciousness, both in God and in man. God's finiteness thus does not mean that he began or will end; nor does it mean he is limited by anything external to himself.[6]

In Brightman's view, then, the evil in the world which has no conceivable good purpose is due not to the fact that God wills evil, but to the fact that he finds *in* his nature a nonrational content which he can no more rid himself of than he can of the laws of his thinking. Both the rational and the nonrational are aspects of his unified nature. His will does not create them, but it has to take both into account in every action. God is morally perfect in that he consistently wills the best he knows. But God's will cannot overcome all the recalcitrant elements in the nonrational Given, that is, those processes in God which might be compared to the sensory, affective, and emotional life of human beings. Yet God is unwavering in his struggle to make the best of every situation. Although he cannot achieve all that he plans, he has managed to control the nonrational content of his nature rather than be controlled by it. Again in Brightman's own words:

> God's will is eternally seeking new forms of embodiment of the good. God may be compared to a creative artist eternally painting new pictures, composing new dramas and new symphonies. In this process, God, finding The Given as an inevitable ingredient, seeks to impose ever new combinations of given rational form on the given nonrational content. Thus The Given is, on the one hand, God's instrument for the expression of his aesthetic and moral purposes, and, on the other, an obstacle to their complete and perfect expression. God's control of The Given means that he never allows The Given to run wild, that he always subjects it to law and uses it, as far as possible, as an instrument for realizing the ideal good. Yet the divine control does not mean complete determination; for in some situations The Given, with its purposeless processes, constitutes so great an obstacle to divine willing that the utmost endeavors of God lead to a blind alley and temporary defeat. At this point, God's control means that no defeat or frustration is final; that the will of God, partially thwarted by obstacles in the chaotic Given, finds new avenues of advance, and forever moves on in the cosmic creation of new values.[7]

We now see that Montague and Brightman would agree that God's will is perfect. Both would also insist that there is that in God which does not have the approval of his will but which he, as the long ages of evolution have shown, is controlling. But Brightman's view of the nonrational Given as part of the unified dynamic process which is God's nature makes it easier to understand why God can and does control the nonrational content of his nature. If the nonrational Given is a phase of God's total unity, and not made of different stuff, there is reason for supposing that God's will could influence it, even as we, for example, influence our emotions. We must here be careful not to think of God's nature as made up of three separate compartments, any more than we think of any moment of our own experience as having three parts. In discussion, Brightman inveighs against "the lump theory of The Given." The basic fact is that the human and divine mind are complex unities within which different functions are distinguishable.

We are emphasizing this point because one of the criticisms of this view which seems to score heavily is the contention that some sort of dualism is set up within God's nature.[8] Thus, one critic says: "Since the nonrational Given is, by hypothesis, neither in the 'eternal reason,' nor an expression of it, nor 'satisfied' by it, it is hard to see how it can be within the framework of causal law or any other intelligible connection."[9]

That fear is understandable but unfounded. It overlooks the empirical complexity of any possible personality, as well as the experience of control. If the nonrational Given were not as interwoven into the very being of God as are his will and reason, then there would be point to the fear that it might stand "outside" the will and reason of God and thus be unresponsive to the volition and thought of God. But Brightman's view is that in the unified Person, the phase which we distinguish as "content" rather than form or activity is responsive to control by rational will and as such must be within the framework of the laws of God's nature. Were this not so, there could not be any control of The Given, a control evidenced by the order of nature and by the realization of value by man. Human beings do not and cannot always control their emotions, but we do not take this to mean that emotions are not within the causal framework of human mind. They are within the framework of our being but not always within the power of the will as it attempts to realize a rational purpose.

ARE OBJECTIONS TO A FINITE-INFINITE GOD VALID?

The first reaction to such an idea of a finite-infinite[10] God, especially if one has believed in a God who controls everything at will, is one of panic. If God's will is not omnipotent, maybe the order of the world will become disorder at any moment, or maybe there will be a reversal of the process of control and God, in turn, will become the victim rather than the controller of The Given.

Can we give assurance that it is absolutely impossible in theory for such a reversal to take place? The answer is no. However, if our conclusions are to be based on the facts at hand, we may confidently estimate such a reversal as highly improbable. The fact that there is a world order, indeed, a world order in which values are achievable, in which human beings may enjoy interaction with nature and cooperation with each other; the fact that cosmic evolution, for all its failures, has nevertheless, at least in our corner of the universe, involved growth and increase of value—here are the basic grounds for believing that he who has controlled the nonrational Given may be expected to continue and improve his control. No other hypothesis is more reasonable.

To be sure, one who has believed all to be absolutely within the control of God's goodness may feel that his universe has lost some of its virtue because he must now face a possibility of disaster and the reality of retardation and struggle. Such a one must be reminded that the value-norms of existence are, and will continue to be, the eternal purposes of the Being upon whom the order of existence and of value depend. He will have to give up the comfort of feeling that *all* is perfectly well in the universe—a dubious comfort often disturbed by the apparition of excess evil. But will he not gain religiously through the realization that in his universe the struggle for increase in value is an eternal process, and through the realization that every human act which makes for decrease of value will be adding to the evil which God is trying to reduce and quarantine?

We are here confronting the final massive objection to the theory of a finite-infinite God. The idea of a finite God, it is claimed, is not acceptable to the religious consciousness. For the religious consciousness demands that a perfect Being, a being consummate in every respect, be real. Now, there is no denying that a profound train of thought and of mystical feeling the world over has insisted that absolutely perfect Being alone can satisfy the mind and the heart. For such philosophers and mystics the theory we defend is only a modern instance of an ancient error: to imagine God as finite, and to have seemed to find God only through some finite idol or person—Christ or the saints—whereas the disciplined mind and heart will stop only at unimaginable perfection as ultimate reality.

Much might be said in actual historical refutation of this claim, which, after all, demands the condemnation of other forms of religious experience in the name of *one* type. But let us raise a more fundamental question. Is the demand for completeness—for nothing-more-to-add, and no-further-goal-to-accomplish—the only ideal which recommends itself to the human mind and heart?[11] Let us grant that in our theoretical, artistic, moral, and religious living there are many moments when a goal is demanded which ends all striving for further goals. We yearn for an end to partiality, to incompleteness, to struggle, to imperfection, and even an end to growth. Surely, we feel, life and existence must be more than a struggle for goals and objectives supplanted, the moment we achieve them, by other goals. In this mood, we assert: Somewhere in the universe there must be escape from the taint of incompleteness and the heartache when, whatever other joy may be present, we come alive to the fact that the realized ideal is inadequate. Can it be that everything in the universe is permeated by a not-yet which disturbs the calm and serenity of life?

Three things should be said in reply. First, if the change in the world were simply change and not growth, there would be more point to this plea. Here, once more, let us seek an analogy. As men realize goal after goal, the past and its good is not lost but rather preserved on a higher level. The same can more surely be said of a being of God's stature. God's present, like ours, is fuller because of the total process of the past. In a universe in which The Given is controlled, there will be no moment when the values of the past are lost to the present and the oncoming future.

Second, as long as there are finite beings about whom God cares, there must be a goal not yet realized for God as well as for these finite creatures. If we suffer, God cannot be conceived as not suffering. If we are incomplete, he still has work to do. When we ask for a God complete in every respect, do we know what we ask? Even if he were *all activity* and no development, it would be impossible to understand how his completeness would be realized if the working out of his plans depended in any way on finite cooperation.

Third, while we as persons know the joy of fruition in some respects, and then think we can understand what complete fruition in every respect can be, we enjoy that fruition in part because we have the joy of arriving at a goal we did not earlier enjoy. Can God have such joy without the consciousness of a task well done as his past? We must not forget that the greatest values we know are not, so to speak, a passive contemplation of static goods. The seeking of truth, the willing of courage and goodness, the creating of beautiful things—in such active striving to build, to fulfill, and to sustain we find our deepest reality as persons. Is perfection our goal? Or is perfection in fact nothing less than perfectibility? Do our minds and hearts crave a point of rest in beauty, truth, and goodness? Or do they yearn that the truth, beauty, and goodness we have be further developed? Does the value of the idea of perfection consist, after all, in its power to energize toward growth?

NOTES

1. Nels F. S. Ferré, *Evil and the Christian Faith* (New York: Harper & Bros., 1947), p. 107.

2. J. Seelye Bixler, "Notes on the Problem of Suffering, "*The Crozer Quarterly,* 1944, p. 291.

3. Edgar S. Brightman, *A Philosophy of Religion* (New York: Prentice-Hall, 1940), pp. 260–61.

4. Ibid., p. 320.

5. Ibid., p. 321.

6. Ibid., pp. 336–37.

7. Ibid., p. 338.

8. Cf. A. C. Knudson, *The Doctrine of God* (New York: Abingdon, 1930), pp. 272–75, and the *Doctrine of Redemption* (New York: Abingdon, 1933), pp. 204–12; L. Harold DeWolf, *The Religious Revolt Against Reason* (New York: Harper & Bros., 1949), pp. 170–72, 184–85; and Andrew Banning, "Professor Brightman's Theory of a Limited God. A Criticism," *The Harvard Theological Review* 27(1934): 145–68.

9. DeWolf, *Religious Revolt,* p. 184.

10. In all other attributes except power and knowledge God is, of course, infinite.

11. See R. A. Tsanoff, *Religious Crossroads* (New York: Dutton, 1942), chap. XII.

Chapter 22

THE SEARCH FOR A POSTMODERN CONSCIOUSNESS: THE SENSE OF MYSTERY

Frederick Ferré

POLYMYTHIC Organicism is a religious posture for those, like me, who find this to be time "between models"—both cognitive and valuational—that might in more settled eras shape a single confident vision of the ultimate. It is a religious stance that affirms as legitimate and exciting the possibility of pluralism in mythic imagery within a context of undergirding fundamental values. It is not a religious reponse *without* organizing imagery but, rather, one with *many* value-focusing sets of myths welcome within it.

Such a religious posture would necessarily sacrifice the sometimes fanatical power that comes from wholehearted and single-minded involvement within a single grand myth. It would require a tolerance for ambiguity that, to some, would seem a far cry from the fervor that we in the West have frequently associated with religious sincerity. But the other side of such tolerance is liberation: liberation from imprisonment is a single set of images that no longer seems quite large enough for life, and liberation from the parochialism of association and imagination that ties us to the mythos of a single community. Polymythic organicism does not mourn over lost certitudes, but rejoices in the new dimensions of possibility that are open to view.

From: Frederick Ferré, *Shaping the Future: Resources for the Post-Modern World* (New York: Harper & Row, 1976), pp. 112–21.

These new spiritual possibilities, though plural, are not shapeless, of course. Some mythic forms simply do not meet polymythic organicism's criterion of appropriateness. The images of unlimited material "progress," for example, or the alienating world pictures of scientism, or the exclusive preoccupation with the Promethean myth, would be resisted on behalf of fundamental organismic values that make this religious posture take on, for all its mythic pluralism, a definite shape.

This shape reflects certain fundamental features of healthy organic life. At a minimum these would include, first, acknowledgement of the constant balance between growth and death (*anabolism* and *catabolism*) that maintains healthy organisms at proper scale and within finite limits. The miracle of homeostasis, in other words, becomes an object of deep valuation.

Likewise, second, a valued feature of healthy organic life must be the balance between local differentiation of function and holistic mutuality of connection. Even in unicellular organisms we find this balance between differentiation and connectedness; much more strikingly we find it exemplified in the higher, vastly more complex organisms wherein local semiautonomy and the general good coexist harmoniously.

And, third, the balance between necessity and spontaneity will be a valued feature of healthy organic life. Living organisms neither are exempt from the general constraints of physical law nor are they mere flotsam on the causal tide of nature; they have the power of invention, of novel stratagems in response to novel challenge; they have some degree—greater in the higher organisms—of creative self-determinism within the larger determinations of the natural order.

These three features: *homeostasis,* differentiated *holism,* and *creativity,* represent fundamental values for polymythic organicism. Drawn from the basic image of healthy life, they are capable of supporting definite attitudes even while remaining hospitably open to a variety of grander mythic exemplifications— Christian, Marxist, astrological, shamanistic, and the like—so long as these are suitably interpreted and lived.

What sorts of attitudes, in general, toward our beliefs, toward nature, and toward our fellows, might be associated with this religious strategy for "living the transition" between the modern and the postmodern worlds?

First, polymythic organicism demands a sophisticated attitude towards our own belief systems. We need a revitalized sense of mystery in knowing. At best our cognitive constructs are only that: cognitive constructs. The better they are the more they reveal the mysteries beyond.

There is a new sense of mystery is the sciences. This, it seems to me, should be perceived as a healthy awareness, to be greeted without fear or despair. And it should be perceived as appropriate to all our cognitive constructs—philosophical, political, historical, religious—as well as scientific. Such a perception will lead to a new sense of limits in all our attempts at knowing, and a new readiness to accept those limits without rage and even with joy.

Our beliefs are finite dwelling places for our minds. We build them as carefully as we can, if we are wise, using the sturdiest materials we can find and then putting them together in the best way we are able. They generally serve us adequately, sustaining and defending us tolerably well. Built spaciously they can house our fellows in great number and can thereby make for civilized community. But it should not shock us that there are other such dwelling places besides ours, or that they will not last forever, or that there are vast domains still outside our highest arching vaults. Even a fine house need not be the only one—or the only type of one. Even a well-constructed house experiences the shocks of weather and the erosion of wear. This means that as we "live the transition" we should school ourselves to be alert to the main alternatives to our own familiar structures, and that we should discipline ourselves to recognize the need for repair, remodeling—or even sometimes moving, since no less finite dwelling places may still be better or worse, larger or smaller, than one another.

Ambiguity need not be destructive or paralyzing, then. It may be liberating and zestful if our attitudes are prepared for it and if our sense of human possibilities is kept wisely in touch with our sense of human finitude. Living the transition to the postmodern world challenges us to such attitudes toward our own beliefs.

Likewise, second, polymythic organicism requires a major change in our attitudes toward the natural environment. We need a revitalized sense of the mystery around us. In that sensitivity we shall regain our feeling for the semi-autonomous "more" in nature that modern consciousness drove out: "more," that is, than we can fully comprehend in our finite theories of nature, and "more" than we can—or ought—to control for narrow human ends. Such a sense of mystery leads directly, then, to the voluntary acceptance of organismic limits on our treatment of nature. It will require us to accept a broader time frame for our policies regarding nature. The larger needs of "then" will need to be more heavily weighed in the balance with the parochial wants of "now." But, further, the very control syndrome itself—the supposition that we have or should aspire to absolute autonomy unbalanced by holistic mutuality, whether in the short term or the long—will need to acknowledge its limits, not out of resignation but out of healthy affirmation of the human situation as properly one of organic partnership with, rather than sheer dominion over, the natural world around us.

For this attitude to be adopted with good will, however, another one is necessary, springing from the voluntary affirmation of homeostatic limits: namely, the acknowledgement of the virtues of thrift, simplicity, or bare sufficiency. As human numbers grow and the earth's resources shrink, the material share we can claim as fairly ours will necessarily diminish with the years ahead. The limits I speak of will be enforced by nature, whether we adopt them gracefully or not; my suggestion is that we seize the moral initiative.

Natural organic limits need not be demoralizing, then. They may spur us to a fuller sense of what besides material consumption constitutes fulfillment in human life. Rather than struggling vainly against the narrowing limits, only to taste the bitter fruit of defeat, we may prepare ourselves now, with dignity, to seek other creative satisfactions. Living the transition to the postmodern world challenges us to newly constructive attitudes toward nature.

Third, and still similarly, polymythic organicism requires that we cultivate distinctive attitudes toward our fellow humans. We need a revitalized sense of the mystery in human variety, creativity, and intrinsic worth. There is urgent need to upgrade our respect for the uniqueness, the privileged "insideness," the subjective stubbornness of human individuals. Each of us, is, in principle, hidden in the center of his or her consciousness from all others. We all see the world from our own point of view. There are structural similarities and holistic connections, of course, or there could be no language, no community, no distinctively human life. But it is also distinctively human to have a certain opaqueness all one's own—the mystery of "me," *my* being, *my* values, *my* birth, *my* death, *my* purposes, *my* creative spontaneity.

In this sense of mystery in dealing with fellow human beings, we shall find the attitudinal basis for the voluntary acceptance of limits, yet again. One of our limits will be felt at the point where we have been accustomed to manipulating other persons. Whether in large numbers or singly, whether for benevolent motives or for selfish ones, the one-way manipulative, controlling attitude is wrong from the viewpoint of polymythic organicism. Technologies of behavior, however well intended, belong to the technolatrous frame of mind. They neglect the precious, mysterious, interior of the persons being controlled. They neglect the creative inventiveness of healthy organic life as well as the proper organic mutuality in holistic controls. What I earlier called the control syndrome is what has brought modern mankind to its present parlous condition: we feel we must unilaterally control every aspect of nature to maximize our wealth; thus, we must control our wealth to enjoy it; thus, we must control our neighbor so that he or she will not steal from us; thus, we must control the society to preserve our privileges; thus, we must control world markets and resources so that our society will prosper; thus, we must control a military establishment capable of controlling the covetous (or hostile, etc.) impulses of other societies who also have military establishments aimed at controlling our similar impulses; thus, we must control the balance of terror . . . if we can! And so it goes, to competition and to war. Unchecked by recognition of the mysterious dignity of others and the need for real mutuality, the control syndrome leads to disaster. *Self*-limitation, in contrast, is always in the context of our subjective recognition of the dignity and freedom of our own selfhood. The dangers of living the transition require much more of the latter (voluntary limitation) and much less of the former (manipulation of others).

Equally, the healthy sense of mystery in other personal centers of experience and value will place limits on our expectation of mythological uniformity. The possibilities of pluralism will be accepted as natural and less threatening. The rich variety of the world may be more cheerfully embraced. We may celebrate our differences rather than attack each other, given these attitudes.

Self-limitation in dealing with other persons need not be demeaning, then. It may be evocative of new, creative social patterns based on mutual respect rather than mistrust, competition, conformity, and manipulation. Living the transition to the postmodern world challenges us to fresh, reconciling attitudes toward our fellows.

This survey of attitudes illustrates the general value stance represented by polymythic organicism, especially as these translate into an ethic for living the transition. But an ethic is not a whole religion. If polymythic organicism adopts such a hospitable attitude toward a *variety* of mythic models, is it not the equivalent of living *without* myths? I suspect that for many the demands of pluralistic openness will be too heavy to maintain; and for them a single religious mythos may be needed for valuational and intellectual wholeness. As long as the religious imagery adopted is compatible with the basic postmodern values we have seen to be needed, no harm is done, though some of the excitement and richness of pluralism is lost.

For others, however, none of the available myths may be "living" to the degree that wholehearted commitment is possible without hypocrisy. If so, perhaps something I wrote exactly a decade ago for the concluding pages of my *Basic Modern Philosophy of Religion* may be helpful here:

> For those who find themselves in this position . . . it may become necessary to learn how to live without religious models. But this is not the same as abandoning all responsible religion. If my general view of religion has merit, a person's religion is not constituted first of all by his allegiance to imagery but rather by his most comprehensive and intensive valuations. A religious life without [commitment to a single set of] imagery is no contradiction, therefore, though I suppose that it must be prepared to sacrifice the help such imagery provides in achieving the practical and theoretical interconnections called for by the ideal of coherence. To this extent, then, it will also be handicapped in attaining the sense of understanding that might be hoped for. But despite this I must confess that the present moment seems to be a time "between models" for me and for many others, a time when we are required to acknowledge our nakedness with whatever rueful dignity we can muster and admit that despite our cravings—of which we need not be ashamed—we do not understand as well as we might wish.
>
> Living with partial meanings and "broken myths" is one thing; but must this then not exclude the possibility of anything like a rich religious life? Must a life

"between models" be parched and shallow, without the heights of worship, the depths of prayer, the breadth of fellowship? So it is often assumed, but I believe otherwise.

At its most general, and aside from the particulars with which it is always concretely found, worship is the unlimited adoration, through whatever forms are taken to be appropriate, of whatever is held to be "sacred," i.e., whatever is valued beyond everything else as most pressingly important and most unavoidably relevant. There is no special posture, no special location essential to worship in this sense. Standing in a picket line may be as much an exalting act of worship as kneeling in a cathedral. I frankly admit that teaching or writing philosophy are, for me, sometimes sacred acts. Likewise prayer, the aspect of worship involving the conscious entertainment in thought and affirmation in will of the sacred is not necessarily forfeit for those who must live "between models." On the contrary, everyone who cares deeply about his values both can and should pause to reaffirm, from time to time, his basic priorities. Philosophers and prophets alike warn us that from the distractions and compromises of our daily pursuits we need to withdraw and regain perspective. Philosophers are inclined to call this movement "contemplation"; prophets call it prayer. If the model of a particular religion has a personal focus in God, as is familiar in Western civilization, it is quite natural that prayers will take the form (often, though not always) of personal address. But this, as is evident from any study of world religions, is not essential to prayer. What is essential in mature prayer is the affirmation, however it may be symbolized, of a value ordering that, whether manifested well or badly in daily affairs, remains normative for one's life. Think for a moment of the types of prayer: the acknowledgment of the (inevitable) gap between profession and practice is the heart of all "penitential" prayer; the focus upon and celebration of supreme values is the basis for "prayers of thanksgiving"; and even where a personal model permits "petitionary" prayer, sophisticated theists have never approved the shopping list approach to God. For Christians the model petitionary prayer is: "Thy will be done." Thus prayer, rightly understood, does not need to be demeaning or superstitious. Without a theistic model it is still possible, I believe, to breathe the equivalent of "Thy will be done": i.e., "May those values that I acknowledge as really sacred, beyond the petty and inconstant willfulness of my momentary desires, find genuine fulfillment." "Thy Kingdom come!" Religious imagery may make one's priorities concrete and vivid, but this is not logically or psychologically necessary for prayer at its most essential level.

What, finally, of fellowship? Must a life "between models" sacrifice the community of shared allegiances that is one of the key benefits of organized religion? In part, I fear, this may be necessary. At present the commonly available institutional religious alternatives do seem to me, at least, to involve imagery articulated by theories that are not honestly affirmable. And so we who cannot participate are cut off by the demand for basic integrity, as we see it, from the offer of such community extended on those conditions.

Men can share basic values, however, without belonging to the same institutions or giving assent to the same images. Perhaps—my analysis of religion suggests this optimistic possibility—sharing basic values, even without sharing traditional ideational forms, is what constitutes sharing a common religion. To this extent we who are on the outside of institutional religion may continue to find meaningful fellowship with others of good will, even apart from the traditional formulas that personal integrity forbids. Is this fellowship important? Indeed it is. *Integrity*, after all, is a poverty-stricken term if it forces a man to shrink into an "integer" standing isolated and apart from other men. It makes all the difference what one's integrity "integrates" into one's life. The ideal kind of integrity, as I have urged in the course of my argument, would make possible wholeness based on some principle that could both give unity to oneself and bring various selves into ever richer, ever widening unities. A wholeness that is always open, a unity that, by its very nature, is hospitable to growth—this is what is needed as the basis for religious maturity and life's fullest integrity.

CONTRIBUTORS

PETER A. BERTOCCI is Borden Parker Bowne Professor of Philosophy, Emeritus, at Boston University. Among his publications in philosophy, religion, ethics and psychology are *Personality and the Good,* with Richard A. Millard (1963), *The Person God Is* (1970), and *Religion as Creative Insecurity* (1958). He is a past president of the Metaphysical Society of America and of the American Theological Society, and a Fellow of the American Psychological Association.

LOUIS DUPRÉ is T. Lawrason Riggs Professor in the philosophy of religion at Yale University. In that area he has published recently *The Other Dimension* (1972), *Transcendent Selfhood* (1976), *A Dubious Heritage* (1977), and *The Deeper Life* (1981). He has also published two books on Marx and one on Kierkegaard.

FREDERICK FERRÉ is Professor of Philosophy and Head of the Department of Philosophy and Religion at the University of Georgia. He is interested in the intersections between philosophy of religion, logic, and philosophy of science, with a special concern for the impact of science and religion on each other, on technology, and on general culture. Some of his books include *Language, Logic and God* (1961) and *Shaping the Future* (1976).

GEORGE L. KLINE is Milton C. Nahm Professor of Philosophy, and Chairman of the Department of Philosophy, at Bryn Mawr College. He is the author of *Religious and Anti-Religious Thought in Russia* (1968), translator of V. V. Zenkovsky's *A History of Russian Philosophy* (1953), translator and introducer of *Joseph Brodsky: Selected Poems* (1973), and (with Lewis S. Ford) co-editor of, and contributor to, the forthcoming *Explorations in Whitehead's Philosophy*.

JOSEPH KOCKELMANS is Professor of Philosophy and Director of the Interdisciplinary Graduate Program in the Humanities at the Pennsylvania State University. He has written books, edited anthologies, and published articles predominantly in two areas, hermeneutic phenomenology and the philosophy of the natural and social sciences. His book *Space and Time*, a study on the special theory of relativity, was awarded a gold medal.

353

JAMES F. ROSS is Professor and Chairman of the Philosophy Department at the University of Pennsylvania. He is the author of *Philosophical Theology* (1969, 1980), *Introduction to Philosophy of Religion* (1970), and of *Portraying Analogy* (1982).

KENNETH L. SCHMITZ is Professor of Philosophy at Trinity College in the University of Toronto. His recent publications include: *Art and Logic in Hegel's Philosophy* (edited with W.E. Steinkraus); "A Moment of Truth: Present Actuality," in *Review of Metaphysics* (June 1980); "Natural Imagery as a Discriminatory Element in Religious Language," in *Experience, Reason and God* (ed. E.T. Long) (1980); "The Ritual Elements of Community," in *Religious Studies* (Spring 1981); "Entitative and Systemic Aspects of Evil," in *Dialectics and Humanism* (Spring 1978); "Shapes of Evil in Medieval Epics: A Philosophical Analysis," in *The Epic in Medieval Society*.

JOHN E. SMITH is Clark Professor of Philosophy at Yale University and currently President of the American Philosophical Association, Eastern Division. He is the author of *Reason and God, Experience and God, Religion and Empiricism, The Spirit of American Philosophy*, and *Purpose and Thought*.

SUGGESTIONS FOR FURTHER READING

George L. Kline

The following bibliography includes key works by such "classical" authors as Aquinas, Hume, Kant, Hegel, Comte, Newman, and William James, but places primary emphasis on the writings of twentieth-century authors.

Part One includes general works in philosophy of religion and "natural theology" as well as studies which focus on special topics such as the concept of the holy. Certain of the general works include discussion of problems treated in greater detail in the works listed in Parts Two, Three, and Four.

The works listed in Part Two examine and evaluate religious reasoning and theological argument, including the "logic of analogy" and the traditional arguments for the existence of God.

Part Three includes works which deal directly with religious experience and its expression, including such topics as religious language, symbolism, myth, and the mystical experience.

The works listed in Part Four examine the relation of religion to science and technology, and to history and culture, giving special attention to the "problem of evil" and the phenomenon of contemporary "alienation."

ONE. THE RELIGIOUS DIMENSION: GOD AND THE SACRED

BERDYAEV, NICHOLAS. *Spirit and Reality* [1937] (tr. by G. Reavey), London: Bles, 1946.
BERGER, PETER L. *A Rumor of Angels,* Garden City, N.Y.: Doubleday, 1969.
BERTOCCI, PETER A. *The Person God Is,* New York: Humanities Press, 1970.
BLACKSTONE, WILLIAM T. *The Problems of Religious Knowledge,* Englewood Cliffs, N.J.: Prentice-Hall, 1963.
BRIGHTMAN, EDGAR S. *A Philosophy of Religion,* New York: Prentice-Hall, 1940.
————. *Person and Reality,* ed. P. A. Bertocci, New York: Ronald Press, 1958.
BULTMANN, RUDOLF. *Essays, Philosophical and Theological* [1954] (tr. by J. C. G. Greig), New York: Macmillan, 1955.
BURTT, E. A. *Man Seeks the Divine,* New York: Harper & Row, 1957.

COBB, JOHN B., Jr. *A Christian Natural Theology*, Philadelphia: Westminster Press, 1965.

COLLINS, JAMES. *The Emergence of Philosophy of Religion*, New Haven: Yale University Press, 1967.

DUCASSE, C. J. *A Philosophical Scrutiny of Religion*, New York: Ronald Press, 1953.

DUPRÉ, LOUIS. *The Other Dimension*, New York: Doubleday, 1972; New York: The Seabury Press, 1979.

FARRER, AUSTIN. *Faith and Speculation*, New York: New York University Press, 1967.

FERRÉ, FREDERICK. *Basic Modern Philosophy of Religion*, New York: Scribner, 1967.

FERRÉ, NELS F. S. *Reason in Religion*, Edinburgh and New York: Nelson, 1963.

FORD, LEWIS S. *The Lure of God*, Philadelphia: Fortress Press, 1978.

HEGEL, G. W. F. *Lectures on the Philosophy of Religion* [1832, 1840] (tr. by E. B. Speirs and J. B. Sanderson), 3 vols., London: Kegan Paul, Trench Trubner, 1895; reprinted 1962.

HOCKING, WILLIAM ERNEST. *The Meaning of God in Human Experience* [1912], New Haven: Yale University Press, 1963.

OTTO, RUDOLF. *The Idea of the Holy* [1917] (tr. by J. W. Harvey), London: Oxford University Press, 1958.

PALEY, WILLIAM. *Natural Theology* [1802], ed. F. Ferré, Indianapolis: Bobbs-Merrill, 1963.

PATON, H. J. *The Modern Predicament*, New York: Macmillan, 1955.

ROSS, JAMES F. *Introduction to the Philosophy of Religion*, New York: Macmillan, 1970.

ROYCE, JOSIAH. *The Sources of Religious Insight* [1912], New York: Scribner, 1963.

THOMAS, GEORGE F. *Philosophy and Religious Belief*, New York: Scribner, 1970.

WHITEHEAD, ALFRED NORTH. *Religion in the Making*, New York: Macmillan, 1926.

TWO. RELIGIOUS REASONING: PROVING GOD?

AQUINAS, THOMAS. *On the Truth of the Catholic Faith* (tr. by A. C. Pegis of *Summa contra gentiles*), 2 vols., Garden City, N.Y.: Doubleday, 1957.

CHRISTIAN, WILLIAM A. *Meaning and Truth in Religion*, Princeton: Princeton University Press, 1964.

DUPRÉ, LOUIS. *A Dubious Heritage*, New York: Paulist Press, 1977.

EMMET, DOROTHY M. *The Nature of Metaphysical Thinking*, London: Macmillan, 1945.

FARRER, AUSTIN. *Finite and Infinite* [1943], Westminster: Dacre Press, 1964; New York: The Seabury Press, 1979.

FERRÉ, FREDERICK. *Language, Logic and God*, New York: Harper & Row, 1961.

FLEW, ANTONY. *God and Philosophy*, New York: Harcourt, Brace & World, 1966.

GILKEY, LANGDON. *Maker of Heaven and Earth* [1959], Garden City, N.Y.: Doubleday, 1965.

HARTSHORNE, CHARLES. *The Logic of Perfection*, LaSalle, Ill.: Open Court, 1962.

———. *Anselm's Discovery*, LaSalle, Ill.: Open Court, 1965.

HICK, JOHN. *Arguments for the Existence of God*, London: Macmillan, 1970.

HUME, DAVID. *Dialogues Concerning Natural Religion* [1779], in *Hume Selections*, ed. C. W. Hendel, Jr., New York: Scribner, 1927, 1955.

KENNY, ANTHONY. *The Five Ways*, London: Routledge & Kegan Paul, 1969.

KLUBERTANZ, GEORGE P. *St. Thomas Aquinas on Analogy*, Chicago: University of Chicago Press, 1960.

MASCALL, ERIC L. *Existence and Analogy*, London: Longmans, Green, 1949.

MAVRODES, GEORGE I. *Belief in God*, New York: Harper & Row, 1972.

MITCHELL, BASIL. *The Justification of Religious Belief*, New York: The Seabury Press, 1974.

————, ed. *Faith and Logic*, London: Allen & Unwin, 1957.

PLANTINGA, ALVIN. *God and Other Minds*, Ithaca, N.Y.: Cornell University Press, 1967.

————. *The Nature of Necessity*, New York: Oxford University Press, 1974.

ROSS, JAMES F. *Philosophical Theology*, Indianapolis: Bobbs-Merrill, 1969.

ROWE, WILLIAM. *The Cosmological Argument*, Princeton, N.J.: Princeton University Press, 1975.

SMITH, JOHN E. *The Analogy of Experience*, New York: Harper & Row, 1973.

SMITH, NORMAN KEMP. *The Credibility of Divine Existence*, New York: St. Martin's Press, 1967.

TEMPLE, WILLIAM. *Nature, Man and God* [1934], New York: Macmillan, 1949.

TENNANT, FREDERICK R. *Philosophical Theology*, 2 vols., London: Cambridge University Press, 1930, 1935.

THREE. RELIGIOUS EXPERIENCE AND RELIGIOUS EXPRESSION

BENDALL, KENT and FERRÉ, FREDERICK. *Exploring the Logic of Faith*, New York: Association Press, 1962.

BUBER, MARTIN. *I and Thou* (tr. by R. G. Smith), 2nd ed., New York: Scribner, 1958.

CASSIRER, ERNST. *An Essay on Man* [1944], New Haven: Yale University Press, 1965.

DILLEY, FRANK B. *Metaphysics and Religious Language*, New York: Columbia University Press, 1964.

DURKHEIM, EMILE. *The Elementary Forms of the Religious Life* [1912] (tr. by J. W. Swain), New York: Free Press, 1968.

ELIADE, MIRCEA. *The Sacred and the Profane* [1956] (tr. by W. R. Trask), New York: Harper & Row, 1961.

FLEW, ANTONY and MACINTYRE, ALASDAIR, eds. *New Essays in Philosophical Theology*, London: SCM Press, 1955.

HEPBURN, RONALD W. *Christianity and Paradox*, London: Watts, 1958.

JAMES, WILLIAM. *The Varieties of Religious Experience* [1902], New York: Crowell-Collier, 1969.

LEWIS, H. D. *Our Experience of God*, London: Allen & Unwin, 1959.

MALINOWSKI, BRONISLAW. *Magic, Science and Religion*, Garden City, N.Y.: Doubleday, 1948.

MARÉCHAL, JOSEPH. *Studies in the Psychology of the Mystics* [1924] (tr. by A. Thorold), London: Burns, Oates & Washburne, 1927; New York: Magi Books, 1969.

O'BRIEN, ELMER. *Varieties of Mystical Experience*, New York: Holt, Rinehart, & Winston, 1964.

OTTO, RUDOLF. *Mysticism East and West* [1926] (tr. by B. L. Bracey and R. C. Payne), New York: Macmillan, 1932, 1970.

RAMSEY, IAN T. *Religious Language* [1957], New York: Macmillan, 1963.

RICOEUR, PAUL. *The Conflict of Interpretations*, ed. Don Ihde, Evanston: Northwestern University Press, 1974.

SANTONI, RONALD E., ed. *Religious Language and the Problem of Religious Knowledge*, Bloomington: Indiana University Press, 1968.

SMITH, JOHN E. *Experience and God*, New York: Oxford University Press, 1968.

STACE, W. T. *Mysticism and Philosophy*, Philadelphia: Lippincott, 1960.

UNDERHILL, EVELYN. *Mysticism* [1911], New York: E. P. Dutton, 1961.

VAN DER LEEUW, GERARDUS. *Religion in Essence and Manifestation* [1956] (tr. by J. E. Turner and H. H. Penner), 2 vols., New York: Harper & Row, 1963.

ZAEHNER, R. C. *Mysticism Sacred and Profane*, New York: Oxford University Press, 1967.

FOUR. RELIGION AND THE HUMAN PREDICAMENT

BARBOUR, IAN G. *Issues in Science and Religion*, Englewood Cliffs, N. J.: Prentice-Hall, 1966.

BELLAH, ROBERT N. *Beyond Belief*, New York: Harper & Row, 1970.

COLLINS, JAMES. *The Existentialists*, Chicago: Regnery, 1952.

COMTE, AUGUSTE. *Introduction to Positive Philosophy*, [1830] translation by P. Descours and H. G. Jones, revised by the ed. F. Ferré, Indianapolis: Bobbs-Merrill, 1969.

DIJKSTERHUIS, EDUARD J. *The Mechanization of the World Picture* [1950] (tr. by C. Dikshoorn), Oxford: Clarendon Press, 1961.

DUPRÉ, LOUIS. *Transcendent Selfhood*, New York: The Seabury Press, 1976.

FACKENHEIM, EMIL. *God's Presence in History*, New York: New York University Press, 1970.

FARRER, AUSTIN. *Love Almighty and Ills Unlimited*, London: Collins, 1962.

FERRÉ, NELS F. S. *Evil and the Christian Faith*, New York: Harper, 1947.

GRIFFIN, DAVID R. *God, Power, and Evil*, Philadelphia: Westminster Press, 1976.

HICK, JOHN. *Evil and the God of Love*, London: Macmillan, 1966.

HOOYKAAS, REIJER. *Religion and the Rise of Modern Science*, Grand Rapids, Mich.: Eerdmans, 1972.

JASPERS, KARL. *Philosophical Faith and Revelation* [1948] (tr. by E. B. Ashton), New York: Harper & Row, 1967.

KANT, IMMANUEL. *Religion within the Limits of Reason Alone* [1793] (tr. by T. M. Greene and H. H. Hudson), New York: Harper, 1960.

LEWIS, C. S. *The Problem of Pain* [1940], New York: Macmillan, 1944.

MADDEN, EDWARD H. and HARE, PETER H. *Evil and the Concept of God*, Springfield, Ill.: C. C. Thomas, 1968.

MONOD, JACQUES. *Chance and Necessity* [1970] (tr. by A. Wainhouse), New York: Knopf, 1971.

NEWMAN, JOHN HENRY. *An Essay on the Development of Christian Doctrine* [1845], London: Longmans, Green, 1966.

NIEBUHR, H. RICHARD. *The Meaning of Revelation,* New York: Harper & Row, 1962.

PANNENBERG, WOLFHART. *Revelation as History* [1961] (tr. by D. Granskou), eds. W. Pannenberg, R. Rendtorff, T. Rendtorff, and U. Wilkens, New York: Macmillan, 1968.

POLLARD, WILLIAM G. *The Mystery of Matter,* Washington, D.C.: U.S. Atomic Energy Commission, Office of Information Services, 1974.

RICOEUR, PAUL. *The Symbolism of Evil* [1960] (tr. by E. Buchanan), New York: Harper & Row, 1967; Boston: Beacon Press, 1969.

SCHILLING, HAROLD K. *The New Consciousness in Science and Religion,* Philadelphia: United Church Press, 1973.

SCHILLING, S. PAUL. *God and Human Anguish,* Nashville: Abingdon Press, 1977.

STENT, GUNTHER S. *The Coming of the Golden Age,* Garden City, N.Y.: published for the American Museum of Natural History by the Natural History Press, 1969.

WHITEHEAD, ALFRED NORTH. *Science and the Modern World* [1925], New York: Free Press, 1967.